Viva la Vuelta!

Viva la Vuelta!

Lucy Fallon and Adrian Bell

Viva la Vuelta!

First published in 2005 by:

Mousehold Press
Victoria Cottage
Constitution Opening   and
Norwich, NR3 4BD
www.mousehold-press.co.uk

Sport & Publicity
75 Fitzjohns Avenue
Hampstead
London, NW3 6PD
www.sportandpublicity.co.uk

Cover design and map: Terence Loan

ISBN 1 874739 40 4

Printed by Wrightsons, Earls Barton, Northants

CONTENTS

Co-Publisher's Note:

The Vuelta has always been a favourite race of mine, and yet, over the years, I have often wondered about its importance and its relevance in the grand scheme of professional cycling. Then you think of the super Champions – men like Anquetil, Gimondi, Merckx and Hinault – who all desperately wanted to add the Vuelta to their grand tour palmarés. They knew their careers would not be complete until they had added this very difficult and fiercely partisan stage-race to their tour victories in France and Italy.

When I was approached by Adrian Bell to co-publish this book with him, I wasn't initially convinced, but when in due course he sent me a first draft, I found I myself learning so many things about the Vuelta that I'd previously had no idea about: the great battles for victory that had ensued over the years; the actual politics of the race; and the complicated and sometimes confusing history of Spain itself – a country we know today as one of the world's truly great cycling nations. I discovered that Spain's often sad, sometimes violent, and relentlessly changing history was as much a part of the race as the actual racing itself. And the organisation of the Vuelta often paralleled the 'State of the Nation', with its highs and lows coinciding with Spain's shifting political and cultural scene. I found the book enthralling, and a joy to read.

It concentrates most often on the battle for the overall victory, rather than being a day-by-day account (although the appendices contain enough information to satisfy history buffs and adds to its overall attraction). It is this direction of the narrative, its concise approach to the overall contenders, with its constant references to the Spanish background that gives *Viva la Vuelta!* its spark.

Lucy Fallon and Adrian Bell have produced a remarkable work that should enthral all lovers of cycle racing, especially if Spain is close to their hearts. It is the product of hard work and a deep affection for Spain and for the Vuelta that is obviously felt by the authors – an English woman who had made her home in Spain and fallen in love with the country and its great cycle race, and a Englishman who lives in Britain but has a special love of things Spanish (having published two books about Miguel Induráin – one of which we produced together – and a book about the Spanish Civil War). This book has something for everybody if they love the country and the wonderful sport of cycling.

Richard Allchin, Sport & Publicity

Authors' acknowledgements:
Researching this book involved reading enormous amounts of sports press, and it's impossible to express enough appreciation for the late Antonio Vallugera, who brought the Vuelta alive in his reports for *Dicen* from 1955 to the paper's end in 1985. It was a privilege to travel into the past and follow the race through his sharp and wise perspective. The other journalist quoted liberally here is Carlos Arribas, who should be awarded a medal for his services to cycling for his original and lyrical dispatches in the national daily *El País*.

We owe a considerable debt to those who once rode the Vuelta and who agreed to be interviewed – Pedro Delgado, José Pérez Francés, Miguel Poblet, John Pottier, Brian Robinson and Ian Steel. We must also thank Chris Sidwells who, on out behalf, interviewed Eddy Merckx and Jean Stablinski about their Vuelta experiences. We must also give a special thanks to another great Vuelta veteran, Sean Kelly, for kindly providing a Foreword to this book.

Marcus Fallon's help was boundless: tracking down people, setting up interviews, fixing computers, reading through chapters with a critical eye are just some of his contributions.

Similarly we are extremely grateful to Richard Allchin for his perceptive and detailed comments on earlier drafts of the manuscript, and for pointing out some of our errors, and to Sue Mullard for her meticulous copyediting of the first draft. For any errors in content that remain in this text, and for any awkwardness in style, we must carry the responsibility.

The photo archivist at *El Mundo Deportivo*, Roberto Ruano Matellán, John Pierce of Photosport International, and Nigel Wynn of *Cycle Sport* were all most efficient and helpful. We are also grateful to Phil O'Connor for his photograph of Sean Kelly.

Raf Van Rooy and Travel Marketing, the publishers of that indispensible annual *Velo* and the superb *Velo Plus*, have been extremely helpful in providing much of the statistical detail of this book and the indices.

In addition, there were numerous people who helped us along the way: Marilyn Bell, Mick Clark, David Duffield, David Harmon and the staff at Eurosport, Luke Evans, Phil Liggett, Frank Quinn and 'Rocky' Turner. Their encouragement turned what seemed a daunting task into something more manageable.

Lucy Fallon and Adrian Bell

FOREWORD

My memories of the Vuelta will always remain with me. I won the race in 1988, and that victory stands at the top of my palmarés. It was the one time I was the overall winner of a major Tour.

I first went to the Vuelta in 1979 – it was my second big Tour after I turned pro (I'd ridden the Tour de France the year before) and I won the first stage. I had a second stage-win a week later, but near the end of the race I became ill and had to pull out. That was a disappointment, but at least I was getting to know the really big Tours, so I suppose you could say it was good experience.

The next season I rode the Vuelta again, and this time I won five stages and finished wearing the points jersey. The big surprise for me, though, was that I was fourth overall. At that time I was concentrating on the one-day races, and supporting the team, and I really didn't think of myself as a big Tour contender.

It was five years before I next rode the Vuelta, and 1985 was the year when Pedro Delgado took the lead from Robert Millar on the last but one stage. I won three stages and the points jersey again, but only finished 9th overall. By then the race was getting a lot bigger and a lot harder – in 1979 there'd only been 90 starters, but by 1985 there was almost double that number. All the same, I had won a few Classics and a good few smaller stage races in the meantime, so I was beginning to think it might be possible for me to win a major tour. The trouble was I raced so much, starting in February, that it was always difficult to be in the special condition you need for a three-week race.

The following year I changed teams and went to Kas – one of the big Spanish teams with a long history in cycling – and I finished third overall. I also won a couple of stages and the points jersey for the third time in my career. The owner of Kas was Luis Knorr, a great cycling fan from the Basque country where there's such a lot of enthusiasm for the sport. He was sure I could win the race one day, and he also told me that he wanted me to stay in his Kas team until I retired. Maybe I would have done, but he died in 1988 and the Kas team folded. I was able to repay his confidence, though – eventually. But not before I reached my worst moments in cycling, and then one of my very best.

In 1987 I had to retire just three days before the finish in Madrid. I was wearing the *maillot amarillo* (leader's jersey) and looking certain for the overall. But for some days I'd been nursing a really bad saddle boil and I just couldn't bear the pain any longer. I had to drop out and leave the race to Lucho Herrera. For the first time in my career I'd been on the point of winning a major Tour, and I had to pull out. That hurt as much as the saddle boil. Later in the season I crashed in the Tour de France and had to retire from that race, as well. It was probably the worst year of my career.

I said at the time that losing the Vuelta like that was a thorn in my side, and I returned in 1988, determined to pull it out. And I did. It was a very special feeling. I also took the points jersey for the fourth time, and had a couple of stage-wins. It still remains the highpoint of my career – my win in the Tour of Spain.

Overall, Spain was always very good to me. I raced a lot there during my 18-year career, and I think the teams I rode for, and those passionate bike fans, appreciated my efforts. They gave me great support, that's for sure – there were times when I felt I could have been at home in Ireland racing in the Nissan. I won the main one-week Tours, in the Basque Country and in Catalunya, more than once, but none of that compared with riding into Madrid with the leader's jersey after three weeks of the Vuelta.

This book takes me back to those years – to the good times and the times of despair. It makes me remember the stages, the riders, the teams and the battles we had, and travelling through that mountainous country. A great race needs a great book like this so that it can live for ever.

Sean Kelly

A COMMENTATOR'S VIEW

I can pinpoint the exact moment when my simmering passion for the Vuelta a España became a full grown love affair. It was stage 19 of the 2002 Vuelta, on the outskirts of Ávila, one of the most beautiful of the many walled medieval towns visited by the race. With a finish inside the town walls at the end of a challenging cobbled rise, it is a stage that rewards the brave, and José García Acosta had launched one of his trademark long drives for the line. Acosta would take the stage win but it was behind him that the true drama was being played out.

Oscar Sevilla, leader of the Kelme–Costa Blanca team, had taken the leader's jersey on a mountainous stage 6, but lost it to fellow Spaniard, Roberto Heras, riding for US Postal Service on stage 13. As the team's grip on the lead had weakened and finally failed, fellow Kelme rider Aitor González, riding in the form of his life and wound up tight like a clockspring, had been forced to wait and watch Sevilla falter under the US Postal onslaught.

At Ávila González knew he was the strongest and, in an explosion of power and will, darted out of the pack and up towards the finish, attacking his team leader against orders and leaving the stunned and shaken Sevilla behind him. The hammer blow to his morale was all too obvious to see.

That day marked out everything thrilling to me about bike racing: the will and conviction of a single man; the shockwaves of defeat; the raw power and aggression of the attack; and the majesty of the setting. That day Spain found a new hero and I found a new love.

The 2002 edition of the Vuelta is also etched in my mind for a different reason. It marked my professional debut as a commentator alongside the great Sean Kelly, a winner of the Vuelta himself in 1988. Since then we have become a regular pairing on Eurosport. A great champion doesn't stop being a great champion just because he hangs up his wheels, and I have learnt more about professional cycling, and life, from Sean than I could possibly recount in this short space.

The Vuelta a España is truly a 'grand' tour: the mountains are longer, the plains drier and flatter, the architecture at once more majestic, and yet wind-blown and sun-bleached and the racing always unpredictable. This beautiful book brings the race and its awe inspiring setting to life in such a way as to re-kindle that love affair for me every time I open it and that is a truly wonderful thing.

When I wrote the above comment the quiet man from Bejar, Roberto Heras, was still under the glare of the Spanish media. A dismal 45th overall in the Tour de France had left many wondering if the three-times Vuelta winner would ever be a Grand Tour champion again.

Now, on my way to the World Championships in Madrid, Heras stands alone as the only rider ever to have won four Vueltas a España.

It was a ride of greatness, achieved with both style and substance against a strong field, including the powerful Russian, Denis Menchov, who refused to give up the fight for victory even without a strong team alongside him.

Not once did Heras falter, even when outclassed by Menchov against the clock, and then stunned by a crash that left him with 15 stitches to the left knee.

The classical 'isolate and attack' strategy finally employed by the Spaniard's Liberty Seguros–Würth team to break the Russian on the vicious ascent of Pajares was cycling poetry of Homeric proportions.

Television pictures of Heras emerging from the fog and rain some five and half minutes ahead of his rival will probably be the defining images of his career. It was the moment when every cycling fan knew that he had greatness, not of the overt nature of former team-mate Lance Armstrong, but the greatness of a champion who prefers to spend his racing talent at home in Spain.

Roberto Heras, who has made my job such a pleasure over the years, has rewritten Vuelta history and shown that, in biking at least, you can be a nice guy and carry a big stick.

David Harmon

Spain – the cities and the puertos

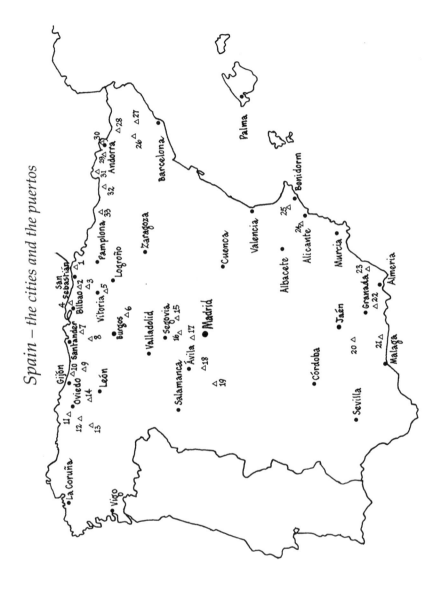

'On that arid square, that fragment nipped off from hot Africa, soldered so crudely to inventive Europe…'

W. H. Auden, *Spain, 1937*

'The northener in search of new sensations has every reason for going there.'

Gerald Brenan, *The Face of Spain*

Prologue

At a quarter to eight on the morning of Monday, 29th April 1935 the Mayor of Madrid raised his green flag, and a peloton of 50 cyclists rode away from the Puerta de Atocha through the streets of the city in front of a cheering crowd of thousands. Ahead of them lay 3,425 kilometres that would take them on a clockwise journey around Spain to end back in the capital 17 days later. It was a bare three months since Juan Pujol, the director of the Madrid daily, *Informaciones*, had announced that his paper would be promoting and organising the first Vuelta a España.

When Henri Desgrange promoted the first Tour de France in 1903, his reasons had been unashamedly commercial – to boost the sales of *Auto* and destroy its rival paper, *Vélo*. Likewise, when Armando Cougnet, cycling editor of *La Gazzetta dello Sport*, announced that his paper would be staging the first Giro d'Italia in 1909, it was only after he'd got wind of *Corriere dello Sport*'s similar intentions. Pujol, by contrast, had no such competition to fear. Spain had, at that time, two races that had acquired some international status – the tours of Catalunya and the Basque Country – but there was scant interest in promoting a cycle race that would emulate the great tours of France and Italy, and embrace the whole nation.

The inspiration for Pujol's venture was an ex-cyclist, Clemente López Dóriga, who'd achieved some modest racing success 20 years earlier. Convinced Spain should have her own national tour, he'd approached the Press – the most likely promoters – only to be met with scepticism and ridicule. The state of the roads – amongst the worst in Western Europe – not to mention the cost and the lack of sufficient accommodation along any likely route, were all advanced as sufficient reasons for considering it a doomed project. The overwhelming opinion was that the country was simply not ready.

López Dóriga's luck changed when he crossed paths with Pujol and infected the newspaperman with his enthusiasm. There were commercial interests at play – the circulation of *Informaciones* would benefit – but Pujol also had the air of a man with a mission. In the pages of his newspaper, he bravely spoke of the Vuelta as an 'incarnation of patriotic exaltation'. Typical nationalistic hyperbole of the times, perhaps, but with civil war a mere 15 months away, it

1

seemed a declaration of blind faith. Only four years earlier, King Alfonso XIII had packed his bags and rejoicing crowds had thronged the streets to greet the establishment of the Second Republic. Fated to be short-lived, it was a period when optimism flourished in defiance of impending catastrophe. In this sense, Pujol's race was entirely in keeping with the spirit of the Republic.

Spain in the thirties was a country of extremes, ranging from the industrialised north, which was competitive with northern Europe, to the undeveloped south, where people's lives could be harrowingly primitive. The traditional powers – the landed families, church and military – recoiled from the new reforms: divorce, votes for women, eight-hour working days. Things were moving too fast. They were unmoved by the dizzying creativity of geniuses like Dalí, Lorca and Picasso. Beyond Spain, storm-clouds were gathering throughout Europe. Fascism, fuelled by economic depression, was on the rise, and the spectre of communism filled the established powers with dread. In an idealistic bubble, the Spanish government continued with their campaign to wipe out mass illiteracy, and Pujol assembled his riders for a national bicycle race.

Seventy years have passed since that April morning and the Vuelta is going strong. It survived the war and struggled though the dark forties before it witnessed Spain's transformation into a holiday playground for northern Europeans, and saw the completion of a circle, as the country left dictatorship behind and became a democracy once again. It has changed hands, been shifted from spring to late summer, seen the triumph of foreign stars like Anquetil, Merckx and Hinault, as well as given a range of top – but less godlike – cyclists such as Lucho Herrera and Sean Kelly the opportunity to taste the glory of winning a great stage race. There have also been the unknowns who came along and surprised everybody by winning out of the blue. And, above all, the Vuelta tells the story of the Spanish cyclists, whose lives reflect the incredible changes their country has undergone in those seventy years.

The course of any Vuelta is a journey through the startling variety of landscapes that form Spain, from the misty green hills and abrupt mountains of Asturias, to the parched desert of Almeria, the vast expanse of the meseta surrounded by purple-hued sierras and an endless coast. The people who live there are just as diverse. From afar there is a tendency to romanticise a country that has remained on the periphery of Europe, apparently unfettered by the strict rules and regulations of the north. Foreigners appreciate that they are at absolute liberty to risk their necks running with bulls during the San Fermines in Pamplona. A legacy of the Civil War is the cliché of lawless anarchists, while holidays on the Med have sowed memories of Flamenco dancing, bull-fights, waiters and siestas. When it comes to stereotypes, Spain has a rich variety of her own: burly, boulder-throwing Basques; superstitious Galicians; penny-pinching Catalans; extravagant Valencians; garrulous Sevillians; serious Castilians. It is an irony that the first European country to be unified, at least nominally – after the expulsion of the Moors in 1492 – should still, half a millenium later, find it so difficult to contain its centrifugal yearnings for regional autonomy or separatism. Today, more than a quarter of its population does not have Castilian Spanish as its mother tongue, and the 'Basque question' refuses to go away.

The story of the Vuelta is also an account of a race trying to establish itself in an international calendar where the Tour de France and Giro d'Italia had the advantage of a clear head-start. It was even more difficult for a country which, after the second World War, found itself a pariah state, diplomatically and economically isolated. For Spain, after being kept at the edge of things for so long, acceptance in Europe has always been important and, likewise, the Vuelta has given prime consideration to the participation of foreign riders. Extravagant 'starting money', which the organisers could often ill afford, would somehow be found and paid to attract them. Or the race profile would be specially doctored to suit their particular requirements: a long early time-trial to please Jacques Anquetil; a plethora of flat stages that would result in bunch sprints which Rik van Looy could dominate.

All of this is in such contrast to the Giro d'Italia, whose organisers would never have dreamed of ingratiating themselves to foreigners, let alone giving them a racing advantage. It was only in 1950 that the Giro was first won by a non-Italian – the Swiss rider, Hugo Koblet. In fact, in all the 32 editions prior to that, only a dozen foreigners had even so much as won a stage. It would be a long time before the Vuelta acquired that kind of self-confidence.

Nor did those foreign stars always repay the organisers' indulgence. All too often they came to Spain with no serious intention to race, but simply to use the Vuelta as a means of quality training for the realisation of a higher ambition – invariably the Tour de France. The Vuelta's traditional April/May position in the racing year – just before the start of the Giro – always condemned it to the possibility of this kind of abuse. Even when, in 1995, the timing of the Vuelta was shifted to September, it remained vulnerable, as Jan Ullrich demonstrated in 2000 when he unashamedly quit the race to prepare for the Olympics. It is impossible to imagine any rider treating the organisers of the Tour or the Giro with such disdain.

The greater participation by foreign riders from 1955 onwards, at least when they were prepared to take the race seriously, immediately demonstrated the limitations of the Spanish professional cyclists. A handful of their number achieved international prominence – most conspicuously, Miguel Poblet, Federico Bahamontes and Julio Jiménez, who significantly all rode for foreign teams – but, below the very top level, there was a naïveté among the Spaniards which the Vuelta frequently exposed. Year after year they demonstrated their climbing prowess – Spain is (after Switzerland) the most mountainous country in Europe, so it is hardly surprising that it nurtured that particular breed – but too often their efforts were wasted. The foreigners bullied them in the sprints, caught them out in echelons, exploited their internal divisions, and rivalries and general lack of tactical know-how.

Yet, just as Franco, if he were resurrected, would be shocked by the metamorphosis of Spain into a tolerant, anti-military, un-churchgoing Western capitalist democracy, he would find Spanish cycling equally unrecognisable. Compare the national team of 1955, arguing and plotting against each other, with the squad that dominated the 2004 World Road Race Championship with an impressive disciplined performance. The stereotype of an anarchic pure climber seems to have been left behind.

The lost years – the four decades of dictatorship – gave Spain an inferiority complex, which occasionally still flickers into life. But this can work as an incentive for improvement. The current organisers of the Vuelta, Unipublic, have approached the race with an innovative spirit, always on the look out for new routes and mountains to climb, and seeking to create dynamic, fiercely contested stages. For many followers of the sport, the most interesting and excitingly competitive racing of the three major tours in recent years has been in Spain, where frequently the outcome of three weeks of racing has been decided only on the last day, with winning margins measured in seconds rather than minutes.

There is a wealth of literature about the Tour de France, but the history of the Vuelta is surprisingly uncharted territory. This book is an attempt to go some way towards redressing that gap.

1935–1936

The Vuelta of the Republic

'They're coming; they're coming! And they're coming naked!'

In a tiny village, far out on the Castilian plain, a little boy shouted in utter astonishment to warn the rest of the inhabitants. In his history of Basque cycling, Javier Bodegas relates this incident, as the GP de la República – a predecessor of the Vuelta – introduced the sight of a peloton of racing men, with their accompanying caravan, to some of the most remote rural areas of the country, where the sight of a professional cyclist with tight-fitting jersey and bare legs would have been virtually extraterrestial.

Originally held in April 1932 to celebrate the Republic's first birthday, the fourth edition, in 1935, was a five-stage race of some 1,150 kilometres from Eibar to Madrid and back again. The Basque town of Eibar, with its BH and Orbea factories, was the centre of the nation's bicycle industry, after a successful conversion from arms manufacture. The Basque Country, together with Catalunya, had long known a passion for cycling, and the rivalry between the two regions was fierce.

1935   The Vuelta was a far more ambitious project, tripling the number of kilometres and stages. It had been the hope of Pujol and López Dóriga that their race would be truly international, but the invitation to participate drew only a patronising smile from many of the foreign aces. 'This Vuelta is a dream' was a common sceptical response. To conceive and organise a race of such length and complexity in little more than a couple of months seemed an impossible task. There was also the matter of its location in the international calendar: the Spanish tour was set to finish just three days before the start of the Giro d'Italia, and it was to Milan that men of the calibre of Leducq, Archambaud, Vietto, Bartali and Guerra were heading. This would be a constant problem for the Vuelta – too close to the Giro, or clashing with the long-established Classics of northern Europe. None the less, the organisers secured a foreign entry of 18 riders (a strong team of six Belgians, plus four Italians, and two each from France,

Austria, Switzerland and Holland) which, in its first edition, was no mean accomplishment.

Set against them would be 32 home riders, the cream of the Spanish peloton, as well as a good number whose total inexperience of a major stage race would give them little real hope of still being there at the finish. Among the battle-hardened veterans who'd already made a mark on the international racing scene were the 34-year-old Valencian, Salvador Cardona, fresh from his win a fortnight earlier in the GP de la República, and who, in 1929, had been the first Spaniard to win a Tour de France stage, in the Pyrenees. Then there was Mariano Cañardo, the strong man from Navarra, whose forceful presence would loom large over the first editions of the Vuelta. He'd triumphed no less than four times in Spain's longest established stage race, the Volta a Catalunya, claimed the Tour of the Basque Country in 1930, where he destroyed double Tour-winner Antonin Magne on the final day, and finished ninth in the 1934 Tour de France. Another ace, perhaps the Spaniard of greatest international renown, was Vicente Trueba. Barely five feet tall and weighing a little over 50 kilos, he'd been the winner of the Tour's first King of the Mountains prize in 1933. Desgrange dubbed him the 'Torrelavega flea'.

It was Trueba who first established the stereotype of the Spanish racing cyclist – small, wiry, fiercely independent and impervious to team discipline, but given to intrepid performances in the high mountains, or rashly suicidal solo breaks. They were built like sparrows but could fly like eagles, and Desgrange loved them. They were his kind of hero, fit for *his* Tour.

Another who seemed to come from the same mould and who lined up for the start of the first Vuelta a España, was Federico Ezquerra. After a series of impressive performances in Spain, this 25-year-old Basque rider had been invited to join the Hispano–Suiza squad for the 1934 Tour, and the pre-race edition of *L'Auto* was ecstatic in praise of his climbing abilities. 'Will he be the revelation of the Tour?' it asked. In the Alps he was dominant, riding everybody off his wheel and setting a new record for the ascent of the Galibier. Desgrange, with his penchant for allotting nicknames to prominent riders, called him the 'Eagle of the Galibier', and later spoke of him as a potential Tour winner.

In spite of such praise, the experience of competing abroad could be overwhelming for the Spanish cyclists. 'I could never believe, after all the years I've been riding, that a race could make such an impression on me in the way the Tour de France did,' commented Ezquerra afterwards. 'I cried; but I wasn't alone. So did Cañardo ... and Trueba confessed that the same had happened to him on his first time.' It was a struggle for them not to feel overawed by their foreign rivals.

The planned route for the peloton of 50 riders was an extensive loop of the country, taking in as many provincial capitals as possible; it was longer than a modern-day Vuelta, but with one week less to complete it. Conspicuous by its omission was Asturias, where the previous autumn a general strike organised by the miners had been brutally crushed by the army. After the national elections in November 1933, a right-wing coalition had taken power, profiting from the splits among the liberal and socialist parties of the first Republican government. The new authorities immediately set about reversing all the social reforms of the previous two years, which provoked an explosion of frustration in many parts of the country, and a determined uprising in Asturias. With Spanish politics becoming ever more bitterly polarised, the government declared martial law. It was, wrote Gerald Brenan in his retrospective book, *The Spanish Labyrinth*, 'the first battle of the Civil War'.

On the eve of the race there'd been a last moment of confusion. To create a semblance of team structure, the cyclists had been divided into two groups, sponsored by Spain's leading bicycle manufacturers, BH and Orbea, and a dispute broke out over who had contractual rights to the Belgians. In the end, BH won, and the focal point of the controversy confirmed their status as pre-race favourites by taking the first stage.

The peloton was barely half-way through the 185 kilometres from Madrid to Valladolid, when Antoon Digneff and Cañardo escaped and, with the Spaniard doing most of the work on the front, the pair stayed clear to the finish. It would have been just, and fitting, if Cañardo had won that historic first stage, and well he might have done because he was no mean sprinter, if he hadn't put a wheel into a tramline. In the struggle to stay upright, his sprint was arrested, and the Belgian was able to pass him a few metres short of the line.

The leadership fell into Spanish hands on the second stage, when Antonio Escuriet rode alone into Santander, having attacked the Belgian star Gustave Deloor on the final climb, the Alto de la Pajosa, ten kilometres from the finish. Digneff had to surrender the orange jersey (as it then was) but Escuriet clearly had little faith in himself. His room mate, Cañardo, reported how he spent half the night calling out in his sleep, 'They are going to take it off me.'

The third stage – regarded as the *etapa reina** – took the riders on a circuitous route through the Cantabrian mountains from Santander to Bilbao. Deloor won the stage and, with it, the orange jersey, when again the sprint went wrong for Cañardo. On the final urban circuit on the Paseo de San Mamés, he gave a tremendous surge over what he thought was the finishing-line. His delusions of victory were rudely shattered when he realised there was another lap to go, and he had to hastily remount. With Escuriet sunk, having lost almost half an hour, exactly as his dreams had foretold, Cañardo was now the principle Spanish hope. He was situated third overall, just behind Digneff, but a full eight and a half minutes adrift of Deloor. The remainder of the race, 11 long stages and the best part of 3,000 kilometres, would centre around Cañardo's heroic attempts to close that gap.

He was a man built for the job: in the lead-up to the '34 Tour de France, *L'Auto* had accurately described him as 'more a Belgian than a Spaniard, in his style and his qualities – strong, heavy and powerful'. Forced to look after himself from an early age – his father died when he was six years old, and he was orphaned at 14 – he was tough inside and out. Bored with his lonely existence as a shepherd in Navarra, he decided to seek his fortune in Barcelona, where he duly discovered a talent for cycle-racing and became one of Catalunya's greatest cycling heroes, able to rival the Basque figures of the time.

In this first Vuelta, Cañardo found himself taking on the combined strength of the Belgians almost single-handed, as those whom he might have called upon for support fell by the wayside: Escuriet (afflicted with a saddle boil) and Ezquerra (suffering from a strained back) both retired on the fourth stage, and Trueba (plagued by a stomach infection from the start) went the following day. Cañardo was still able to rely on the veteran Cardona, and the valiant Italian Paolo Bianchi, who was the only foreign rider grouped in the Orbea team to stay loyal to the Spaniard, but, for all that they rode their hearts out on his behalf, they were no match for a squad of disciplined Belgians committed to preserving their leader's considerable advantage.

---

* literally, the 'queen of stages', the one alleged to be the toughest

The journey from the Basque country to the Mediterranean was completed in just two gigantic bounds, stopping off at Zaragoza, the capital of Aragón, where Cañardo won his first stage. During this day of torrential rain and intense cold, the Barcelona newspaper *El Mundo Deportivo* reported that many shivering cyclists were forced to dismount and take refuge in people's homes 'in search of hot coffee or a sack to protect themselves a little from the inclement weather'. On the following stage, towards the end of the interminable 310-kilometre ride to Barcelona, Cañardo punctured, and despite a desperate chase to recuperate lost time, was forced to yield a few more seconds to Deloor.

With Barcelona came the sun and the Mediterranean heat that the Spanish riders had set their hopes on. Here they had thought the Northern Europeans would be vulnerable, but they were to be disappointed. On the road to Tortosa, Cañardo, supported by Bianchi, launched an attack, but Deloor and his men annulled it, and the following day black clouds rolled back in. On stage 8, Cañardo, Bianchi and Cardona pressed from the fall of the flag, but to no avail: the Belgians countered every move. In those torrential downpours, with the roads churned to mud, they couldn't have felt more at home if they'd been riding the Tour of Flanders.

On the 265-kilometre ninth stage, south from Valencia to Murcia, it seemed that Cañardo's slender resources were going to be reduced still further. After one more fruitless attack through Benidorm, and another deluge, Bianchi came down in a violent multiple pile-up, after he'd thrown himself from his bike to avoid an oncoming car. Torn and battered down the length of his right side, and in real pain, he none the less refused to abandon. 'I cannot leave Cañardo by himself,' he said. And so he climbed back on to his bike, barely able to pull with his right arm and his right leg stiffening up. Yet, with an extraordinary effort of will, he got back to the peloton before the finish, his bandages soaked in blood, and, against every prediction, he was on the starting-line the following morning for the tenth stage. 'I said I would help Cañardo, and I will do so, whatever the cost.' Already, the Vuelta was beginning to create its own legends.

The remaining 31 survivors faced 285 kilometres in pouring rain, climbing through the Sierra Nevada before dropping down to Granada, after eleven and a quarter hours in the saddle. Max Bulla, the Austrian winner of the stage, commented afterwards to the reporter from the organising newspaper, *Informaciones*: 'The race is very hard, so hard that, believe me, not only the Spanish riders, but the majority of European cyclists wouldn't have come if they'd known what the route was going to be like.' This was a seasoned professional talking, who'd won the inaugural Tour of Switzerland two years previously. For Cañardo, the stage was a partial success: the gap to Deloor remained a stubborn 8'–39" – the Belgian finishing on his wheel – but he did take more than a minute out of Digneff and so moved up to second place on general classification.

It rained all the next day, too, on stage 11 to Sevilla, and there were times when Cañardo found himself surrounded on all sides by the Belgians. Such fierce marking prohibited any further attacking moves. There was a welcome rest-day in Sevilla, but while listening to the Spain versus Germany football match (won by Spain) on the radio, Cañardo bloated himself with fruit. After spending the night vomiting, he needed all the support Bianchi and Cardona could provide him simply to stay in touch with the leading group.

The next attack, when it did come, was on the penultimate stage, and it was initiated not by the Spaniard but by Digneff. In an effort to take back his second place overall, he escaped on the climb of Béjar, crossed the summit alone and after a furious descent was clear away, with 150 kilometres still to ride to Zamora. Two kilometres back down the road, somewhat recovered from his previous day's ordeal, Cañardo was organising the chase. Cardona, and the Italians Paolo Bianchi and Edoardo Molinar came up in support to drive the group, and although they could never get rid of the other Belgians, they gradually reeled the fugitive in.

Relative calm returned to the leading group, but as they were approaching the outskirts of Zamora, the misfortune that had dogged Cañardo throughout struck again. His chain, which had already slipped from the sprocket twice that day, broke. He quickly borrowed a bike from a young enthusiast at the side of the road, but in just six kilometres he lost almost five minutes. Deloor, the man he'd been chasing ever since the fateful second stage, was now irrevocably out of reach, and the brave man from Navarra bitterly admitted defeat on the finishing-line. To compound his disappointment, he'd been relegated to fourth overall: Digneff was back in second place, now a comfortable 3'–47" ahead, and Molinar, who'd won the stage, was third, 20 seconds behind him.

All that remained was the final 250-kilometre stretch through the Sierra de Guardarrama to Madrid. The miserable weather that had accompanied them for the preceding week continued with constant drizzle in the air. It was bitterly cold over the Alto de los Léones but there, impelled by the desire to snatch back his second place overall, Cañardo took flight. Fearless as his descent was, it was never going to be enough to dislodge Deloor from his back wheel, nor to get rid of Max Bulla, who seemed to thrive in the most arduous conditions, but it was sufficient to pull the three of them away from their chasers and to keep them clear all the way to the capital. When they arrived at the Casa de Campo track, to a huge ovation from the many thousands of spectators, it was with a comfortable ten-minute advantage.

Appropriately, Gustave Deloor, who'd controlled the race so effectively since the third stage, with the help of his strong and disciplined colleagues, took the sprint, while Cañardo, who'd kept the battle going throughout the race despite all his set-backs, regained his second place – the only Spaniard to finish in the top ten overall. The organisers, Pujol and López Dóriga, had been vindicated: they had demonstrated to the doubters and the sceptics that in Spain it was possible to stage a race of such magnitude; and, for two weeks at least, they had managed to divert Spanish public attention away from fratricidal politics.

The day after the Vuelta concluded, Cañardo, accompanied by the Minister of Culture, went to visit the President of the Catalan government, Lluis Companys, who was imprisoned in Madrid. At the same time as the miners' revolution in Asturias, Companys had declared Catalunya an independent republic – it was a very short-lived affair. Cañardo presented him with his hard-won runners-up trophy and bouquet of flowers. 'In return, he gave me his book, *Catalunya and Companys,* with a dedication I'll never forget. It said, "To my friend and great sportsman, from between bars, Lluis Companys".' Only five years later, the Gestapo would arrest the exiled President in Paris and hand him back to Franco's regime. He died before a firing-squad in Barcelona's Montjuic castle, after having taken off his shoes to feel his homeland beneath bare feet.

* * * * *

In the wake of the left-wing Popular Front's election victory in February 1936, politics degenerated further into violence. The election result boosted recruitment to the fascist Falange party, whose terror squads fought running street battles with Republicans, and assassination attempts became almost daily events. In the south, Anarchists – Spain was the only country in which Anarchism took hold as a serious political force with a mass following – began reclaiming what had once been common land, while the rich *latifundista* retreated to Madrid, or to the safety of Biarritz. In the parliament any pretence towards moderation was abandoned: deputies scuffled with each other, while the violence of their rhetoric matched that in the streets. And, in the Officers' Mess, rebellion was being plotted.

In this climate, not surprisingly, many politicians urged the cancellation of the second Vuelta. Only intervention by a Government minister, anxious to rebut the Falange's accusation that they were incapable of preserving law and order, ensured that the race took place. In the event, it was run off without disturbance, apart from once having to be re-routed to avoid a demonstration in Oviedo.

For their part, the organisers appeared to have paid heed to the advice of Max Bulla, who'd finished fifth overall in the first Vuelta. If they didn't reduce the length of the stages, he'd warned them, only the Belgians and a few other foreigners would ever arrive back at the finish in Madrid. In the second Vuelta the average stage length was reduced from 245 to 207 kilometres. On the other hand, the race was extended to a full three weeks – 21 stages – a total distance of 4,353 kilometres, just a fraction short of that year's Tour de France and fully 600 kilometres longer than the Giro.

1936

Whether racing cyclists elsewhere in Euope had been put off by the chronic unrest in Spain, or they'd been listening too much to Bulla, foreign participation in the second Vuelta was reduced to just eight men: four Italians and, once again, a strong team of four Belgians led by the Deloor brothers. There were absentees among the home riders, too, most notably Federico Ezquerra, who complained of an extra week's labour for a reduced fund of prize money.

As in the previous year, the physical demands of the race were exacerbated by the weather: frequently the riders were numbed by the cold and soaked by torrential downpours. At one point, it seemed likely that the organisers would have to improvise an alternative route through Navarra to avoid the flooded roads; as it turned out, the waters subsided sufficiently for them to keep to the original plan and the cyclists only had to wade for 100 metres on one stretch of road still inundated by the flood waters of the River Ebro.

In some respects the race resembled its inaugural edition: Gustave Deloor gained a substantial early lead and held the orange jersey through to the finish. With the unwavering support of his three team-mates – his brother, Alphonse, who finished second overall, Alfons Schepers who won three stages and Joseph Huts, who won the first stage from Madrid to Salamanca – the Belgian gradually increased his advantage to win by a margin of almost 12 minutes. Only once was he severely tested, when he crashed on the 294-kilometre 12th stage from Barcelona to Zaragoza. With the Spaniards in the leading group combining to take advantage of his mishap, and with his bike damaged in the fall, it took 50 kilometres of hard chasing to regain contact. That day apart, he had a trouble-free ride, his lead never seriously endangered.

Indeed, on the second stage from Salamanca down to Cáceres, he seemed to be leading a charmed life. After battling through a torrential storm, the peloton found itself on a road that had deteriorated into a pot-holed, gravel-strewn mud track. Riders were puncturing one after another, and two Spaniards were brought down by an untethered mule, forcing one of them to retire on the spot. Worse was to come: Cañardo crashed into a dog crossing in front of him, injuring himself and wrecking his front wheel. Through this mayhem Deloor rode unscathed to finish alone, four and a half minutes ahead of his brother, Alphonse, the Italian Antonio Bertola, and a few Spaniards. With a time-bonus of two minutes (awarded to a stage-winner who finished more than three minutes ahead of the second man) he put on the orange jersey, already with an advantage of almost seven minutes. Any thoughts Cañardo might have entertained of revenge were gone for good: he was 17'–59" in arrears – and this, after just two stages.

The Valencian Antonio Escuriet, who'd worn the leader's jersey for a day in 1935, moved up to second place on the fourth stage from Sevilla to Malaga. A repeat of the previous year's drawn-out battle seemed in prospect, as Escuriet would presumably be aiming to eliminate the 7'–38" that separated him from Deloor. But, whereas in 1935 Cañardo had attacked the race leaders at any and every opportunity, however unlikely his chances of pulling back time, Escuriet preferred to defend. Even when ideal occasions for attack arose, such as when both Deloor and Schepers punctured 70 kilometres from the stage-finish at San Sebastián, he chose to save his forces.

It was a conservative strategy in which all the leading Spanish riders colluded. Although riding for different trade teams – BH and Orbea – they'd agreed to form a coalition against the foreigners, with Mariano Cañardo, their most experienced and respected rider, as effective team leader. Denied any chance himself of a top position overall, Cañardo had instructed them all to ride in defence of Escuriet's second place. In this impasse, stages were decided all too often in bunch sprints and the sprinter Vicente Carretero was the only obvious beneficiary, taking a total of five stages.

Settling for second so early in the race began to look like bad tactics when Escuriet saw the gap to the race leader gradually extending while his own advantage over third placed Alphonse Deloor was simultaneously whittled away. As the race moved into the mountains of the north – on the very stages when the Belgians should have been most vulnerable to Spanish attacks – it was left to another foreigner, the Italian Bertola, then in fourth place overall, to make the running. His aggression on stage 13 between San Sebastián and Bilbao split the peloton, and resulted in Escuriet losing a further two and a half minutes to Gustave Deloor, while his second place overall now hung by the slender thread of 1'–29" – with 1,500 kilometres still to race.

Through Asturias and into Galicia the race descended into a slow, boring routine: natural climbers like Fermín Trueba and the young up-and-coming talent Julián Berrendero had to contain their frustration. They stuck to Cañardo's orders, knowing that any adventurous moves might imperil Escuriet, who would not be capable of following them. The organisers became increasingly impatient, as did the one remaining Basque rider in the race, Francisco Goenaga, who took off on his own on stage 16. Cañardo, who had the arms of a stevedore, immediately chased him down and thumped him, ordering him to get back into the peloton. Goenaga complained to the officials, who did nothing, so he went off again. And again Cañardo caught him and this time hauled him back by his shorts.

At the end of stage 18 from La Coruña to Vigo, ridden at an average of less than 25kph, the organisers had had enough. Desgrange, director of the Tour de France, knew how to deal with riders on a go-slow – he would threaten to turn the next stage into a time-trial – and the Vuelta organisers took a leaf from his book. In the end, they relented, but only after the riders had promised to race with more vigour – in their own interests as much as to preserve Escuriet's position, because 178 hilly kilometres all the way to Verín, raced individually against the clock, would surely have finished him off.

It was a more lively stage, won by Fermín Trueba, and the Spanish coalition still managed to keep Escuriet in second place overall. With just two days left, it looked as if self-restraint, coupled with Cañardo's physical discipline, would succeed and Escuriet would be able to ride into Madrid in the second position that collectively they had defended since the fourth stage. That night in Verín, however, the pact was about to explode.

Staying in the Spanish riders' hotel was veteran Oscar Leblanc, winner of the San Sebastián–Madrid race in 1913, and Spanish National Champion the following year. He complained bitterly to Berrendero and Trueba about the poor performance of the Spaniards. When the two climbers who could have made it a different kind of race explained the strategy that lay behind their flaccid performance, the old champion urged them to break the pact, promising even to take care of whatever financial repercussions might ensue. 'It has been said so often and it is certainly true,' wrote Berrendero in his autobiography, years later, 'that we Spaniards have a poor team spirit, and at the moment when the prizes are at stake, or our own interests, or just for the applause, each one looks out for himself.'

So, on the first hard climb, nine kilometres out of Verín, the two conspirators launched their surprise attack. It wreaked havoc on the peloton. At the summit, only race leader Gustave Deloor and the Italian, Bertola, had been able to withstand their acceleration, while the second group, containing Escuriet and Cañardo, was already at two and a half minutes further back down the hill.

Once over the top, Berrendero and Trueba were delayed by punctures – at one point they were some three minutes behind – but they were joined by the Belgians Schepers and Alphonse Deloor and together they made contact again. The six strongest riders in that year's Vuelta were finally all together, and throughout the day the gap back to Escuriet, with the faithful Cañardo always alongside him, steadily grew. Bertola won the sprint from Berrendero, and Escuriet was sunk, ceding 16'–42" and dropping to fifth overall.

The general classification was now headed by the two Belgian brothers, ahead of the Italian, while Berrendero, the ambitious young man from Madrid, who would one day become the first Spanish victor of the national tour, was up to fourth place. And that is how the second Vuelta a España ended, 24 hours later in Madrid.

The last stage of a major tour normally signals a cessation of hostilities, with the major issues already decided, but not this time. While the foreigners who had dominated, and been allowed to dominate the race, were able to sit back and enjoy the final 250 kilometres between Zamora and Madrid, it was a day of fratricidal battling among the indigenous riders. 'Those who two days before were our friends attacked us,' wrote Berrendero. 'Now they were all against Fermín and me; but we responded to all their attacks, and dominated them to the point where, in the end, we were the attackers.' The only one to join their rebellion was Emiliano Alvarez, who had given his spare tubulars to Berrendero and dropped back to support him earlier in the race. On this final day he received his reward: he was allowed to go clear for a solo stage-win, 2'–54" ahead of Berrendero, with Trueba third. For the 50,000 Madrileños in the Metropolitan Stadium, it represented some compensation to set against the Belgians' second consecutive overall success.

Even after the race, there were still matters to be resolved in the Spanish camp. On the final two stages Berrendero and Trueba had won considerably more money than all the others in Cañardo's pact put together, and there were a lot of disgruntled cyclists who wanted their share. The two rebels were disinclined to split their earnings, arguing that the agreement had been broken. The end was ugly, with fists flying and Berrendero escorted by guards from the offices of *Informaciones*.

It would not be the last time in the story of the Vuelta a España that Spanish cooperation degenerated into enmity and personal feuds, but it would be some years before it would again be put to the test. Berrendero described that fateful penultimate stage as 'a coup d'état, a revolution, an explosion'. A somewhat grandiose claim, in the circumstances: six weeks later there was to be an infinitely more serious coup d'état, followed by a real social revolution, and Spain would explode into a ferocious civil war.

1941–1942

The Negro with the Blue Eyes

The Vuelta was resurrected in 1941 in a country devastated by war and gripped by the military fist of Franco's regime. The Nationalists had defeated the Republicans, and they would spend the next years putting the boot in at their leisure. Under Franco, there was no magnanimity in victory, nor ever any attempt at reconciliation. War for Spain was over, but for many the nightmare had just begun.

Democracy was replaced by *el Movimiento* (the Movement) – a coalition of the fascist Falange party, the Church, the army, and various monarchist groups, presided over and held together with political astuteness by *el generalisimo* Franco. But even many of his allies, imagining the regime to be a temporary solution, would have been horrified to know Franco would stay entrenched in power for the next 36 years.

It's impossible to put a definitive figure on the total number of casualties of the Civil War, but Hugh Thomas' estimate of half a million is now widely accepted, and it's an indication of the cruelty of the conflict that probably less than half that number met their death on the battlefield. The others were the result of summary executions or reprisals and, of these, perhaps half took place in the decade after the war was concluded. The mood of revenge was so vicious that you could be sent before the firing-squad or into a forced labour camp merely for having failed to show active support for the Nationalists, regardless of any political connection to the left.

To compound the suffering, the country's economy was wrecked. Industrial and agricultural production had plummeted and average income was at 19th century levels. While defeated Republicans suffered the most – denied work and their property confiscated – for much of the population life was reduced to a struggle for survival. These were the years of hunger, with ration cards issued for food and tobacco. Even the relatively affluent felt the pinch. A fashionable cocktail in '40s Madrid was the *porto flip*, consisting of Oporto sherry, egg yolk and hazelnuts: it was, above all, nutritious.

By 1942 an estimated two million people had passed through the prisons or concentration camps. One of these was Julián Berrendero, the *Madrileño* whose precocious show of talent in the 1936 Vuelta had indirectly sealed his fate. Having impressed everyone in the race that year, the 24-year-old from Madrid had been asked to join the Hispano–Luxembourg team that Desgrange invited to the Tour. There, and most particularly in the mountains, the Spaniards had excelled, albeit with a characteristic disdain for co-operation. Cañardo finished sixth overall; Berrendero was eleventh, and took the climbers' prize, after an elbow-to-elbow battle through the Alps and Pyrenees with his team-mate Ezquerra, who was 17th overall. Their duel caused a sensation: they were nicknamed 'the Siamese twins of the Mountains'. But, midway through the Tour, on the very day that the Spanish papers were printing photographs of Ezquerra leading over the top of the Galibier, the generals had made their *pronunciamiento*, which was to plunge the country into civil war.

Fêted in Paris, the Spanish riders now faced the dilemma of whether or not to return home, finally opting to remain in France, and continue racing there. In Spain, a few were critical of their decision: they were 'avoiding their responsibilities to the Republic' as one *El Mundo Deportivo* journalist put it. But, it has to be said, they were encouraged by the government to remain abroad and continue flying the Republican flag, and their popularity at home remained largely undiminished. When the 1937 Tour – from which the Spanish riders donated half their earnings to war orphans – passed through the Pyrenees, thousands of miltiamen took time out to cross the frontier and cheer them. And they had plenty to cheer: Cañardo won the stage into Ax les Thermes; Berrendero – the 'negro with blue eyes' as he had been nicknamed because of his particularly dark complexion offset by strikingly blue eyes – took the *etapa reina* from Luchon to Pau two days later.

When the Civil War ended in 1939 an estimated 300,000 defeated, bedraggled Spaniards trudged wearily into an exile that for many was to last the remainder of their lives. Julián Berrendero travelled in the reverse direction. Unable to bear separation from his girlfriend and family any longer, one evening in September he turned his back on a comfortable life in Pau, where he'd established a bicycle shop, and crossed the border at Irún. He anticipated being reunited with his family in Madrid within a few hours, but the last part of that return journey took very much longer. Arrested on the station platform, he spent the next 18 months in a succession of concentration camps.

Perhaps he'd been blacklisted for comments made during the '36 Tour, when he had the world at his feet and a future of sporting glory ahead of him. On the rest-day in the Pyrenees, Berrendero had spoken to some journalists, condemning Franco's attack on the Republic. To his amazement, when the peloton arrived in Paris, he was enthusiastically cheered by the sympathising crowds, even more than the winner, Sylvère Maes. 'The French Press exaggerated what we said,' he commented later.

After Franco's death in 1975, Berrendero would recall those days, but none of this is mentioned in his autobiography, published in 1949 when everything in print was subject to strict censorship; his time in prison is euphemistically spoken of as the period he was denied a racing licence! But his book does offer an insight into the stoical resilience that saw him lining up for the Vuelta in June 1941, a mere three months after regaining his licence. 'Life brings more sorrow than joy,' he wrote, 'and we have to take what comes if we're to live it.' Behind that mixture of resignation and protest so much had to be left unsaid.

Undoubtedly his physical strength helped him survive life in the disease-ridden, flea-infested camps, with their pitiful food rations. One day, the prisoners were standing for inspection when the captain stopped and stared fixedly at him, finally ordering him in a stern voice, 'Follow me.' Frightened, Berrendero obeyed, but once in the office, the captain embraced him with tears in his eyes. 'You don't recognise me,' he said, overcome with emotion. It turned out they were cycling buddies from before the war; Berrendero's luck had changed. He would always remember the two fried eggs and potatoes his friend served him: 'They tasted like heaven.'

1941 While the rest of Europe was now embroiled in its own war, Spain was too shattered to do anything but follow events from a distance. As the economy deteriorated even further and the food shortage worsened, Franco's government began to feel the strain. Setting up a national cycling race in these conditions might seem utter folly, but it offered an illusion of normality. The third Vuelta was a gesture of defiance in the face of ruin, organised primarily by the Ministry of Education and Leisure, outside whose offices in Madrid, on 12th June, the pathetically small peloton of 32 gathered on the starting-line. After the compulsory singing of 'Cara al sol' (Face to the sun) – the anthem of the Falange party – with riders and spectators raising their arm in the fascist salute, the general who had been appointed president of the Cyclist Union (there was no organisation, however remote from politics, that was not headed by one member of el *Movimiento*) dropped the flag to set the race in motion.

The small group of riders had a daunting task ahead. They were scheduled to return to Madrid in a month, after covering 4,406 kilometres, which would take them to all the corners of a battle-weary nation. The two bicycle manufacturers, Orbea and BH, that had been so prominent in the pre-war years were no longer in a financial position to sponsor any cycling teams. In their absence, some leading riders were affiliated to the two Barcelona football clubs, sporting the blue and white jerseys of Español, and the scarlet and blue of FC Barcelona – but these were loose coalitions rather than hierarchically organised teams. The majority were effectively 'Independents', riding in the anonymous grey jersey adorned with the Ministry of Education's emblem. Finally, to justify the 'international' label, four undistinguished riders had been rounded up from neutral Switzerland.

By the end of the first week, having crossed the empty rolling plains of Andalucia in stifling heat, and begun a slow toil up the Mediterranean coastline, in nine- or ten-hour stints, the peloton had been reduced to 19 riders. Fermín Trueba, the brother of Vicente, the 'Torrelavega Flea' who had so captivated Desgrange, was wearing the leader's jersey (this year white). Half of the Swiss contingent had already retired. Throughout the history of the Vuelta the Spanish cyclists have complained about foreigners receiving preferential treatment. In '41, while they soaked their leathery meat rations in a vain attempt to make them more digestible, the Swiss were given more edible fare. Ironically, it was overeating that defeated one of them. Trying to cope with the high temperatures, he consumed numerous ice-creams and abandoned with a strong stomach ache. Berrendero survived on memories of the abundant food he was given the first time he went to race in France. 'In the *etapa reina*, there, I managed to eat three chickens, one after the other. Three chickens, a steak, soup, anything they put in front of me.'

In this era, apart from tough climbs or strong rivals, a racing cyclist lived in fear of punctures. Fermín Trueba, the third Español

21

rider to wear the white jersey, owed his position almost entirely to good luck on the tyre front. Certainly, his team were overwhelmingly stronger than FC Barcelona, which had been considerably weakened by Mariano Cañardo's decision to pull out on the starting-line. The veteran had realised that only his team were using the crudely constructed, puncture-prone tubulars supplied by the organisation. The Español team and the Swiss had opted to bring their own superior quality tubs, so Cañardo, instead of struggling on with such an enormous handicap, feigned a leg injury and went home. His withdrawal effectively turned the Vuelta into a battle between individuals racing in the same colours.

Prior to Trueba, the other two *Españolistas* to briefly lead the race were Julián Berrendero and Delio Rodríguez. Galicia, traditionally one of the poorest regions of Spain, has produced few cyclists of note, but in the 1940s the five Rodríguez brothers from Pontevedra were the exceptions; their bad luck was to race during Spain's most isolated period, which prevented them from making any international impact. The eldest, Delio, was a fine sprinter who won 12 stages in the '41Vuelta – more than half of the total – thereby setting a record that wouldn't be beaten until Freddy Maertens won 13 in 1977.

Before reaching the cooler respite of the mountainous north, the peloton had to cross the burning Monegros desert *en route* to the Aragonese capital, Zaragoza, in a mammoth 294-kilometre stage. It was here that Berrendero's pre-war rival, his 'twin' Ezquerra, lost all hopes, losing 19 minutes. But Ezquerra couldn't disappoint his Basque countrymen, and recovered some lost honour by winning the Bilbao stage, three days later.

They were now in Spain's cycling homelands, where enthusiasm for the sport was strongest. Throughout the rest-day prior to the 14th stage between Bilbao and Santander excitement mounted. Cantabrian race leader Trueba was assured of fervent support from his compatriots. He knew these mountains better than Berrendero, but the Madrileño was expected to put up a serious challenge. The race had boiled down to a duel between the two climbers, both in Español colours, and separated by 1'–56" in the overall classification, and a handful of points in the mountains competition.

There were three cols to be surmounted, and Trueba wasted no time, attacking strongly at the foot of the first, the short but steep Puerto de Azón, with Berrendero in tow. By the summit, they had left the rest behind. At the top of the Puerto de Sía they were still together, and their lead on the peloton was even more substantial. Berrendero had punctured earlier, but a rapid tyre change allowed him to catch Trueba without undue stress. When Berrendero punctured again, he was equally lively in getting back to his rival. But no sooner was he on Trueba's wheel when he punctured for a third time. Grimly, he carried out the repair and set off in pursuit, once again making contact. But it wasn't his day: his tyres let him down twice more – a total of five punctures in some 45 kilometres. When Trueba, still climbing as strongly as ever, crested the third and final obstacle, La Braguía, Berrendero was trailing at 8'–40", and it seemed the Vuelta belonged to the Cantabrian.

But the *Madrileño* had other ideas. After so much experience of racing in France, he was too ambitious to settle for only the Mountains prize. In a daredevil descent of La Braguía, and then a fierce ride over the flatter run-in to Santander, he channelled his exasperation into slashing Trueba's hefty advantage down to little more than two minutes. His rival had won the stage and the overall gap between them had grown to 4'–05", but Berrendero was still in the race.

It was a glorious moment for Trueba, riding alone into Santander to an ecstatic reception. Despite wearing the white jersey for 11 days, until now he'd barely had to make an effort, merely watch his rivals fall away one by one. But today he'd ridden superbly, attacking without inhibitions from the first climb and consolidating his lead. He could presumably face the remaining stages with confidence.

The next day was a split stage: a 194-kilometre ride along the coast to Gijón, followed by a 53-kilometre individual time-trial through the hills to Oviedo. It was an all-round success for Delio Rodríguez who, after sprinting for victory in the morning, won the time-trial in the afternoon, demonstrating he was not 'just' a sprinter. While Berrendero also rode strongly and finished within a minute of the winner, Trueba's luck deserted him. He punctured in full flight, forfeiting 4'–44", and had to surrender the white jersey to his rival.

Berrendero's 36-second margin was slim, considering there were still 1,100 kilometres to go. But for the remains of the race, all fight seemed to drain away, not only from Trueba, but the whole peloton. As the temperatures soared – it was now July – the cyclists wearily rode through Galicia, their average speed dropping to below 24kph. On the relatively short Vigo to Verin stage, during which Ezquerra dropped out because of saddle boils, the 16 suffering survivors needed more than seven hours to cover 168 kilometres. The jury punished them by refusing to part with any prize money. 'Things look fine from inside the car,' commented Berrendero, 'like taunting the bull from behind the barrier.' The truth was everyone was exhausted. 'Nobody wanted to ride – nobody had the energy, enthusiasm or combativity. I didn't have any more spirit left than anybody else.'

Having gone penniless the previous day, the riders were even slower on their penultimate session in purgatory. The longest stage of the race turned into a route march over 301 kilometres, in suffocating heat, on an appalling road that yielded a total of 83 punctures during more than 13 hours in the saddle. In the closing kilometre Berrendero showed he still had something left in reserve by jumping clear to steal an additional cushion of 31 seconds, pushing up his margin on Trueba to 1'–07". There was, after all, always the remote possibility of an ambush on the final stage, which, after passing through Segovia, would lift them over the 1,860-metre Navacerrada in the mountains north of Madrid. He needn't have worried. On this final climb it was he, Berrendero, who set the pace, slowing down only so Trueba could consolidate himself as King of the Mountains with the final points.

The crowd in the Metropolitan Stadium welcomed back their hero, overjoyed that a Madrileño had won in a sport so dominated by northerners. The reception was warm but the financial rewards modest, as Berrendero described in his autobiography: 'If the team had had this triumph in the Tour de France, we could have lived on the prize money and all the subsequent earnings for eight or ten years; here, we had to be thankful if it lasted a year.' But he did qualify that, after 18 months of what he called 'enforced retirement', riding the French race would have been a disaster. 'We were nothing more than a handful of invalids.'

The state-controlled Press painted a rather different picture from Berrendero, unable to cover the event without lapsing into characteristic pomp. *La Vanguardia*, for instance:

> The world reputation of our national cycling will have risen after this tough and passionate fight among our men, because we have invested all our honour in it, and when peace is reborn and normality returns to international cycling, this

Third *Vuelta a España* will stand as an example of tenacity, stamina and enthusiasm.

Complaints about prize money would have been unforgivable: it was understood that, above all, the cyclists were motivated by duty to *la patria*.

Meanwhile, from the other end of Europe, came news of another type of patriotism. In support of Germany's invasion of Russia the Falangists had rapidly formed the 'Blue Division' – a unit of volunteers deployed on the Eastern Front to help the Nazis overcome 'the Bolshevik barbarians'. It was at most a token gesture – all that Hitler could extract from Franco, who was restrained not only by a war-torn economy near to collapse, but also by his reliance on fuel and grain supplies cleverly drip-fed by the UK and USA. Spain remained detached from the turmoil in Western Europe: while front pages were covered with photographs of soldiers, tanks and corpses, a national cycle race was being celebrated.

On the home front, the regime was busy 're-Christianising' Spain. Divorce and civil marriage were outlawed, kissing in public was punishable by a fine, and prostitutes and homosexuals were sent to concentration camps. They got round to making adultery illegal in May 1942, shortly before the next Vuelta was due to start.

The race organisation had reverted to the newspaper **1942** *Informaciones* and once again football clubs backed the teams, Real Club Deportivo de La Coruña fielding most of the Spanish stars. To help shoulder the cost, commercial firms were roped in for added sponsorship, including some with a cycling connection, such as Hutchinson and Michelin, and others with none, such as Cinzano and sherry producers González Byass. When *extra-sportif* advertising appeared on cycling jerseys in Italy and France in the early 1950s, it provoked a shocked reaction. Tour organiser Jacques Goddet was fiercely opposed and the UCI passed a resolution condemning it. Yet, more than a decade earlier, economic realism already held sway in the backwaters of Spanish cycling.

The organisers had more success in recruiting foreign riders that year, although issuing passports in wartime proved a lengthy affair. Teams from Belgium, France and Italy had all signed up to be on the starting-line in Madrid on 16th June, but as that date approached there was no sign of them, and *Informaciones* secured permission to delay the race by a week. By 23rd June, only the Italian, Pierre

Brambilla, had appeared in Spain, and so another request was sent to the Spanish Cycling Union and the start was put back again. By 30th June, a full complement of six French riders, led by René Vietto, together with two more Italians had arrived; there was still no word from the Belgians, but there could be no further postponements. Against these nine foreigners, there were 31 Spaniards, so creating an initial peloton of 40 riders.

This was nearly reduced to 39 when, as they rode through the neutralised first kilometres in the streets of Madrid, Delio Rodríguez slipped on paving slabs that had been watered down for the occasion and fell heavily. Despite damaging his elbow, he was able to remount and join the rest of the riders as they raised their arms in salute to the presiding general's shouts of 'Arriba España' before setting off on their 245-kilometre first stage to Albacete.

It was an epic day, full of incidents, with attacks and counter-attacks waged beneath a blazing sun, so much so that, by the end, the Vuelta was all but decided. Not only did Berrendero win the stage, outsprinting his escape partner Antonio Sancho, after the pair of them arrived clear of the peloton by a massive 22'–53", but two of his most serious challengers were forced to abandon: Fermín Trueba broke the frame of his bicycle and retired after a fruitless chase, and Dante Gianello crashed. Crashes were the order of the day and by the second stage a fifth of the peloton had retired, due to injuries or, in the case of Antonio Escuriet, an urge to see his newborn baby.

Berrendero led the race from start to finish – another record that wouldn't be equalled till Maertens came to the Vuelta in 1977 – but it was not until stage 10 that he finally disposed of Sancho. Until then he'd been wearing the leader's jersey (orange once more) by virtue of having won the first stage, but they were equal on time. In 1941 it was in the Cantabrian mountains where, despite five punctures, Berrendero had avoided losing the Vuelta; in 1942 it was where he would conclusively win it.

Attacking at the foot of the Puerto de Asón, he immediately went clear; only Brambilla was able to briefly hold his wheel. Away from all his pursuers, on the descent of the Asón and over the eight-kilometre climb of the Puerto de Alisas, Berrendero's gap grew steadily. He rode into Santander after a solo escape of 124 kilometres, giving a performance reminiscent of his glory days in the Tour de

France. By the end of that day, Sancho had been distanced by more than 13 minutes.

With the race in his pocket, Berrendero could now concentrate on beating Brambilla, albeit narrowly, in the mountains competition, while his team-mate, Delio Rodríguez, accumulated eight stage-wins. For the second year running, the *Madrileños* could cheer their hero's triumphant return to the capital. His double victory wouldn't be matched until Asturian José Manuel Fuente won his second Vuelta in 1974.

The fourth edition of the Vuelta had not been much of a success. Even the Press couldn't raise the enthusiasm for hyperbolic accounts: the word cropping up most was 'monotony'. *La Vanguardia* urged its comrades in *Informaciones* to fix a stage limit of 200 kilometres and avoid the hottest time of year in the future. With its delayed start, the Vuelta was still on course on 18th July, the anniversary of *el Alzamiento* (the Nationalist uprising) – always an excuse for lavish military parades. On that day, even the sporting Press ceded their front pages to enormous portraits of Franco.

Among the 18 survivors who managed to arrive to Madrid's Casa de Campo were René Vietto, who'd won two stages, and Pierre Brambilla, who'd won another as well as figuring prominently in the battle for the King of the Mountains prize. These two cyclists, so comprehensively beaten by Julián Berrendero, would be the principal animators of the first post-war Tour de France: the Frenchman would hold the yellow jersey for 15 days; the Italian would lose it only on the final stage. But there would be no place for Berrendero or any other Spaniard in the French race. It would be years before Spain emerged from its isolation – and three years before it even had another edition of its own national tour.

1945–1950

The Years of Hunger

As the forties wore on, dogs and cats vanished from the city streets: they'd either starved or been eaten. The collapse of the rural economy, coupled with droughts in a number of years, made for deprivations that were worse than anything encountered elsewhere in post-war western Europe. Even middle-class families, reported Gerald Brenan after spending some months in Spain in 1949, could afford to eat no more than once a day, and only the black market was buoyant. But for General Perón's food supplies, there would have been genuine famine, for nobody other than the Argentinian dictator was prepared to offer any relief. Diplomatically ostracised, refused a seat at the United Nations, denied support from the Marshall Aid Plan and subject to an imposed trade embargo, the country suffered from its isolation. Yet Franco saw sport as a way of demonstrating the splendour of his vision of Spain and so, undernourished and ill-equipped as they were, the cyclists went forth to ride the Vuelta.

A witness of those harsh conditions was Jefke Jansenn, one of the Dutch team that participated in 1946. Years later, he spoke of their problems securing even the most adequate supply of food – potatoes, for instance, had become a rarity, unseen in urban areas since before the war. He abandoned half-way through the race and, on the flight back to Holland, 'I gobbled up my meal, and the remains of those around me in such a way that an American sitting next to me thought that I was returning from a concentration camp.' It was unsurprising that many stages turned into tired promenades, the peloton picking up retinues of local cyclists who would tag along for the ride.

On 10th May 1945 war in Europe officially ended and, three days later, the Vuelta was on the road, promoted as a celebration of peace. Always quick to exploit any situation for its propaganda value, Franco credited himself for keeping Spain safe from the horrors of the worldwide conflict, although at the same time Hitler's death was reported as the fall of a hero who fought against the Bolsheviks till his last breath. The demise of his counterparts in Germany and Italy had the Spanish dictator wondering if it was his turn next. To placate the western democracies, the most overt fascist elements of the regime were immediately toned down – stiff-arm salutes were phased out – and a new image created around Catholicism.

That year the Vuelta had no participants from across the **1945** Pyrenees; organised by the Catholic daily paper *Ya*, it was an all-Iberian affair – 43 Spaniards joined by eight Portuguese riders. The race began, not unexpectedly, with the favourite, Julián Berrendero, forcing the pace on the first major climb, the Alto de Los Leones, with Fermín Trueba and the Portuguese climber, Joao Rebelo on his wheel. This was to prove the one brief glimpse of Trueba's climbing talent – stomach cramp and colitis would force his retirement on stage 8 – but the sight of Berrendero and Rebelo locking horns in the mountains was to be one of the abiding images of the Vuelta. Their race-long battle, though, wouldn't be for the general classification, but for the lesser crown of King of the Mountains: the top prize was effectively decided on the second stage, and not in favour of either of them.

It began quite innocuously with a five-man break forming after some 25 kilometres on the road between Salamanca and Cáceres. Punctures soon reduced the group to two, of whom only one, the Galician sprinter Delio Rodríguez, could be considered a dangerous man. He and his accomplice put their heads down and worked perfectly together, while behind them the peloton dawdled, and the gap grew. As they passed through Plasencia (after 130 kilometres, and still with another 84 to ride), it had stretched to a yawning 35 minutes, and still there was no reaction from behind. Over the final 30 kilometres Rodríguez found himself alone as his companion weakened, but he was a sprinter who could time-trial and finished still with half an hour on all those with any serious pretensions. Barring an accident, the race was over.

The peloton's passive attitude can partly be explained by remembering that cycling in Spain was still evolving into a team sport. In Italy, the Giro had been promoted as a 'race for teams', while in the Tour de France, Henri Desgrange had pursued the other extreme, forever inventing obstacles to thwart the power of the trade teams, which he felt stifled the race and made it too predictable. Desgrange died in 1940, but had he lived a little longer he might have come to envy the Vuelta, because until the mid '60s, Spanish cyclists were loathe to conform to the discipline of a tightly structured team, and tended towards the first Tour director's ideal of heroic individuals.

In 1945, Delio Rodríguez was lucky to be riding for the team that came closest to a modern conception of one, sponsored by the tyre manufacturers Galindo. There was another sponsor from the tyre business, Pirelli, but the riders who wore their strip could barely be considered a team as such. The support they received was limited to a supply of tubulars and a bonus if they won a race. The bonds between the Pirelli cyclists were inevitably weaker than in the Galindo set-up, although even here there were divisions, as riders formed groups within which they shared out prize money. To complicate matters further, loyalties also depended on which local cycling club they belonged to.

The Spanish Cycling Federation then took the situation to an even higher level of complexity by restricting the sponsors to fielding only six riders – they'd hoped, in vain, that more teams would appear. That left the peloton with six official Galindo riders, with eleven affiliates hovering around, six in Pirelli colours, with another four using Pirelli tubulars, eight Portuguese and assorted 'Independents'. Although he proved to be a tough nut to crack, tested to the limit in the final week and winning six stages, Delio Rodríguez was allowed to establish his advantage far too easily. With nearly half the peloton sharing the same sponsor as himself, and given the tenuous links of the Pirelli 'opposition', no one had taken the initiative to reel him in. His Galindo team-mate Berrendero later regretted letting the Galician go, although he did well financially from the arrangement. The race would have lost all interest had it not been for the struggle for the mountains title that dominated the final week.

The stifling heat of the south now left behind, a total of 28 survivors pedalled out of a rainy San Sebastián to begin stage 13, with four major *puertos* ahead along the 207 kilometres to Bilbao. Joao Rebelo attacked at the foot of the first climb but Berrendero rode him down and led over the summit: first blood to the Madrileño. A comparative truce was declared on the second ascent, but when the Portuguese broke free again, he was unstoppable. As he crested the Urkiola, there were still two others clinging to his wheel but, on the final climb, the Sollube, Rebelo was alone and he plummeted down to Bilbao to a sensational solo victory, 40 minutes ahead of the scheduled arrival time. His remarkable performance earned him enough mountain points to lead Berrendero by 26 to 24. The *Madrileño* might have relinquished the overall classification – he was in third place, 38 minutes down on Rodríguez – but he had no intention of giving up the Mountains prize. The closing stages saw a tenacious struggle, as the two men grappled for points.

On the stage to Santander, any thoughts Rebelo might have had of consolidating his position were quashed by a combined Spanish effort, leaving Berrendero to come away with the lion's share of the points; he now led by 32 to 31. But, the following day, the prospect of one of Spain's most feared ascents, the Puerto de Escudo, inspired the Portuguese climber. He was first over the top and won the stage to boot, which left him once more ahead of Berrendero by a solitary point – 36 to 35. Then, two days later, the *Madrileño* showed that anything Rebelo could do, he could match, as he claimed the Puerto de Pajares and won the stage into León. Now they were equal on 40 points each, and everything would hinge on the 1,500-metre Alto de los Leones on the final day.

Everything, that is, except the general classification, where Delio Rodríguez was still sitting comfortably on his 30-minute lead, and looking forward to a triumphant ride back to the capital. And joining him in the celebrations was the local hero. A few kilometres from Madrid, Julián Berrendero crested the final climb a mere wheel's width ahead of the little man from Portugal, whose constant aggression in the final week had enlivened the race. The struggle to be King of the Mountains had come down to a mountain-top sprint.

It had been a hard race, Berrendero conceded, with the high temperatures and the dreadful state of the roads, harder even than any of his Tours de France. Only 26 of the original 51 arrived back at Metropolitan Stadium in Madrid. One of those who abandoned the struggle, exhausted by the heat and daily grind, was the Basque rider Máximo Dermit, who returned from his voyage round Spain to the green valleys of the Basque Country in a state of shock:

> It's too horrible to imagine. There's nothing comparable, not even the Alpine stages of the Tour de France; there are moments riding through some places where it seems like you're in another world – not a living soul, or a single house for kilometre after kilometre. Just huge bare, rocky mountains. And water! That's an expensive liquid. In some places, like

in Totana, if we asked for water, they preferred to give us wine. There was no water to waste on the likes of us.

He was almost certainly not the last rider to be touched by agoraphobia in the vast plains and harsh sierras of Andalucía, which, in the years to come, were to become increasingly depopulated as the desperately poor and the unemployed drifted to the cities of the north in search of work.

1946 As for lack of water, the following year it was rather too abundant. Much of the 1946 Vuelta was run in incessant rain, turning the dusty, flint-strewn roads into muddy tracks, which only increased the likelihood of punctures. The *parcours* was similar to that of the previous year, but unfortunately for the Rodríguez clan, it made no excursion into Galicia. While Delio was summing up stages (five this year), his younger brother Emilio, riding only his second Vuelta, was crowned King of the mountains, ahead of race favourites Langarica and Berrendero.

In the 1940s, Dalmacio Langarica was one of Spanish cycling's great heroes. Born in the Basque village of Otxandiano, his fate was set at the age of 16, when he saw Gino Bartoli ride the Tour of the Basque Country. Stout-hearted and strong, he was a truly powerful *rouleur*, who could also sprint, climb and race against the clock. He was often let down by the inferior material of the age, forever crashing and puncturing. Bikes seemed to disintegrate beneath him, as if unable to resist so much unleashed power. In the future he would employ this energy in taming the fiercely individualistic Spanish riders and become one of the most respected team directors Spain has produced.

The year of 1946 was truly Langarica's *annus mirabilis*: prior to the Vuelta he'd enjoyed a string of early season successes and by the end of the year he would have accumulated 12 prestigious victories. His principle challengers were the perennial favourite, Julián Berrendero, who'd recently won the Tour of Catalunya, and two foreigners – Joao Rebelo, aiming to improve on the previous year, and Jan Lambrichts, the one rider of class in an otherwise undistinguished team of five Dutchmen.

On only the second day, Langarica made his intentions apparent. It was a split stage, of the sort that the Vuelta's organisers were becoming increasingly fond – a 73-kilometre time-trial in the morning, and twice that distance *en linea* in the afternoon. At the end the Basque was wearing the leader's jersey – white with a red band bearing the inscription *Ya*.

But he was soon to pay for his efforts: on the morning of the fourth day he woke with severe pains in both legs. Facing the prospect of a 218-kilometre ride to Sevilla, he gave warning: 'I don't know if I'll be able to finish today.' But he was underestimating his own combative instinct. After sitting in the bunch for 175 sodden kilometres, he decided to launch an attack on a short incline. It was an impetuous move, gaining him no more than a few hundred metres, before being quickly annulled. What was worse, it provoked a fierce counter-attack to which his aching legs couldn't respond. He finished the stage three and a half minutes down on a Berrendero–Delio Rodríguez tandem, which had no compunction about taking advantage of a wounded team-mate. The *Madrileño* took the stage; the Galician acquired the leader's jersey; and the Basque dropped to third overall.

All the signs suggested that the future of the race would revolve around these three strong men: after all, they were the stars of the Spanish peloton. Yet a challenge to their monopoly came from unexpected quarters.

After the rest-day in Sevilla, which Langarica spent on the physiotherapist's table, the peloton set off on stage 6 to cover the 251 kilometres to Granada. It was an early morning start, and in the gloom and the rain, one of the lead cars made a wrong turning, drawing the Dutch leader Lambrichts and two other riders behind it. Eventually the mistake was realised, and the race was brought to a halt while officials went off in search of the three lost sheep. Once they had been returned to the fold, the race was restarted, now 34 kilometres down the road. Whether in anger, or simply because he was thoroughly warmed up by now, Lambrichts was almost immediately off the front again, this time taking in tow the little-fancied Catalan rider, Manuel Costa.

It was to be another of those days when an indifferent peloton gave licence to a couple of determined men to gain an outlandish advantage: within just 70 kilometres the gap had stretched out beyond half an hour. Only when a resuscitated Langarica took command was any time clawed back, but the fugitives still had 27 minutes in hand at the finish in Granada. Costa was first over the line, only to be relegated to second position after he was spotted hauling back Lambrichts by the saddle. Not that this loss would have bothered him too much: his profit on the day's venture was a white and red jersey, and a 22-minute overall lead.

But was Costa a serious contender? Nobody thought so. Although the Catalan was sponsored by Galindo, he hadn't been picked for the team. It was surely simply a matter of time before one of the aces – of whom Langarica was now best positioned – displaced the upstart.

The very next day, and despite the continuing rain, Langarica was in a sufficiently belligerent mood to take the stage, but all he retrieved was a miserly 52 seconds. When fighting for the next stage in Murcia, he had a typical run-in with his own bicycle, ripping the tubular from the rim of his back wheel and crashing heavily. Then, on the road to Barcelona he punctured while leading a five-man break (which included the irrepressible Costa) and it took a good hour of forced labour before he brought himself back up to the leader. The 'Independent' was proving surprisingly resilient.

When the race reached San Sebastián, the cyclists had a day off, but judging from the scheduled programme, there was scant opportunity to rest. In the morning, the foreigners were taken out sightseeing, and at 11.00 a.m. there was a memorial mass for Vuelta organiser López Dóriga's recently deceased daughter. Before lunch, there was also time to visit the offices of the Regional Cycling Committee, while in the afternoon, they attended a game of *pelota*, the popular Basque sport. The highlight of the day came at the very end, when they were all invited to supper.

The Catalan sports daily *El Mundo Deportivo* was following Costa's progress with particular interest and they sought him out on the rest-day to gauge his morale and find out if he had any serious hopes to last out the race as leader. He had headed the classification for ten days so far, and his margin was still a healthy 15'–39". 'Physically, I'm very well', he told the reporter, 'although a little frightened by what's to come, especially by tomorrow's hard stage.' As for his biggest threat, Langarica, Costa was sure the Basque would be even more dangerous in front of his countrymen but he was convinced that by measuring his own strength, he could limit his losses.

The next day, however, was to prove Costa's undoing. If not outright defeat, it was certainly the beginning of the end of a glorious run. The action began at the foot of the Urkiola, where in the vanguard were the blue Galindo jerseys of Langarica, who was intent on swapping his for white, and Emilio Rodríguez, who wanted mountain points. Half-way up the climb they were joined by another small group that included the ever-determined Costa.

No sooner had they begun the descent when Manuel crashed into a car that had invaded the race. *El Mundo Deportivo* described the anguish of the moment:

> We saw Costa crying at the side of the road while his cuts and grazes were dressed and we understood his pain. His bicycle was lying on the ground with a broken wheel, and the service lorry was far away, far behind the last of the cyclists who in this phase of the stage were separated by a great difference of minutes.

Costa was faced with a dilemma: should he wait or persuade another in that leading group to exchange a wheel? Whether it was panic, or a rational calculation as to the time that he might lose before the service lorry arrived, Manuel opted to 'borrow' a wheel – a clear violation of the regulations, which he knew would incur a ten-minute penalty. Up ahead the two Galindo men were not waiting; they shed all their unwelcome company on the Sollube to finish together in Bilbao. And Costa must have ridden his heart out to end the day within four minutes of them. But, coupled with the time penalty, his advantage over Langarica was now reduced to a slender 1'–40".

Two days later it had evaporated entirely. On the two climbs between Santander and Reinosa, churned into a heavy mud-bath by the continuous rain, the Basque *rouleur* showed his strength. Hampered on the final descent by broken spokes in his rear wheel, he no longer needed to take any chances: after 12 stages of chasing – half the route of the Vuelta – the white jersey was now his. All that remained was to consolidate his lead, which he did consummately in the final time-trial – not for nothing was he known as the 'Titan of Otxandiano'. Poor Costa lost nearly eight minutes that day, in just 53 kilometres. As so often happens, the leader's jersey had given him wings; stripped of it, he slumped. All the will and strength with which he had defended his unlikely leadership drained from him in the final days as first Berrendero, and then Lambrichts, relegated him further down the general classification.

While Costa had been race leader, Galindo didn't hesitate to change their original line-up and include his name in their daily advertisements. Understandably, they wanted to cash in on his glory, although officially he continued to be an 'independent with affinities' and had to fend for himself. Given the precarious nature of the teams, it was understandable that Langarica should suffer palpitations on the last stage, when his team-mate Berrendero escaped from the peloton and disappeared in search of victory in Madrid. In fact, Berrendero, a man of his word, only wanted to win the stage in his own backyard and had no plans to 'betray' Langarica, even to the extent of checking the time difference, to make sure the gap didn't grow too wide. But the Basque wasn't taking any chances, and pledged a good portion of his prize money in securing aid, especially from the Dutch, to keep the gap low.

The first Basque winner of the Vuelta, he returned home to a hero's reception, with bands playing in the streets of Bilbao, while Manuel Costa could only dream of what might have been, little realising at that moment that the story would be repeated the following year.

1947   The 1947 Vuelta, despite its May date overlapping with the Giro d'Italia, was the most international edition since before the Civil War, a fact which sent the sports daily *Marca* into raptures, as it prematurely enthused about the end of Spain's isolation, which it painted as wholly unjust:

> The reality is that today an embassy of foreign riders is coming to Spain to witness at close-hand the organisational capacity of our people, to compete against Spaniards, to win or lose – that is the nature of sport – and then to proclaim the hospitality of this land which, bit by bit and with faith in its destiny, is struggling in every area of life with unbridled passion and a charming optimism.

So much for the regime-pleasing rhetoric; the reality was five Belgians, four Italians and three Dutchmen. In fact, some of them were classy riders who, between them, would collect a total of seven stage-wins. With the Spanish riders, however, the organisers had more difficulty. Those affiliated to Barcelona's Union Deportiva de Sans, including talented Bernardo Ruiz from Alicante – who in 1952 would become the first Spaniard to reach the podium in the Tour de France – were unable to come to a financial agreement, and Langarica refused to use the official Galindo tyres, since he was sponsored by rival Dalton–Auto.

The Spanish cyclists had a love–hate relationship with Galindo tubulars. Miguel Poblet, who became Spain's Classics king in the 1950s, remembers:

> We were always very short of material here in Spain. Galindo only manufactured car tyres, but due to the lack of material, any cyclist who had a tubular – old, good quality and foreign-made – gave it to them to study and they created their own.
>
> But as always happens when you don't have much experience in something, it turned out that they were smaller than the wheels, and to put them on, you had to use your teeth, and when you punctured, you'd take the new tubular and hang it from the branch of a tree and then pull…

There must have been many broken branches in trees across Spain in the 1940s but, apart from its over-blown 24 stages, the '47 edition of the Vuelta barely lived up to *Marca*'s hubris. The first 2,000 kilometres were a passive procession, with nobody showing the slightest inclination to dislodge Delio Rodríguez from the lead he'd established on the first day. Only in the Basque mountains did it come to life, and the animator was a man with memories to expunge – Manuel Costa, no longer an 'Independent' but sporting the team colours of Galindo.

On the morning of stage 12, as they set out to ride the 212 kilometres from Bilbao to Santander, Costa was lying fourth overall, at 10'–35". That evening he was in the lead, five minutes ahead of the Belgian Edouard Van Dyck on general classification. Not only had Costa ridden superbly, first and out alone over the three major cols, he was the principle beneficiary of a ten-minute penalty given to Delio for holding on to the back of a car.

Yet there was little optimism that he could hold that advantage. In fact, the prevailing opinion was that he'd probably forfeit his gains the next day on the same Santander–Reinosa road where he'd finally succumbed the previous year. But, to general surprise, he held on and continued to preserve his lead. At one point, Van Dyck closed the gap to 15 seconds, but three days later in Galicia he punctured and, since it was in all their interests, a fast-travelling group of Spaniards went to the front to prevent the Belgian from bridging the gap: Costa's breathing space was back to 2'–16". 'It'll all be resolved in the Astorga–León time-trial,' he said. 'I'll have to battle, but the truth is that I'm in great form.'

But all that self-confidence was to no avail. However good his form and high his morale, he was up against a man who could ride against the clock better than any Spaniard. Van Dyck covered the 47 kilometres four and a half minutes quicker than Costa, and it was all over. In little more than an hour, ten days of sweat and a year of dreaming were to end again in tears.

Not that Costa collapsed this year. He preserved his second place overall, and, indeed, he was back on the offensive during the final run-in to Madrid, but the Belgians and their Dutch allies were far too wily to allow any last-minute surprise. The home riders had to be content with the consolation of Delio Rodríguez's eight stage-wins and Emilio's mountain prize. Van Dyck's win was a premonition of a future when foreigners would obliterate the Spanish climbers with their superior time-trialing skills.

Two days after the Vuelta's conclusion, the regime was treated to a rare official visit from abroad. 'Evita' Duarte de Perón, representing Spain's lone ally, Argentina, arrived in Madrid and swanned around the city in her furs and jewels, despite the summer temperatures and the tightened belts of the citizens. Franco's wife, prim and plain, but with a taste for baubles, was horrified by the competition.

1948   Another small foreign contingent of cyclists came in 1948, but as this year the Vuelta overlapped with the Tour de France, the Belgians brought nobody of the calibre of Van Dyck (who finished 14th in the French race that year), and the Italian, Felix Adriano, who'd won four stages in 1947, was not in the same form twelve months later, and abandoned the race early on. The 1948 Vuelta turned, therefore, into a battle between the two men who were currently the strongest in the Spanish peloton – the two major absentees of the previous year – Dalmacio Langarica, the '46 winner and the 23-year-old Bernardo Ruiz.

Despite the impetus given to the race by their struggle, this was to be the slowest Vuelta on record. In a scorching heatwave all the way up the Mediterranean coast, the peloton slugged it out, the lead changing repeatedly. Riders withdrew with sunstroke, and some stages were run off at little more than 20kph, which, inevitably, resulted in the organisers withholding half the prize money. When the race turned inland after Barcelona the heat became even more unbearable.

Racing was out of the question; the only aim was survival. It took the peloton seven hours to cross the 160 kilometres of arid, semi-desert between Lérida and Zaragoza in temperatures that touched 43 degrees, with not a living soul venturing outdoors into that furnace to watch them pass. Bunched close together, the cyclists rolled along at the pace of a farm wagon, stopping at each village to fill up their bottles and douse themselves with buckets of water begged from the locals. Ignoring the organisers, they gave their own signal to set off again, braced to endure the fiery sun till the next oasis.

Only in Zaragoza did the heatwave mercifully break and conditions become more favourable, luckily in time for the mammoth split-stage of 276 kilometres to San Sebastián. Setting out at seven in the morning, and with an hour's break for lunch in Pamplona, it was half-past eight in the evening when the riders climbed off their bikes. Langarica won that day (his third stage-win of the race), his lead over Ruiz extending to 2'-42", with the mountains of his Basque homeland still to come.

In a drizzle, which turned to snow at the top of the climbs, the 34 survivors of the original 54 set out from San Sebastián to cover the 269-kilometre loop to Bilbao, still reeling from the abrupt change in climactic conditions. Once on to the first major obstacle, the Urkiola, the race leader predictably began to force the pace. This was Langarica's territory, where he'd effectively won the race two years before; he knew the terrain intimately and was out to press his advantage. He was first over the summit – which meant another minute's bonus – having gradually ridden most of the peloton off his wheel.

One of the few who kept up the pace was Bernardo Ruiz, a young man who'd had to learn the art of survival at a very early age. The son of a poor agricultural labourer, he was only 13 when his father had been sent off to the Republican trenches in the Civil War. In the years after the war the family had suffered under the reprisals, which only stopped in 1945 when the local Guardia Civil saw Bernardo's photograph in the pages of *Marca*: he'd won a race organised by the Falange youth movement – and there he was in the sports paper, receiving the trophy from the hands of a Falange official. Soon after that, with just 350 pesetas in his pocket, the 20-year old took the train to Barcelona to ride the Volta a Catalunya. He knew nobody there – he'd never travelled beyond Valencia – and he had to win prize money almost daily simply to keep going. When he duly won the race, his 350-peseta investment had yielded a return of 17,000; on the bicycle he'd found his means of escape from hunger and poverty.

With 80 kilometres remaining of that 12th stage to Bilbao, Langarica punctured. In a flash, Ruiz, Emilio Rodríguez and three others had swept past. Since it benefited each one to put time into the Basque, they worked in close unison to maintain the gap. Behind them, the Titan was justifying his nickname and his reputation, holding them at a minute and a half, or less, for kilometre after kilometre, through Guernica, down to Bermeo and then back inland and on to the Sollube. On that short, but steep ascent, the leading group fell apart, but by now Langarica's long solo chase was starting to take its toll. On the 10-per-cent slopes, the gap started to widen, and Ruiz was already the leader on the road as he crossed the summit, just ahead of Emilio Rodríguez. On the long descent into Bilbao towards his third stage-win, he increased his advantage by a further minute.

The next morning, Bernardo Ruiz was at the starting-line in the leader's jersey, but with 1,600 kilometres still to ride, a two-minute advantage on his rival seemed negligible. As the peloton left Bilbao, the race between the two strong men was still wide open. Yet eight hours later, in Santander, it was all but over, and for the second day running, it was punctures that did for Langarica.

The first came after just 25 kilometres, but it was too early in a day of heavy climbing for anybody to pay much attention. The second came moments after Julián Berrendero had attacked on the lower ramparts of the Azón, the day's second major ascent. The negro with the blue eyes was now 36 years old, and on the edge of retirement. His powers may have been on the wane, but on those famous Basque slopes where he'd once been invincible he could still soar. It wasn't his attack that provoked the reaction from Ruiz, however – at 13th overall, 48′–59″ down, Berrendero was no longer a threat – but Langarica's repeated misfortune with his tyres.

Berrendero was first over the top, hotly pursued by Ruiz and a small posse of team-mates from the Catalan Sans Cycling Club, out to put distance between themselves and Langarica. The Basque arrived five minutes further back but, lacking the team support that Ruiz was enjoying, he was losing ground all the time. Then, when the gap had opened up to nearly eight minutes, he punctured a third time, and it was all over.

On the approach to Santander, Berrendero was caught by the Asturian rider Bernardo Capó, who'd escaped from the Ruiz group, and then, almost in sight of the finish, the *Madrileño* punctured. After having initiated the action of the day, he had to settle for third place on the stage. It would be Spain's last glimpse of the great man at his most majestic.

For Langarica, it had been two days of frustration. His countrymen had been forced to witness how he lost his white and red leader's jersey, before dropping to third overall behind Delio Rodríguez, with all hope gone of a repeat of his 1946 victory. His promise that there would be 'no peace until Madrid' was a forlorn gesture. In fact, he wouldn't even make the podium in the capital because, four days later, as the peloton wound its way through Galicia, he broke his handlebars on a fast descent and crashed heavily. It says much for his resilient spirit and physical strength that he was able to continue with such deep contusions, but even 'the Titan' could not prevent Capó from ousting him from the podium.

Once more, the final outcome of the Vuelta had been shaped by the chance factor of who punctured, when and where. A matter of luck, except that some riders seemed particularly prone to suffer that misfortune; others, such as Bernardo Ruiz, were less often afflicted. Ruiz, it was said, loved his tubulars: he bought the best ones he could, cured them properly and, in a race such as the Vuelta, changed them often – before they punctured. Later, when he became wealthy – and he was the first Spanish cyclist to become rich – he bought the very best Italian Clements and Pirellis, and would have some 60 hanging, maturing in his garage. He'd learned from a young age that such care paid dividends.

On 4th July Ruiz arrived back in Madrid a dual winner – first on general classification and King of the Mountains. The bouquets on the final podium, however, were reserved for Berrendero, who'd retired two days earlier on learning of his father's death. Of the seven Vueltas he rode, this was the only one he failed to complete: he had won twice, finished second twice, and also taken the Mountains prize twice. The last surviving cycling hero of the Republican era was close to hanging up his wheels, and certainly didn't deserve the ignominious ending to his career that lay in wait.

* * * * *

The morale of Spaniards by the end of the forties was very low. Shunned by most of the world, and paralysed by the regime's defiant and unrealistic self-contained economic policy, there was no sign of an emergence from the post-war depression. Countries that had endured the Second World War were already well ahead. Foreigners who travelled in Spain at that time reported conversations with despondent people, bitter and exasperated at how low their country had fallen. In his autobiography, Eric Hobsbawm remembers how: 'Time and again ... people would say things like "This is the worst country in the world" or "People in this country are poorer than anywhere else".'

Unsurprisingly, the cinema became a favourite place of escape, but even there Spaniards felt cheated. In 1948, Fritz Lang's 'Gilda' was released, but the suspicion spread that the Church had censored the famous scene where Rita Hayworth sensuously removes one of her long opera gloves during her performance of 'Put the Blame on Mame'. Audiences were convinced that the rest of the world was enjoying a full-blown strip-tease.

Spanish cycling had also suffered the consequences of isolation. In 1946, the director of the Swiss team observed with surprise how differently Spanish races were run:

> The speed is intermittent: either flat out or at a snail's pace. That's not the way cyclists ride abroad. The strong men work from the beginning without letting up, seeking to tire out their opponents. Those who can't keep up, fall behind and never catch up. That explains the frequent averages of 35 to 40kph in French, Belgian and Swiss races.

So, when Jacques Goddet stretched out a neighbourly hand, inviting a Spanish team to take part in the 1949 Tour and selecting San Sebastián as a host town, the six cyclists chosen to represent *la Patria* were filled with foreboding. Ill-equipped and ill-prepared, only their captain, 37-year-old Berrendero, had experience of racing abroad. Their opponents would be well-paid, well-fed professionals – while they were expected to dig into their own pockets to meet all the expenses. The Federation promised 75 kilos of sugar, which vanished, destined for the black market, and provided a team director who was stone deaf.

None of these handicaps mattered to the regime – on the contrary, it was a chance for Spanish blood to show the world what could be achieved when the odds were down. Any grumbling about money was silenced: the team needed to realise that it would not be riding for financial gain, but for the honour of representing abroad the glory that was Spain. And, of course, they didn't even last a week.

The Press reported the event as if the cyclists abandoned through lack of back bone, although Langarica made it clear that had they received the same technical service as other teams, they would have survived to the mountain stages. When his gear mechanism broke, the rest of the team were ordered to wait with him, but it was 38 minutes before the team-car arrived, and they had no chance of making the time cut. To the embarrassment of the regime, there were no red and yellow national jerseys in the peloton when it reached San Sebastián. Pilloried as the 'dwarfs of the road', the cyclists were punished by having their racing licences revoked.

Goddet was more relaxed about the debacle and, at the reception in San Sebastián, extended an invitation to the following year's Tour. The invitation was declined. Perhaps the administrators had finally realised the truth in what Bernardo Ruiz had been saying to them all along: 'We are not ready to go to the Tour de France'.

So, there was no Tour for the Spaniards in 1950, but there was another Vuelta. In 1949, López Dóriga had been too involved organising the Tour expedition, but now, for one more year, the Catholic daily *Ya* managed to find the budget to reinstate the race in mid August. In a meagre peloton of 42 riders, the foreign contingent of five Belgians and three Italians had little more quality than it had quantity. Although the Italian sprinter, Umberto Drei, won four stages, he was never a serious threat overall, and the principle Belgian, Omer Braeckeveldt, returned home demoralised, after losing six minutes on the fourth stage. The race was dominated by the Rodríguez brothers: Emilio repeated Delio's success of 1945 (and also won the mountain prize, for the third time) while his younger sibling, Manuel, was second overall.

1950

It was altogether a dull affair in which public interest declined as the race progressed through its interminable 24 stages towards a predictable finish. On several occasions the racing was so devoid of commitment that the organisers threatened to resort to Desgrange's trick of converting the following day's stage into a time-trial. In truth, the sponsors could hardly have felt that they received a good return on their investment. Indeed, not only would it turn out to be their last sponsorship of the Vuelta, but it would be five years before any other organisation was prepared to take on the task.

1955–1958

Two Roosters in the Farmyard

Although the worst 'years of hunger' were over, Spain was still struggling with acute economic problems, which its hopelessly archaic government was ill-equipped to deal with. In Franco's musty utopia, the military and the church were in charge of keeping corrupt modern values at bay, although the reality of widespread poverty and rumbles of unrest among workers and students was threatening to intrude. But the dictator, whose hold on power would last for nigh on four decades, was a man with a sharp instinct for survival. While Europe was turning its back on Spain, Franco was able to present himself to the USA as a solid ally against the pressing threat of communism. A deal was struck in 1953: in return for allowing US military bases on Spanish soil, the economy would receive a generous injection of much-needed dollars. And in 1957, the *Caudillo*, who knew next to nothing about economics, was persuaded to bring into the government a number of younger, better-educated 'technocrats', whose more enlightened policy would eventually bring benefits to the country. And as for morality: if in the forties State censors were drawing vests on photographs of boxers to screen their nudity, by the sixties women were free to wear bikinis on the beaches, as Franco realised that tourist-generated wealth would breathe life into his regime.

It was still the grey, pessimistic period of the mid-'50s when Alejandro Echevarría stepped in to save the Vuelta. He was the director of a Basque newspaper, *El Correo Español–El Pueblo Vasco*, whose unwieldy name was the result of a fusion of two publications after the Civil War. When he took over the newspaper in 1951, Echevarría set about modernising it and, once this was accomplished, scouted around for a new focus for his considerable energy. A photograph shows a brash-looking man, wearing sunglasses and a flamboyant necktie, exuding self-confidence. Luckily for the Vuelta, he was a great sports enthusiast and brave enough to invest the then astronomical quantity of six million pesetas needed to resurrect it.

1955   One look at the international line-up of the 1955 Vuelta confirms that Spain was no longer a pariah. For the first time there were over 100 participants: 60 Spanish, 12 French, 12 Italian, six Swiss, two German and, last but not least, six British cyclists made up the 106-strong peloton divided into small teams of six. Few Spanish cyclists had raced abroad, so the Vuelta would be an invaluable opportunity to ride and learn alongside the foreigners. The route had been considerably reduced since the previous edition: 2,740 as opposed to 3,932 kilometres, with 15 rather than 24 stages. A shorter, livelier race had come back after five years of absence.

As in the Tour de France, the teams represented their nations, and Spain's main rival was considered to be Italy, led by Fiorenzo Magni – Italian Champion, winner of the 1951 Giro, and shortly to win it again in 1955. The French leaders were Gilbert Bauvin, Louis Bergaud and Raphaël Géminiani (later to become Anquetil's *directeur sportif*). The six Britons had been nominated by the impoverished National Cyclists Union; among them was John Pottier:

We went by air to Madrid and when we arrived we had to pay the costs of the extra baggage – our bikes and equipment. We had to pay for that ourselves, so we ended up eating bananas and bread rolls. That was all we could afford; we had no money left. We were taken up to the start in Bilbao in a Spanish army lorry.

The Spanish cyclists were divided among eight regional and two national teams: 'A' and 'B'. The 'A' team was the showcase for the cream of Spanish talent, and fairly bristled with egos. All the cycling nations have had their famous rivalries: Bartoli and Coppi in Italy, Anquetil and Poulidor in France. In Spain, it was Jesús Loroño and Federico Bahamontes who gripped and divided the nation with their battles both on and, when passions ran high, off the bicycle.

While Bahamontes is internationally famous for his exploits in the Tour de France, which he won in 1959 as well as claiming the King of the Mountains prize six times, Jesús Loroño forged his palmarés almost exclusively in Spain, and remains largely unknown outside her borders. His rivalry with Bahamontes marked an era of Spanish cycling, with *Loroñistas* and *Bahamontistas* trying to convince each other that Jesús was a more complete rider or that Federico was a better climber.

Born in a farmstead in Larrabetzu, in the Basque province of Vizcaya, the eighth of nine children, Loroño was 11 years old when the Civil War broke out. The village was near to the 'iron belt', a front line established to defend Bilbao, and Jesús dug trenches for a *duro* (five pesetas) a day. He was young enough to avoid being imprisoned in a labour camp, a fate suffered by five of his brothers when the Basque Country fell to the Nationalists. When his father died in 1941, Loroño had to work hard, cycling into the mountains to chop wood, as well as helping on the farm. He started competing in local races, sneaking out to train at night while his mother threatened to take an axe to his bicycle, fretting that he would catch TB with all that sweating in the cold damp air.

About to emigrate to Chile to join one of his brothers, Loroño was called up to do his military service and was lucky enough to have a cycling *aficionado* for a captain, who encouraged him to keep training. One day in 1947, Loroño asked permission to take part in a local race, but was refused; the captain would only grant him leave if he went to Asturias to compete with the professionals in the classic Climb of the Naranco, which Fermín Trueba had won the previous two years. He could hardly disobey orders, so Loroño found himself in Oviedo lining up with the 'cracks' to take part in what was then a two-day race, without enough money in his pocket for the journey home. By coming third on the first day, he won enough to cover his expenses, and approached the second stage more confidently. With astonishment, the experienced cyclists turned to look at this sturdy young Basque with black curly hair and strong features, who dared to attack at the foot of the Naranco. Instead of dropping back as expected, he won – not only the stage, but the overall and the combative prize as well.

His career was launched, although not at an opportune moment. Spanish cycling was still years away from recovery, as the 1949 Tour fiasco showed. When Loroño made his debut in the '53 Tour, he won the Mountains prize and a stage in the Pyrenees; he would achieve his best classification, fifth, in 1957. It was his bad luck to be competing at a time when Spanish cyclists abroad were too obsessed with stocking up on the quality bicycle material that was unavailable at home to dedicate themselves wholeheartedly to the team effort. There's good reason for thinking that, with proper support, Loroño could have achieved much more, perhaps even matching the exploits of his younger rival, who enjoyed better opportunities.

Far from the green valleys of the Basque Country, Bahamontes was born on the sun-scorched Meseta, near Toledo, where from a young age he worked delivering fresh produce, towing it in a cart behind his bicycle. In an interview to mark his 70th birthday, Bahamontes reminisced about growing up during the 'years of hunger': 'I worked the black-market and ate fried potato peel and cats, roasted as if they were rabbits. At the age of 17, I was loading my bike with 150-kilo sacks of potatoes. And I only weighed 56.' Back-breaking work, which would toughen him up for his future career.

Fame arrived in 1954 when Bahamontes won the Mountains prize in the Tour de France, the year after Loroño, and 17 years after Julian Berrendero. The story of how he stopped for an ice-cream at the top of a col as he waited for the peloton to catch up is now legendary, but in fact he was only continuing a tradition among Spanish cyclists: in the 1930s, Berrendero and Ezquerra would often dismount for a quick beer at the top of a climb. Securing the Mountains prize was considered next best to winning the Tour, as it guaranteed publicity and lucrative contracts. The overall was discounted, of course, and going for stage-wins was considered a waste of energy better reserved for picking up mountain points.

From the start Bahamontes was regarded as a 'character', his wiry figure instantly recognisable as he flew away from his rivals – back straight, hands gripping the centre of the handlebars, bobbing head marking time with a swift pedal cadence. His typical tactic was to give an experimental acceleration to see how it affected his rivals. He would then force the pace again, and few could or dared to follow, for they would surely pay the price later.

Although direct rivals, for years Bahamontes and Loroño were forced to compete together in the same team. To make a modern comparison, imagine if Oscar Sevilla and Aitor González, after their clash in the 2002 Vuelta, had both been obliged to continue in Kelme and compete in the same races instead of going their separate ways. The atmosphere would have been intolerably tense. Loroño and Bahamontes were more restricted in an era when a place in the national team was every cyclist's dream. Yet their rivalry was not wholly negative: in the words of Angel Giner, biographer of Bahamontes: 'A hero, whether cyclist or warrior, can never reach such heights without an enemy to defeat.'

Thrusting them together only emphasised how radically different their characters were. Loroño, the 'Lion of Larrabetzu', was a reserved man, with immense pride, who would be inspired by the fervour of the Basque fans to give everything he had. The 'Eagle of Toledo' was voluble and volatile, given to acting on strange whims and apparently impervious to any hopes placed on him. One day, he would be living up to his nickname, leaving everyone in awe as he soared apparently effortlessly up the steepest mountain, and the next, behaving like a flustered hen. His quitting of the '57 Tour is another legend: claiming his arm hurt from a calcium injection received that morning, he flung off his cycling shoes in mid-stage and invaded a French family's roadside picnic, curling up in a foetal position, deaf to all entreaties. He would not budge, not for his mother, his wife, Spain or Franco. But people forgave him in the end, as a genius can be pardoned for his foibles.

But they were not the only stars in the national team: Miguel Poblet and Salvador Botella were also contenders for overall victory in the resurrected Vuelta of 1955, and they were accompanied by Francisco Massip and veteran Bernardo Ruiz, who still had some shots up his sleeve. In a situation redolent of what sometimes occurs in the World Championships today, most notoriously in the Italian team, Julian Berrendero was presented with this dazzling line-up and given the unenviable task of directing it.

On 23rd April, at 11.48 a.m. precisely, the Mayor of Bilbao cut the yellow and red tape, and the 106 cyclists set off surrounded by huge cheering crowds on the first of three stages on the steep hills of the Basque Country. It was an ideal day for the Spanish riders to show off their climbing prowess, but to their chagrin, Bauvin escaped on the Azcarate and crossed the line with 1'-18" on the field to take the first yellow jersey. Then came an historic day when, for the first time, the Vuelta left national territory and entered France (while remaining in the Basque region) with a finish in Bayonne. Bahamontes and Loroño launched a strong attack on the first-category Jaizkibel – the climb that is used today in the Clasica San Sebastián – but just as they were crossing the frontier, the Frenchmen Bauvin and Bergaud caught them up, determined to defend their gains on home ground. Bauvin went on to win his second stage. On the following day, however, he cracked on the Puerto de Velate, and to immense national satisfaction, Loroño was the new leader.

He was in yellow, but without a moment's peace to enjoy it, as the stage to Zaragoza saw a constant battle and the Spanish nationals were unable to control the race. When he punctured, Loroño was already losing four and a half minutes to Bauvin. Poblet handed him a wheel, and the team chased furiously, managing to catch Bauvin's group just ten kilometres from the finish.

Nothing much was expected to happen between Zaragoza and Lérida: it was considered a transitional stage to connect the North with the Mediterranean. Not so this year. Skirmishes broke out immediately and the peloton splintered. By kilometre 120, the leading group with four French nationals had 12 minutes on Loroño. The Spanish team's tactics were in disarray: Bahamontes and Poblet were completely worn out, having struggled long and hard to catch up after a puncture, while the threesome, Ruiz, Botella and Massip, were somewhere ahead in no-man's land.

At this point, the Basque cycling correspondent for *La Gaceta del Norte*, Francisco de Ubieta, decided to intervene. Acting as an unauthorised *directeur sportif*, for which he would be penalised, he drove up to Loroño and warned him that unless he reacted immediately, his team-mates would destroy his hopes for the overall. Loroño began the chase, working alone for 60 kilometres, until Fiorenzo Magni took pity and joined in. There was nothing in it for the Italian leader, other than to hone his form for the Giro, the principle reason he'd come to the Vuelta (although he wasn't averse to picking up a couple of stage-wins: the Barcelona time-trial, and the thirteenth stage between Madrid and Valladolid.) With Magni's help the renegade Spaniards were rounded up, not far from the finish.

Loroño criticised them bitterly for leaving him behind, but they were unrepentant. As far as Botella was concerned, Loroño had betrayed *them* by working to close the gap. While the Spanish nationals squabbled amongst themselves, the French showed they were the strongest, with Raphaël Géminiani the new leader, and the Italians were about to begin their own festival: of the ten stages left to dispute, they would win nine.

Taking advantage of the rest-day in Barcelona, the sports correspondent of *El Correo Catalan* went to the hotel where the Spanish nationals were staying to gauge the atmosphere in the team and find out what lay behind all the disputes. First, he knocked at the door of Poblet and Loroño. The Catalan sprinter tried to avoid the issue: 'Don't ask me. I'm always at the back, doing my best not to get dropped. I don't see anything.' So the journalist turned to Loroño with a direct question: 'Why do you argue so much?' 'Because we all want to win, and only one of us can,' was his terse reply.

Realising no more was forthcoming, the journalist continued up the corridor to Ruiz and Botella's room. 'So, what happened after the Lérida stage?' he asked, referring to an incident involving the Basque journalist, Ubieta. 'He insulted us and said things I wouldn't put up with from anyone,' replied Ruiz, stressing his own self-restraint in the matter. His room-mate Botella was more concerned to make his own ambitions clear: 'I fully intend to win the Vuelta.'

There remained only the Massip–Bahamontes room to visit. On the question of team friction, Bahamontes put the blame solidly on his rival: 'Five of us are united, because we're fed up with Loroño and what he says.' Massip staunchly defended the tactics of the Lérida stage: 'It doesn't matter that Loroño lost the jersey and dropped to second, if we put four men in the top ten. The problem is that this Basque journalist is turning his head, and now he thinks he's a bigger star than Bobet.' The reporter shut the door on this blast of indignation.

After Barcelona the yellow jersey remained in French possession, although it changed hands. Small, skinny, dark-haired Jean Dotto had leapt to the top of the classification in two giant bounds. The first was on the stage from Lérida to Barcelona, where he was in an escape that finished eight minutes ahead of the peloton. The British rider Ian Steel was prominent in that group – in fact, at one point, Dotto had to call to him to slow down. The second was on the tenth stage, when Dotto's group arrived in Cuenca nearly 12 minutes clear. Regardless of Géminiani's personal feelings about relinquishing the leadership, the French team closed ranks around Dotto, defending his position to the end.

Many teams had lost several riders before the day of the team time-trial held in Madrid's Retiro Park, so the organizers had to group them together. By now, the British team had been reduced to one sole survivor – Ian Steel. His last remaining companion, John Pottier, had retired after suffering an allergic reaction to an anti-tetanus injection in Valencia, and in Madrid, Steel, also, called it a day. He was still in good physical shape and well placed overall, but he felt isolated, having no one in the peloton to talk to.

'Loneliness,' said Steel, 'is one of the biggest handicaps any British rider suffers in Continental racing.'

The next day, enthusiastic crowds accompanied the cyclists in cars and motorbikes as they left the capital to the top of the Alto de Los Leones, the pass that links the provinces of Madrid and Segovia. It was another disastrous day for the Spanish team. As the peloton entered the streets of Valladolid, Loroño's bicycle was playing up, and he swapped with Bahamontes, who was very low on general classification, plagued by a knee injury that would keep him out of the Tour de France that year. Bahamontes promptly crashed as the handlebars gave way. He finished, bruised and bloodied, riding a bike lent him by a spectator.

The final stage of the race began and ended in Bilbao, and Loroño, desperately wanting to redeem himself in front of a home crowd, tried to attack on the Sollube, but he didn't have the power to get away. Jean Dotto thus became the first Frenchman to win the Vuelta, with his team-mate Raphael Géminiani in third place. The Spanish had to console themselves with the revelation Antonio Jiménez Quiles (another beneficiary of uncontrolled escape groups), who took second place and the green points jersey.

Discounting the foibles of the national team, Alejandro Echevarría and company could be satisfied with the way their Vuelta had gone: there had been enormous public interest and each stage was closely fought. *La Vanguardia* reported with pride that the French sports critic Gaston Benac 'has declared that its atmosphere and organisation give the Tour of Spain a category similar to that of "Le Tour".'

As the Press ruminated on the lack of Spanish team spirit, for which the hapless Julián Berrendero was taking much of the blame, the United States was petitioning for Spain to be admitted to the United Nations. Formal acceptance was granted in October. This same year also saw the release of one of the most memorable films produced under Franco's dictatorship: 'Death of a Cyclist', directed by Juan Antonio Bardem. Its bleak portrayal of life in contemporary Spain somehow avoided censorship, and Bardem was awarded the Cannes critics' prize. He was languishing in jail for his affiliation with the Communist Party at the time, but international clamour won his release, at least temporarily.

The Vuelta's new organisers, always on the look out for foreign stars who would give their race lustre, were disappointed not to sign up the great Fausto Coppi for the 1956 race, but happy to secure the participation of Frenchman Louison Bobet, winner of the previous three Tours de France, and the Swiss 'pedaller of charm' Hugo Koblet, now in his veteran years but with an impressive palmarés (1950 Giro, 1951 Tour, 1954 World Champion). These two guests of honour arrived in flamboyant style, causing a sensation in austere Spain. Koblet drove as far as San Sebastián in a gleaming Alfa Romeo, where he parked and cycled into Bilbao. Bobet flew to Biarritz in his private plane.

Altogether there were nine teams of ten riders each. Bobet was **1956** accompanied by the leading French cyclists Jean Dotto, Gilbert Bauvin and Louis Bergaud, while the star of the Belgian team was top roadman sprinter Rik van Steenbergen, World Champion of 1946, and about to reclaim the title in 1956 and 1957. The Italian leaders were Angelo Conterno and Giuseppe Buratti, who'd finished as King of the Mountains in the 1955 Vuelta. Riding with Koblet in the mixed Swiss–British selection was Brian Robinson, although, as usual in these hybrid formations, there was scant team spirit. Robinson explains: 'Koblet made it clear that he wasn't going to share the prize money. So you thought, "Well, if you're not going to share the money, I'm not riding for you. I'll ride for myself."' That strategy would earn Robinson an eventual eighth place overall, which coupled with another eighth place in the Tour of Switzerland, secured him an invitation to the Tour de France that year.

Persuading the Spanish riders of the necessity to work together for the common good was the task of the new Spanish team director Luis Puig – the man who would save the Vuelta in 1979. He assured everyone that the mistakes of 1955 would not be repeated, but when questioned about who was team leader, side-stepped the issue. He explained that no one took pride of place, and everyone had their allotted task: Salvador Botella would fight for the general classification, Poblet was to go for stage-wins, while Bahamontes and Loroño would collect mountain points.

Interpreting his director's words to mean only one thing, Loroño couldn't hold in his fury: 'Botella has no right to be leader. I've just beaten him in the Tour of Eibar but apparently this means nothing to Luis Puig. It's intolerable. I'm the strongest, so if anyone's to be leader, it should be me.' And so the conflict and tension had begun even before the race had started. Bahamontes tried to explain the problem in plain language: 'Ten who want to win, don't win, while one or two helped by eight or nine, can win.' Very logical, and convincing, but … who was to be the one? The aces hadn't fought their way up to the national team only to serve as mere *gregarios*, a thoroughly undervalued role in Spanish cycling of the fifties. Bahamontes once complained that if you asked a supposed *gregario* to fetch a waterproof from the team-car, you'd be told to get it yourself.

Apart from the national team, Spain also fielded four regionals, representing Cantabria, the Central-South area, the Pyrenees and the Mediterranean. The route would be similar to the previous year, beginning in the north, visiting Asturias, before heading south across the Meseta, and reaching the east coast in Alicante. Skirting the Mediterranean northwards, the peloton would return to the Basque country for several hard hilly stages. An area without a cycling tradition, Andalucía, was excluded, although when the Vuelta got underway, the area was hosting a different kind of tour, as Franco conducted a lengthy trip around southern Spain, addressing Falangist rallies and inaugurating reservoirs.

The General certainly enjoyed better weather than the peloton as, during the first stages, the cyclists were drenched, battered by winds and even snowed upon. The third stage, between Oviedo and Valladolid, should have crossed the Puerto de Pajares, the pass through the Cantabrian Cordillera, but there was too much snow to let the peloton through and the icy descent would have been treacherous. Shortened to 175 kilometres, the stage was disputed at great speed, perhaps to ward off the cold, and Miguel Poblet won the sprint. Van Steenbergen had taken the first stage, so the battle was on between the two leading sprinters. Poblet was currently the most highly rated Spanish cyclist abroad, but at home he was something of an anomaly. He didn't come from a poor background and he was a Classics specialist, not a climber. Just like Oscar Freire today, Poblet had to emigrate, finding a niche for himself in Italian cycling.

The race leader at this point was an Italian rider from Turin, Angelo Conterno, who had attacked on the second day, and obtained a margin of 3'–05". He was in good form, but not expected to hold the yellow jersey for long. The weather changed on the stage between Albacete and Alicante, as the cyclists reached the Mediterranean. The peloton relaxed, the riders warming their bones in the hot sun, as they followed the coast for three consecutive days.

The temperatures were high but no one was sweating. Even when Louison Bobet punctured three times in one day, no one was interested in making a move. Exasperated by this lack of activity, the organisers retained 10 per-cent of the prize money on the stage to Tarragona, as a wake-up call. Coasting along the sparkling Mediterranean, the peloton went by in a sunny haze, except for a few electrifying moments on the finishing-lines. In Albacete, Poblet had snatched victory from under Van Steenbergen's nose just as the Belgian was beginning to celebrate. The diminutive Catalan was on a roll and won again in Alicante. He was about to repeat victory in Valencia when Koblet blocked his path, giving Van Steenberg a clear run to take the stage. The Belgian also won the following day in Tarragona, so they were drawing three-all. The Spanish Press were not at all indignant about a foreign alliance against their man, they only wished their riders would show the same initiative.

The tenth stage was divided into two sections, with a 21-kilometre team time-trial held in Barcelona, consisting of four laps round Montjuic. It was a close battle which the French won by a mere second from the Spanish team. Louison Bobet was still regarded as the favourite to win overall, despite Conterno having held on to the yellow jersey for so many days. Everyone was sure that the decisive fight would occur when the peloton returned to the north but, in fact, it occurred much sooner.

After the time-trial, there was a short and apparently innocuous route of 133 kilometres inland to Tarrega, but it turned out to be as decisive as the most demanding mountainous stage. An extremely dangerous foursome broke away: Loroño attacked and was quickly followed by his team-mate Botella, the Italian race leader Conterno, and Frenchman Bauvin. After the peloton had shattered in a fuitless pursuit, Bauvin beat the other three to take the stage, 50 seconds ahead of Bahamontes' group, while Koblet and Bobet came in nearly five minutes later and Poblet trailed in at 16 minutes. There had been serious carnage.

While Koblet pulled out almost immediately, Bobet waited a couple of days before packing his bags, alleging a heavy cold. So much for the big stars. Louison tried to excuse his weak performance, arguing that his original plan to deal a decisive blow on the Puerto de Pajares had been foiled by the snow. Poblet also abandoned, demoralised to find himself half an hour down. In the race, Conterno was beginning to look increasingly comfortable as leader, followed by Bauvin in second place and then the three Spaniards: Bahamontes, Botella, and Loroño. Robinson, who'd had the bad luck to puncture when he was well placed on the Tarrega stage, was holding 11th place overall. His director, Raymond Louviot, was confident that he would finish the race in the top ten.

The stage to Bayonne provided a peculiar spectacle. As they reached Pamplona, Navarran Jesús Galdeano and the Italian Giancarlo Astrua were 16 minutes ahead of the peloton. Shaking off his escape companion with a spectacular acceleration, Astrua increased his own lead to 29 minutes, becoming virtual race leader. Some distance later he began to foam at the mouth and wobble all over the road. The stimulants he'd swallowed had worn off and now he could barely stay on the bike. Despite everything, he showed remarkable tenacity and finished 17'–38" ahead of the field. He promptly lost those 17 minutes in the time-trial the next day, cutting such a ghastly figure that he was pulled in for a medical check-up as soon as he crossed the line.

That time-trial kept the excitement level high because Conterno turned in a very weak performance, while Bahamontes finished second, which placed him just eight seconds behind the Italian on the general classification. He hoped to take the yellow jersey in the second sector to Pamplona that afternoon, but suffered an ill-timed puncture in the dusty pot-holed road. Still, what were eight seconds to the Eagle with four mountain stages ahead?

Expectations gathered around stage 15, ending in Bilbao after the traditional climbs of Jaizkibel, Elgueta and Urkiola. The Spanish and Italian teams were watching each other closely when another piece of bad luck struck Bahamontes: his headset suddenly jammed and he suffered a hard fall. He was escorted back to the group by four team-mates in time for the final climb and, despite his injuries, made a strong attack on the Urkiola. For a while Bahamontes was leader on the road, but his hopes were dashed as Conterno appeared by his side on the descent, after a frenetic chase: descending was never the Toledano's strong point. He would have preferred today's Vueltas, with plenty of summit stage-finishes.

It was now Loroño's turn to make a move and he attacked on the short climb of Santo Domingo just outside Bilbao, arriving at the finish in a small group with a minute on Conterno and company. Bahamontes was deeply frustrated by his bad luck while Loroño went to bed that night mulling over his own prospects: he was now third overall, only 43 seconds behind Conterno and 35 seconds from his team-mate.

The Vuelta had nearly come full circle as the riders set off for Vitoria, welcomed back by the heavy rain so characteristic of the Basque country. The balmy Mediterranean seemed far away. It was a miserable day for Bahamontes and not just because of the weather. When he first punctured in Logroño, nothing untoward happened, but when he punctured again near the Herrera, the Italian team made a concerted attack and Loroño went with them. Bahamontes fought desperately to make up lost time, but his luck had deserted him: he punctured again on the descent of Peñacerrada, and yet again two kilometres from the finish. He crossed the line nearly four minutes behind the Italians, and dropped to fourth place overall.

Here, the French team, with a great deal of fuss, announced that most of them were going home, claiming the sandwiches provided by the race organisers had given them food poisoning. Alejandro Echevarría, outraged, held a Press conference, and suggested it was all a smoke screen. The French, having lost their leader, were slinking off demoralised because their chances for success were blown. Echevarría invited the other teams to lodge complaints, but none did.

Loroño had one day to win back 43 seconds from Conterno. He was on home ground in front of his own people, but he held all of Spain's hopes. Conterno had strongly defended the yellow jersey for 14 days but he'd woken up with a high fever and his prospects seemed uncertain. Sure enough, he began to struggle on the Sollube when the Basque attacked, backed up by Bahamontes and Rene Marigil. Loroño crested the Sollube with over a minute on Conterno, but the Italian was rescued by willing hands pushing and pulling him to the top. Apart from his own team, Belgian, Swiss and French cyclists were all happy to help. Van Steenbergen, the winner of the stage, later confessed that his team and the other riders hired themselves out. Many years later, long after hanging up his wheels, Loroño still felt bitter about what happened that day:

The last straw was that I punctured on the descent, and Luis Puig took an eternity to give me a new wheel. In the end they caught me on the way through Las Arenas, and all the favourites finished together. The judges, who should have disqualified Conterno for climbing the Sollube without pedalling, turned a blind eye, and they gave him a ridiculous sanction of 30 seconds, which left me 13 seconds from victory. The times that I have remembered that Vuelta...

Being the moral victor was of no consolation at all.

And the Brits? Steel and Tony Hoar had retired well before the finish, but Robinson, riding strongly but discreetly throughout, had fulfilled his director's expectation and finished in eighth place overall.

1957   In 1957 all the tension that had been brewing between Loroño and Bahamontes exploded. After the disappointment of the previous year, Luis Puig was particularly determined to secure a Spanish victory. The perennial anxiety about who should be team leader was dealt with by agreeing that the responsibility would fall on whoever was best classified. The international participation was deemed satisfactory since it included the complete podium of the previous year's Tour de France: Frenchmen Roger Walkowiak and Gilbert Bauvin, and the Belgian Jan Adriaenssens. The Italian leader was Gastone Nencini, who would go on to win the Giro the following month, and find even greater glory in 1960 when he won the Tour. The route of this year's Vuelta was as short as in 1955, with only 15 stages (after losing one to snow) but what it lacked in length it made up in difficulty: it was a climber's race, filled with mountains.

Three days into the Vuelta, the peloton was on its way from Santander to the Asturian mining town of Mieres. Nationals Bahamontes and Botella were alert, and formed part of an early breakaway of thirteen. Loroño was caught napping and his error became evident when the group rapidly built up an advantage of 15 minutes. This was Bahamontes' day. Every time the road steepened he would force the pace. When they reached the Asturian capital of Oviedo, the break was still ten-strong but, shortly after, Bahamontes made the definitive attack and he crested the third-category Padrun alone. He reached Mieres 14 minutes ahead of the peloton and, for the first time ever, put on the Vuelta's yellow jersey.

Glory for Federico, and disaster for Loroño. The Basque was furious, as he'd begun the day as team leader, due to his third position in the overall. Where had been the support owed to him? Let down, he'd dropped to tenth place at nearly 13 minutes. He planned his revenge for the Puerto de Pajares, which the peloton had to cross to reach the next day's finish in León. Encouraged by the wet and cold conditions, and knowing that Bahamontes was less resistant to bad weather, he escaped in a group of nine. But Loroño's luck ran out as the race was 'neutralised' after 63 kilometres. It was the first time the Vuelta ever had to cancel a stage. The snow was already falling heavily, so higher up conditions would have been impossible. Loroño was riding with such anger, he had to be forcefully pulled off his bike. The cyclists were sent back to Mieres by train, finally reaching León at midnight. Meanwhile, the Asturian civil guard asked for help to rescue the 500 hapless spectators who were trapped by the snow at the top of Pajares.

Between Valladolid and Madrid, the leadership changed although it remained in Spanish hands. It all began after only eight kilometres when a spirited Italian, Gianno Ferlenghi, jumped clear, quickly joined by six others, including Salvador Botella, and their lead grew rapidly. Back in the peloton, Bahamontes was gnashing his teeth and arguing with his director, Luis Puig. He made a futile bid to close the gap, only to be rapidly reabsorbed. It's pretty certain that Bahamontes didn't find much consolation in the fact that the new race leader was his team-mate, Botella.

The next stage was a classic round trip over the Sierra of Madrid and Bahamontes channelled some of his frustration in an explosive climb of Los Leones. There was a rare incident of companionship, that day: when Federico punctured, Loroño waited for him and saved him from losing excessive time. Talking to the Press that evening, in a good mood after Botella had lost the yellow jersey to a member of the Central-South regional team, and having moved back up to second place at 54 seconds, Bahamontes stated confidently: 'Loroño will win the mountains. That's not my aim, as I'm going for the overall.' Loroño's opinion of this prediction could only be imagined.

Madrid to Cuenca was a day on the flat, but Bahamontes handled it expertly, getting into the right break with the French leaders. In spite of puncturing in the outskirts of Cuenca, he was able to retake the yellow jersey, while Walkowiak won the stage. The Toledano could seriously begin to hope for final victory. His rivals within the team were no longer a threat: Botella was suffering from a leg injury and Loroño was 11th at nearly 16 minutes. Yet, two days later, his world was turned upside-down.

The peloton had reached the Mediterranean and were following the coast northwards from Valencia to Tortosa, situated near the mouth of the River Ebro. As in other years, the proximity of the sea seemed to induce a holiday spirit and the cyclists dawdled along. But not everything followed the habitual script: a group had been permitted to escape early on, and they were to finish 22 minutes ahead.

There was a loose cannon in that year's Vuelta – Bernardo Ruiz, who some regard as the best cyclist Spain produced until Induráin came along. The veteran Ruiz hadn't been picked for the national team where, as he put it, his duties had been to act as 'Bahamontes' nanny'. It was a task he'd performed without relish, since the two cyclists were sworn enemies. In the '57 Vuelta, relieved of that irksome chore, he was enjoying his freedom as leader of the Mediterranean regional team, and spent the whole race riding aggressively to finish on the podium in third place.

Bernardo Ruiz remembers that when he decided to attack that day, on the road to Tortosa, he muttered in Loroño's ear, 'Come with me'. When Bahamontes realised that the escape was in earnest and his own position in danger, he became anxious and tried to react. But his director, Luis Puig, blocked the road with his car while team-mates held on to Federico's shorts. In Tortosa, Loroño was in yellow and Bahamontes was ignominiously dislodged to third place, six minutes behind the Basque, and three minutes behind Ruiz.

That night at dinner, Bahamontes couldn't contain himself. Overwhelmed by the injustice of it all, he unleashed an incessant tirade of indignant complaints, aimed mainly at Loroño. Finally, the quiet Basque could put up with no more. He got up and walked over to Federico. Grabbing him by his shirt-front, he enquired: 'What's your problem?'

There was instant silence. It was as if a plug had been pulled. Without another word, Bahamontes retreated to his room, from where he refused to move. He demanded his meal be sent upstairs, because Loroño was 'threatening to beat him up'.

Part of Bahamontes' indignation must have stemmed from a conviction that he was the strongest member of the team. He was probably right. Probably he should have won the '57 Vuelta, so what went wrong? The truth is he didn't have enough allies, and he lacked the qualities of a leader, rarely showing gratitude to his team-mates. Often they would escort him to the front of the peloton only to see him immediately drift to the back again. Then, if the peloton broke up, they would have to wear themselves out to close the gap, and, on top of all that, have to listen to Bahamontes complaining that they'd abandoned him. In contrast, Loroño had two particularly faithful *gregarios* – the Basques, Cosme Barrutia and Jesús Galdeano – who were ready to leave their skins on the road for him, or hang on to Bahamontes' shorts, if necessary.

Bahamontes was as unpredictable as a firework: he could explode with dazzling brilliance, or fizzle out, a damp squib. Luis Puig felt safer with Loroño in the lead: he could be counted on. He didn't shine with the genius of the Eagle, but he was as solid as a rock.

With Loroño now race leader, Bahamontes was reduced to going for mountain points. Tension between the two remained high, skirting on violence, and the Press had a field day. *La Gaceta del Norte* ran a headline: 'Bahamontes = Loroño's enemy number one.' The tough, 81-kilometre time-trial from Zaragoza to Huesca took place in an atmosphere of explosive rivalry. Both men did brilliant rides, Loroño winning and Bahamontes only six seconds behind him. It was the ideal expression of the friction between them, infinitely preferable to brandishing bicycle pumps at each other. Luis Puig had received a stern telegram from the Spanish Cycling Federation, threatening to exclude both riders from the race if they didn't stop warring, so he seized the moment to organize the 'Armistice of Huesca'. *La Vanguardia* captured the moment: 'We have seen how Loroño and Bahamontes shook hands as a sign of victory and friendship while a band played a series of military marches.' That night all the Spanish nationals drank a toast to unity.

In the remaining stages, Bahamontes challenged Carmelo Morales for the Mountains prize. In Bayonne they were equal, and then, during the stage to San Sebastián, Federico dazzled everyone with his climbs of the Jaizkibel and Vidania. No one could threaten him in his territory.

The final stage was a day of umbrellas and vast crowds, overjoyed to see a Basque win the Vuelta. As the spectators and cyclists gathered in San Sebastián's Reina Regente Avenue, mass was said from a portable altar. It wasn't Sunday, but the fifties were a heyday for the Catholic church in Spain. Among its many state-granted privileges, such as freedom from taxes and power to censor anything it considered offensive, was the right to keep people waiting in the pouring rain before a bicycle race. First to cross the line in Bilbao was the Madrileño, Antonio Suárez, who in the near future would carve his name even more decisively on the race. When Loroño arrived, the crowds went crazy. The whole of Spain could be proud since the podium was an entirely national affair: Loroño, Bahamontes and Ruiz.

Another event of national significance in 1957 was the production of the first Seat 600. It was a sign of changing times. Although not especially cheap, and without the necessary contacts you might be on the waiting list for months or even years, it was sturdy and reliable, doing a maximum of 90kph on the flat. The motor, situated at the back, had a tendency to overheat, so the boot was often kept propped open when in transit. In a country still largely devoid of cars, it was destined to become a familiar sight in sixties Spain. The inevitable increase in car traffic was one of the factors that led Loroño to contemplate retirement. But not just yet.

1958
He was back again at the start of the following year's Vuelta, together with Bahamontes. There were some modifications in the 1958 Vuelta. Instead of Bilbao, it finished in Madrid, on 15th May, when the capital was in full festivities in honour of its patron, San Isidro. The regional teams had been scrapped: it seemed pointless to break up the existing trade teams just for the Vuelta. Each participating country, however, fielded one national squad, although in the case of Spain, the riders were all picked from the trade team 'Faema', thereby creating a curious type of compromise. Luis Puig was in charge, but when trouble developed, it was the Faema director, Miguel Torelló, who was summoned to deal with it.

When Luis Puig made a typically evasive declaration, it was clear that nothing had changed: 'At the outset Loroño is the team's strongest element, but Bahamontes will have the same privileges.' When asked if the friction between his stars would be a problem, he optimistically announced that he welcomed such friction 'as long as it fits in with the ethos of sportsmanship – it shows the athletes want to surpass themselves'.

In the first part of the 1958 season the Belgians were unstoppable, notably Rik Van Looy, or Rik II, as the heir of Rik Van Steenbergen was sometimes called. Considered one of the top 20 cyclists of all time, he held the record for winning Classics until the advent of Eddy Merckx, and in his prime no contemporary could beat him in a sprint. A strong personality, he knew how to impose discipline on a team moulded around his needs. By the time he came to Spain that year Van Looy had already won the Milan–San Remo, the Paris–Brussels (which he'd snatched from Seamus Elliott, whose frame broke at the worst possible moment) and come third in the Paris–Roubaix.

So it was understandable that the Belgians were the most feared team in the Vuelta, although there was speculation as to whether their leader would be able to survive a long stage race. *La Vanguardia*'s reporter wrote that 'in the mountains I do not think they will overshadow our cyclists' before nervously mentioning that the morale of their best climber, Hilaire Couvreur, was high after winning the Tour of Levante, an area comprising the regions of Valencia and Murcia.

The most difficult part of the Vuelta was concentrated at the end. After a short sharp mountainous introduction, the race turned to the Mediterranean, following the coast southwards from Barcelona to Valencia before veering back onto the Meseta and finishing with an extended tour of the mountainous north, through the Basque Country, Cantabria, and Asturias. So the first two days were important for the Spanish team: they had to establish themselves before the lengthy flat section, which everyone predicted would be one long party for the Belgians.

The race began in unusually hot sunny weather. Rather than shivering in rain and snow, the riders were pouring water over themselves to cool off, and after two days of combative cycling in the Basque hills, the Spanish nationals could be satisfied with their spoils. They had fended off Couvreur's attacks, taken both stages, and the Catalan Miguel Pacheco was in yellow, with three team-mates in the top five where Couvreur sat like a cat among the pigeons in third place. The only worrying detail was that Loroño seemed to be struggling to find his form. After looking disconcertingly exhausted on the first-category Velate climb, he was classified 15th at 5'–09" and would have lost far more time without the services of his faithful *gregario*, Jesús Galdeano.

Then, in the dust and heat on the road to Zaragoza, the Nationals' excellent start disintegrated. Early on, Jean Stablinski broke away from the peloton in search of the escape group up ahead, and Bahamontes, deciding it was too dangerous to give the Frenchman any leeway, went in pursuit. Soon, Bahamontes, Stablinski and nine others had fused to form a strong cohesive group. This was when Loroño committed a colossal error.

Without thinking twice, the Basque made his own move, and didn't desist when Couvreur and two others stuck to his back wheel. Powering this group of four, it seemed that for Loroño the rest of the peloton had vanished. Only he and Bahamontes existed. After a tremendous effort, he bridged the gap and thereby catapulted Couvreur into yellow, robbing Bahamontes of the honour. That night, Puig gave Loroño a severe dressing down, even threatening to send him home. He obtained promises of better behaviour, but the situation would only deteriorate.

During the stage to Barcelona, Bahamontes took advantage of the confusion at a feeding station to slip off, hoping to put distance on Loroño. Puig blocked his path, driving him off the road and forced him to wait for Loroño, who was struggling, undoubtedly paying the price for his previous day's exertions. The director's ability to manage his team of hotheads was foundering. In his anxiety to impose his authority, Puig forgot his tactical sense. As Bahamontes was clearly the strongest in the team that year, he should have allowed him to chase the group in which Van Looy was travelling.

Once in Barcelona, with the help of Faema director Miguel Torelló, the two 'roosters' made their peace with yet another of their public handshakes. Sports paper *Dicen* commented sarcastically: 'Remember that famous "Pact of Huesca" of the previous Vuelta? Well, now it seems we have the "Pact of Barcelona".' And they suggested that Spain could look forward to a whole new series of pacts as the race progressed. But it was all too late. The hot weather had turned to cold and the mountains to flat lands. The setting was perfect for the Belgian 'greyhounds', and Van Looy took his first bunch sprint, having threatened to win every flat stage left.

Down the Mediterranean, the pace was lively this year as the Belgians controlled the peloton. They chased down every escape, and Van Looy rounded off the effort with two more consecutive sprints to victory. Although third overall, at 7'–26", Van Looy was accumulating bonuses at such a rate (one minute for a stage-win, 30 seconds for second place) that people began betting on him as the final winner.

Stablinski had held the yellow jersey for two days and in Valencia, it passed to the Dutch rider Daan De Groot. Any attempt by the Spanish nationals to reassert themselves was effectively crushed by a Dutch–Belgian coalition. This was particularly frustrating for

Bahamontes the day they arrived in Toledo, with a home crowd eager to see him win. While the Dutch–Belgian Pact controlled him, a group containing Stablinski stole the opportunity to escape. The Frenchman took the stage and moved up to second place.

The peloton rediscovered the mountains in the Sierra de Madrid, where De Groot abandoned. Bahamontes' climb of Los Leones was spectacularly fast, but the Stablinski group caught him on the descent. The nationals attacked again on the Navacerrada but Van Looy implacably swept down after them and was first over the line in Madrid. The moment that many had predicted had come – Van Looy was in the yellow jersey. His position was still insecure, however, with Stablinski on his heels, only four seconds behind. The Belgian rectified that by winning his fifth stage in a sprint finish in Soria the following day.

The return to the mountains of the north saw Bahamontes and Loroño working together to shake off Van Looy, but to no avail. An invincible sprinter, it seemed he could also defend himself when the road steepened. At least, he could until stage 12. That day as the peloton covered the 173 kilometres between Vitoria and Bilbao in heavy rain, negotiating the slippery curves, the news came through that the Belgian was in trouble. Surrounded by his team, he was struggling with a knee injury. At the foot of the Sollube, he was out of the race and Stablinski inherited the yellow jersey.

Bahamontes, meanwhile, had been amassing more mountain points, but neither he nor Loroño had manged to improve their positions. However, a new, unexpected Spanish hope had emerged: Fernando Manzaneque, a modest member of the national team. A solid all-rounder, he was now in second place, 2'–27" behind Stablinski. His steady progress up the general classification had gone virtually unnoticed at the margin of the Bahamontes–Loroño furore. It was further eclipsed by another big story – one that was supposed to have been kept secret until after the race: Luis Puig was resigning. He had taken the decision in Madrid, informing the President of the Spanish Federation that he was tired of the constant criticism. A cartoon in the weekly cycling magazine *Rueda Libre* ('Free Wheel') showed Luis Puig with a packed suitcase, ready to go, announcing: 'I would like to present the ideal director for the Spanish team.' Behind him stood a gruff, whip-toting lion-tamer, with a docile lion perched on a stool.

The bad weather continued as the peloton moved westwards through Cantabria and Asturias. The French were nervous at the prospect of climbing the Puerto de Pajares, gateway to the Meseta. After all, the danger-man, Manzaneque, now theoretically had the support of *domestiques de luxe* Bahamontes and Loroño. But the two fell out again. They had stormed up Pajares together, but Loroño became annoyed when Federico wouldn't let him cross the top first, since the Toledano had already secured the mountain prize, while the Basque was trying to distance Couvreur for second place in that category. They could never be at peace for long. Sulking, Loroño refused to work on the descent, and the pair were soon caught. To complete an unsatisfactory day, half a kilometre from the finish in Palencia, Manzaneque was involved in a mass fall, causing him to lose 21 seconds. It was enough for the Italian, Lino Fornara, to take over second place.

There was a flurry of suspense on the last stage. The reduced peloton of only 46 surivivors confronted the remaining mountainous obstacle before Madrid, Los Leones. On the frenetic descent Stablinski was brought down by a dog that ran in front of him. He still remembers the moment well:

I was hurt and lost all my lead before I got going. I was really shaken, but my team-mate, Jean Graczyk saved the day. He was a very fast rider, and the run-in to the finish in Madrid was flat. He waited for me and made the pace until I recovered. Then we worked together and just managed to regain all my time back by the finish. It was tough, though; Fornara, who was second, wasn't waiting. I was so tired I collapsed at the finish.

The Vuelta trophy was taken away to France by Stablinski, whose victory was hailed as well-deserved, despite Van Looy's withdrawal. The Spanish Press couldn't fail to acknowledge that he'd been backed by a strong, united team, rather than a band of guerillas, always ready to stab each other in the back. It would be the last year that Loroño and Bahamontes competed in the same team.

When interviewed in 1992, Bahamontes declared: 'The Loroño–Bahamontes rivalry was the invention of a journalist, Señor Ubieta, to improve his reports. Some things were true, but others were imaginary. Loroño never gave me any trouble.' Jesús had his own verdict: 'Our rivalry? It was logical, because we were two roosters in the same farmyard. Both of us were very ambitious, and always wanted to win, which created friction between us.' They were fated never to agree.

1959–1961

'The race is over. May God forgive it.'

For the first time in its short history, the Vuelta had come back for a fifth consecutive year. Its apprenticeship was over, and for Spanish cycling enthusiasts, April was now synonymous with their national stage race, although it had to share the month with another annual fixture: the celebration of 'Victory'. Every 1st April, the country was relentlessly reminded of how the Republican forces had been crushed in 1939. Franco's vindictive enthusiasm for this anniversary showed no signs of abating: 'It was 20 years ago today that Spain saved the West,' crowed a typical headline, implying that without Franco, Europe would have been overrun by communist hordes. In 1959, the anniversary was celebrated with particular fervour, coinciding with the official inauguration of the 'Valley of the Fallen'.

This cavernous basilica was built at enormous expense, at a time when Spain was struggling to recover from the devastation of the Civil War. Intended to be a burial place for those who fell during the conflict, what Franco really wanted was a pyramid for himself where he could be entombed in what he considered to be appropriate grandeur. With its towering cross jutting out of the Sierra of Guadarrama, it's now a curiosity on the tourist trail, and seen by many as a memorial for the Republican prisoners who were maimed or killed in its construction.

Trapped in the past, Franco wanted endlessly to relive his moment of triumph but, at the end of the fifties, Spain was poised on the edge of a far-reaching transformation. It was understood that if the regime was to survive there was no choice but to agree to the Stabilisation Plan proposed by the International Monetary Fund, which aimed to turn the country into a free-market economy. Holding back the tide of modernisation would soon be impossible.

The Vuelta had also reached a watershed: for a while there had been almost a sense of disbelief that, after so many years of ostracism, an international race was successfully taking place in Spain. So, while the national cyclists were often the target of irate criticism, there'd only been words of praise for the organisation. But the honeymoon was coming to an end. The ideal of an exciting hard-fought race proved frustratingly elusive. It was generally agreed that a strong foreign line-up was vital if the Vuelta was to be a serious event, but when the well-paid figures didn't live up to expectations, the choice of invitations began to be questioned. The participation of Fausto Coppi in the 1959 Vuelta, so proudly announced, was inevitably a disappointment. Nearly 40, he was a ghostly presence in the peloton, and rarely seen. On the home front, Loroño was on the wane, his best years over and the way seemed clear for Bahamontes. Yet he, unpredictable as ever, only brought more headaches.

Controversy was courted when the Vuelta decided to follow the example of the Giro and give full acceptance to the trade teams that disputed the rest of the racing calendar. The Tour de France was more reluctant to abandon the national team formula, and wavered between the two systems until 1968. Invariably, cyclists were in favour of the innovation, but many commentators were unconvinced. *Dicen* argued that some notion of sporting purity had been lost: 'It is no longer a fight between men, but has turned into a defence of commercial interests.' *La Vanguardia* reported that the spectators missed the thrill of seeing a Spanish team emblazoned in the national colours of red and gold. But Mariano Cañardo, the prominent pre-civil-war cyclist, was adamant: 'The formula of national teams is condemned to disappear, since the cyclists cannot be rivals one day and friends the next.' He pointed out that the sponsors who paid the riders all year round wanted to reap the benefits from the maximum exposure to be gained in the major stage races. The question remained: could a cyclist still be heroic if he were plastered in advertisements?

The foreigners who would make the greatest impression in 1959 were 'the Emperor', Rik Van Looy of Belgian Faema (Italian coffee machine trademark), and the young, ill-fated hour record-man Roger Rivière of Rapha–Géminiani. Just for the duration of the Vuelta, Bahamontes had signed a contract with Kas – sponsored by a Basque soft drinks company – a team with a long and glorious future ahead. Bernardo Ruiz had hung up his wheels and was directing Spanish Faema, whose riders included Loroño and Salvador Botella.

The Vuelta began in Madrid and turned south towards the heat **1959** of Andalucía, stopping off in Toledo, where Van Looy won and became the first leader, much to Bahamontes' irritation, as he had marked that stage for himself, and had attacked repeatedly. As the days went by, Bahamontes became increasingly disgruntled. He was convinced there was a conspiracy against him, telling a French journalist: 'Everyone is against me in this Vuelta. The Spanish just as much as the foreigners. I've got the impression that my compatriots would prefer to see Van Looy or Rivière win before me.'

He channelled his frustrations into an outstanding performance on the Sevilla to Granada stage, considered ideal terrain for Van Looy and his team. When Bahamontes attacked, only two riders could follow his wheel, Fernando Manzaneque of Licor 43 and Jan Adriaenssens of Peugeot. A duo who had escaped earlier were caught and Federico set a blistering rhythm for the group of five, not looking for anyone's help.

Back in the main field, Van Looy, Rivière, and Botella worked to close the gap, but Bahamontes accelerated again and dropped his escape companions. Adriaenssens gave up altogether in exhaustion, while the other three hung on in pursuit. The Toledano crossed the line 45 seconds ahead of Manzaneque, with four minutes on the peloton. It was a formidable display of what Bahamontes was capable of when he put his mind to it. On this day his grievances had fuelled his attack rather than his tongue. The crowds in Granada, who had followed his progress on the radio, gave Bahamontes a wild welcome. Worn out but happy, his demons temporarily laid to rest, he climbed from eleventh to third place overall and saw the leadership within reach.

There was great excitement: if Bahamontes had taken four minutes off Van Looy in the Belgian's territory, what would he achieve once the Vuelta reached the mountains? Rik II shrugged it off, even suggesting the Spaniard was rashly burning himself out: 'The Eagle has shortened his flight.' But he was clearly stung because the next day, on the stage to Murcia, despite the African temperatures, Van Looy tried to form an escape after only eight kilometres. It was quickly curtailed by a vigilant Bahamontes, who then attacked with Rivière: an extraordinarily combative mood had infused the leaders.

After another regrouping there was a brief interlude of calm, until the intermediate sprint in Lorca, where a mixed group of French and Belgians formed, with the interloper Bahamontes in their midst. The escape came to an end when Van Looy's frame broke, but the peloton continued at a breakneck pace, stretched out in a line in the shimmering heat. Antonio Suárez of Licor 43 seized his chance by attacking at a level crossing, and maintained his lead to win in Murcia, 29 seconds ahead of Van Looy. Bahamontes' group came in at 59 seconds: he was now second on general classification, only 55 seconds behind team-mate Antonio Karmany.

The organizers were thrilled at how the race was developing: the 'aces' had engaged in battle and a national star was poised to become leader. But when the peloton turned north to follow the Mediterranean, hostilities gave way to a type of truce. A strong crosswind sent high waves crashing against the normally tranquil shore and obliged the cyclists to make an extra effort. A breakaway was allowed to win an alarming advantage, with no one willing to organise a pursuit. Bahamontes' inertia was particularly inexcusable since Kas' first and second positions were rapidly slipping away. When the peloton rolled in 30 minutes after Antón Barrutia, instigator of the escape and stage-winner, race director Luis Bergareche clutched his head, repeating endlessly: 'This is completely intolerable.' He found the cyclists' attitude inexcusable: the overall had been turned upside-down, and it was uncertain if the stars could recover their losses before Bilbao. 'We make a big effort to give brilliance to our Vuelta, bringing over the best people, and for what? If things don't change, if this absurd attitude doesn't disappear,' Bergareche continued threateningly, 'they can all go to hell!'

To make amends, Van Looy won the next two stages, but Bahamontes slipped even further down the classification, making ill-timed attacks and missing the important moves. When the peloton turned inland after Barcelona, heading for the mountainous finale in the north, there was more drama to shred Bergareche's nerves. Bahamontes' mood was getting worse: he'd threatened to abandon in protest after five members of Spanish Faema, his arch-enemies, were pardoned for arriving outside the time-limit. Then, early on the 11th stage to Pamplona, when Van Looy and other rivals disappeared up the road, his morale fell even more. The last straw was when Loroño took off in their pursuit, accompanied by Rapha–Géminiani's Pierre Everaert, who'd taken over the race leadership. Bahamontes got off his bike, and when questioned why he was retiring, spat out: 'Because it's easier to go by car'.

Meanwhile, Van Looy was giving a demonstration of power. The Belgian could be a cruel boss: after the Paris–Roubaix of 1959, his *domestique* Armand De Smet found himself out of a job when Rik, furious at only coming fourth, stripped him of the team jersey there and then on the finishing-line. His performance on the road to Pamplona showed why he was entitled to be so exacting, as well as nearly proving catastrophic for the Vuelta. After instigating and driving the break, Van Looy won the stage and nearly eliminated the bulk of the field, which turned up 30 minutes later. It was the type of ride that would make him a legend.

A very agitated Bergareche, with a bellyful of Bahamontes, was aghast as he drove over the Yesa reservoir to see Roger Rivière leaning against the bridge, furious and ready to quit, having already lost ten minutes. Rivière had been quick to join Van Looy when the Belgian attacked, but his adventure ended when he punctured twice in quick succession and ran out of tyres. He could only curse his director for preferring to accompany team-mate and temporary yellow jersey holder Everaert, who was somewhere on the road behind with Loroño. Losing two stars in one day would have been seen as pure carelessness, and Bergareche didn't hesitate to help himself to one of Kas' spare wheels and hand it to the young Frenchman. Although rule-bending was clearly not restricted to Spanish races, some sharp criticism followed: how could the Vuelta be taken seriously if the rules were just so much 'wet paper'?

Rivière might have lost all chances in the general classification, but his impressive victory in the demanding time-trial convinced many that he would have won the Vuelta had it not been for the puncture of Yesa. On the 62 kilometres between Eibar and Vitoria, including the climbs of Elgueta and Urkiola, he overtook no less than six riders. It was also a great day for Antonio Suárez: already with two stages in the bag, he finished second and became the new leader. Coppi suffered terribly, despite the warmth and encouragement of the spectators, and in Vitoria, he packed his bags and quietly slipped away.

In his euphoria, Suárez had announced he would die to defend the yellow jersey: such extremes were not required, but he did have to put up a desperate fight. On the penultimate stage from Santander to Bilbao, after the long, punishing climb of the Escudo, Suárez found himself isolated at the head of the field amongst a group of French Rapha–Géminiani riders. They tried to drop him but he resolutely responded to each attack. Then bad luck struck when he hit a stone and crashed, falling back to the second group. With immediate rival Everaert ahead, Suárez's position was in danger, until Van Looy came to the rescue. The Belgian was ill and had suffered horrendously on the Escudo, but now he made an immense effort to defend his third place on the podium, and crossed the gap to Suárez's group, towing various Spanish Faema and Kas riders in his wake. There ensued the unusual spectacle of different Spanish teams working together, and Everaert's gains were substantially reduced. Suárez survived to take the Vuelta – an unexpected winner, praised for his tenacity and courage. Bahamontes' *gregario*, José Segu, finished second and Van Looy came third, and also took the points jersey.

The only award for Bahamontes was a feather duster, a symbolic booby prize *Dicen* handed out weekly, given to Federico for dishonouring the Vuelta with his selfish conduct. Of course, his sins were forgiven that summer when he became the first Spaniard to win the Tour de France. Bahamontes undoubtedly profited in the Tour from rivalry between the French stars that was more characteristic of the Spaniards, but his victory was also thanks to the work of director Dalmacio Langarica, whose undivided attention coaxed out a disciplined and constant performance. The cost was high, for Langarica had to exclude his old friend Loroño from the team and consequently endure relentless hostility from outraged Basques. The windows of his bicycle shop were smashed and even his wife was spat at in the street. On Bahamontes' return to Toledo, they unlocked the enormous gates to the city and he passed through like a conquering hero. It was considered deeply meaningful that the Tour had finished on 18th July, and the Spanish anthem played in Paris on the anniversary of the Nationalist military uprising (yet another annual celebration).

This same year, a group of young Basques pledged to create an independent homeland, founding an organisation – Euskadi Ta Askatasuna ('Basque Fatherland and Freedom'). All of Spain would be shaken by their impact, including the Vuelta.

* * * * *

'The race is over. May God forgive it!' Such was the epithet *Marca* gave the Vuelta at its conclusion in 1960, as the sorry-looking peloton of 24 survivors crossed the final finishing-line in Bilbao. If 1959 had been a difficult year, far worse was to come.

1960   The omens had been bad from the beginning. Van Looy had to forgo his lucrative fee in Spain when he was required to compete in a minor one-day event in Belgium by a UCI regulation that aimed to force the top figures to compete in their own countries. Then Rivière had to be turned down because his asking price was too high. The Belgian Groene Leeuw ('Green Lions') sent a young and inexperienced team, the Portuguese pulled out at the last minute, while the lacklustre French team, Rochet-Margnat, were to pass by without trace. This shortage of stars focused attention exclusively on the promised confrontation between the 'Eagle of Toledo' and Charly Gaul, the 'Angel of the mountains'.

Eyebrows were raised when Bahamontes signed for Faema: how would he function in a team directed by his old enemy Bernardo Ruiz? Bahamontes and Antonio Suárez watched each other suspiciously. The previous year's Vuelta winner lay down a challenge: if the Eagle expected him to work as a *gregario*, he had to demonstrate his superiority first. The team got off to a bad start, when in the opening time-trial a crash brought down the two rival leaders; Suárez would be nursing his injuries throughout the Vuelta.

Beginning in Gijón, on the coast of Asturias, the race would make a rare visit to Galicia, reaching the west Atlantic coast in Vigo, before crossing the country to the Mediterranean shores of Catalunya in the east. Having gone no further south than Madrid, the peloton would finish up in the Basque country as usual. The length of the stages was erratic: the fourth stage, Vigo to Orense, was 105 kilometres, followed by a 287-kilometre slog from Orense to Zamora. It was on this longest day that Bahamontes broke the Vuelta record for solo escapes: he spent 243 of its kilometres alone, and since he was caught 32 kilometres from the end, it was considered a spectacular but pointless waste of energy. It was his way of dispelling doubts about his form.

This year's other big star, Charly Gaul, had an impressive palmarés: the Tour of 1958, and Giros of 1956 and 1959, and when he showed himself on the Sierra de Madrid during the seventh stage, it seemed the race had truly begun. Gaul first decided to try his strength on the climb of Los Leones, catching up with a small breakaway. He attacked again on the Navacerrada, flinging off his cap to show he meant business, with only Vicente Iturat of Ferrys hanging on. Storming up behind was Bahamontes' group, with Loroño and Belgian Franz De Mulder, who were within a minute of

74

Gaul by the summit. Defying death, De Mulder managed to cross over to the leading pair on the descent, and after Iturat's derailleur broke, the Belgian and Luxumbourger were left to work in perfect synchrony, until De Mulder sprinted past Charly in the Sports Palace of Madrid. Bahamontes came in at 4'–40". As *La Vanguardia* put it: 'Round one to Gaul'.

Yet the excitement was short-lived. There were two factors working against the Guadalajara to Zaragoza stage: it was sandwiched between two mountainous days, and there was a strong, cold head wind. The cyclists had requested an extra feeding station because of the late start and the long route ahead (264 kilometres). When the race directors refused, they mounted a semi-strike, employing only the minimum of effort. The expected average speed was 37 kph, but as the peloton crawled along the final stretch in the light of car headlamps, listening to disapproving whistles from the dark road-sides, they had managed an average of 28.4kph. They arrived in the Romareda Stadium at 9.20 p.m., greeted by 30,000 irate cycling fans who had been impatiently waiting for up to 3 hours. In the uproar, no one cared who won (it was actually Arthur De Cabooter) and no prize money was awarded.

The lethargy of the 'Stage of Hunger' inexplicably held for four more days. In Barcelona, there was another reception of whistles and boos, after an 11-strong breakaway had borne De Mulder to race leadership, while the peloton, like a ship without a captain, drifted in at 37'–38". Unaccountably, Faema were unwilling to take the helm, even though they had held the yellow jersey with Manzaneque. The professionalism of the cyclists was called into question as each day the script remained the same: the peloton would ease itself over the finish half an hour after an obligatory escape group. Luis Bergareche held an emergency meeting with all the directors: his Vuelta was dying, so could they please act and save it.

The race was rekindled at last on stage 13 between Logroño and San Sebastián, thanks to Bahamontes, who escaped alone in the very first kilometre, with a challenging route ahead. The climbs of Lizárrega and Jaizkibel were lined with spectators, delighted to witness one of Bahamonte's solo flights. A strong group formed intent on reeling him in and began wearing down his lead, which had reached a maximum of 13 minutes. When Federico punctured, for a while it seemed all was lost, but he redoubled his efforts to arrive in San Sebastián 2'–32" ahead of Marigil, with 5'–06" on the pursuing group and 12 minutes on the peloton. It was a shame that after such a display it was too late for him to make significant inroads in the overall. Positioned 20th overall, Bahamontes had no choice but to concentrate on the Mountains prize.

Long, solo breaks were the vogue, Suárez setting yet another new record in the *etapa reina* between San Sebastián and Vitoria, after riding 260 kilometres alone. In contrast to the light and effortless elegance of Bahamontes, strapping Suárez was a picture of fighting spirit, gritting his teeth against the pain of his time-trial injuries and refusing to be defeated by gale-force winds on the Urkiola. He came in 11'–05" ahead of Bahamontes, with the other riders trickling in one by one. The original peloton had been small, but by now its 80 riders were down to 36. Charly Gaul, after a meagre contribution, became the latest to abandon, draped in a blanket lent him at a farmhouse. The rest of his team, EMI, would soon follow.

Meanwhile, undeterred by his low classification, Bahamontes was planning an audacious strategy. Before the *etapa reina*, he'd given strict instructions to Julio San Emeterio, his most loyal *gregario,* to take it easy and save his legs for the day after. While the rest of the peloton were still recuperating, the pair would launch a pitiless attack, aided by San Emeterio's intimate knowledge of the local roads through the Basque hills to Santander. Inadvertently, Suárez had sabotaged the plan, when his outstanding solo ride had left San Emeterio disqualified for arriving outside the time-limit.

When Bahamontes demanded his *gregario* be readmitted, Licor 43 announced they would abandon *en masse* if the rules were flouted so flagrantly. With only 36 cyclists left in the peloton, it was a serious threat. Fuming, Federico dragged San Emeterio along to sign on before the stage, but the race judge was implacable. Refusing to accept defeat, Bahamontes then sought out the Vuelta boss, reminding him of the Rivière tyre incident of the previous year. Bergareche was not amused: 'I will not be blackmailed. Do what you want. I'll be reporting everything to the Federation.'

For a while, it seemed Bahamontes would channel his anger into a blistering performance, but this would have saved the race, and he was only interested in revenge. He slowed down to a snail's pace, dismounting at one point to let off steam, attacking an abusive spectator with his pump, and arrived late enough to be disqualified. All hell broke out. The Press were outraged, while the people of

San Emeterio's home town, Torrelavega, put up a sign for the Vuelta director to ponder when he passed through the next day: *'Bergareche, San Emeterio será tu cemeterio!'* (Bergareche, San Emeterio will be your cemetery!) The implication was clear – he might soon be out of a job.

Despite everything, the Vuelta staggered on to its finish in Bilbao. Only two years previously Franz De Mulder had been working as a miner and now he experienced the glory of winning a major stage race. On the penultimate stage he attacked very early and only Loroño reacted. The Basque punctured twice on the descent of the Escudo, but the Belgian wisely waited for him and the duo made good time. De Mulder beat Loroño at the finish, which secured him the yellow jersey, and another of the Green Lions, De Smet, finished second on the podium. Miguel Pacheco of Licor 43 took third place amid anger that the Spanish riders had not rallied round him to challenge the Belgians. Calls were made for trade teams to be scrapped: for many, it was incomprehensible that national loyalty didn't come first.

Dicen awarded one feather duster to the Vuelta itself and another to be shared by Gaul and Bahamontes. Disillusion had set in: cycling had been reduced to a fratricidal fight between makers of sausages, cognacs and men's underpants. Already critics were looking back longingly to a more epic age. They found it hard to accept that, in the words of Bernardo Ruiz, 'a cyclist can't live from glory alone. He's a professional in a hard job from which he has to try and get some benefit.' The race organisers were attacked for designing interminably long stages and paying large sums to stars who would only abandon. But the most popular target for these diatribes was Bahamontes. Here was the best cyclist Spain had yet produced, letting down the nation. The 1960 Vuelta should have been a celebration of his great victory in France. He, of course, refused to take any blame for the fiasco, reminding everyone that he'd given up the better-paid Giro to ride at home. Feeling unloved, in the future, Bahamontes would concentrate his efforts abroad, signing for a French team, claiming 'my potential has never been exploited in Spain and I regret not having gone to France earlier'.

The hardship of his early years forged Bahamontes as a cyclist, and also marked him for life. Even when at the peak of his success and highly paid, he could never shake off his black marketeer's opportunism, selling sought-after Spanish cycling gloves to the foreign riders on the side. His follies are easier to understand if it's remembered that he belonged to a generation of riders who were self-made men who had to fight against extremely hard odds. At a recent edition of Barcelona's end-of-season classic, the 'Escalada a Montjuic' (Montjuic hill-climb), Spain's Tour de France winners were invited to do a lap of honour, perched in the back of open cars. While Delgado and Induráin both seemed slightly embarrassed by the whole affair, Federico smiled benignly, bestowing regal waves on his subjects, the cycling public, who applauded enthusiastically. With so many of his contemporaries no longer around, it was gratifying to see him enjoying his status: he was a born-survivor.

So, too, was Bergareche. Stung by the debacle in 1960, the following year he sought a breathing space. When asked what he wanted most for his race, he solomnly replied, 'Dignity'. A certain degree of calm was guaranteed by Bahamontes' absence, but there were no foreign stars either. The field was young and enthusiastic, the three most outstanding Spanish cyclists all under 25: good-looking José Pérez Francés, who Tour boss Jacques Goddet nicknamed 'the Rudolf Valentino of the peloton', Antonio Gómez del Moral and Angelino Soler – all complete riders rather than mountain specialists. It was hoped that the '61 Vuelta would act as a trampoline for a new international star.

1961   A glance at the route reveals there were no stages over 250 kilometres long, unlike in 1960 when there had been six. The organisers had learnt that what was acceptable in the Tour, which still included stages of over 300 kilometres, did not necessarily work in the Vuelta. In fact, there were only four days when the cyclists had to cover more than 200 kilometres. The balance of the race was tipped in favour of flat terrain when at the last moment the planned incursions into France had to be cancelled, because of unrest over the Algiers crisis, and, as a consequence, two first-category Pyrenean climbs were lost.

For the first time there was a stage-finish in Benidorm, newly established on the map by a fast-developing tourist industry. Visas for Western Europeans had been abolished in 1959, when the mayor of Benidorm, who had seen the potential of what was then still a sleepy fishing village, made a legendary trip to Madrid on his Vespa. In oil-stained trousers, he obtained an audience with Franco, and persuaded him to lift the church-imposed ban on bikinis. The high-rise hotels were then only a matter of time; by 1973 the number of tourists visiting Spain would have jumped from three million to 34 million.

As usual, the Mediterranean belonged to the Belgian Green Lions, who secured the yellow jersey with Marcel Seynaeve, a humble *domestique*. But as the temperatures climbed, some of the northern Europeans began to flag, the inexperienced Dutch team pulling out, exhausted. On the baking Meseta, Pérez Francés decided to make up the time he'd earlier lost through a crash and mechanical problems. Leading a five-strong breakaway, which the Belgians failed to control, he finished off his display of class by winning in Albacete. He was now placed sixth, while the Belgians had three riders in the top five.

In the mountains of Madrid, a young Julio Jiménez pocketed the 8,000 peseta prize for cresting the Navacerrada in first place. The ease with which he climbed was beginning to draw attention, but the Spaniards were demoralised to see how strong André Messelis was on the climbs; although Seynaeve was surprisingly still in yellow, Messelis was the real Belgian candidate for the general classification and duly took over the race leadership the following day in Valladolid. The Green Lions were also strong favourites for the team prize; their only challenge could come from Faema, since Pérez Francés' Ferrys were out of the running, with the team reduced to three riders.

Some Spanish hope was rekindled when the Belgians didn't perform as well as expected in the 48-kilometre time-trial between Valladolid and Palencia, which Antonio Suárez won while Messelis came 16th. Then came the *etapa reina*, 235 kilometres of sinuous mountain roads from Santander to Vitoria, and it was here that the order of the race changed significantly. The first-category climb of Orduña proved too tough for Messelis, who cracked as he was mercilessly attacked by a mainly Spanish formation that included Suárez and Pérez Francés, and drew support from several teams. 'They rode like infuriated demons,' wrote *La Vanguardia's* reporter, clearly impressed by the frenetic pace, which was maintained to the finish, where the Frenchman François Mahé outsprinted Pérez Francés to take the stage.

The Belgians licked their wounds and complained about excessive collaboration among the Spanish riders – not a frequently heard accusation. Messelis had lost nearly nine minutes, although he was still clinging to the yellow jersey, with Angelino Soler classified second at 1'–24", Mahé third at 2'–15" and Pérez Francés fourth at 3'–47". In the unforgiving Basque hills of the final two stages the Green Lions were definitively sunk, and 21-year-old Soler emerged as the youngest ever Vuelta winner.

There was a frightening moment in the streets of Bilbao, when someone's wheel got trapped in a tramline but, fortunately, the ensuing pile-up only resulted in cuts and bruises, although Soler's bike disappeared under a lorry. Aside from this last-minute shave with disaster, the Vuelta had passed without undue incident, to the immense relief of Bergareche. Accompanying Soler on the podium were Mahé and the other Spanish revelation, Pérez Francés. The Belgians, who had promised so much, finally went home empty-handed. In future years, the '61 Vuelta would be held up as a shining example of how to defeat the enemy.

Julián Berrendero – 'the Negro with the blue eyes' sprang to
prominence in the Vuelta of 1936. After the Civil War he survived
18 months in concentration camps to become the first Spanish
winner of the Vuelta in 1941, and the last surviving rider from
the Republican era when he retired in 1949.

Mundo Deportivo

Mariano Cañardo, described by *L'Auto* as 'more a Belgian than a Spaniard, in his style and his qualities'. Most of the first Vuelta revolved around his battle with the Belgian winner, Gustaaf Deloor.

Mundo Deportivo

Dalmacio Langarica, nicknamed the 'Titan of Otxandiano' in the leader's jersey, 1946. The newspaper *Ya* sponsored the Vuelta during the 1940s.

Delio, the eldest of the Rodríguez brothers, winner in 1945,
and still the record holder with a total of 39 stage wins.

Langarica, a strong *rouleur*, leads a break.

Federico Bahamontes in his element. In the 1950s few roads
outside the towns had a tarmac surface.

One half of Spain supported Bahamontes…

… the other half supported Jesús Loroño.

When rainbow jersey Rudi Altig won the Vuelta in 1962, there was talk of betrayal. The St Raphaël strategy had been to keep the yellow jersey rotating within their ranks (Shay Elliot wore it for a week) before handing it over to their leader, Jacques Anquetil. Altig had his own agenda.

1963 – Jacques Anquetil wins the Vuelta at his second attempt, leading from start to finish.

José Pérez Francés, the Spaniard Jacques Anquetil feared most. His Vuelta palmarés, twice second and twice third overall, does not reflect his prodigious, unfulfilled talent. Jacques Goddet nicknamed him 'the Rudolf Valentino of the peloton'.

Kas, the first Spanish super-squad, in full flight. The team time trial was a perfect opportunity to show off their power and discipline.

Felice Gimondi, one of only four men to have won the Giro d'Italia, the Tour de France and the Vuelta a España.

1962–1965

Stars and Water-carriers

The Spanish economy experienced a spectacular boom in the sixties, with productivity doubling in ten years. Foreign investment poured in, both from America and Western Europe, since labour was cheap and strikes completely illegal. When Miguel Poblet retired from cycling in 1962, it was a sign of the times that he established a factory in Barcelona to build Ignis fridges, after riding in their colours for five years in Italy.

It was also a time of massive social upheaval as traditional ways of life disappeared. Rural communities shrank – or vanished entirely – as people from the poorest regions of Spain flocked to the northern industrial cities, and settled in squalid shanty towns on their outskirts. Others went further: between 1960 and 1973, around 1.3 million people were driven abroad in search of work, mainly to northern Europe. The cultural gap meant that an Andalucian newly arrived in Barcelona was regarded as much an 'immigrant' as a Spaniard in Germany.

It wasn't just the rural poor who made up this army of economic migrants: the top Spanish cyclists, including Bahamontes and Vuelta winners Suárez and Soler, followed suit and went abroad in search of brighter opportunities, and better wages. The exception to this trend was José (Pepe) Pérez Francés, although he later came to admit that renewing his contract with Ferrys in 1963 was the biggest error of his career. It undoubtedly explains why, in the words of the Barcelona writer, Manuel Vázquez Montalban, Pérez Francés was 'a complete rider who was on the point of becoming one of the greats, and only got half-way there'. His palmarés, including four podium positions in the Vuelta and a third place in the 1963 Tour de France, does not reflect his prodigious, unfulfilled talent.

Notoriously bad-tempered, Pepe had to cut short his Vuelta debut in 1960 after laying into the Belgian team director with his pump. He jokingly attributes his irascibility to being born during the Civil War in a bomb shelter, as the Nationalists bombarded Santander, but his family was lucky to avoid the worst privations of the years of hunger. Pérez Francés grew up surrounded by bicycles, which his father made and repaired – a good business when this was such a common mode of transport. A few kilometres outside of Santander was a large steel works, and everyday the roads were filled with hundreds of cyclists going to and fro.

A boyhood memory has him sitting on the front doorstep during a stage of the Vuelta, fascinated as the cyclists came by in ones and twos at lengthy intervals: 'they seemed like extraterrestials'. One of them, Langarica, would be his director in the future.

When his parents separated, Pérez Francés moved to Barcelona with his mother, already, at the age of 17, wearing the Spanish colours as amateur Spanish champion. There he found a thriving amateur scene – 'every other shopkeeper would organise a team, with its own jersey'. He was soon earning decent prize money and was signed by Ferrys – a team sponsored by a successful underwear company, whose boss was a cycling enthusiast – Pérez Francés throws doubt on his first team's professional status: 'we were just a group of friends'.

After reaching the podium in the '63 Tour, he was approached by both Italian Faema and the top French team San Raphaël, but the owner of Ferrys was willing to match any offer. And when his star remained unconvinced, he resorted to blackmail: 'If you don't sign, I'll disband the team – there'll be no one left.' Pérez Francés bowed to the pressure, with the condition of a substantial increase in salary for everyone, and the promise of some serious reinforcements. Sadly, his boss was killed in a car crash the following year, and with him died the project of a revamped Ferrys: 'Everything went downhill.'

In the Vueltas of the sixties, apart from the disadvantage of riding in a comparatively weak team, Pérez Francés was also at times handicapped by the organisers' zeal to secure a foreign winner. They were anxious to consolidate the position of their race – the Spanish tour – in the international racing calendar, and succeeded in attracting several top stars at the height of their powers with succulent financial inducements and tailor-made routes. Blatant favouritism towards the foreigners understandably sparked irritation among the national riders.

The cyclist making the most headlines in the early sixties was Jacques Anquetil. In 1961 he'd won the second of his five Tours de France, holding the yellow jersey from the second day all the way to Paris, and in 1960 he'd taken the Giro d'Italia. So it was a triumphant moment for the Vuelta organisers when they announced he would be on the starting-line in Barcelona in 1962. When asked if they'd designed the route specially for the French star, Bergareche irritably replied, 'What an absurd hypothesis. When the course of the Vuelta was planned, it wasn't known Anquetil would be in the race.' True, but there'd been no harm in trying to lure him over. The bait consisted of a mainly flat or gently undulating route, with only a dozen climbs of any significance in the entire 2,800 kilometres. And most tempting of all, two stages from the finish, there was an individual time-trial between Bayonne and San Sebastián of no less than 82 kilometres. Irresistible for a cyclist whose victories were based on his excellence against the clock and who, with the Vuelta in his palmarés, would become the first man to have won all three of the major tours.

In case anyone doubted he meant business, Anquetil came surrounded by a powerful Helyett–St Raphaël team, which included Jean Stablinski (winner of the Vuelta in 1957), the superb sprinter, Jean Graczyk, tough *rouleurs* like Seamus Elliott, Jean-Claude Annaert, Mies Stolker and Albert Geldermans, and the reigning World Pursuit Champion, Rudi Altig. It was directed by Raphaël Géminiani (third in the Vuelta in 1955) who had developed the *colmatage* strategy, whereby the team would work to neutralise every move of potential threat, leaving their leader free to claim the yellow jersey in the time-trial. The approach didn't make for exciting racing, but it proved hugely effective.

A true star, Anquetil had a glamorous blonde wife, and he and Géminiani were notorious for celebrating their victories with champagne parties long into the night. Yet when he arrived for the start in Barcelona, he was noticeably tired and gaunt, as if the season were coming to an end rather than barely begun. The warm April sun cheered him up, though: 'When it's hot I'm in top form. If this weather continues, I'll definitely win.'

Although the opening stage – ten laps of a nine-kilometre circuit over and around Montjuic – was won by Kas' Antón Barrutia, the Spanish riders would be mere onlookers for much of the race. With crushing authority, Anquetil's dream team would pick up 12 of the 17 stages.

They seized control on the second day *en route* to Tortosa, the beginning of a long journey down the Mediterranean coast. The stage began quietly enough: after 26 kilometres Antonio Karmany led over the third-category puerto del Ordal to score the first points that would ultimately reward this Kas rider with the King of the Mountains prize. But on the descent, St Raphaël *en masse* moved to the front and Géminiani ordered his troops to attack. They rode the next 140 kilometres as if it were a prolonged team time-trial, and at such a pace that only seven other riders – the very best of the Spanish opposition – were able to hang on to their coat-tails, while the gap back to the main field steadily grew. On the banks of the River Ebro, Rudi Altig took the sprint and, with it, the overall leadership.

With the peloton finishing almost a quarter of an hour down, the essential selection of the race had been made – nobody who wasn't in that leading group of 13 in Tortosa would finish among the final top seven in Bilbao. It was a tremendous psychological blow. By giving such an early demonstration of their superiority, the French team had thoroughly demoralised the opposition. From now on, or so everyone thought, Géminiani's men would simply keep the yellow jersey safe until the moment came for their leader to assume it.

For the next two days Altig was its guardian, then, in Benidorm, the leadership passed to Elliott, after St Raphaël had squashed an early show of ambition from Pérez Francés. He was the one Spanish rider Anquetil was always very careful to control: he considered him 'the most dangerous of all'. The thriving sea resort was also the scene for a 21-kilometre team time-trial, which the French team covered in 25'–25", with only Ferrys, whipped along by Pérez Francés, finishing within a minute of that time. This left Géminiani's riders occupying the first five places on general classification in the order: Elliott, Altig, Stablinski, Anquetil and Stolker. With a mixture of admiration and despair, Dalmacio Langarica, director of Kas, pronounced: 'St Raphaël are the Real Madrid of cycling.'

In Cartagena it was the turn of the fast-finishing Frenchman, Jean Graczyk, to bring them their stage-win, and then Altig won in Almería, the one-minute bonus putting him back in yellow. The St Raphaël strategy seemed to be working to perfection: they now held positions one to six overall. Except that it was Anquetil who was in sixth place, 4'–51" down on his own *gregario*. In an effort to quell any idea that he might be contemplating an act of treachery, Altig reaffirmed publically that his team leader would take over the yellow jersey on the day of the Bayonne–San Sebastián time-trial. Anquetil, however, was becoming increasingly unhappy and suspicious of the German's intentions. Altig had joined the team earlier that year only to be told by Géminiani that, while he might ride the Vuelta, he was too inexperienced as yet for the Tour de France. The brash young German had been unable to disguise his disappointment. Were ideas of revenge passing through his head?

Anquetil's misgivings were given further confirmation on the last Mediterranean stage, finishing in Málaga, which followed what had now become the daily routine. Early Spanish attacks, a number of which were initiated by the proud Pérez Fancés who, most especially, chafed at the French stranglehold, were all comfortably chased down by St Raphaël troops. Then, with 71 kilometres still to ride, a solo bid for freedom was made by Spaniard René Marigil, on to whose back wheel Annaert immediately latched. The Licor 43 rider posed no threat, and with St Raphaël's interests more than adequately represented, he was allowed to go clear. But, forced to do all the work on the front, Marigil had nothing left to contest the sprint in Málaga, and Annaert had no difficulty in marking up St Raphaël's fifth stage-win. What was telling, however, was the visibly strenuous effort Altig made at the head of the main field to keep the margin down to 1'–20", and thereby preserve his jersey. If he had genuinely been riding for his team leader, would it have mattered if it had passed to a fellow team-mate? Anquetil clearly thought not, for the following day, when the race finally turned inland, all the tension in the French team which, until then had been mere peloton gossip, came out in the open.

On the ninth stage, to Córdoba, the 76 riders left in the race soon encountered the first-category Puerto de la Reina – the first major climb of the '62 Vuelta. On the descent a group of 15, including Anquetil, came together at the front, while Altig found himself 1'–18" adrift. With no intention of making life easy for his water-carrier in the yellow jersey, Anquetil began organising the relays at the front to keep the tempo high. This was tantamount to a declaration of war – civil war within St Raphaël's ranks. But back down the road, Altig forged a temporary alliance with the Belgian team and was able to make contact with the leaders.

The decisive break came some 50 kilometres from the finish when a mixed group of six riders got clear: trusted lieutenant Elliott was sent forward to represent the French team's interests, while Anquetil himself controlled the rearguard. This time there was no stage-win for St Raphaël. The local boy, Antonio Gómez del Moral, not known as much of a sprinter but no doubt inspired by the home crowd, took the stage for the Spanish Faema squad. The yellow jersey was once more on Elliott's shoulders, after Altig was penalised by half a minute for receiving food outside the feeding station.

Anquetil could be satisfied with his day's work. 'I am fed up with Altig's stage-wins – they make me nervous,' he said after the stage. 'That's why I didn't allow the six escapees to be recaptured in the final kilometres.' Altig said nothing, and simply kept his powder dry.

Pérez Francés, on the other hand, had plenty to say. Ferrys had all but collapsed around him, sinking from second to sixth in the team competition, and he berated them for 'coming in puffing and panting behind everybody'. And his strictures were not confined to his own team. 'The French,' he maintained, 'have begun to weaken, but Kas and others are playing into their hands, so it's impossible to take any time back on them.'

Any signs of debility were not reflected in the French team's champagne bill. Apart from holding the yellow and green jerseys with Elliott and Altig, the St Raphaël men were still wedged in the top five positions overall, and they continued picking up stage-wins. The iron grip they had imposed upon the race was in no way extenuated by the Anquetil–Altig jaundice. The sports paper *Dicen* couldn't help but admire the way the French team saved their rows for the privacy of the hotel, unlike the Spaniards who would freely shout at each other in the peloton.

But Pérez Francés had a point, nonetheless: there was a weakness in the French team. Over and above the division within their ranks, Anquetil had been showing persistent symptoms of flu ever since the third stage.

There was an enormous sense of anticipation when the long-awaited time-trial arrived. It was the cue for Anquetil finally to assume his rightful position, but his heart must have sunk when he saw the day dawning dark, cold and wet. Nothing was going right: during her stay in Madrid, his wife had fallen down some steps and broken her ankle, while Anquetil had developed a fever and couldn't eat, or sleep. The hot weather he loved so much had been left behind in the south.

Géminiani tried to keep his team leader's spirits up. Altig had no chance, he insisted. For all his power over the pursuit distance of 5,000 metres, he wouldn't be able to resist the world's supreme time-trialist over the 82 kilometres to San Sebastián, which involved scaling the second-category Alto de Ibardin. But the German had secretly planned for this day, slipping off in Bayonne to buy a 13-tooth sprocket. It served him well for, in pouring rain, the unthinkable happened: despite his losses on the col (where Anquetil made the second-fastest ascent), the *gregario* who'd been told he was too inexperienced to ride the Tour pulled back enough time to beat his team leader by a solitary second. Revenge was sweet. Back in the yellow jersey for the third time, Altig now stood 4'–52" ahead of second-placed Anquetil in the overall classification and 7'–14" up on Pérez Francés, who had made a superb ride against the clock.

The Vuelta was effectively over for Anquetil, but Pérez Francés still entertained hopes. There were two days in the Basque mountains before the finish in Bilbao and it might yet be possible – on the first-category slopes of the Lizárraga or the Sollube, for instance – to ambush the race leader; it would all depend on how San Raphaël responded to the 'traitor' in their midst. And that, it turned out, depended on money.

Jean-Claude Annaert spoke for all of them:

We'll help Altig if he shares the winnings in the same way Jacques was going to. If not, we stand to lose more than a million francs, and he can hang out to dry in the days that remain.

Of course, Altig soon put their minds at rest and in the remaining two stages the St Raphaël machine was back in motion as if nothing had happened, chasing down any move that promised a threat to their new 'leader', and getting their sprinter, Graczyk, into position to score his fourth stage-win in Vitoria.

That night, before the final stage to a rain-soaked Bilbao, where the Minister of Sport, no less, castigated the Spanish teams for their poor showing, Anquetil abandoned the race. He set off back to Normandy with a sick note signed by the Vuelta's doctor confirming he was suffering from a 'gastric infection'. He was indeed ill, and probably shouldn't have been racing – some weeks later, after a visit to the Pasteur Institute in Paris, viral hepatitis was diagnosed – but few can doubt that his decision was provoked more by bitterness at the sight of Altig's yellow jersey.

As Antonio Vallugera wrote in *Dicen*: 'Anquetil has a constellation of stars for *gregarios*. And sometimes a star doesn't accept the *gregario*'s role.' It was the risk of riding with a dream-team. The mechanic, Eduardo de Gregorio, who was assigned to act as Anquetil's interpreter for the duration of the Vuelta, had been a privileged witness of all that unfolded. He revealed that Géminiani had repeatedly urged his leading star to show the team who was boss early in the race, but Anquetil preferred to save himself for one final strike, and let his team-mates pick up some glory in the meanwhile. De Gregorio was much taken with such generosity: 'He's a great companion. He doesn't just leave a few crumbs for the rest. He wants them to sit at the same table.' But, in return, as Stablinski remembers, 'Anquetil expected total loyalty from his team in a stage race he wanted to win, even if he wasn't going well.'

The irony was that, after all the suspicion and rancour, Altig was selected to ride the Tour de France that year. Géminiani was able to persuade Anquetil that Spain had been more a matter of his illness, rather than Altig's treachery, and that, anyway, he was going to need the German's support to combat the threat of Van Looy, who would be making his first venture in the French race. That July Anquetil won his third Tour, Altig took the green jersey, and St Raphaël the team prize, but the challenge of being the first man to win all three of the major tours would have to wait at least another year.

1963   In 1963, the Vuelta began in Asturias, with a short road-race from the mining town of Mieres to Gijón on the coast, followed by a 52-kilometre time-trial back to Mieres. This town was still recovering from events of the previous year. The Asturian mines were profitable but conditions for the miners were so grim that in 1962 a strike had broken out in Mieres, and spread until 60,000 Asturian miners had downed tools in the first serious social protest since the Civil War. The regime was sufficiently shaken to call a state of emergency, and the strike was brutally suppressed, with many miners tortured and imprisoned. Even so, their example proved an inspiration: strikes spread into the Basque Country and university students turned out to demonstrate their support. Was it a coincidence that the Vuelta should begin here?

It was in this same part of Asturias in 1934, even before the Civil War, that Franco had first employed his troops to crush, with extraordinary savagery, a general strike that had been initiated by the miners. One year later the organisers of the first Vuelta had studiously avoided the region for fear of sparking a protest. Not so in 1963: it wasn't in the nature of the regime to be cowed by opposition or to ignore an opportunity to impose its authority. The Vuelta could start in Mieres.

One survivor of the retribution that followed the 1962 strike, attending an anniversary reunion in 2002, remembered that during his trial in a military court, a colonel had looked him in the eye and said, 'Well I never, with all the weeding out that we did in Asturias, there are still some roots left.' Behind the contempt, there is a certain note of reluctant admiration, for it was indeed impressive that all the merciless reprisals before and after the Civil War had failed to crush the miners' spirit. Society was stirring again.

As for the overall route of the '63 Vuelta, Bergareche was again hotly denying that he'd shaped it with Anquetil in mind. It was the honest truth: Van Looy had been the intended guest of honour but injury had forced him to pull out. Although Anquetil hadn't touched his bike since winning the Paris–Nice, he accepted the last-minute invitation to come to Spain. A route that might favour a Flandrian sprinter would surely do for him, too. At 2,442 kilometres, it was the shortest Vuelta ever, concentrating its most difficult stages in the first week, when the peloton would cross Cantabria and the Basque Country. After Pamplona it was virtually flat all the way to Madrid.

This time there would be no mistakes. Altig had been left behind, and Anquetil was backed up by the reliable Elliott and Stablinski, the latter resplendent in his World Championship jersey. Without any preamble, on the first afternoon Anquetil set to work, comfortably winning the 52-kilometre time-trial, with 2'–51" on the best Spaniard, Pérez Francés, who finished third. The winner's bonus meant Anquetil was already three minutes ahead of his rivals and the fate of the Vuelta seemed sealed. 'The foreigners are the spoilt children of the organisers,' grumbled one Faema rider after he'd finished nearly seven minutes down. 'We might as well all go home and leave them to it.'

Fortunately for Bergareche, they didn't, and the days to come were constantly punctuated by spirited Spanish attacks. All the key men of Kas, Ferrys and Faema had their turn, but each and every time one or more sought to escape, they would look over their shoulder to see one or other of Géminiani's men pegged to their back wheel, and another dutifully accelerating the peloton.

Stablinski, in particular, was tireless in this defensive role – a *domestique* in a rainbow jersey is truly a *domestique de luxe*. For all that Raphaël's troops were sometimes made to sweat, their general's yellow jersey was not once seriously in jeopardy.

As the mountains came into view, Faema rider Julio Jiménez – 'the Watchmaker of Ávila' – tried to escape the St Raphaël strait-jacket. A quiet, mild-mannered man, he'd spent years cooped up in a workshop, hunched over the intricacies of watch mechanisms, all the while day-dreaming of open skies and steep mountains. The shortage of cycling teams in Spain forced him to compete as an Independent: when he finally turned professional he was already 27 years old, and 30 when he rode his first Tour. Like his predecessor, Bahamontes, he preferred racing in France, reigning over the Tour mountains between 1965 and 1967. In his era the Vuelta wasn't designed for a specialist climber: the now-famous ascents to the Lagos de Covadonga or the Angliru were still decades away.

Nonetheless, he gamely made the most of what was available. The fifth stage was a 191-kilometre venture into the Basque mountains, beginning and ending in Bilbao. On the first-category Puerto de Sollube, with the effortless acceleration that is the true climber's hallmark, Jiménez strung out the peloton. First over the summit, he showed none of Bahamontes' anxieties on the descent, and it took a furious chase by Anquetil and his Dutch henchman, Bas Maliepaard, to absorb him back into the leading group of 11 men. Then, in the streets of Bilbao, it was the familiar story: Maliepaard broke clear to be first under the Westinghouse Refrigerators banner that marked the finishing-line, consolidating his lead in the points competition and denying any Spaniard the time-bonus that would have closed the gap on the Yellow Jersey.

As a veteran of the '61 Vuelta, when the Spaniards had waited for the most propitious moment to launch a united attack and crack open the apparently invincible Belgian opposition, what exasperated Pérez Francés was the tactical naïvety they had generally shown ever since. They suffered from a *perro hortelano* syndrome: the curse of the gardener's dog. As the Spanish proverb observes, the dog guarding the vegetable patch can't eat the cabbages, but it won't let anyone else near them either. The Spaniards' erratic guerrilla warfare could make little impact against St. Raphaël's disciplined forces.

A heavy crash had left Pérez Francés on the verge of retiring, but he steeled himself for an offensive on the last mountainous stage, from Tolosa to Pamplona. After an early break had been quashed, Kas sent Pacheco away at kilometre 42 and Maliepaard was dispatched to guard him, but they were immediately joined by Pérez Francés. Once again Géminiani's men raised the tempo of the peloton and erased the danger. But the Ferrys captain was not going to be denied. Today he was in rampant mood. After lying low for just five kilometres, he was off again, with Pacheco for company once more. Now on the lower slopes of the first-category Jaizkibel, St Raphaël's climber, Guy Ignolin, was sent forward to police the escape and then Anquetil himself took charge and brought the breakaway pair under control.

But Pérez Francés was irrepressible. After further short-lived skirmishes on the road to Pamplona, the stage was finally decided in a sprint and it was taken by the jubilant Ferrys leader. With his bonus, Pérez Francés was able to pull back time that he'd lost to Anquetil on the first day of the race. He was now up to third place, just behind Barrutia and 2′–16″ down on the race leader.

The relentless pace and constant battle of the Pamplona stage had taken its toll on Anquetil. Worn out, he asked permission to go straight to the hotel, skipping the yellow jersey ceremony. He had plenty of time to recover, for stretching ahead, all the way to Madrid, was a long flat route with barely a climb in sight. With this prospect, even Pérez Francés, for all his stubborn refusal to concede to the St Raphaël steamroller, knew in his heart that the race was probably lost.

An air of resignation took hold of the Spaniards, who suffered a disastrous day on the Zaragoza to Lérida stage. Pérez Francés punctured repeatedly and, with the field blown along at a fierce pace by a strong following wind, he was never able to retrieve the leaders; his Ferrys team-mate, Manzaneque, who had waited to try and relay him back, crashed and damaged his gear mechanism; and the Kas rider, Barrutia, second overall that morning, missed the crucial selection and finished six minutes down. The only potential challenger left was José-Martin Colmenarejo and, in the streets of Lérida, Stablinski again did his job to perfection, and deprived the Faema man of the winner's time-bonus.

The last straw to demoralise Pérez Francés came on the morning of the 12th stage. The final time-trial would be held in the afternoon, but first there was an 80-kilometre circuit of Montjuic in Barcelona. Pérez Francés's mother ran a bar at the foot of the hill, so he was literally on home ground. It was Sunday and the Barcelona public were out in force to roar their approval when their man won the sprint. But the judges disqualified him, declaring he'd been given a hand-sling, and awarded the stage to the Belgian, Frans Aerenhouts. The spectators clamoured long and loud. Would the rules have been applied so strictly if a foreigner had done the same? It was difficult to imagine the same scenario in the Giro d'Italia. Pérez Francés lost the will to fight and retired the next day in disgust.

In the time-trial that afternoon an off-colour Anquetil finished second, beaten by a splendid Miguel Pacheco who lifted himself into third place overall. But the 'Colmenarejo miracle' that the Spanish fans had prayed for didn't materialise – a mere 20 seconds down at the half-way time-check, he went on to lose 1'–44" by the finish. It was good enough to hold on to second place overall – just 26 seconds ahead of Pacheco, but now 3'–06" down on Anquetil. At the second time of asking, the Frenchman had completed his collection: all the major tours were his.

The Press could no longer grumble about slack foreign stars not pulling their weight. For the second year running the best team in the world had come to Spain, ridden like true professionals and cleaned up most of the prize money. Instead, the criticisms were reserved for the home riders, accused of giving away the race too easily. A cartoon in *Dicen* showed Anquetil riding along immersed in a newspaper, and behind him a Spaniard, cooling him down with a fan, with another alongside bearing a tray of refreshments. It was, perhaps, rather unfair criticism; they would have far more reason to complain the following year, when the anarchy that had plagued the Spanish nationalist team in the fifties erupted with a vengeance in the Ferrys squad.

1964   Anquetil did not return in 1964; instead, the French challenge was led by Raymond Poulidor. Those legendary rivals, one an icon of smart, urban modernity, the other an incarnation of honest, rural tradition, never battled it out face-to-face in the Vuelta. They chose to come separately. Poulidor's presence in 1964 did not unduly worry the Spaniards. To be sure he was the favourite to win the long time-trial that was slotted in two days before the finish, but that year there were plenty of mountains for the Spaniards on the way there. And if the Ferrys men thought back to the last Tour de France, they could take heart in Pérez Francés' third place overall and Manzaneque's win of an epic Alpine stage by a full five minutes.

The other top contender on the starting-line in fashionable
Benidorm was Classics master Rik Van Looy, at the head of his strong
Solo–Superia squad. Looking distinctly battle-worn, the Belgian
appeared grateful for a respite from the dreary rain and tension of
racing back home. His domineering nature had earned him quite a
few enemies over the years and the season wasn't going smoothly
for him but, he told *El Mundo Deportivo*, 'with only four days in
Spain, with this fantastic sun for company, I already feel like a new
man'.

He had gone to the Tour de France the previous year arguing
that time lost in the mountains could be more than compensated
for by his stage-win bonuses. The theory, however, had been
comprehensively falsified by Anquetil and Bahamontes in the Alps:
although Van Looy won four stages (and the green jersey points
competition) he finished tenth overall. Perhaps the lower mountain
ranges of Spain would provide more propitious terrain.

Certainly, the 199-kilometre second stage was perfect for him –
pancake-flat with a strong cross-wind – and it was here that he made
the first decisive move of the race, breaking clear at 103 kilometres.
First to get across was Pérez Francés, who knew Van Looy from the
Tour and had seen the skill with which the Belgians set up their
echelons when the wind was on their shoulders. Twelve other men
made the bridge and when they rode into the *vélodrome* in Nules,
where Van Looy easily took the sprint and the yellow jersey, they
were seven minutes up on the peloton. A fortnight later, in Madrid,
only one rider who missed that crucial break – Julio Jiménez – would
finish in the first six overall.

Roads in Spain badly needed improving, not only for bicycle
races, but to cope with the needs of the rapidly expanding economy
and car ownership – the country had discovered the joys of holiday
traffic jams. The variety of road surfaces added an extra element of
risk to the Vuelta. On the way to Salou, another burgeoning seaside
resort, the long, flat stage was enlivened by a ten-kilometre stretch
of broken, flint-strewn road, which produced innumerable
punctures and, for a while, splintered the field. The most
distinguished victim was Poulidor, and his Mercier–BP colleagues
had to work like Trojans to bring their man back to the leading group,
which was being whipped along by the Belgians. The unspoken
rule that you don't attack a rival delayed by a puncture has always
been honoured more in the breach than in the observation.

At the very end of the day, however, the French exacted their revenge: in the final charge they were able to get their sprinter, Frans Melckenbeeck, over the line ahead of Van Looy. But immediately behind them, Van Looy's team-mate, Ward Sels, had elbowed a well-placed Pérez Francés out of contention for the important time-bonus. Now Pérez Francés was a man who knew how to look after himself, not only in a sprint, and after the stage-finish he went looking for his man. Shouted accusations turned into a fist-fight and only after the Spaniard had hurled his bike at the astonished Belgian were they separated by spectators and officials.

In the Pyrenees, the next road casualty was Van Looy. He crashed on the sinuous, pot-holed descent of the Puerto de Tossas, which Julio Jiménez had crossed alone to win the stage in Puigcerdá. Mountain areas would have to wait for the development of a skiing industry to see their roads improved. Van Looy remounted and continued, but there were rumours of a broken collar-bone. This seemed to be refuted as, despite obvious discomfort, he was able to climb on to the podium to receive the yellow jersey – he had retained his overall leadership – before being taken to the clinic. Later that evening the Vuelta's doctor announced that there was no fracture, just bruising around the shoulder. Whether or not the race leader continued would, he said somewhat pointedly, depend primarily upon his strength of character.

Leaving himself up for judgement, before seven o'clock the following morning Van Looy was on his way back to Belgium, in a car driven by his *gregario*, Edgard Sorgeloos (who was fined 1,000 pesetas by the Technical Jury of the Vuelta for his unjustified departure from the race). They were no doubt well into France by the time the sixth stage got underway, with Pérez Francés having inherited the yellow jersey much sooner than he could have hoped. Digesting the news, the peloton was in a quiet mood and the day ended in a sprint finish where Melckenbeeck gained another stage-win and Pérez Francés, untroubled this time by Sels, consolidated his leadership with a half-minute bonus for second place.

'In questions of tactics, we're still in nappies.' Such was the rueful verdict of the president of the Cycling Federation of Navarra, Ignacio Orbaiceta, after witnessing the following stage from Pamplona to San Sebastián. That morning, as the peloton set out under a leaden sky, Pérez Francés seemed a solid race leader, at the head of a team capable of resisting the expected attacks from Kas. When a group of

11 men went clear, 70 kilometres from San Sebastián, with a Kas trio in the vanguard, Ferrys sent Luis Otaño to safeguard their leader's interests. As a local man (from Rentería, next door to San Sebastián), he would know the road.

Convinced there were better ways of using that knowledge, on the ascent of the Puerto de Aguiña, still some 36 kilometres short of the finish, the defender suddenly switched to the attack. Otaño's move took everybody by surprise and he crested the summit with a 15-second advantage, which he steadily augmented on the run-in to San Sebastián, where his solo victory was enthusiastically cheered by his countrymen. With the benefit of the one-minute bonus he found himself the new race leader, with Pérez Francés relegated to second place.

There was widespread incomprehension. The veteran Belgian star, Rik Van Steenbergen, who was in Spain participating in a series of criteriums, was amazed to see the Ferrys leader working at the head of the peloton in his effort to limit the gains of his own *gregario*. 'A man of his class must constantly impose his authority without allowing anyone to waste a single gram of his strength,' he said. 'What happened with Otaño, no one with an iota of cycling sense could hope to understand.'

For all his protestations that he'd never wanted to strip his team-mate of the yellow jersey – he'd only been looking for the stage-win, he insisted – Otaño's action inflamed all manner of passions within the Ferrys team, whose strong point was not discipline. Their director, Damián Plá, was well-liked by his cyclists, for he was a warm-hearted man with impeccable manners, as well as being an excellent administrator – he'd been plucked from his job as factory manager and told to run his boss's new cycling project. But he was often out of his depth – Pérez Francés considers he lost a Giro d'Italia because Plá couldn't bring himself to offer money to another team for additional support, which was a common enough practice. He was also helpless at imposing order when faced with rebellion, which is what he had on his hands when the third of Ferrys' heavyweights, Fernando Manzaneque, joined the fray, complaining that he was being given no opportunities to show off his excellent form.

Manzaneque's grumbles increased everyday and he threatened to attack at the slightest opportunity. True to his word, on stage 12 from Vitoria to Santander, 40 kilometres from the finish on the Puerto de Alisas, Manzaneque launched an offensive which, once it was supported by several other opportunists, managed to stay clear. One of those in the break was Barry Hoban, representing Poulidor's team, Mercier–BP, and he seized what was for him the ideal opening of a small-group finish to become the first Englishman to win a stage of the Vuelta.

Race leader Otaño arrived with the main peloton, 1'–05" later. 'It's now up to each man to defend his own interests,' he declared. Manzaneque, meanwhile, was promising further attacks: 'As far as I'm concerned, the team doesn't exist.' Pérez Francés opted for something more pragmatic: 'The important thing is that one of the team wins, whoever it may be.'

And how could one of them not win? Ferrys now occupied the first three places on general classification: Otaño was followed by Pérez Francés at 1'–32", with Manzaneque third at 2'–06". Apart from their inability to set aside their individual ambitions in favour of the collective interest, the other stick in the spokes was Raymond Poulidor. He'd kept a low profile, but now he was lurking only a few seconds behind this leading trio, and counting the days until the 73-kilometre time-trial of stage 15.

The day following Ferrys' anarchic display at Santander produced no overall change as the peloton wound its way westwards along the coast to Avilés, and Hoban, again taking advantage of a small breakaway near the finish, secured his second stage-win. The next stage, though, would surely witness plenty of action. Its route carried the race through the Cantabrian Cordillera, and over the first-category Puerto de Pajares towards León. It would be the last opportunity to distance Poulidor.

The stage was, indeed, full of incident, albeit of a totally unexpected kind. Long before Pajares came into sight, a lowly placed rider, Angel Gutiérrez, set off on a solo mission and, since he represented no danger to the leaders, he was given his freedom. At the foot of Pajares his lead over the dawdling peloton was nearly ten minutes, while behind him, half a minute in front of the peloton, was Julio Jiménez, intent on securing the mountains title. He wasn't considered a threat either, having missed the Van Looy express on the second stage.

By the time Gutiérrez had crested the top and could gaze down upon the province of León, the Vuelta's top climber was only 1'–40" behind, while the indifferent Ferrys trio was trailing by four minutes. With 62 kilometres still to ride, there was plenty of time to reel in the Kas rider, but that would have required a measure of cooperation among the Ferrys men which they were unwilling to invest.

Up ahead, Jiménez caught and passed Gutiérrez, and still there was no reaction from the peloton. The gap continued to stretch until, with 30 kilometres to go, the little climber became the leader on the road. Even then, with Otaño's overall lead completely dissipated, his team continued its impassive way.

Jiménez won the stage to León by a massive 7'–12", and with it, the yellow jersey. He was under no illusion that he'd be able to hold on to it over the flat, 73-kilometre time-trial the following day, but that, he said, could not diminish his pride in having been leader of the Vuelta a España – if only for 24 hours.

As expected, in the time-trial Poulidor clocked the best time and, in doing so, secured the yellow jersey, and nudged Otaño and Pérez Francés down to second and third place. While Anquetil had exerted a tight domination of the race, Poulidor had been content to let the Spaniards take centre stage while he watched the drama from the wings, only to step in at a crucial moment and steal all the limelight. Never one to mince his words, Pérez Francés was dismissive of the Frenchman's achievement: 'This is the only great race that Poulidor will win, and it's because we gave it away.'

Throughout the nation there was general incredulity that Ferrys could have thrown away a race so rashly. The President of the Spanish Cycling Federation, Manuel Serdan, had difficulty in digesting the truth: 'Who could have imagined this disaster when there were four Spaniards at the top of the classification?' His bewilderment rapidly turned to anger: 'One has to remember that the prestige of Spain is at stake, and it must be respected as it deserves to be.'

That year a Spanish victory in the Vuelta would have been particularly gratifying for the regime because 1964 was the 25th anniversary of the end of the Civil War and of the start of Franco's rule. Gloating about the country's increasing prosperity, they celebrated their domination with the slogan 'Twenty-five years of peace'. It was an ironic choice of words considering that, in April of 1963, Julián Grimao, a leader of the clandestine Spanish Communist Party, had been sentenced to death after a trial for alleged crimes committed when he was a policeman in Barcelona during the Civil

War. He was executed despite world-wide disgust and pleas for clemency from the Pope.

One brave voice did confront the propaganda machine, with compelling clarity. The Abbot of the famous Catalan monastery of Montserrat, Aureli María Escarré, declared:

> Where there is no real freedom, there is no justice ... We do not have 25 years of peace behind us, but 25 years of victory. The winners ... have done nothing to end the division between the victors and the vanquished. This represents one of the most lamentable failures of a regime that calls itself Christian, but whose State does not follow the basic principles of Christianity.

These were words that could never have been published in Spain; they appeared in *Le Monde*, but they carried far and wide. The regime was affronted at being attacked from the Church, and the Abbot, like so many who had dared to be critical of the regime, was forced into exile.

In 1965, the question that was uppermost in the minds of those Spanish cyclists who hadn't had the opportunity to move abroad was not national prestige so much as money. They were becoming increasingly disgruntled at the disparity between what they received and the sums the race organisers paid out to the foreigners. Bahamontes, whose best years had been spent in the pay of the French Margnat team, was now in the last months of his cycling career. Nevertheless, he'd been invited to the Vuelta, and his hefty appearance fee was particularly galling.

1965 When the race began, in the Galician fishing port of Vigo, Poulidor looked a firm favourite for overall honours. This evaluation appeared to be vindicated when he took over the yellow jersey as early as Stage 4, a 41-kilometre *crono-escalada* – an individual time-trial, up to the summit of the Puerto de Pajares. The Frenchman was untouchable: Francisco Gabica was second fastest at 2'–52"; Bahamontes ceded four and a half minutes; and Van Looy, who'd worn the jersey up to that moment by virtue of claiming the first two stages, lost 7'–49". This result demonstrated once again the impossibility of winning a three-week tour on time-bonuses alone. In this edition of the Vuelta Van Looy went on to win eight stages in all (the closest anybody had come to Delio Rodríguez's record of

12), but virtually all his sprint-won advantage was dissipated in that one solitary climb.

In the next few days Poulidor's grasp on the race began to look decidedly uncertain as breaks full of dangerous men were repeatedly allowed to go clear – stage 5 went to Manzaneque and stage 6 to Pérez Francés. In Benidorm, after the end of stage 7, Bahamontes was predicting that Poulidor would lose the yellow jersey before they reached Andorra.

In the event, it was a conservative estimate, since he lost it the following day. After 31 kilometres, a small international group accelerated away and, on the monotonously flat road to Sagunto, their ever-increasing lead over the peloton went unchecked. At the finish the advantage had stretched to a huge 13'–40". Sitting in on that six-man break, representing Mercier–BP's interests with perfect correctness, was Rolf Wolfshohl. He was the new Yellow Jersey, five minutes up on his team leader and, of course, protesting his innocence – he had never sought to take over the leadership from Poulidor; he'd simply been carried there by the escape group.

Echoes of Otaño and Altig resonated. In just three years the Vuelta had seen several facets of the *gregario*–leader relationship enacted – treachery, loyalty and complete implosion. In 1965 it was a simple case of role reversal, for Mercier–BP did not rip itself apart as Ferrys had done, nor did this shift of the normal order of things unleash the jealousies that had riven St Raphaël. The fact was that Wolfshohl, an ex-World Cyclo-Cross Champion, was at that moment the stronger of the two, and Poulidor had the good grace to admit it.

In the days to come, in the Pyrenees and then in the heat of the Aragón plain, the German *gregario* revealed himself to be capable of defending the yellow jersey with far greater conviction than Poulidor had previously shown. Antonin Magne, Mercier–BP's *directeur sportif*, let it be known that the team would be supporting Wolfshohl, and only if he failed would Poulidor resume his status as their prime option. As with so many cyclists, Wolfshohl's slender figure was deceptively fragile. He was strong and alert, responding personally to attacks as the days went by. His only 'failure' was to finish second, just 33 seconds behind his team leader, in the final time-trial.

As for Poulidor, he'd never been fully committed to the race. His mind was almost certainly elsewhere. In the previous year's Tour he'd finished a mere 55 seconds behind Anquetil, and had beaten his *bête noire* on that memorable day on the Puy de Dôme. This year Anquetil would not be riding: it was a chance Poulidor simply could not let slip. So there were no complaints from him as he watched his German *gregario* finish in Bilbao with a comfortable 6'–36" advantage overall. The only thing that mattered was July.

For the organisers, the '65 Vuelta was not an altogether happy race. The home riders had failed to mount any serious challenge: there'd been talk of a Jiménez–Bahamontes duel, which never materialised. Surprised by his passivity, journalists asked Bahamontes if he was planning to abandon, but he just grinned and assured everyone he'd arrive in Bilbao, without question. After all, one of the conditions of his considerable fee was that he completed the race. Bergareche was understandably annoyed: 'He is sneering at the organisation and the Spanish fans.' In response, Bahamontes did make one brief attacking move – on the last major climb of the race – but he desisted the moment Jiménez latched on to his wheel. It was, in reality, the final fluttering of the Eagle's wings. In the Pyrenees, two months later, midway through the Tour, he'd climb off his bike for good.

As far as Pérez Francés was concerned, it was the organisers' fault that the Spaniards were so apathetic. 'Many riders, on seeing the amount that the foreigners were getting paid, just to start, have preferred to take it easy,' he argued. But they had plenty of energy to mark an extravagantly paid Bahamontes, encircling him in a moving prison.

There had been another, by now obligatory, run-in with the Belgians, inevitably involving Pérez Francés. It was rumoured that Van Looy had been offered nearly a million pesetas to ride the Vuelta, but on the condition that he won five stages. His team's particularly gung-ho tactics seemed to corroborate this.

Cheered on by a cosmopolitan Benidorm crowd, where swimsuit-clad northern Europeans outnumbered the Spanish spectators, Van Looy had won his third stage and he was determined to score another in the beach resort of Salou. As he triumphantly crossed the line in first place, various riders were left sprawling in his wake. Pérez Francés was one of the worst hurt, rushed to hospital with a suspected jaw fracture and severe bruising on the back. For once in no condition to talk, he left his battered team-mate Antonio Bertrán to explain what had happened. Speaking painfully, with the mark of a bicycle wheel seared across his back like a whiplash, and feeling as if his ribs had been 'ground in a mill', Bertrán described the final moments of the sprint: 'Pérez Francés was ahead with Mercier–BP's Melckenbeeck when Van Looy came up from behind, pushed by [team-mate] Desmet . . . Sels obstructed us and we all fell.'

It was all part of a day's work for one of Van Looy's *domestiques* – fending off irate rivals after the finish. So Sels couldn't have been surprised when Melckenbeeck, his shorts shredded, tried to thump him. Bertrán was equally incensed: 'The Belgians are doped. They arrive at the finish like madmen. It's impossible. These characters are taking stimulants.' There were fervent demands that judges be posted in the last metres to police the sprints, just as they are in the Tour de France.

The organisation had slipped up on other occasions, too. Poor signposting at the entrance to the vélodrome in Gijón caused some riders to take the wrong route, among them Van Looy and Barrutia, who were contesting the sprint. Their protest was dismissed. When the same happened at the finish in Palencia, the consequences were far more serious: a badly placed barrier caused the Belgian and Rudi Altig to crash. Altig sustained a broken leg, which lost him the rest of the season, and a furious Van Looy threatened to withdraw from the race. This lack of professionalism marred a race that was rapidly growing in international stature. Now that Bergareche had succeeded in enticing some of the very best European cyclists to Spain, he couldn't afford to let the organisation lag behind.

1966–1969

Waiting for a Champion

'Lá, la la lá; la la lá, la la lá.' As lyrics for a Eurovision Song Contest entry, they were a stroke of genius, and in 1968 Spain won, beating Cliff Richard's 'Congratulations'. A minor triumph but another small step out of isolation. The ebullience of sixties pop culture was at odds with the spirit of Franco's regime, but it penetrated the country all the same. There was a new, self-confident generation that wasn't haunted by memories of the Civil War, and if you had a reasonable job and kept out of politics, there was a sense that life was improving. There were small pleasures to aspire to: perhaps even a car, certainly a new domestic appliance; the newspapers were packed with advertisements for fridges.

The ever-growing legion of tourists was another link with the outside world, and the Vuelta organisers began to complain about the shortage of hotel rooms on the coast. Foreign participation in the race remained strong; indeed, the last three editions of the decade were all won by Tour de France winners. The only exception was in 1966, and that was a year when the race almost didn't take place. Grave economic difficulties experienced by the organising newspaper, *El Correo Español–El Pueblo Vasco*, brought them to the point of announcing that the Vuelta would probably not be held. Considering the importance that Franco's regime gave to sport, it came as no surprise when the Minister of State for Sport intervened to avoid the embarrassment of cancelling such an international event.

1966 But the last-minute reprieve couldn't save the race entirely. *El Correo Español* hadn't been in a financial position to arrange contracts with major foreign teams, and by the time government money came to the rescue it was too late: they'd already made their plans for the season. The only foreign competition capable of making a significant impact on the 21st edition of the Vuelta came from Dutch Televizier. Packed full of sprinters, they took nine stages, yet their top rider on general classification, Cees Haast, finished only eighth overall, and he was the sole foreigner in the top 15. After four years of counting on the presence of some of the world's most outstanding riders, in 1966 the race was essentially an all-Spanish affair.

102

In fact, it turned into an exhibition of a single team – the Vitoria-based Kas. Under the expert hand of Dalmacio Langarica, who'd won the Vuelta in 1946 and then, as director, had guided Bahamontes to victory in the Tour de France, they had evolved into a dynamic and compact unit whose domination of Spanish cycling would make the other teams weep in frustration. At their peak, it was claimed they drove sponsors away from the sport, as they offered no one else a look-in.

Langarica's aim was to get rid of the apparently inherent individualism that had plagued Spanish cycling. He never tired of insisting that: 'the important thing about Kas is that there's no such thing as a pivotal man'. He was adamant that: 'in my team, everyone has the role of *gregario* and leader'. The strong team spirit he engendered brought results in the 1964 Tour de France when Kas won the team time-trial; the only other Spanish squad to emulate them has been Manolo Sáiz's ONCE, three decades later. They went on to win the team prize in the Tours of '65 and '66, as well as picking up stage victories and the Mountains prize with Julio Jiménez in 1965. Their star climber received some tempting offers from other quarters, but he was keen to stay in Kas, requesting only a modest increase in salary which, he suggested, could be kept secret from the rest. So strong was Langarica's commitment to the egalitarian ideal, he rejected the idea out of hand. Reluctantly, Jiménez went abroad to ride in Anquetil's team.

The now retired Federico Bahamontes, catching up with the 1966 race in Madrid, predicted a Kas victory. The only issues, he said, were which of their riders it would be and where the selection would take place. And that, he insisted – never one to waste an opportunity to pour scorn on the new generation – would not happen in the mountains, 'because there are no climbers in the Vuelta'. It was more likely, he thought, that the final outcome would be determined by the 61-kilometre time-trial between Vitoria and Haro on stage 15.

His prediction began to prove accurate on the seemingly innocuous seventh stage – a mere 105 kilometres from Catalyud to Zaragoza – when Kas sprung an ambush and placed eight men in a 12-strong breakaway. The average speed was 48.5kph – 'a hundred kilometres of biting the handlebar', as *Dicen* described it. This stage also served as the coming out in society of a new rivalry to polarise Spanish cycling, although one between teams rather than individuals. The new Basque squad, Fagor, fought fiercely to bridge the gap, to no avail. Six days later, however, they took revenge by launching a counter-offensive 35 kilometres from the finish in San Sebastián and putting nearly two minutes into Kas' yellow jersey, Valentín Uriona. The aim had been to save face in front of a home crowd, but the main beneficiary was an intelligent opportunist who'd been quick enough to sit in on both the Kas and Fagor breaks: Dutchman Cees Haast, who, after winning the sprints on both occasions, became race leader.

'I understand that the rivalry between the Spanish teams is very strong,' said Haast, obviously hopeful of his chances, having corroborated that the stories about fratricidal tendencies were true. But he underestimated the difficulty of the 1,100-metre high Alto de Herrera, situated in the middle of the all-decisive time-trial, three days before the finish. There, he was utterly sunk, dropping to eighth overall. It was on the descent of the Herrera that Kas' Francisco Gabica, throwing all caution to the winds, overhauled his better placed Kas team-mates to claim the yellow jersey back for the team. A taciturn man from the province of Vizcaya, like his predecessor Loroño, Gabica became the second Basque to conquer the Vuelta and the jubilation in Bilbao knew no bounds. Kas had secured the whole podium, placed eight men in the top 15 and walked off with almost half the prize money. It wouldn't be so easy for them next year.

1967   With financial difficulties now resolved, the 1967 line-up was much more impressive. Together with the winners of the three previous editions – Gabica, Wolfshohl and Poulidor – there were two ex-World Champions – Jan Janssen (1964) and Tom Simpson (1965). The Spanish teams Kas and Fagor would pay scant attention to the foreign competition, absorbed as they were in their own running battle. They had locked horns since the start of the season: of the eleven Spanish races leading up to the Vuelta, one had gone to Ferrys, and the remaining ten were equally divided between the two Basque teams. Langarica recognised that this obsessive fight reduced Kas' chances of repeating victory.

The route wouldn't be much help either. Given that the Tour de France had always served as a model, when the French race became dominated by time-trials, the Vuelta followed suit. In 1967 there were three, ranging from a five-kilometre prologue-style opener in Vigo, to two challenging stages of 44 and 28 kilometres in Cantabria and the Basque Country. Although the Spanish riders were improving in this speciality, it was not their strong point. 'A true climber will never be able to win the Vuelta,' observed *Dicen*, uneasy with what they considered undue eagerness to mimic the French race. Poulidor was automatically judged a favourite: he only needed to repeat his strategy of '64, saving his forces till the last part of the race – a prognostication that somewhat ignored his less impressive performance in '65.

Dicen was even more critical of a new rule that would rob Julio Jiménez of the Mountains prize since, to be eligible, a rider had to finish in the top 15 on general classification. Ironically, the idea was originally conceived in France to thwart Spanish dominance in that category, but eventually discarded for being mean-spirited. Yet the Vuelta, not content with designing a route ideal for a specialist against the clock, connived not to reward Jiménez for his 'titanic effort to win in non-existent mountains', as an exasperated Antonio Vallugera wrote: 'We are used to copying everything that comes out of France, because we think that if it proceeds from beyond the Pyrenees, it must be good.'

Such a lack of self-confidence was again in evidence during the first week, after the Italian sprinting ace Michele Dancelli, Vitadello's top rider, was fined and penalised one minute on general classification for blatantly hanging on to cars during a climb. When his team threatened to withdraw, race organiser Bergareche capitulated. Claiming it had simply been an error, he cancelled the penalty, which cleared the way for Dancelli to take the yellow jersey from Fagor's Txomin Perurena. It seemed a particularly submissive gesture, especially considering the Italian readily confessed to journalists that his team 'had only come to the Vuelta to prepare for the Giro'.

He was not the only well-paid star training for a greater prize. In 1967 Tom Simpson only had one ambition, and that was the Tour de France. His unusually restricted participation in the Northern classics that year was all part of his preparation for an assault on the Tour. So, too, was his involvement in the Spanish race. In fact, he had decided to quit the Vuelta in Salamanca, only riding the next day because that was the easiest way to get to the airport in Madrid! But having won the stage, and won it in some style – 42 seconds ahead of escape partner Pérez Francés (riding for Kas this year) – he decided to stay on. He took a second stage later in San Sebastián, where he'd won his world title 18 months earlier, but never had any intention of being a serious candidate for the overall classification.

From the race-start, in the north-west province of Galicia, the peloton had been crossing Spain in a south-east direction aiming for the Mediterranean coast. It was during the sixth stage, between Albacete and Benidorm, that the men with serious aspirations came to the fore, and the first selection to have lasting significance occurred. After just 20 kilometres, a group of 16 was allowed to break clear from a seemingly indifferent peloton. Although the escape contained the patently dangerous Janssen, accompanied by two of his capable Pelforth *gregarios* – Jean-Pierre Ducasse and the Luxumbourger Johny Schleck – the reluctance of the main field to chase them down was perhaps understandable, since all the Spanish teams were well represented up ahead. Nevertheless, Fagor faced an acute dilemma – to chase or not to chase? In the main field they had José López Rodríguez in the yellow jersey, but their strongest man, Luis Otaño, was being born away in the escape group. Finally, they opted to let the break go.

Ninety kilometres further on the gap had risen to an alarming 12 minutes, and the leading group had shed only two of its members. When Bic's sole representative, Graczyk, was ridden off the back his team assumed control at the front of the peloton, but it was all too late, and they crossed the line in Benidorm still more than seven minutes adrift of the leaders. So, the yellow jersey passed to the Frenchman, Ducasse, with Otaño in second place at 5'–16", only a handful of seconds up on Janssen, ominous behind his dark glasses.

Blown up the Mediterranean coast to Barcelona by a strong tail wind, the Spanish riders waited impatiently for the *etapa reina* between the Catalan capital and Andorra, which would take the riders over three major cols – Tosas, Puymorens, and Envalira – evocative names, seeped in Spanish climbing history. The Col de Puymorens had regularly figured in the Tour de France since 1913: Ezquerra had been first over the top in 1936, and Berrendero the following year. More recently Julio Jiménez had led over its 1,915-metre summit on the way to his first Tour stage-win in '64, as did Pérez Francés *en route* to his stage-win in Barcelona in '65, the triumph of his career. It was a propitious day to put Pelforth to the sword.

The attacks came almost from the start. Initially they were contained, but at kilometre 37 – with the mountains still 100 kilometres in the distance – a group of five went clear, with Fagor and Kas represented by one rider each. When they'd established a lead of two minutes, the young Vicente López Carril jumped away from the peloton to reinforce Kas in the leading group, and Schleck immediately followed to defend Pelforth's interests. Together they bridged the gap, which, at the foot of the Collada de Tosas, had grown to almost six minutes.

When it was the peloton's turn to tackle the climb, Yellow Jersey Ducasse began to suffer, and to rub salt into the wound, Pérez Francés leapt away and embarked upon an extraordinary solo gallop up the mountain to further strengthen the Kas presence up ahead. Incredibly, he bridged the gap before the 1,865-metre summit. But the hero of the day was Fagor's Mariano Díaz, who jumped clear just before Pérez Francés made contact to lead over the top by 35 seconds, and, impressively, he held off the Kas trio and all other pursuers to take the stage, two *puertos* later, in Andorra.

The Kas offensive, which had promised to reverse the entire order of the race, evaporated on the final climb. In reaction to his monumental efforts on the Collada de Tosas, Pérez Francés suffered a true *pájara**, and was overtaken by the Yellow Jersey group. It was also a fairly disastrous day for Fagor; they'd have to take consolation in their stage-win, since their man for the overall, Otaño, crashed on the long 29-kilometre descent of Envalira, losing nearly six minutes. Ducasse remained race leader.

With the Pyrenees a wasted opportunity, the Spanish teams also failed to make any impact in the time-trials. The first, held in Cantabria in pouring rain and a swirling wind, was won by Poulidor, who gave virtually his only demonstration of strength in the entire race. With Anquetil now thinking of retirement, and the prodigy Merckx still to arrive, there was perhaps a final window of opportunity for him in the Tour this year – he'd squandered his chance in 1965, losing to Felice Gimondi, and the previous year, finishing third behind Lucien Aimar. So, like Tom Simpson, he was using the Vuelta merely as a training exercise. Pérez Francés was prompted to comment acidly on the extortionate fee the organisers had paid for Poulidor's one afternoon of real effort.

---

* *pájara* – Spanish cycling jargon meaning a sudden complete loss of energy, equivalent to the 'bonk' in British cycling argot, but with more dramatic overtones.

But the true winner that day was Janssen. Although three and a half minutes slower than Poulidor, he had leapt to second overall with a performance that was sure to secure him overall victory. Although the brave Ducasse still led the race, it was with a mere 50-second advantage. Dutiful *gregario* as he was, he kept the jersey warm for his leader during 11 days, finally to present it to Janssen after the last time-trial in the Basque Country; his consolation was to hang on to second overall. The first Dutchman to win the Vuelta, Janssen, had rehearsed a rather conservative strategy that would win him the Tour the following year. He owed his victory to being attentive at all times, getting in the right breaks and reserving enough strength to secure a winning margin in the final time-trial.

On what was supposed to be a leisurely last run into Bilbao, the peloton were rudely interrupted. As the cyclists rounded a bend on the descent of the Sollube, some 30 kilometres from the finish, they found the road strewn with nails and sprayed with oil, which provoked numerous falls and punctures. Here was an act of sabotage by the Basque separatist movement Eta against the Spanish tour that would be repeated, with more deadly intent, the following year. It had no effect on the immediate outcome of the race, but it cast a sombre shadow on its future.

The atmosphere at the finish was starkly different from the previous year, with disappointed fans booing the Kas and Fagor riders. As the peloton approached Bilbao, some of the cyclists, including the 1966 winner, Gabica, preferred to quietly slip off home so as to avoid the hostile crowds. Tom Simpson had observed that for an escape to succeed in the Vuelta, it was essential to be either very badly placed on general classification or have at least one Kas and one Fagor rider present. While they were so distracted by marking each other, the Spanish teams couldn't hope for overall victory. The situation was aggravated by the dominance of only these two teams: with others in the fray, tactics would automatically have become more complex. Of course, such rivalry wasn't limited to Spain, but elsewhere teams were capable of holding a truce if it served their interests. A ready example was provided a few weeks later, in the Giro d'Italia, where Anquetil was on the point of taking advantage of Italian in-fighting, until the national teams stopped him in his tracks. Once the foreigner had been eliminated, the Italians returned to fighting it out among themselves, Felice Gimondi emerging as the strongest.

Gimondi was the man of the moment, and in 1968 he came to **1968**
Spain with one purpose in mind – to emulate Jacques Anquetil and
become only the second man to win all three major tours. In 1965,
at the age of 22, he'd won the Tour at his first attempt, and he would
conquer the Giro three times during his career. *Dicen* described his
strong Salvarani team as 'a two-headed dragon', since at Gimondi's
side was Rudy Altig, Anquetil's rebellious *domestique* from '62.
Among the Italian's rivals were Janssen, and the 1966 Tour winner,
Lucien Aimar, at the head of Bic, while against this array of talent
were ranged the best of the Spanish riders, and many *aficionados*
must have wondered if this might finally be the year of José Pérez
Francés.

As the peloton tracked down the Mediterranean, one of the
successful sprinters was Michael Wright, who became the first
Britain ever to wear the Vuelta's yellow jersey, although it should
be added he barely spoke any English. Having been brought up in
Belgium, French was his natural tongue, and Flemish his natural
style of riding. Two stage-wins, in Barcelona and Salou, allowed
him to take the leadership from Altig.

Wright didn't stay long in yellow: after only one day, Altig
reclaimed the leader's jersey in Vinaroz with another fierce display
of finishing speed. This time he didn't relinquish it immediately: all
he did lose during the following two days that took the race down
to Benidorm was 100 pesetas – the fine he incurred for 'bad conduct',
his crime being to have snatched three oranges from one of the many
trees that lined the road south of Valencia.

Although practically an established tradition, the foreign
ownership of the first week, with all its prize money and important
bonuses, was beginning to rankle. Apparently sprinters could only
grow in certain countries, and it was Spain's destiny to produce
nothing but climbers, albeit in the abundance with which it grew
oranges. When asked why Spaniards couldn't sprint, Altig thought
it was due to a lack of practice: 'They hardly ever go to the
international Classics.' On the other hand, Pérez Francés considered
the most crucial factor was strategy: 'The foreigners beat us because
their teams position four or five riders working together in the
finishes.' Or perhaps the Spaniards weren't reckless enough: 'The
foreigners launch themselves like mad men,' said a disapproving
López Rodríguez of Fagor. 'They're always grabbing each other. If
you join in, you're risking your life.'

Nevertheless, some good home sprinters had emerged. In the previous year's Vuelta, both Ramón 'Tarzán' Sáez and Txomin Perurena had won stages, which in Perurena's case secured him the yellow jersey for two days. He was at the start of a long, exceptionally successful career, and no other Basque cyclist has managed to equal his number of victories. Curiously, and as proof of his versatility, Perurena became the last Spaniard to win the King of the Mountains jersey in the Tour of 1974, reminiscent of another great all-rounder who began life as a sprinter – Laurent Jalabert.

On the eighth day of the race Altig did lose his yellow jersey, and in the most extraordinary of circumstances. The riders left Benidorm in blazing sunshine to begin the 167-kilometre ride inland towards Almansa. After just 14 kilometres, Manuel Martín Piñera, the 37-year-old 'grandfather' of the tour who was riding for the minor Spanish Karpy team, accelerated out of the peloton. Even discounting his age, he was clearly no threat – currently lying 45th on general classification – and so was given leave for his brief moment in the limelight. But what nobody could have realised was that this was no spur-of-the-moment opportunism: it was an ambush that had been planned as far back as the first stage in Zaragoza. When Martín Piñera had studied the route guide he'd guessed that after seven days on the flat those foreign legs would need time to accustom themselves to the hills. It was a stage that would break the mould of the first week and he calculated he could take advantage of it.

When 'grandfather' Piñera rode away from the indulgent peloton there was no hint of desperation in his flight: he rode steadily, fully aware that he would need to measure out his strength over more than 150 kilometres. At no time did his lead over the main group extend beyond four and a half minutes, and for much of the time the presence of a couple of more dangerous men attempting to bridge the gap kept everyone alert. With more than 120 kilometres covered, and his lead down to under two minutes, it seemed as if Piñera would soon be reeled back in and his solo flight become one more case of heroic Spanish failure. But he rallied, the leaders relaxed their tempo, and he rode to a rapturous reception in Almansa, where he jumped into a fountain as soon as he crossed the line, 3'–36" up on Gimondi who led in the peloton. When he planned his stage-winning strategy eight days previously, he never imagined it would reward him with the yellow jersey as well, nor that his adventure would bring about the retirement of no less than 14 other riders, who arrived outside the time-limit.

The following day, Altig took the yellow jersey for the third time. The route was flat – 230 north-west to Alcácar – but the riders were buffeted by a cross-wind blowing down from the Meseta. Under the guise of nothing more aggressive than competing for an intermediate sprint, the German attacked with a vigour that split the peloton in three. Martín Piñera was trapped in the second group and from there to the finish the gap steadily widened to an unassailable 11′–20″. After his 24 hours of glory, 'grandfather' was back in 31st position overall and five riders more, unable to hang on to the coat-tails of the trailing echelon, had been eliminated.

Today's Vuelta, held in September, has lost an epic element. A springtime journey around Spain is full of contrasts: while Andalucía basks in summer temperatures, the north can still be shrouded in winter. The diversity of climate is still in evidence at the tail-end of summer – there is always the uncertainty as to whether thick mists and rain will descend to make the stages in Asturias invisible – but the unpredictability of spring accentuates the contrast between the north and south much more. In 1968, as the peloton left the Mediterranean ever further behind, the temperature dipped overnight, and the next three days turned into a nightmare for the beleaguered cyclists. Not only were they battling into a constant cold, northerly headwind throughout the 650 kilometres past Madrid, Palencia, and up to the coastal town of Gijón, they also had to contend with rain, hailstorms and, on the climbs, swirling mist and snow. Riders crashed on roads made treacherous by hail, or simply abandoned through sheer misery. And in blinding snow, Altig's time in the yellow jersey came to an end.

On stage 12, climbing the Puerto de Pajares by the gentler southern slopes, the riders remained in a more or less compact unit. Once over the top, now just 85 kilometres from Gijon, they rode into a white-out – a blizzard streaming out of the low clouds brought visibility down to a few metres, and turned the road into a virtual ice rink. Only Vittorio Adorni and Aimar had the suicidal nerve to attack, and in their wake the peloton splintered into fragments: Altig was one of many who descended slowly, opting for discretion as the better part of valour. He was destined to lose more than ten minutes that day, and ten more men were to abandon the race or finish outside the time-limit.

Once on the flat a small leading group came together and, then, with less than 30 kilometres to the finish, Pérez Francés attacked, and only the Belgian, Joseph Spruyt, was able to follow his back wheel. Mud-splattered, they arrived together at the velodrome in Gijon, where the Spaniard took the sprint. They were 1'–47" ahead of the chasing group, which, coupled with the 40-second time-bonus, presented Pérez Francés with the yellow jersey. The margins at the head of the general classification remained very close, however. Janssen was second, 20 seconds down, while Gimondi, although seventh overall, was only 1'–16" from the new race leader.

It was four years since Pérez Francés had last worn the Vuelta's yellow jersey and the next day, as if in celebration, the sun shone. Kas director Langarica instructed his troops to shackle any serious threats on the road to Santander and the race leader rode in triumph into his native town.

Stage 14 was the *etapa reina*, carrying the riders over three cols during its 224-kilometre trek to the Basque provincial capital of Vitoria, the town of Kas' headquarters. The third and final climb was the hard Puerto de Orduña, its 900-metre peak 47 kilometres short of the finishing-line. A seven-man break, into which three Kas riders had infiltrated, was allowed to go clear on the descent of the Alisas, the first climb of the day. Their lead continued to extend, as Gimondi and Pérez Francés kept watch over each other. Then, with three kilometres to go to the summit of the Orduña, Gimondi accelerated into a rhythm that the Spaniard couldn't follow. The Kas advance guard served simply as a moving target for the Italian: the closer he got to them, the more distance he was putting into Pérez Francés.

His descent was every bit as dramatic, and stylish – the Italians were renowned for descending with the speed and grace of downhill skiers – and at the bottom of the col he had succeeded in putting two minutes into the race leader. In the final kilometres, the fighter Pérez Francés pulled back a handful of seconds, but not enough to preserve his jersey. Gimondi now led the Vuelta by 11 seconds.

Pérez Francés recalls Langarica as 'a man who was obsessed with winning by teams' and in his attempt to secure a symbolic win in Kas' home town, the director had sacrificed rather than protected the leader's position. Also flowing through Langarica's mind were thoughts of next July. The year before, the Tour de France had reverted to national teams, and not a single Kas rider had represented Spain. In 1968 Langarica was in charge of the Spanish squad, and he intended to pick its members entirely from Kas. Until then he lost no opportunity to show the Spanish Federation how strong his men were. It was a cruel twist of fate that, after leaving the undisciplined Ferrys, Pérez Francés should end up in an outfit at the other end of the spectrum, where at times there was no room for individual ambition or glory.

The next stage began in Vitoria in front of a huge and enthusiastic crowd that had braved the steady rain. It was scheduled to take the race 128 kilometres through the Basque mountains to Pamplona, but only reached the half-way point. As the peloton began the descent of the Puerto de Urbasa, a bomb detonated at the side of the road. The threat that Eta had hinted at the previous year had become a much more serious reality.

Obsessed with the unity of Spain, Franco systematically repressed any expression of regional identity, particularly in the Basque Country and Catalunya. When the rebel generals took Bilbao in the Civil War, he proclaimed: 'Here is the end of separatism, and from here on, there is nothing more than Spain, which is eternal, immortal.' The inevitable response to such repression was a heightened sense of regional nationalism and the legacy of Franco's regime, from which Spain still suffers, was Eta. The terrorist organisation's first killings would occur in the summer of 1968, when they targeted a notorious torturer and police chief in San Sebastián, Meliton Manzanas. In the spring, they turned their attention to the Vuelta, as the presence of such a symbolically Spanish event in the Basque Country was an affront to their separatist aims. If the race acted as a link between the regions of Spain, they wanted to cut their homeland loose.

Had the explosion occurred a few minutes later, the consequences would have been far graver. As it was, there were no casualties, only a bunch of very scared cyclists. With extraordinary insouciance, the Vuelta's organisers asked them to continue racing, once they'd overcome their immediate alarm, and pushed their bikes through and around the debris of the ripped-up road. The riders were completely opposed to the idea, and leading their protest was Pérez Francés, who informed the organisation that 'I've already done my military service in Africa.' When an officer of the civil guard accused him of being on Eta's side and wanting to sabotage the Vuelta, the incensed cyclist threatened to abandon. Everyone was conscious of the foreign Press in attendance, and the repercussions on the race if the rider classified second went home, so the Lieutenant Colonel was persuaded to retract his words and the stage was annulled. The hotheaded Pérez Francés suddenly found himself very popular: 'It was the first time that all the riders were on my side.'

That night it was feared that the Vuelta would have to be cancelled. Some cyclists, including Gómez del Moral of Kas, had received anonymous threatening letters and wanted out. The team directors talked until the early hours, and were in favour of continuing, so as not to give in to the terrorists, but they decided the cyclists should have the last word. There was another heated meeting the next morning, and Bergareche passed on the message from the Spanish Cycling Federation that any rider who refused to start the stage would have their license confiscated, to which Pérez Francés retorted: 'No, you're not going to take away my license, because I'm going to give it to you.' But eventually, after promises of increased security, the riders allowed themselves to be persuaded.

So, three-quarters of an hour behind the scheduled departure time, a nervous and tightly bunched peloton rolled out of Pamplona *en route* for San Sebastián. Before long, the events of the previous day seemed forgotten, and the riders got down to their business of racing. It was a lively stage, but not one that produced any changes at the head of the general classification: Gimondi was still in the yellow jersey.

The penultimate stage, and the last real opportunity for significant change, was the individual time-trial, which covered 67 kilometres and included two third-category climbs: it was a test of strength rather than specialist skill. A huge roar of applause greeted the arrival of Pérez Francés in Tolosa – he had comfortably beaten the best time recorded up to that moment – but the precipitous appearance of the Italian signalled what the home crowd feared. In the '68 Vuelta, with an overall advantage of 2'–15", Felice Gimondi was the strongest man. He'd given a master class in how to win a grand tour, lying low at first, using Altig as a smoke-screen, until Pérez Francés struck his blow. Then, no longer willing to risk everything in the final time-trial, the Italian had retaliated – attacking from afar, and taking Kas by surprise. Although once more the Vuelta had eluded him, Pérez Francés could be proud of putting up a hard fight, helping to turn '68 into a vintage edition.

The 1969 Vuelta began with arch rivals Fagor and Kas having to share the podium. A rider of each team had completed the preliminary morning time-trial of 6.4 kilometres with exactly the same winning time and, since fractions of a second hadn't been recorded, it was impossible to establish the first yellow jersey. But the happiness of the Kas rider, Gómez del Moral, was short-lived, as he was called away to Córdoba by the sudden death of his mother. It was a bad omen, and the team from Vitoria made little impact on the rest of the race; for once they were outshone by their adversaries.

Giving an early warning of his good form, bony, baby-food-gulping Roger Pingeon, leader of Peugeot and winner of the '67 Tour de France, clocked the second-fastest time. This year he was the only serious foreign challenger. It was bad news for the Vuelta that the Tour had reverted to commercial teams for, after its brief decline brought about by the national team formula, the French race was once more the absolute focus of the racing calendar. So the Vuelta was left by the wayside, the organisers finding it impossible to secure the line-up they wanted. No Eddy Merckx for them.

The race had begun in Extremadura, in the south-western corner of Spain, where summer arrives early. In hot sun, Michael Wright won the first of two stages and, for the second year running, put on the yellow jersey. But by the time the peloton had reached Madrid they were riding through torrential rain and strong cold winds. In the Meseta, the Belgian Raymond Steegmans took advantage of the echelons to win a reduced-group sprint; he'd wear the yellow jersey for five days in all.

But this was the year of the Spanish sprinters. When the race reached the Mediterranean , 'Tarzán' Sáez won in Nules by a clear margin. The day after, Steegmans rose to the challenge, and the pair fought tenaciously over the final metres in Benicasim. For the observers, it was too close to call, but the judge, as if by reflex, handed victory to the Belgian, without even consulting photographic evidence. Only later was it shown that the first wheel over the line had been Sáez's and the positions were officially reversed. Tarzán was in roaring form, and his team, Pepsi, kept the pace high on the following stage, to deter any adventurers. He nearly won a third consecutive sprint, beaten by López Rodríguez into second place, but, with the 20-second bonus, he was the new race leader. The Spanish fans' delight was completed on stage 10 when 'Grandfather' Piñera topped another of his heroic escapes with a win on the elegant

Paseo de Gracia in the centre of Barcelona, on Saturday afternoon. For a change, the Spaniards were not pushed into the background in the buildup to the mountains.

'What mountains?' a climber might have asked, looking at the route of the *etapa reina*. The most demanding stage of the race would take the peloton from the Costa Brava resort of San Feliú de Guixols, over five cols of only medium difficulty to Moyá, a town in the Catalan interior. To give these climbs the categories of first and second seemed pompous, wrote Vallugera in *Dicen*. It was a tough stage, certainly, but hardly epic material.

The Spanish landscape is famous for its mountains. Apart from providing a hide-out for bandits, they are responsible for shaping Spain's diversity, isolating regions from each other and encouraging them to develop their own culture and language. Although there are no colossal passes as in the northern Pyrenees, Alps or Dolomites, the Vuelta organisers' argument that 'Spain doesn't have enough mountains to decide a race' never rang true. In the '60s, when the balance of the race was weighted heavily towards time-trials, the anathema of any slightly built *escalador*, Bergareche would respond to criticisms with his stock answer – 'I can't bring the Tourmalet to Spain' – refusing to acknowledge the potential of the country's rugged terrain.

It was the weather that came to the rescue and provided the day with the necessary epic touch, and a suitable scenario for the emergence of a new hero. The Spanish teams were now internationally recognised as among the strongest; unbridled individualism was something of the past, so it was frustrating that such strength was not being translated into results. A champion was required to finish off the work.

The day was cold, with persistant rain and mist on the cols to freeze the cyclists to the bone. The peloton shattered on the first climb and, by the top, the leading group had been reduced to two men: Roger Pingeon and current Spanish Champion, Luis Ocaña. Riding for Fagor, 23-year-old Ocaña was considered to be a reasonably promising young cyclist, but by the end of the stage his attitude and ambition had impressed everyone, and hopes were raised that the longed-for saviour of Spanish cycling might have arrived.

When Ocaña attacked Pingeon showed excellent judgement in sticking to his wheel. Unconcerned by his shadow, the young

Spaniard powered onwards, establishing a gap of two minutes on the main field. The far more experienced Frenchman bided his time, conserving his strength and, 15 kilometres from Moyá, Ocaña blew – he'd paid the price for his generosity. Knowing the Vuelta was within his grasp, Pingeon seized the opportunity and flew to the finish, where he was presented with the yellow jersey. Ocaña lost over three minutes, but he delighted everyone with his spirited declaration: 'It's clear that Pingeon is strong, but as the race isn't over, I haven't given up. I'm going to try and recover lost ground or, at least, make Pingeon sweat.'

In the stages leading up to the two time-trials in the Basque Country, held over the final three days, Pingeon secured some help from the Belgians, since his own Peugeot team was decidedly ineffective. But his main ally was the irrepressible Fagor–Kas rivalry, which diverted the Spaniards' attention and allowed him to preserve his lead unchallenged. In the first time-trial, a course of 25 kilometres between Irún and San Sebastián, Ocaña beat Pingeon by 54 seconds; it moved him up to second place, but there was still a yawning gap between them of 3'–48". Then came the penultimate stage into Vitoria, the occasion of a historic cease-fire, when Fagor allowed a Kas rider to win in their home town – the only Kas victory this Vuelta. It was, after all, in their interests to let an escape go and avoid a sprint finish, because if Michael Wright had won a third stage his bonus might have threatened Ocaña's second place.

In the final 29-kilometre time-trial into Bilbao, Ocaña gave an exhibition, beating Pingeon by 1'–32". The Frenchman's winning margin had been reduced, but not eliminated. He had won on the back of the young cyclist's impetuous riding on the Moyá stage. But instead of frustration, the reaction in Spain was of excitement. Deeply impressed by Ocaña's style and strength, *Dicen* declared him 'the best time-trialist that Spanish cycling has ever had, and the best cyclist of the moment'. The new President of the Spanish Cycling Federation, Luis Puig, summed up the mood of optimism: 'We've lost the Vuelta, but found a Champion.'

1970–1975

Cycles of Pain

After three decades of Franco, it was hardly surprising that so many Spaniards had finally accommodated themselves to the regime, or at least come to value the security it offered them, but there were unmistakable signs that an era was coming to an end. The dictator was now approaching 80, and no amount of photographs depicting him engaged in outdoor pursuits could disguise his growing fragility. The prospect of his death worried some to the point of panic, while others were filled with hope.

Despite the population's general political indifference, in the early '70s the regime had its hands full trying to suppress dissent. The steady undercurrent of worker and student unrest of the '60s had swollen into a tidal wave of strikes and demonstrations in the cause of decent wages and political freedom. Assertions of national identity in the Basque Country and Catalunya were gathering momentum and were often backed up by the church, much to Franco's consternation. The regime could only react with violence, but as the repression grew fiercer, so did the solidarity among the different groups that dared to challenge the status quo.

The dramatic events – the states of emergency, show trials and death penalties – provided a distant background to the Vuelta. It was one of Spanish cycling's most exciting periods when two stars appeared almost simultaneously: Luis Ocaña and José Manuel Fuente, also known as 'Tarangu', which in Asturian dialect means 'unconcerned about himself'. Two extraordinary cyclists, whose lives were marked by success and tragedy, and neither of whom are alive today.

Both were prodigious climbers, although Fuente was 'purer' in this sense and less of an all-rounder. Both were born into poverty: Ocaña's family left their native Cuenca to emigrate to France in 1957 when he was 11 years old, and Fuente grew up in a small Asturian village, Limanes. Both felt like outsiders, finding it difficult to fit in. Riding in a French team, Ocaña had to constantly assert his Spanish identity: on either side of the border he was regarded as a foreigner. Fuente had fought so hard to break away from the misery of his background, he never really learnt to relax his guard. He entitled his autobiography *The Cycle of Pain* and every victory was scoured from a destiny mounted against him. Of all the obstacles destiny threw their way, perhaps the cruelest was Eddy Merckx.

The Vuelta's organisers dearly wanted to contract Merckx in 1970 to celebrate their 25th anniversary in style, but he was unavailable, and the eventual line-up was poor. They claimed that foreign teams had pulled out as soon as they discovered that doping controls, already in effect in the Tour de France, were to be introduced. 'A sanction at this stage of the season would mean missing the Giro and the Tour. They don't want to take the risk,' accused Bergareche.

That year the Vuelta smelt of the sea, tracing half of the entire Spanish coastline, beginning in Cádiz by the Atlantic, and following the Mediterranean round as far north as Barcelona for a distance of 1,600 kilometres. It was a voyage through a new Spain, the one the tourists saw: a land of sun, sand and hotels. It was the first time the Vuelta had begun in Andalucía; ignored for so long, the region would feature prominently in the new decade. Its new wealth was much in evidence; the coast was transformed, some would say destroyed, and an improved road network was taking shape. The race correspondents were delighted with the weather, the foreign girls in bikinis and picturesque views, but the route didn't make for exciting racing. Each day the cyclists were blown from start to finish by a strong tail wind that kept the speed high and the peloton compact. The stages were resolved in mass sprints, still the speciality of the foreigners. There was a growing impatience to reach Barcelona, so that a selection could take place and the Spanish cyclists might play a bigger role in events.

Following the Tour's example, there was a prologue, which Luis Ocaña won by four-tenths of a second from the Dutch rider René Pijnen, who fell 20 metres from the finish and had to run over the line, bike on shoulder. Ocaña, a strong favourite to win overall, became the first race leader, but it seemed only fair that Pijnen should take the jersey after the first stage in Jerez de la Frontera. The surprising thing was that he kept hold of it for eight days. Lacking action to report, journalists produced travelogues, describing the glittering sea, the snow-capped Sierra Nevada, the orange blossom and the fighting bulls who lifted their noble heads to watch the cyclists pass.

1970

By the time the Vuelta abandoned the coast, the Belgians had picked up six victories and the classification was exceedingly tight. The Barcelona–Igualada stage into the interior must have brought back memories for Ocaña, for it was here that he made his heroic if unsuccessful bid for victory the previous year. Billed as the *etapa reina*, it didn't yield as much battle as expected; skirmishes were restricted to the last climb of Montserrat, the emblematic mountain of Catalunya, on whose slopes Pijnen was definitively dropped. Ocaña attacked three kilometres from the top and only Agustín Tamames responded: it was the first sign of what would be main duel of the race.

The two were caught by an advance guard of the peloton five kilometres from the finishing-line, which Tamames crossed first, but Ocaña was the new leader thanks to the time-bonus he'd picked up on Montserrat. An initial selection had been made but the top positions were still extremely close: Miguel María Lasa and Herman Van Springel were joint second at eight seconds and Tamames only one second further behind.

The peloton was now in deep Spain, far from the cosmopolitan atmosphere of the coast. They took two days to cross Aragón, stopping off at Zaragoza – where bikinis were still banned in the swimming pools – and Calatayud. The tail wind from Calatayud to Madrid was so strong, the cyclists barely had to pedal and arrived an hour ahead of schedule, forcing the organisers to choose girls from the spectators to present the bouquets, since the contracted hostesses hadn't arrived yet. The race was literally turning out to be a breeze. Apart from the wind, Spain's new network of high quality roads was easing the cyclists' way. While Ocaña's elegance and polished style was much admired, those expecting an epic gesture were disappointed, as he was quite content to live off his Montserrat gains.

With the classification so tight, the time-bonuses became crucial. The Werner team devised a strategy to get Tamames, their leader, into yellow on the Soria stage. Rather than wait for the finish, Tamames attacked on the Somosierra climb, picked up the prime and then let Werner control the race. Tamames declared he fully aimed to defend the yellow jersey until Bilbao, although for the moment his advantage was only one second. 'I can't deny that to win the Vuelta I need to get two minutes on Ocaña before the time-trial. Ocaña is much better than me against the clock,' he said, realistically surveying his chances.

The tail wind disappeared, along with the good road surfaces, as the peloton crossed the Meseta to Valladolid. Here the riders had to dig out woollen gloves and waterproofs, as they were battered by hailstones. Despite the wintry weather, the roadsides were packed with people who were off work to celebrate Ascension Day, and since Valladolid was close to Tamames' home town of Salamanca, the leader had a strong contingent of fans, friends and family to support him. The peloton continued northwards to Burgos, fighting the wind and cold, and keeping Isidro Salinas, the Vuelta doctor, busy treating bronchial illnesses. 'The continuous changes in climate that the cyclists have to endure are enough to kill a horse', he reflected.

The mountainous finale was a disappointment because the *puertos* were invariably climbed from the easy side and the freezing head wind discouraged attacks. On the Santander stage, a young Fuente crossed the Puerto of Alisas in second place. He was beginning to attract attention, wearing the 'Tiger' jersey for best young rider making his debut in a long stage race.

On the eve of the 29-kilometre time-trial in Bilbao, the climax of the race, Tamames had managed to distance himself from Ocaña by a grand total of nine seconds. After more than 3,000 kilometres, everything was to be resolved in the Vuelta's final hour. Van Springel was Ocaña's only serious rival, but the route was too technical for the Belgian, who needed long straights to pound along, not short ramps and nervous corners. He came in 1'–07" behind Ocaña, winning third place on the podium, while Tamames lost 1'–15", and stepped down to second in the overall classification.

After receiving his trophy, 24-year-old Luis Ocaña declared, 'Today I feel more Spanish than ever.' He was conscious of certain reservations towards him, although his technique was admired, his position on the bicycle held to be perfect, and his victory had been skillfully calculated, with no waste of energy. Resident in a more developed country, it was natural he should take advantage of the most up-to-date training methods, and *El Mundo Deportivo* called him 'a modern champion, from the laboratory'. This was the complaint against him – that he was a far cry from the old-school Spanish heroes, who rode from the heart. All the past winners of the Vuelta were gathered in Bilbao to celebrate a special silver anniversary dinner, and some of them, as veterans are wont to do, regretted how easy and conservative modern cycling had become. Clearly, no one realised what kind of new champion they had on their hands.

Ocaña's family had moved to France looking for a new life and better conditions for their sickly son. After leaving school, Luis worked as a carpenter's apprentice and raced in his spare time; later in life, he would confess that he far preferred carpentry to cycling. The director of Fagor, Pedro Machain, was very impressed when he saw Ocaña competing in an amateur race in Spain in 1966, and immediately offered him a job as a professional. Luis hesitated, unconvinced, but an incident at work made him rethink his future. When he witnessed his boss threatening and humiliating a Spanish workmate, his anger spilled over, out of control, and he hurled the first object that came to hand. His boss managed to swerve in time, while the axe stuck quivering in the back of the door. Jobless, only then did Ocaña accept one of several offers, first opting for Poulidor's team, Mercier, and then Fagor in 1968, before signing for Bic in 1970.

That Ocaña was a romantic, with a profound sense of his Spanish identity, is captured in his autobiography. At the beginning of his first professional year with Fagor, on his way back from the Tour of Andalucía, he'd stopped to visit his native village of Priego, by then seriously depopulated. It was at the time when his father was dying of cancer:

I rediscovered forgotten memories and the perfume of the olive trees of my childhood. But my heart was torn thinking that my father would never again come back to his village, or this abandoned house open to the wind. Those who hadn't emigrated formed a tanned legion grown old under the harness of poverty, but I received their show of friendship like a token of faith. I embraced those shy Castilians who recognised in me somebody of their race and their blood.

So much for the clinical, calculating 'Frenchman' the journalists mistrusted.

Throughout the 1970 race the long-standing controversy about the Vuelta's unchallenging *parcours* had gathered new momentum. Taking the peloton round the new motorways ensured a high average speed, but also tedium. The foreign journalists could report back home that Spanish roads had now reached European standards, but 'this work of promotion corresponds to the Ministry of Public Works, not the Vuelta', wrote *Dicen*, sardonically. 'Mountains are what the Spanish rider needs', argued *El Mundo Deportivo*. The race organisers would eventually bow to this growing pressure with the help of the skiing industry. In the meantime, the race's saving grace had been Ocaña's victory. He went back to Mont de Marsan to prepare for the Tour and to put the finishing touches on his new house. He had a great future ahead – but for an impoverished immigrant, he'd come a long way already.

At the end of the year, the attention of the world was turned on Spain when the regime organised the show trial of Burgos, putting 16 Eta activists in the dock for the murder of secret police chief, Meliton Manzanas. The lawyers were the stars of the trial, using it to draw attention to the Basque separatist cause. The miltary court doled out a total of nine death penalties and 500 years of prison, while a national state of emergency was declared, as demonstrators clashed with police. When Franco announced in his end of year speech that he had lifted the sentences of execution, it was not from a sense of mercy. By kidnapping the German consul, Eugen Beihl, Eta had rudely twisted the arm of the regime: the Spanish economy was too dependent on Germany for their demands to be ignored.

The Vuelta of 1971 began in Spain's south-east corner in Almería and followed the Mediterranean coast to Barcelona. Then it swung to the west, skirting the Pyrenees *en route* to the Basque Country. The final stretch would be the journey to Madrid, via Segovia and Ávila. As in the previous year's race, there was a lack of serious mountains, but as far as Ocaña was concerned, there was another glaring omission – a decent time-trial. 'When Anquetil raced the Vuelta they gave him time-trials of 70 or 80 kilometres. Now they've forgotten. What a shame!' He took it as a personal affront.

1971

At least the line-up had improved. Foreign names on people's lips were Poulidor, apparently unscathed by the passing years and riding in Fagor–Mercier, and young Joop Zoetemelk of the Belgian team Mars–Flandria, second in the 1970 Tour but with a reputation as a *chuparruedas* or 'wheel sucker' – someone who takes advantage of the work of others. The strongest foreign squad was Peugeot, although without a particular contender for the overall, and on the home front Kas and Werner were the most solid. Ocaña, who'd just won the Tour of the Basque Country, upset everyone by rebelliously declaring that he was only riding the Vuelta to train for his real obsession, the Tour. He was yet to leave his mark on the French race 'because bad luck and misfortune have preyed on me'. Already he was chafing under a sense that destiny was weighted against him.

To celebrate Almería's film boom, the first stage would begin in the desert of Tabernas, where a western town had been constructed for shooting 'spaghetti westerns'. When *Dicen*'s reporter went to Ocaña's hotel to interview him, he passed Ursula Andres in the corridor and then had trouble concentrating on his work. There was an atmosphere of cowboys, with horses and gunslingers, and cyclists posing for photos on horseback.

In time-honoured tradition, the coastal stages were disputed among the fast men. There were some outstanding sprinters in the peloton, such as Cyrille Guimard in Poulidor's team and Walter Godefroot in Peugeot, who were not ruled out for the overall because of the rate at which they amassed time-bonuses. One of the few Spanish cyclists tempted by a sprint was López Rodríguez of Werner. He tried his luck in the second stage ending in Calpe, only to be grabbed by the Dutch rider Gert Haring as they hurtled along the last few metres. 'I'm married; I've got two children', said a shaken López Rodríguez. 'And I don't want to leave behind a widow and two orphans. If this is the way people are going to ride, I'll abandon the Vuelta, and cycling, too. It's inadmissible what the foreigners do. They're mad.' Afterwards, Haring found himself surrounded by the Spaniard's irate team-mates, who were prodding the Dutchman in the ribs with a wheel.

The Calpe stage was also the scene of a brief strike organised by the cyclists to protest against the fees Spanish television wanted to charge for showing the publicity on their jerseys. In the daily resumé, the TV cameras would focus primarily on the landscape, showing only fleeting images of the riders or just their legs pumping up and down. More than a decade would have to pass before the television company realised the potential of cycling to attract viewers.

The race took some unpredictable turns: first of all Walter Godefroot won the *etapa reina* from Barcelona to Manresa in a mass sprint – so much for the mountainous stage that was supposed to make the first selection. Then he repeated his victory in Jaca, an alluring gateway to the Pyrenees that the organisers had seen fit to ignore. A third sprint finish was expected in Pamplona, yet this apparently innocuous day dramatically overturned the general classification. After 60 kilometres, the peloton fractured on a small climb. Agustín Tamames explained that he'd jumped ahead before the Puerto de Aibar to stop Zoetemelk getting the mountain points in defence of his own Werner team-mate Luis Balagué, who was also disputing this prize. 'And without really knowing how, we found ourselves with the peloton cut in half.' When the 20-strong leading group realised that Ocaña was missing, together with Pijnen, Godefroot and Guimard, they began to bowl along. Behind, Ocaña had little assistance and the gap widened.

As the breakaway approached Pamplona, the tension grew because three men, Lasa, Tamames and Zoetemelk, all had a chance of donning the yellow jersey: it was a 'simple' matter of winning the stage. Tamames, permanently wearing a cap since a crash in the Tour of the Basque Country had left him with 16 stitches in the head, proved to be the strongest. Ocaña's group came in at 5'–08".

It seemed the big favourite had been eliminated. Downcast, for he'd been serious about the race after all, Ocaña refused to make any excuses. 'I've lost the Vuelta because I haven't been intelligent enough to be in the right place at the right time.' As for his team, 'they want to help me but can't … they're a complete disaster.' But he swore revenge on those who'd worked so hard to eliminate him that day. 'I'm ready to make them sweat blood.'

He waited two days to keep his word. Between Bilbao and Vitoria there were two demanding climbs: the Orduña, and the Herrera. It was a propitious stage for Ocaña, and the sunny weather augured well for a cyclist who functioned at his best in the heat. He attacked at the foot of the Orduña, but with no collaboration forthcoming from those who had stuck to his wheel, he let himself be caught by the peloton on the descent. Another group broke free, but Ocaña bided his time until the Herrera came in sight. When he struck again, Ferdinand Bracke of Peugeot and Wim Schepers of the Dutch team Goudsmit–Hoff quickly latched on, but Luis paid no attention to them, and soon caught the breakaway, whereupon he continued setting the pace. 'Here comes Ocaña!' was the cry all the way up the Herrera, which he crested alone, the others left 50 seconds behind, while the peloton was at four minutes.

Thirty kilometres from the finish, Ocaña began to weaken and repeatedly looked round, expecting to see the pursuers closing in. The deserted road must have been a heartening sight, for he redoubled his effort and rode the time-trial the organisers had denied him. Incredibly, he reached Vitoria 2'–01" ahead of the Bracke group and 7'–25" up on the peloton. There was jubilation: Ocaña had shown everyone that he was without doubt a great champion. It was a flash of the form he would display in the Tour that summer. Now it was the turn of others to look crushed: the hopes of Tamames, Lasa and Zoetemelk had been destroyed; their Pamplona offensive had been avenged, and the monotony of the Vuelta shattered.

The new leader was the Belgian, Ferdinand Bracke, whose quick thinking in following Ocaña's wheel had paid off. Although the Spaniard's performance inspired everyone to believe he could still win the yellow jersey, for the moment he was third at 2'–27". He warned the optimists that he'd seen Bracke surprisingly strong on the Herrera, but his radiant face betrayed his own hopes. Highly emotive moments always made him reassert his identity: 'What bothers me most of all is when people call me "the Spaniard of Mont de Marsan". If that's where I live, it's because my parents went there in search of better prospects. I'm Spanish.'

The stage to Burgos, two days later, was considered Ocaña's best chance to oust Bracke, with four mountains to climb. In the cold and rain it seemed at first that nothing would ever happen; the peloton remained huddled together as if to keep warm. Then on the mist-shrouded Tornos, Lasa and Manuel Galera jumped clear, soon to be joined by Wilfried David of Peugeot and Désiré Letort of Bic who sat in as observers while the Spaniards did the work. With 75 kilometres to go, they'd built up an eight-minute advantage, turning Lasa of the modest Orbea team into the virtual leader.

Closely marked throughout the day, Ocaña finally managed to break away on the last climb, Las Mazorras, with Zoetemelk for company. Working together, the two made inroads on the gap to Lasa's group and it was Ocaña's turn to be the leader on the road, albeit briefly. His team-mate, Letort, was instructed to drop back and help. Up ahead, Lasa was running out of fuel after his near-solo effort, and Bracke's Peugeot team-mate, David, pounced without mercy, 10 kilometres from the finishing-line, disappearing up the road towards stage victory. It was a testing moment for Lasa's morale, as he was suddenly left alone with only his fatigue for company. 'I thought I wouldn't even make it to the finish,' he recalled afterwards.

Further back, Yellow Jersey Bracke was suffering badly on Las Mazorras. It was Godefroot who took charge and guided him home, helped by the well-surfaced, gently undulating road into Burgos. Afterwards, Bracke freely admitted that Godefroot had saved his skin.

As far as the general classification was concerned, it couldn't have been more disappointing for the Spaniards. Despite their huge efforts, Ocaña and Lasa moved down to fourth and fifth. Bracke remained on top, with Wim Schepers of the Dutch team Goudsmit–Hoff second, while David had jumped to third place. Ocaña looked drained and exhausted. 'I've worn myself out more than in the Vitoria stage. And all for nothing.' Feeling the defeat intensely, he cried with rage. 'Why does it have to end like this?' His conviction that the Vuelta had been within reach was shattered.

After the stage, the journalists in the Press room were rudely interrupted by a fuming Gaston Plaud, director of Peugeot. He burst in, shouting, 'You Spanish are corrupt and worthless! I'm never coming back to Spain, and I dare you to write this down.' It turned out that the judges had penalised Bracke 30 seconds for illegally accepting a bidon from Plaud, thereby losing the yellow jersey to Schepers. Enraged by what he saw as an abusive sanction, Plaud threatened to pull his team out. Not for the first time, the organisers backed down, and the *comisario* was forced to say he had accidentally jotted down the wrong number, even though Bracke was the most unmistakable member of the peloton in his luminous yellow jersey.

There was bad feeling after this incident. Plaud's bullying reinforced the conviction that the organisers did not have the *cojones* to stand up to the foreigners. Earlier in the race, the Werner team had complained about the way Zoetemelk was pushed uphill by his team-mates. When photographic evidence appeared, the judges fined the Dutchman a paltry 100 pesetas. Werner's director snorted with disbelief, declaring he would hire a taxi to pull their mountain prize candidate, Luis Balagué, up the remaining slopes.

The last chance for Ocaña was the Segovia to Ávila stage. On the Alto de Los Leones, Bracke was losing 1'-25" but only Tamames and Ocaña were working in the leading group, where Bracke's team-mate, David, kept a vigilant eye on any movement. After the regrouping, Zoetemelk escaped alone to win the stage. He also left the Vuelta with the Mountains prize, the first foreign rider to win it since 1956, while the points jersey went to Guimard.

The Spaniards turned a disappointed eye on Ferdinand Bracke; he was not their idea of a worthy winner. He was quite surprised, himself. Tall, bony and grey-haired, he was at the end of a career whose highlights had been beating the hour record in 1967, when he'd crossed the 48kph threshold, and a third place in the Tour the following year. A distinguished *pistard*, he'd also been World Pursuit Champion in 1964 and '69. In 1970 bad health almost forced him to retire, his lungs damaged from the days he worked as a miner. The first Belgian to win the Vuelta since Frans De Mulder, 11 years earlier, Bracke's victory was based on team work. Peugeot had given him solid support and even if the bidon sanction had been confirmed, the race would have remained in Peugeot's hands, because Schepers was finally demoted from second to 15th after failing a dope test, which left David second and Ocaña third. Poulidor, who'd kept a low profile throughout the race, summed it up thus: 'Ocaña was the strength, but Bracke the intelligence.'

* * * * *

In 1972, Ocaña was conspicuous by his absence. Apart from requesting a hefty fee, he'd demanded that the organisers include a 40-kilometre time-trial. Bergareche explained: 'We tried to set up a Merckx–Ocaña duel, but it wasn't possible for two reasons. The Conquense [someone hailing from Cuenca] made the demands of a super-diva, and the Belgian's sponsors wouldn't let him come.' Business came first, and as Molteni's meat products were not sold in Spain, they wanted Merckx to concentrate on their main markets, Italy and France.

1972

If the Vuelta lacked an outstanding figure, there was no doubt about the strongest team. Kas were entering their golden age: they had dominated the early Spanish season, with Miguel María Lasa taking the Catalan Week and José González Linares the Tour of the Basque Country. True to their style, no one was cast in the role of leader, but the rider most talked about in terms of victory was Lasa. A talented all-rounder, fast and intelligent, he was also favoured by the sponsors of his team, who wanted a Basque winner. His rivals among the foreigners were the tough Portuguese rider Joaquim Agostinho, a veteran of the Angola war who'd made a great impression in the 1971 Tour, and Willy Planckaert, riding for Goldor under the management of Rik Van Looy, who was making a debut as director.

In one respect, the 1972 race was a turning point. The developing skiing industry had opened up tempting possibilities for Spanish cycling: for the first time, the Vuelta had a mountain-top stage-finish, in the Pyrenean resort of Formigal. Bahamontes and Julio Jiménez could only look at the route book in envy. And the new profile didn't stop there, for the following stage finished on the classic Arrate climb in the Basque Country. Bergareche said proudly: 'It's the toughest Vuelta we could have organised. Thirty *puertos* and some of them of the highest category. The final stretch will be terrible.'

In the first week, there was panic on the stage to Tarragona when Agostinho, trying to avoid overhanging branches, crashed into a milestone, and his heart momentarily stopped. Mouth to mouth respiration revived him, but he was unconscious for several hours. The peloton watched in troubled silence as the ambulance bore him away. Fortunately, fears of a skull fracture were proven wrong, but it was a blow for the Vuelta to lose one of its main contenders.

By the time the peloton turned its back on the sea in Barcelona, Kas had secured the top four placings overall, with Txomin Perurena in yellow. The days went by monotonously, as if the riders were lying low in anticipation of the Pyrenees. The tenth stage, ending in the lakeside town of Banyoles in the north of Catalunya, had all the ideal elements for an ambush, with hills, pouring rain and slippery roads, but the bunch arrived intact, and Perurena reinforced his lead by winning the mass sprint.

The following day, on the eve of the mountains, there was a reminder of how cycling had changed. No sooner had the cyclists set off from Manresa than Luis Balagué, the Asturian rider of Werner, decided to make a solo escape. No one rated his chances, but through dogged persistence he managed to cross the line in Zaragoza, 259 kilometres later, with ample time to dry his sweat before the peloton rolled in, ten minutes behind. 'I noticed that a lot of people had aching legs from the rainy Banyoles stage,' he explained, and dedicated the victory to his mother. After so many colourless stages, the organisers were enraptured and awarded him a special 15,000 peseta prize. He'd been only one kilometre short of the Vuelta record for lone escapes, established by Antonio Suárez in 1960. But the days when the leaders would take off alone at the beginning of a stage were gone for good: now only the lowly placed would consider such a risky endeavour.

On stage 12, another Asturian had the chance to be a hero. The peloton was heading across the plains of Zaragoza towards the Pyrenees, visible on the distant horizon, when Werner's José Grande jumped clear. Kas director, Barrutia, moved one of the many pawns he had at his disposal. He chose Fuente, 2'–21" down in the overall, and not figuring in anyone's predictions. Fuente dutifully sat in on Grande's wheel, but even without any contribution from him the pair soon established a sizeable gap. When they were three minutes clear, Fuente decided to collaborate and their advantage increased rapidly. Behind, the peloton was drifting without anyone to seize the helm, so used the riders were to being pulled by Kas. Taken aback by the situation, Barrutia was uncertain about what strategy to pursue, but Perurena convinced him to let Fuente go.

At the foot of Monrepós, the pair were 4'–45" clear, but on these first serious slopes of the day, Grandé's legs were suffering, which inspired Fuente to ride off alone. He reached the summit with 1'–30" on his escape partner, and descended at full tilt to increase his lead further, while the peloton continued to coast along, as if it were in an entirely different race.

By Sabiñanigo, Tarangu had a leeway of seven minutes. After so many kilometres alone, he would surely start flagging on the Formigal. But, surrounded by snow-capped peaks, he maintained his implacable rhythm to the end. It was a sensational victory, nearly nine minutes ahead of the peloton!

Overnight, Fuente was famous. Until now, no one had paid him much attention: his two stage victories in the 1971 Tour de France in Super-Bagnères and Luchon had been completely eclipsed by Ocaña's terrible crash on the Col de Menté, which had cost him the race. And Fuente's own ambitions had been humble: 'I began the Vuelta with the mission of helping Lasa to win and trying to win the Mountains prize if the occasion presented itself.' Struggling to choose a definitive leader, Barrutia had been undecided between the two Basques, Perurena and Lasa, but now Tarangu had solved his problem. There was only one lingering doubt about the Asturian's triumph: how much was it due to the passivity of the peloton? There was great interest to see how he would defend himself over the demanding days to come.

As the race approached the Basque Country, it was briefly caught up in the unrest. A small explosive went off on the Lizárraga climb in the north of Navarra, where the sense of Basque identity is strong, but the organisers had time to cover up the wide breach in the road before the cyclists passed. The stage would end in the outskirts of Eibar, home of Orbea and BH bicycles, on a hard eight-kilometre climb to the medieval sanctuary of Arrate. It was the scene of an annual pilgrimage as well as a major annual cycle race, which had been won by Bahamontes five years running between 1958 and 1962, and by Ocaña in 1971.

When the peloton reached Eibar, the attacks began and Fuente ably defended himself on all fronts. He crossed the line one second behind Tamames, and threw his bike down in a rage: 'I could've done what I did in the last Tour, and won two mountain stages together. I think Tamames blocked me.' Calming him down, Perurena pointed out that the flat final kilometre had favoured his opponent much more. Tamames, now classified third, was full of admiration for Fuente: 'He's very strong. I tried to shake him off three times, and he responded amazingly easily.' Another Tarangu admirer was Julio Jiménez: 'I like him because he's a rebel and doesn't bow down before anyone.' He made a wistful comment about the route: 'When I raced the Vuelta, it wasn't decided in the mountains.'

Fuente had confirmed his strength, but his most spectacular move was yet to come. On the penultimate stage finishing in Vitoria, Lasa's second place came under pressure from Bic's Désiré Letort. The Frenchman had attacked on the slopes of the Puerto de Orduña, and Kas had been unable to control him. Finally, Fuente decided to act alone: as soon as he observed that Tamames was in no condition to follow, the Asturian made a sharp acceleration. Before long, he was passing remnants of Letort's group, and then the Frenchman himself, two kilometres from the top. Fuente crested the Orduña alone, leaving behind a peloton in complete disarray. It was an impressive demonstration of his explosive climbing powers, which would be thrilling the Italians later that month.

Instead of racing on to take the stage – Kas' headquarters were in Vitoria after all – Fuente waited to help his team-mates, and consequently, it was Tamames who was first over the line. Kas could not complain: they'd held the yellow jersey in every stage but one, and in Fuente they'd found an indisputable champion, someone who could bring stability to a team whose great spirit of camaraderie was sometimes strained by too many riders vying for top place. On receiving his trophy, Fuente showed his gratitude for being given a chance: 'I dedicate the victory to Barrutia. He trusted in me and took a big risk.'

When Fuente first rented a bicycle to take part in races, he was looking for a way out of poverty. In his autobiography, he wrote, 'I never had a real childhood, nor a real youth.' He remembers catching scarlet fever, which left him blind for 11 days, and the family's damp old house, where they constantly had to paper over the leaking ceilings. When he left school at fourteen to start a metalworker apprenticeship, his future seemed mapped out: minimal wages and long hours for the rest of his life. He'd seen his parents wearing themselves out, labouring from dawn to dusk, and was desperate to escape the poverty trap. As he dedicated more and more time to racing, his anxious parents fretted that he would lose his job while he struggled to succeed in a cycling world where connections were often worth more than talent.

During his professional years, Fuente was sometimes accused of lacking technique or having an ungainly style. A self-taught cyclist, he bemoaned that no one had given him any advice in his formative years, but he was proud that he'd achieved everything on his own. 'From the start I was a fighter.' He never tired of trying to escape, and throughout his career that would be his speciality – reckless attacks that could be suicidal, or spectacularly effective. After his debut in the 1970 Vuelta, the only year the organisers introduced the 'Tiger' jersey for neo-professionals, which he wore from start to finish, Langarica signed him for Kas. When he won two stages and the mountains in the 1971 Tour de France, they tripled his salary and he could finally afford to marry his girlfriend. Four days after surprising everyone by winning the 1972 Vuelta, he was riding the Giro as team leader. In Italy, for a while he had Merckx against the ropes after gaining 15 minutes on him, and with a more calculating strategy, he would surely have won the race instead of finishing second. It was not easy being Fuente's director. Restraining him was impossible, when his natural instinct was always to attack, even when tactically it made no sense. His stubborn hotheadedness had taken him far; it was too late to change now.

* * * * *

At last they'd hooked him. After years of trying, the organisers had persuaded Eddy Merckx to fill that irksome gap in his palmarés. With the biggest star of world cycling, the 1973 Vuelta was guaranteed to be a success. It had never attracted so much publicity, or drawn such large crowds. People were eager to see a clash of the titans, Merckx and Ocaña, on Spanish soil.

The *parcours* was a throwback to the '60s Vueltas, designed to **1973** appeal to Merckx by avoiding the mountains and offering plenty of flat stages. The generous sprinkling of bonus sprints certainly didn't favour the Spaniards, either. Kas had wisely reserved Fuente for the Giro and Tour, and was fielding a mainly young, inexperienced team. Worryingly for Ocaña's chances, Bic also failed to present a strong squad. For there was no question about it, Merckx had come to win. As Lucien Acou, his father-in-law, said: 'For Eddy, all competitions have the same importance.'

The prologue took place in Calpe, a thriving resort on the Costa Blanca, in brilliant sunshine and an atmosphere of high expectation. There was an avalanche of journalists, particularly from Belgium. Merckx wanted to begin the Vuelta in yellow, partly to assuage his insatiable hunger for victories and also to undermine his rivals psychologically. He finished the six-kilometre circuit with the best time, Joaquin Agostinho providing the surprise of the day by coming second.

There were echoes of Anquetil in the way Merckx's team were able to control the peloton with a fast tempo that dissuaded would-be attackers. The German-based team, Rokado, were given free rein in the sprint finishes, their Dutch rider Gerben Karstens taking the yellow jersey from Merckx on the third stage in Albacete. The Spaniards had to sit back and observe as the foreigners mopped up all the prize money.

This frustrating impasse was broken when Kas' captain José Pesarradona escaped on stage 4 on the hilly road to Cuenca, accompanied by Merckx's *gregario* Jos Deschoenmaecker. Merckx later claimed the Vuelta radio gave inaccurate information about Pesarrodona's advantage. Fifteen kilometres from Cuenca, Molteni's director suddenly discovered the gap was not of one minute but four, and after chasing hard, Molteni only managed to reduce the difference by half. Since Deschoenmaecker had been sitting in on guard duty, he easily won the stage, but Pesarrodona had the immense satisfaction of becoming the new race leader. Merckx was annoyed at how the race had slipped out of his control. On the steep rise to the finishing-line in Cuenca's old quarter, he effortlessly dropped the rest of the field. Pocketing the bonus for third place, his campaign to recover the yellow jersey had already begun. If the terrain were not propitious for outright battle, he would engage in a war of attrition.

Often criticised for lacking a fighting spirit, and too easily conforming to his role as a *gregario*, Pesarrodona had been given the chance to show his worth, while the other Kas big-hitters were engaged elsewhere. Always a realist, he aimed to keep the yellow jersey until Manresa, his home region in the heart of Catalunya.

Molteni resumed their draconian control of the peloton and Merckx, whose calm had been ruffled, launched an implacable campaign to eradicate the 1'–25" gap between himself and Pesarrodona. No intermediate sprint was beneath him unless he was saving himself for the finish. On the eighth stage to the beach resort of Calafell, his day's booty was suspiciously low: only two seconds picked up on the Alto de Santa Cristina. Suspicions were fulfilled when he attacked as soon as the peloton entered the final sprint zone. A close duel evolved with compatriot Eddy Peelman, which seemed to be going in Merckx's favour when his opponent was propelled over the line by a timely hand-sling from a team-mate. A normal enough occurrence, but no one could tread on Merckx's toes like that. Peelman received his flowers on the podium, only to be informed that the judges had heeded the complaint lodged by Molteni, and not content with stripping him of the stage, they also sanctioned him with 30 seconds.

Merckx won again in Ampuriabrava, the last seaside stage of the race. The following day would be more challenging, with three mountains to cross before arriving in Manresa, where Pesarrodona's countrymen awaited him. The Catalan was hanging on to yellow by six seconds, while Ocaña was already over a minute behind the Belgian, without having engaged in any direct battle. Merckx's strategy was proving very effective.

These numerous bonus sprints were the main controversy of the '73 Vuelta. Some argued that they gave far too much advantage to the sprinters, although it was recognised that without them the race would have been even more lack-lustre. At least it came alive at certain moments. Merckx refused to answer any more questions about the matter: 'It annoys me to talk about *bonificaciones*. They are available for everyone and it wasn't me who made the rules.' He also challenged the idea that they were in some way his gift from the organisers: 'It's always dangerous to dispute a sprint,' he insisted. Merckx's easy dominance was not providing exciting racing, but it was fascinating to watch his ruthless progress.

At last a selection was made, thanks to the 30-kilometre climb of Coll Formic, which gives a view of the Mediterranean on one side and the Pyrenees on the other. The eight-man break that was first over the top included all the favourites – Merckx, Ocaña, Pesarrodona and Bernard Thévenet. The descent of Coll Formic was reckless, almost suicidal, and from then on there was a tense vigilance all the way to Manresa, where they arrived six minutes clear. Ocaña and Pesarrodona were helpless to stop Merckx picking up the bonus seconds on the final climb and the intermediate sprint. Despite working hard all day, and having already secured the yellow jersey, Merckx was aiming for another stage-win, but this time without success: 'I started the sprint very early, convinced that no one would catch me. I was very surprised to see Thévenet shoot out from the left like an arrow.' The *grimpeur* had shown his strength earlier, first to crest Coll Formic.

The Press had taken to keeping an alternative general classification, where no time-bonus was counted, and according to this, Pesarradona was still leader. Asked if he were demoralised at his loss of the yellow jersey in front of a home crowd, the Catalan replied: 'No. Because I haven't *lost* the yellow jersey. The regulations have taken it away from me. I know that we all accepted them from the start but that doesn't mean they are fair. This stage has shown that in the mountains, Merckx lacks a team and has to do everything himself. I'm sure that with some real mountain stages and without the time-bonuses, the Vuelta right now would not be resolved.'

Ocaña was even more scathing. The parallel general classification had him as 15 seconds behind Merckx in third place instead of fourth at 1'–46". 'The point of this Vuelta is to win bonus sprints – the more, the better. It's clear that the organisers designed the route for Merckx to win. There are hardly any mountains and there are bonus sprints even in the hotel doorways.'

To reach the north, the peloton had to cross the plains around Zaragoza, fighting a losing battle with the *Cierzo*, the fierce north-westerly wind that sweeps the area. Not for the first time, the cyclists arrived in Zaragoza way behind schedule, Karsten winning the sprint. Heeding the weather forecast, the organisers shortened the following stage by 35 kilometres, moving the start to the tiny village of Mallén, where the inhabitants were amazed to see stars like Merckx and Ocaña in their sleepy streets.

Escapes seemed out of the question, but 20 kilometres from Irache, Txomin Perurena of Kas took advantage of a lull in the wind to break free and he maintained his 20-second gap to the end. It was his way of venting frustration after the race judges had sanctioned him with ten minutes for failing a doping test. His crime? Taking cough syrup prescribed by the race doctor, who had worked in the Vuelta since 1955 and found the new regulations preposterous.

If there had been any doubt about the final outcome, it disappeared in Torrelavega, when Merckx assured his victory by winning the 17.5-kilometre time-trial. His team-mate, Roger Swerts, was second at 32 seconds, Ocaña third at a disappointing 36 seconds and Pesarrodona, bravely defending his second place overall, was fourth at a commendable 53 seconds.

There was only one mountainous obstacle where Ocaña could make a challenge: the Puerto de Orduña. He attacked at its foot, and only Merckx and Thévenet could keep up, both eventually ceding ground. As the spectators chanted his name, Ocaña reached the top, resplendent in the national champion's red and gold jersey, which he wore in defiance of all those who persisted in calling him *El Francés* – 'the Frenchman'. But his two rivals were barely half a minute behind and, working together, they hunted him down 27 kilometres from the finish in Miranda del Ebro, where Merckx again came out triumphant.

Ocaña had to be content with second place on the final podium, while Thévenet took third. Nearly two years previously, in the 1971 Tour, Ocaña had impressed the world by defeating Merckx in the Alps. It had been exciting beyond words to see the invincible Belgian brought to his knees, at least for those few days before the Spaniard was forced to retire after crashing heavily in a torrential storm on the Col de Mente. But in Spain, Ocaña could do nothing. The terrain had tied him down.

The 'Cannibal' could go home satiated, having gorged himself at will. Apart from the race, he'd won the points jersey and come second in the mountains, picked up six stage-wins, including the prologue and two short time-trial sectors. He admitted the victory had been served to him on a plate: 'If they don't put obstacles my

136

way, I'm not going to create them.' Ocaña's conclusion was terse: 'Didn't they bring me here to play the role of Merckx's rival and to finish second? Well, I did so.' And what about the verdict of the unofficial bonus-free general classification? Who was the 'real' winner? Inexorably and inevitably, Eddy Merckx.

At the end of the year in Madrid, on 20th December, there was an almighty explosion in the centre of the capital. A car was blasted high in the air and seemed to disappear. It was discovered later in an interior patio, having flown clear over the nearby buildings.

The assassination of the recently appointed Prime Minister, the Admiral Carrero Blanco, was Eta's most spectacular coup and a heavy blow for Franco, who'd lost a guarantee of the regime's future after his own death. Carrero Blanco had believed a strong, authoritarian government was necessary for the country's welfare. Under a pseudonym, he'd written that establishing a democracy in Spain was as risky as giving a job to a reformed alcoholic. When the satirical magazine *La Cordoniz* noted that he had broken the high jump record, their office was closed down, and their writers imprisoned.

Spain's political future might have been thrown into uncertainty, **1974** but 1974 was a vintage year for the Vuelta. It was one of the most exciting and hard fought, and provided moments that José Manuel Fuente would carry with him to the end of his days, helping to assuage the bitterness of his eventual untimely retirement. He'd been planning his season around the Giro and Tour but, after learning that the Vuelta would pass through Asturias, asked to be included in the team. Neither he nor Ocaña were in top form, both with minds set on the other major stage races; Ocaña was aiming to do all three, and the Vuelta was supposed to be a gentle build-up. Yet when the moment of truth arrived, neither could hold anything back. The rest of the season seemed to fade away, as they gave everything to the fight in hand.

The tension between them was at its height. To understand the situation, it's necessary to go back to the previous summer, when the Spanish teams had agreed to work together in the Tour de France to ensure a maximum share of the booty. The idea was that Ocaña would take first place, with second overall and the Mountains prize for Fuente. But Tarangu was unable to keep to the arrangement: it stuck in his gullet. However slim his chances, he wouldn't be at peace with himself unless he had a stab at overall victory and that

Tour will always be remembered for the Spaniards' hand-to-hand on the Galiber, where Ocaña taught the Asturian a lesson. Fuente's rebellion brought a lot of grief for Kas. A vengeful Ocaña used every tactic and alliance at his disposal to block them, and they had to sweat to scrape together two stage victories, while Fuente lost the Mountain prize to Pedro Torres. The Casera rider had pleaded to have the polka-dot jersey on a temporary basis, but when the fratricidal hostilities broke out, Tarangu found himself thwarted at every opportunity to amass points, as Ocaña sought to humiliate him. Finally, Fuente was third on the podium, while Ocaña's victory was overwhelming, nearly 15 minutes ahead of second-placed Bernard Thévenet.

The conflict between the two Spaniards had smouldered through the winter and was waiting to reignite, as they lined up – each with one Vuelta in his palmarés. Meanwhile, the rider most tipped to win was Miguel María Lasa, fresh from victory in the Tour of the Basque Country and visibly more in form than any of his Kas team-mates. His morale was high, knowing he was also the favourite of Kas' sponsors. Sharing captain's duties with Ocaña in Bic was Joaquim Agostinho, whose thoughts were on events back home, as Portugal underwent the peaceful 'Carnation Revolution' on 25th April. The world was rid of a dictator, to the disquiet of hardline Francoists across the border. Completing the presence of the entire 1973 Tour podium in the Vuelta was Bernard Thévenet, riding in Peugeot colours.

In the first week there was an extensive tour of Andalucía's most important cities, after which the peloton would make a bee-line for the north, where two mountain top finishes awaited them in Asturias and the Basque Country and a time-trial in San Sebastián on the last day. After the monotony of the previous year, the organisers had devised a challenging route.

The prologue in Almería was won by Roger Swerts, previously Merckx's top lieutenant, who'd finally tired of serving his lord and master. On the second stage, the peloton began the day at sea-level and finished in Granada at 900 metres. The sharp rise to the Alhambra provided an exciting finish. An edgy Perurena attacked first, and succeeded in stretching out the peloton, but he'd mistimed his move. Next to jump was Thévenet, but he was unable to shake off sprinter Eric Leman, who won the stage after a strenuous effort in the final metres. Thévenet's consolation prize was the yellow jersey, which he kept for two days until Perurena claimed it by winning enough bonus sprints. Throughout their sojourn through Andalucía, the peloton was accompanied by unseasonable cold and rain, but the inclement weather failed to hamper Sevilla's April Fair. It was in full swing when the peloton arrived, and loud enough to disturb the cyclists' sleep.

The word *Dantesco* is well-loved by cycling commentators in Spain and it was used liberally during this Vuelta, one of the harshest in terms of weather. As the peloton turned northwards, the 211 kilometres to Ciudad Real became a six-and-a-half-hour endurance test in freezing rain, fog and strong wind. The appalling road surface added to the suffering, the team-cars running out of spare tyres for their riders. Just as it seemed the peloton would arrive bunched together, Belgian Julien Stevens attacked when the terrain levelled out, and provoked a three-way split. Stranded in the last group, Thévenet would lose a precious 1'–39". Sodden and caked in mud, his national champion's jersey unrecognisable, the Frenchman ruefully admitted his mistake in not being more attentive, but gamely stated: 'I still think I can win the race, but now it's going to cost me much more.' The history of the Vuelta is littered with race favourites who have fallen foul of the winds of Castilla.

The rain held back on stage 7, with a finish in Toledo on top of the Alcázar hill. This time Perurena didn't make the mistake he'd made in Granada; positioning himself at the front of the strung-out peloton he won with authority. Kas confirmed their strength by winning the team time-trial in Madrid, held in the Jarama motor racing track. For Casera – the team managed by Bahamontes – this day was a disaster. They suffered a spectacular fall, and among the scattered bodies and bicycles, two of their strongest riders, Pedro Torres and Andrés Oliva, lay unconscious, their seasons ruined. José Luis Abilleira, Casera's contender for the mountains, overcame his amnesia and shocked everybody by turning up at the start the next day, bandaged like a mummy. The race doctor refused to authorise his participation, and made him sign a document that he was continuing at his own risk.

On the first mountainous day in the Sierra de Madrid Fuente launched an audacious attack on the Alto de Los Leones. Only Ocaña responded but he couldn't match Tarangu's pace, trusting instead to the most likely outcome – that he would be caught on the downhill run to the finish in San Raphael. Yet Fuente managed to hang on to his lead, arriving 31 seconds ahead of a quintet that included Ocaña, Thévenet and Lasa. He was now only five seconds behind Perurena overall, while Lasa was in third place. Ocaña was fourth, a minute behind Perurena, with his options intact, but the panorama looking complicated with three Kas riders lodged in front of him.

Driving Fuente was an overwhelming desire to arrive in Asturias in yellow. He had one more day to achieve this: the stage to Ávila, which was proceeded by an extremely short uphill time-trial, only five kilometres, but with a brutal gradient. His wish was fulfilled when he registered the second best time after Ocaña's *gregario* Raymond Delisle, and became the new race leader. The rest of the day was uncommonly hard, more like a Belgian Classic than a stage of the Vuelta in May. When they set off from San Raphael after this short 'warm-up', it was snowing. By Segovia it had turned to sleet, and in Ávila it was raining torrentially. Fuente would remember this day in his autobiography, when he paid tribute to his *gregario*, Juan-Manuel Santisteban, who died in 1976 after crashing in the Giro.

It must have been two or three degrees below zero, but he was wearing only a short-sleeved *maillot*, as if it were 30 degrees. To defend ourselves from the strong wind, we formed an echelon. I was sheltering behind his large back. The pace was very fast, and I remember that in the middle of the storm, Santi turned round and said, 'Taranguin, I'd tuck you in my pocket if I could.'

He was a large, reassuring presence for a slightly built climber, always ready with a joke, and never begrudging in his services.

After a permitted escape, Martín Martínez won the stage, and the cyclists repaired to the hotels to thaw out, more than 50 of the 75 survivors suffering from bronchitis. Doctor Isidro Salinas threw up his arms in despair, unable to administer treatment because of the newly introduced doping controls. The harsh conditions didn't favour Ocaña, who flourished in the heat and sun: 'All this cold and rain is killing me,' he complained. He was 1'–39" down on Fuente as the Vuelta returned to mountainous terrain.

The peloton set off from León on what was to be a brilliant stage. Ahead loomed the Puerto de Pajares, beyond which lay Asturias.

Early on, a breakaway of eight men formed, building up a lead of four and a half minutes. Half of this group was made up of Kas men, including Lasa, who was classified second, only 24 seconds behind Fuente. But there was a dangerous presence among them: Agostinho, classified sixth, only 40 seconds behind Lasa. Kas director Eusebio Vélez decided it was too risky to let the group go and ordered his riders to stop working. Lasa was deeply unhappy, and there were moments of tension in the Kas camp.

Pajares was gripped by thick fog. Its long, wet descent was extremely dangerous as the riders hurtled into the oblivion, and there were several crashes. Electrified to be on home ground, Fuente jumped clear with team-mate Santiago Lazcano to reach the group ahead. Ocaña was left without allies: Thévenet's knee had seized up in the cold, and Delisle was afflicted with severe bronchitis. Ahead, Fuente was taking risks to force the pace. Behind, Ocaña had to do the same.

Impressively, he bridged the gap to Fuente's group, but the effort cost him dearly. Tarangu waited for the penultimate climb of San Esteban de las Cruces to accelerate, and Ocaña could only keep up for a few metres. There was no stopping Fuente, buoyed by the delirium of thousands of his countrymen. On the final climb of the Naranco, with the finish at the top, they were driven wild to see their hero, alone, and storming in 1'–10" ahead of Lasa.

For Ocaña, the last climb was an ordeal. His legs were not responding and he had to deal with tremendous hostility from the crowds, who spat at him and shouted 'French dog'. They hadn't forgotten how Ocaña, still vengeful after the Tour, had forced the national selector to leave Fuente out of the Spanish team for the World Championships held in Barcelona. After the stage, Fuente reproached the public for their unsporting behaviour, asking them to give his rival a big cheer the following day. Perurena had climbed the Naranco in Ocaña's group and was full of admiration: 'He's never looked a champion as much as today. I've seen him suffering and the constant insults of the public cut me to the bone. It made me sad to go ahead in the last metres and leave him behind. Luis had to fight alone for 100 kilometres.'

Surrounded by legions of ecstatic fans, Fuente remained calm: 'In the time-trial, I'm sure I will cede time to Ocaña. I had to do my stage today, and it turned out much better than I'd hoped.' He had two and a half minutes on his rival, but there were still many stages left and after such a strong start, Kas might wear themselves out before the end.

Next morning, Ocaña was greeted by cheers, the public wishing to make amends. Fuente sought him out to apologise for the spectators and they embraced. The peloton had shrunk, as Gaston Plaud, director of Peugeot, had decided to pull out Thévenet and Delisle, both affected by the bad weather. He didn't mince words: 'Thévenet knows that he has an appointment with the Tour. And that is much more important.' He expressed surprise that Ocaña was risking his season by continuing despite persistent bronchitis, but the Spaniard was too busy planning revenge on Fuente to think about the rest of his racing calendar.

It was the second day in Asturias and the cyclists had to climb the hardest mountain of the Vuelta, the Fito, only ten kilometres from the finish in Cangas de Onis. No sooner had the peloton turned onto its steep, narrow slopes, when Ocaña attacked. Fuente tried to respond, but his chain slipped off and he found himself at the tail end of a strung-out field. He reacted explosively, speeding past one rider after another until he'd caught Ocaña, and the two approached the final metres together, straining after their supreme effort. Yet it was Ocaña's team-mate, Agostinho, who was first over the summit.

A formidable cyclist, the Portuguese attacked on the descent, with Fuente in fearless pursuit. Agostinho won the stage, moving up to third overall, but the Asturian had defended himself honourably. Ocaña ceded 21 seconds, admitting he hadn't dared keep up with them. Although he was fifth at 3'–26", he and Agostinho seemed to be getting stronger by the day: they were now threatening Lasa and Perurena, placed second and fourth. The Kas ship had also been rocked by stormy scenes in their hotel in Oviedo, as Lasa, convinced that he could have had the Vuelta sewn up if the director hadn't interfered, lashed out at what he saw as a betrayal. The race would decide who was right.

As the peloton moved eastwards, there was a brief lull, during which minor players had their say. Kas' *gregario*, Santisteban, an expert in long futile escape bids, finally had a day of glory, winning in Laredo, very near the village where he was born. On the stage to Bilbao, Abilleira, the bandaged survivor of the Jarama crash, picked up enough points to secure the Mountains prize.

Demonstrating that his form was improving, Ocaña gave Kas a hard time *en route* to Miranda del Ebro, where the winner was Agustín Tamames, riding for the Portuguese team, Benfica, after surprisingly being turned down by all the Spanish teams. After the stage, Fuente admitted: 'Today, Ocaña rode up the Urkiola frankly very well. I tried to follow his wheel and couldn't.' There was one day left in the mountains, and Fuente would be able to sleep more easily if he used it to distance his rivals before the final time-trial.

This penultimate stage finished on top of the Arrate in the Basque Country, and there were worries in the Kas camp about possible aggression from the roadside against Fuente because Lasa's countrymen were not happy about the sidelining of their hero. The day was bright and sunny, which must have lifted Ocaña's spirits and on the Elgueta he was first to attack. On the descent, the intensity of their rivalry caused Fuente and Ocaña to crash as their handlebars locked together. While Ocaña picked himself up with barely a scratch and was able to continue immediately, Fuente was bleeding copiously from head and face injuries, and his bike needed to be changed. Half stunned, he tried to block out all thoughts except 'chase', but his rivals were doing their utmost to gain as much time on him as possible, and remained out of reach.

If the Basques were planning a special 'welcome' for the Asturian on the slopes of the Arrate, they rapidly cancelled it at the sight of him fighting desperately to save his position, his head dripping blood. In the end he only lost 14 seconds to Ocaña and six to Agostinho. Ocaña was now an unlikely threat, but his Portuguese team-mate, strong against the clock, was uncomfortably close, at 2'–35".

Sore all over, and extremely nervous, Fuente lay awake, chain-smoking through the night. The time-trial was just under 36 kilometres, finishing in the Anoeta velodrome in San Sebastián. The atmosphere among the spectators was electric, especially when Ocaña overtook Perurena and equalled the leading time so far of 48'–47", set by Swerts. Then Agostinho caused a furore with an unbeatable 47'–42". It seemed that the Portuguese rider had destroyed all of Kas' work in the very last moment. The crowd held their breath.

When Fuente rode into the stadium, there was an eerie silence. He said afterwards: 'When I arrived at the Anoeta, a chill ran through me. That silence, those faces, gave me the impression that the worst had happened.' He finished in agony, sweating, forcing every pedal stroke. Then the silence was broken as it was announced that Fuente had won the Vuelta – by eleven seconds!

The stadium was delirious, any hard Basque feelings against Fuente long gone. The crowd loved it when he announced that 'without the stimulus of Lasa's friendly rivalry, I would never have won'. Agostinho was inconsolable: 'When I saw I was catching up with Lasa, I was sure I was going to win. Eleven seconds are a mere whisper.' It was the closest the Portuguese rider would ever get to winning one of the major tours.

*   *   *   *   *

Twelve months later, as the 1975 Vuelta got underway, yet another state of emergency was declared in the Basque provinces of Vizcaya and Guipuzcoa. Franco's last days dragged on in slow motion, but the regime's oppressive instincts were not tempered by the approach of an uncertain future. The campaign of intimidation in the Basque Country, the random arrests and brutal interrogations, was storing up a poisonous legacy for the future. Meanwhile, at the other end of the country, the Vuelta was touring some of the principle Mediterranean holiday resorts – from the jetset playground of Marbella, with its recently inaugurated leisure port, to the more down-market Benidorm and – as the race ventured off the mainland for the first time – Palma de Mallorca

1975

How many riders were dreaming of victory in the peloton? Everyone expected another Ocaña–Fuente duel, while in their shadow, cyclists like Lasa, Perurena and Tamames were keeping their ambitions to themselves. Ocaña was riding in the new, Navarra-based team, Super Ser, with Tamames his right-hand man, while Lasa was the second-in-command for Kas. The Vuelta would evolve into an intense battle between the two teams, but neither of their leaders started on a good footing. Ocaña was unhappy and on edge, claiming Kas director Barrutia had shielded Fuente with his car in the Prologue, and then accusing Lasa of sheltering behind the film crew after he'd unexpectedly won the short eight-kilometre uphill time-trial in Benidorm. Fuente, meanwhile, lost time after crashing on the Almería stage, and only managed to finish sixth in Benidorm, despite the favourable *crono-escalada* course. He had no excuses –

'To be honest, I didn't climb very well.' He could only hope to pick up form as the race progressed.

When Lasa won that time-trial, he'd already been the race leader for several days, having claimed the yellow jersey in Granada, after Perurena let him cross the line first. When asked how he rated his chances in the final outcome, Lasa replied: 'I've come to the conclusion that it's better not to dream.' Victory had been within his grasp before – in his opinion especially in 1971 when he was riding for the lowly Orbea team – always to be snatched away. Lasa, Tamames and Perurena were all great cyclists, but they lacked the genius of Ocaña and Fuente, who in turn were eclipsed by the mighty Merckx. Perhaps after all the disappointments, they'd learnt to keep their feet on the ground.

As the grumbling cyclists were herded onto the night ferry to Mallorca, the general classification was very cramped – a reflection of how anodyne the racing had been. Ocaña was fourth at 52 seconds and Fuente 14th at 1'–32". The scenic island stage, finishing in Castillo de Bellver, with its splendid panoramic views, saw some lively skirmishes between Kas and Super Ser. On the final ramps leading to the castle, Andrés Oliva of Kas tried an attack, but Tamames shot after him, winning easily, with Lasa finishing in second place

Back on the mainland, the running battle between the two Spanish teams continued as the peloton turned northwards to Tremp, within sight of the Pyrenees, where a stage finishing at the Formigal ski station awaited them. Not for the first time, a day of transition unexpectedly produced an upheaval in the overall, when Perurena and the Kas workhorse, Santisteban, made a break, which was immediately joined by Super Ser's Santiago Lazcano and José Gómez Lucas. With Santisteban pulling tirelessly, the group acquired a lead of nine minutes. It became a war of nerves. Would Super Ser defend Ocaña and reel in the escape? Were Kas going to forget about Lasa and hedge their bets on their sprinter, Perurena, with the mountains just around the corner? Apparently so, as Perurena won the stage with five minutes on the peloton and took the yellow jersey from his team-mate.

After the stage, the team's strategies were called into question. Gabriel Saura, Super Ser's director, concluded: 'It's clear they wanted to distance Ocaña. But they are also putting time into their own strong men. I think there's only been one victim here, and that's

145

Lasa.' Barrutia repeated the Kas mantra: 'For me there are no individuals, only the team.' Lasa made no comment.

All eyes were on Ocaña and Fuente: there would be nowhere for them to hide in the Pyrenees. Kas controlled the stage until the foot of the Formigal, where the peloton fractured under the impetus of Ocaña's attack. Perhaps his move was too early and the climb not as difficult as he expected, since the road had been resurfaced and some of its gradient smoothed out. At any rate, Lasa was able to reach him and remain firmly on his wheel. Tamames rode up to Ocaña, but received orders to save himself – Ocaña had to improve his classification, but Lasa could not be allowed to take the stage. As planned, Tamames easily broke away in the last metres for his third stage-win, leaping from twelfth to fourth place overall.

But where was Fuente? Early on, he'd worked to help Kas control the race, but on the Formigal suffered a *pájara* – something that was becoming worryingly characteristic of the Asturian. For Tarangu, the dream of being the first to win three Vueltas was over. His teammate Perurena was still in yellow, however, having defended himself well, arriving at the top in seventh place at 1'–53".

The race would have been more interesting with a consecutive mountainous day to maintain the pressure. Instead, there was a flat route across Navarra to Irache, and the ever-alert Perurena reinforced his lead by picking up an intermediate bonus, and finishing second. The winner was Tamames, but no one seemed to grant much importance to his fourth stage victory, which left him 17 seconds ahead of Ocaña overall; he was applauded for snatching the bonus from his team leader's rivals, as a good *gregario* should, but wasn't considered a contender in his own right. He didn't feature in any of the calculations that were hastily being made: Lasa was checking records of past Vueltas to see how much time Ocaña had taken off him in the time-trials; Perurena was gloomily wondering how much he would lose on the Urkiola, the next mountain-top finish. Barrutia was trying to appear calm by announcing he could win with either of them.

The events on the Urkiola evolved as they had on the Formigal. Once again, Ocaña attacked at the foot and broke up the peloton. He was under tremendous pressure to perform that day – his last chance to assert himself as leader. But all his and Tamames' combined efforts were not enough to fend off Lasa and the Dutch rider Hennie Kuiper. Tamames was trying to lead Ocaña when his leader called to him: 'Go on, Agustín, Lasa's coming!' With these words Ocaña surrendered the race, and without hesitation, Tamames shot off to take an impressive fifth stage.

Although Ocaña was not completely ruled out, Kas openly admitted that Tamames was now the one they feared. Perurena had survived the mountains in yellow, but his lead was precarious: he had 54 seconds on Lasa and 1'–17" on Tamames. Everything would be decided in the final time-trial in San Sebastián. 'I've never been so close to winning the Vuelta, that's the truth,' confessed Perurena. 'I've never known what it's like to reach the last stage in yellow. I couldn't forgive myself if I lost the race in 32 kilometres.' Perurena's earlier cautious pessimism had given way to a desperate longing to win. He didn't waste any opportunities on the stage to Bilbao, picking up all the intermediate time-bonuses, and was fighting for the stage-win when he punctured practically at the finishing-line. The Italian sprinter, Marino Basso, who'd taken six of the coastal stages, had been concentrating so hard on his Basque rival that he didn't notice the Australian Don Allan slip past to win.

The final day of the Vuelta was split into two sectors. The morning road-race was uneventful since the favourites had their minds on the time-trial, which was held in an atmosphere of great tension that afternoon. All the excitement lacking in the previous weeks was concentrated in these 32 kilometres, on a dangerously wet circuit – the rain appearing as if on schedule. The spectators in the Anoeta stadium were naturally backing their countrymen, Txomin Perurena and Miguel Lasa, and when Ocaña and Lasa both registered poor times, all their attention focused on Perurena. He had a cushion of 1'–19" but this year it didn't work out for Kas. He lost 1'–33" on that very last afternoon, and had to relinquish the yellow jersey to Tamames. Those 14 seconds were as bitter to Txomin as the 11-second margin had been to Agostinho the year before. At the age of 32, he would never have such a chance again. He'd forgotten Lasa's advice and let himself dream. He must have remembered certain moments: voluntarily ceding six seconds to Lasa on the Alhambra, losing a photo-finish sprint to Tamames, the puncture in Bilbao ... there are endless ways to find 14 seconds.

Astonished by the transformation in his career – 'Last season there was no room for me in any Spanish team and now I've won the Vuelta' – an emotional Tamames embraced his director. His successful early years had been disrupted by illness, and Gabriel

Saura had rescued him from the minor Portuguese team where he was riding for a modest wage. Although always an impeccable *gregario* for Ocaña, Tamames admitted that he'd been thinking of winning the Vuelta ever since the Formigal stage, when he found he could keep up with his leader.

For Ocaña there was no end to the tunnel. Always an intense and troubled man, he'd suffered a season without any important victories; his self-confidence was low and he was desperate to vindicate himself by winning another big stage race. Saura reflected: 'In the crucial mountain stages he jumped too soon, and couldn't consolidate the escape.' But the director was very proud: to win the Vuelta in a team's first year was a great achievement. And Ocaña would have another opportunity in the Vuelta next year. Not so, José Manuel Fuente.

In the Tour de France that year, Fuente abandoned professional cycling. A photo shows him with his face a deathly mask, his eyes sunken and lost, as he grips the handlebars. Medical tests revealed that his kidneys, weakened by the ineptly treated scarlet fever he'd suffered as a child, could no longer cope with the pressures of racing, or the amphetamine usage rife in the peloton of that era. On the penultimate day of what turned out to be his last Vuelta, Fuente had abandoned the race in an ambulance. Alerted by Barrutia that he would be summoned for a surprise doping test – normally reserved for only the first three to finish – he loosened his front wheel and staged a crash. Reminiscing many years later, he spoke at length with typical frankness about the doping habits of 'the doomed generation', the shared injections and lack of medical supervision. His comments were not well received by his cycling peers.

Fuente found it hard to accept his career in cycling was over so suddenly and tried to make a comeback in Italy, before retiring to his sports shop in Oviedo and managing a new cycling team, Clas. His autobiography, published before he'd come to terms with the turn of events, is a veritable storm of bitterness. The front cover is graced with a photograph of his bloodied face, taken after the fall that nearly stopped him winning the '74 Vuelta. His solace was to see his parents comfortably installed in a brand new house in Limanes. The cold, damp, perennially leaking home of his childhood had disappeared from their lives for good.

Finally, the long-awaited event arrived. On 20th November, Prime Minister Arias Navarro sobbed in front of the television cameras as he announced Franco's death. Flags flew at half-mast, thousands queued to pay their last respects by the coffin; elsewhere champagne bottles were uncorked and children enjoyed a day off school. Now the country held its breath, wondering what would happen next.

1976–1982

The Transition

The passage from dictatorship to democracy in the years following Franco's death – 'The Transition', as it's known in Spain – was a period of uncertainty and trepidation for everybody. Although it was accomplished with far less bloodshed than many feared might be the case, it was by no means an entirely peaceful process. Even before Spaniards had their first opportunity to cast a vote, there had been riots, shootings, and bombings in which over 20 people met their death in politically motivated killings.

That cold late November, as the echoes of the canons fired in honour of the dead dictator faded away, the immediate prospects for a more representative government looked rather discouraging. The new Head of State, King Juan Carlos, had been personally groomed by Franco since the age of 10 to be his successor and whenever the opposition parties took to the streets – and since they were still illegal they had little alternative to street demonstrations – among their favourite chants was: *España, mañana, Será republicana* ('Spain, tomorrow, Will be republican'). The misgivings gave way to total dismay when the King appointed Adolfo Suárez as Prime Minister, a man whose entire career had been spent in Franco's service. 'What a mistake,' rang one headline in *El País*, echoing widespread opinion. Few suspected how committed both men really were to a democratic Spain.

Within three months, working with unforeseen determination and political acumen, Suárez had steered a reform bill through the Spanish parliament that would re-establish democratic government, and the following month it was endorsed by 94.2 per-cent in a national referendum. The reforms continued to come thick and fast. In early 1977, political parties (including the Communist Party) were legalised; so, too, were trade unions, with the right to strike re-established. The *Movimiento* was abolished, and the date of the first general election in more than 40 years was set for July of that year. Then, in 1978, a new constitution was approved – again with overwhelming support in a referendum – which ceded substantial amounts of autonomy to regional assemblies.

Aside from this rush of constitutional reform, Spanish society was changing vertiginously. It was the age of the *destape*, or 'uncovering': newspapers were filled with advertisements for erotic sex shows and there was topless sunbathing on the beaches. Demonstrators clamoured for the legalisation of divorce, abortion and the pill.

In the social and political whirlwind of these years, it would have been impossible for the Vuelta to emerge unscathed. In fact, the race came very close to disappearing, rescued only at the last moment by a new organisation. Part of the problem was that Spanish cycling was going through a protracted barren period, which some saw as an inevitable result of progress. It seemed it was necessary to be poor and oppressed to be able to endure the sport's inherent hardship and that cycling had no place amid Spain's new liberalism and affluence.

Observing how the sport was slipping into the doldrums, Dalmacio Langarica, still working for Kas as technical advisor, thought it was a problem of attitude: 'We've arrived at a totally conservative style of cycling, where only a few are willing to take risks, and as a spectacle it's losing force.' The Vuelta of 1976 turned out to be one of the last opportunities to see a survivor from a more heroic era. Fortunately for the race, Luis Ocaña, although now on the downward slope of his career, was too impulsive and proud to play it safe.

The strongest foreign team that year was Ti–Raleigh, directed **1976** by the suave Peter Post, and the race was expected to evolve into a fight between their Dutch rider Hennie Kuiper, the current World Champion, and Ocaña, still leading Super-Ser. Yet it was guaranteed that Kas would be looking for revenge for the previous year, when victory had been snatched so cruelly from Perurena. Without Fuente, Kas were once again missing a clear leader. Their director, Eusebio Vélez, juggled five names when considering which of his men could spearhead their attack, but he omitted to mention José Pesarrodona, the Catalan rider who'd briefly fended off Merckx back in 1973. A quiet, affable man with little concern for personal glory, Pesarrodona fitted in perfectly with the Kas ethos of brotherhood.

The first half of the race took place in Andalucía and the Mediterranean area, where, as usual, the Spanish teams' strategy was to limit their losses, and not allow the Dutch and Belgians too much leeway before the final week in the north. Ti–Raleigh exerted their dominance, keeping the yellow jersey within their ranks throughout the first week with three different men, although the last of these, Gunther Haritz, and his successor, Erik Jacques of the Belgian team Ebo-Cinzia, both failed to pass doping controls. The yellow jersey fell back into Raleigh's hands, with their talented 21-yearold German rider, Dietrich Thurau, in only his second season as a professional, instated as the legitimate race leader.

The issue of doping was becoming ever more intrusive, implicating cyclists at all levels, although positive tests were regarded as more of a nuisance than career-threatening. Sanctions were still in a rudimentary phase and lenient by today's standards: apart from small fines and suspensions that were easy to side-step, ten minutes would be added to a rider's time, with consequences that could be negligible, or – as would happen in the 1982 Vuelta – scandalous. The sports Press generally sided with the cyclists, unhappy with the UCI's list of forbidden products. In spring 1976 the weather in Spain was particularly changeable and it seemed absurd that the coughing, fever-wracked peloton was unable to take even the most innocuous syrup that would be prescribed for children. The team directors, many of them veterans who'd raced unencumbered by tests, struggled to come to terms with the new regulations, while the cyclists deeply resented the way their sport was being singled out. And, as always, the serious stuff was going undetected.

As customary in these opening stages, the Spaniards had largely taken a back seat, but when the peloton reached Asturias there was a change of momentum, as well as scenery. Seventy kilometres after setting off from Gijón, Kas sent Perurena ahead to toughen up the stage, and the main field soon dwindled. Once on the Fito, situated only 18 kilometres from the finish in Cangas de Onís, it was Ocaña who attacked, and left the rest struggling. Thurau, who'd been wearing the yellow jersey for nearly a week, made the novice's mistake of attempting to match the Spaniard's rhythm. For the uninitiated, the Fito's unrelenting ramps can come as a disagreeable surprise, especially when others are intent on lifting the tempo. On the frenetic descent, a group of nine came together and the Asturian Vicente López Carril gave Kas the stage in front of an appreciative home crowd. The Fito had claimed 3'–12" from Thurau, and the yellow jersey passed to Teka's leader, Joaquin Agostinho. Pressing close at nine seconds was Hennie Kuiper, upon whom all Ti–

Raleigh's hopes were now concentrated, while Ocaña was third at 31 seconds. Not far behind was Pesarrodona of Kas.

When the peloton moved eastwards to Cantabria, swallowed up by the mist and saturated by cold rain, it was Agostinho's turn to be targeted. After Ocaña forced the pace on the Sierra Collada, the Portuguese began to suffer, and he was finished off on the next first-category climb, the Palombera. As Ocaña flew downhill towards Reinosa, he was joined by a group of six, including the two strongest Ti–Raleigh men. It was an altogether satisfactory day for Peter Post's team, with Thurau first over the line and Kuiper the new Yellow Jersey, but he could hardly feel secure with Ocaña breathing down his neck.

Such was Ocaña's exhibition of strength – in two days he'd single-handedly eliminated Thurau and Agostinho, without any help from his ineffectual team – there was a general conviction that he would storm the final time-trial in San Sebastián, pull back his 25-second deficit on Kuiper, and carry off the Vuelta. At least, that's how the plot should have unfolded, if only as a reward for having seized the race and shaken it out of its complacency. After the stage, Ocaña said: 'I only ask that my strength continues responding.'

There was one more mountainous stage, culminating in the abrupt climb to the Santuario de Oro in the south of the Basque Country. It was there that Ocaña finally ran out of ammunition, and had to be pushed up the last metres. With the passing of years, his powers of recuperation were not the same. Deeply disappointed, he remarked: 'Forces spent need to be paid for, and I've paid for them at the crucial moment. I've had to fight on many fronts.' Kuiper also lost time because of mechanical problems, when for once Peter Post was not immediately at the scene, after having terrorised the peloton almost daily with his reckless driving. In the general classification, Ocaña was still close behind Kuiper, but in his heart he knew it was all over.

Banesto's well-known team director, José Miguel Echávarri, once said of Ocaña that 'everything he did was tinged with heroism and tragedy'. Spanish cycling would miss his intensity, for the '76 Vuelta was effectively his parting shot, the last time he came seriously close to winning an important stage race. Ocaña's future lay in directing teams, without much success, dabbling in radio commentary, and cultivating his vineyards in France, before turning a gun on himself in 1994, when he was 49 years old.

In the final time-trial in San Sebastián, Ocaña finished eighth at 1'–02", but he was not the only one who failed to deliver. The most disappointing rider was Kuiper, who only managed 20th, two minutes slower than his triumphant team-mate Thurau, and it relegated him to sixth place overall. For Ti–Raleigh the only compensation was that Thurau's fifth stage-win confirmed him as winner of the points jersey, but the race, against all odds, went to the man who was placed second in the time-trial: Pesarrodona, the first Catalan to win the Vuelta.

Pesarrodona's victory was down to his consistent good form and his knack of passing virtually unnoticed. True to the Kas philosophy, he insisted his excellent time-trial had merely been the final touch to a solid team effort. 'I have to repeat one and a thousand times,' he told the Press, 'that it isn't Pesarrodona who has won the Vuelta, but Kas.' But above all, he'd known better than anyone how to reap the benefit of Ocaña's work. The downcast leader of Super Ser had to make do with second place on the podium.

In fact, this was to prove the season's high water-mark for both Ocaña and his team. Although he was the animator of what turned out to be the decisive stage of the Tour he finished 14th overall, and at the end of 1976 Super Ser disappeared. Big projects, grandiose plans, all came to nothing. Apart from the dearth of new figures in Spanish cycling capable of capturing the public's imagination and winning races, the European recession, prolonged by the energy crisis, was biting hard. The following year this was more than apparent in the Vuelta's shrunken peloton, with only 70 riders taking the start.

1977

There was an alarming beginning to 1977 when right-wing extremists ran amok in Madrid, furious at Suárez's political reforms. One January night a group of armed men entered trade union offices on Calle Aotcha and shot dead three lawyers and two others, all affiliated to the Communist Party. This was a time of 'Communists without wigs' wrote Miguel Mora in *El País*, referring to the freedom of political exiles to return home undisguised. One of them was the Communist Party leader, Santiago Carillo, who with hindsight, described the atrocity as 'the final gasp of a regime that refused to die'. Despite nervousness about the army's possible reaction, the party was finally legalised that April and the tanks stayed in their barracks – at least, for the time being.

At the end of that anxious month the smallest peloton since 1950 assembled for the 32nd edition of the Vuelta. Its start was jeopardised by an Iberia airline strike, so buses had to be organised to ferry the cyclists to Alicante, and a plane chartered for the VIPs. The race also began without the Swiss-based Kanel team: their riders had been left stranded without their bikes, which had been sold off by the mechanics, tired of waiting for their salaries. Even the Tour de France would struggle to complete its roster this year; instead of fighting for invitations, teams stayed away and the French race would begin with three unfilled places.

The organisers of the Vuelta had at least secured one of the biggest figures of current cycling, Freddy Maertens, even if they weren't able to provide him with any decent opposition. The Belgian sprinting star was burning very brightly when he came to Spain. In 1976 he'd achieved an extraordinary 54 victories, including eight stages in the Tour de France. He proceeded to leave a scorched trail through the Vuelta, breaking records, and filling his bank account. The rest of the field could only look on helplessly.

Maertens was at the head of the Belgian Flandria squad, where he enjoyed the undivided attentions of the talented *domestique* Michel Pollentier. They'd been friends since their amateur days, and Pollentier was to Maertens what Stablinski had been to Anquetil. During the race, observers of how the partnership worked were drawn to wondering if Pollentier wasn't the stronger of the two. Maertens was undoubtedly one of the best-ever road-sprinters, but only an average climber.

One of the few stages Maertens failed to win was the time-trial in Benidorm, when he was brought down by a Belgian tourist stepping too close to take a photograph. The honours went to Pollentier instead, who afterwards declared he was quite satisfied with his role as Maertens' right-hand man. Financially he did very well, with plenty of invitations to races and criteriums: 'Where Maertens goes, so do I,' he insisted. Regularly referring to him as 'Maertens' third leg', the Press pondered if the real reason Pollentier was not a star in his own right was simply that he was balding, short and looked ungainly on the bike.

The headline in *El País* after the second stage was: 'This Maertens thing is boring already.' He'd collected the leader's jersey after the prologue – on a whim the organisers had reverted to orange – and never let it go, becoming only the third rider, after Berrendero and

Anquetil, to lead the race throughout. He steadily consolidated his position by having Flandria control the peloton, allowing him to sprint to victory and pick up the time-bonuses.

Acknowledging defeat, the rest of the field chose to ignore Maertens, and concentrated on the battle for second place. After all, the weather and the landscape might vary from day to day, but the final 100 metres were always the same. The only variation was that sometimes Flandria would set Maertens up in a bunch sprint, and at other times he'd fight it out on his own in a reduced group. It was towards the end of the Mediterranean stretch, in Salou, that Maertens secured his eighth stage-win to equal Van Looy's score of 1965. The next day, the peloton moved up the coast to Barcelona, where a short time-trial of 3.8 kilometres, followed by a 45-kilometre road race through the city's streets awaited them. Both sectors went to Maertens, who now set his sights on Delio Rodríguez's hallowed record of 12 stage-wins, set way back in 1941.

Sprinters normally retreated after the first week, but not this year, given the particularly undemanding *parcours*. The organisers, conscious of Maertens' reluctance to come to Spain, had done their best to erase any mountainous difficulties. The so-called *etapa reina* finished at the Formigal ski station in the Pyrenees, but the peloton arrived at the bottom of the climb fresh and intact, and Maertens crossed the line only a few seconds after the winner, Pedro Torres of the Spanish team, Teka. Even the Belgian was surprised at how easily he'd been let off: 'Aren't there any mountains or climbers in Spain?' he queried.

To be fair, Miguel María Lasa, no mean climber, had intended to pressurise Maertens on this stage, but his tactic backfired. It was a fashion among cyclists at the time to drink a small bottle of Cava towards the end of a stage for its brief euphoric lift; on this occasion, however, it left Lasa feeling whoozy, and instead of attacking, he rapidly found himself drifting backwards.

The only suspense left was whether Maertens could set a new record: he equalled Delio Rodríguez's dozen on the 16th stage finishing in Cordovilla, part of Pamplona's industrial belt. There, the peloton found itself enveloped in the tense, heated atmosphere generated by the pro-amnesty week being held in the Basque Country and northern Navarra. A series of meetings, strikes and demonstrations demanding freedom for all political prisoners had been met with fierce resistance by the police. People had been killed and scores injured and arrested. Only the day before, in Rentería, the Civil Guard had sprayed the demonstrators' legs with machine-gun fire. This police brutality did nothing to calm the situation.

The Basques' love of cycling meant they turned up in droves to see the Vuelta, but it was impossible in the current climate for any gathering not to evolve into a political demonstration. As the peloton left Cordovilla the following morning, heavily armed police escorted them for the first 50 kilometres. It was dubbed the 'stage of the *ikurriña*' – the recently legalised Basque flag. Its mere presence was a taunt to any one with allegiance to the old regime – and the route was lined with them. The day finished uneventfully in Bilbao, the peloton allowing Luis Ordiales, a modest rider of Novostil, nearly an hour down overall, to escape. Bergareche rapidly began negotiating an alternative to the planned finish in San Sebastián; the traditional time-trial ending in the Anoeta stadium would have to be cancelled.

On the penultimate stage, with its summit finish on the Urkiola, the peloton managed to skirt barricades and scattered nails, which left several team-cars stranded at the foot of the climb. Kas' José Nazábal broke free at the last moment, Maertens finishing a few seconds behind, on Perurena's wheel. Then there was chaos, as *ikurriñas* and amnesty banners were unfurled and confrontations with the police broke out. Shots were fired, causing a blind panic.

The final stage was hurriedly set up – a mere 104 kilometres to Miranda del Ebro in the province of Burgos. After all the commotion, and with the race completely resolved, everyone was anxious to pack up and go home. The only rider upset by the cancellation of the time-trial was Maertens, who saw it as a missed opportunity to distance himself from second-placed Lasa. Conscious that an overall victory based purely on bonuses lacked authority, he attacked at kilometre 64, with the support of three team-mates. His attempt to gain time on the Spaniards was foiled when three Teka riders, including Lasa, latched on, but they couldn't come between Maertens and his bid for a new record of 13 stage-wins. The big losers on the day were Kas: only González Linares made the break, and then, on director's orders, he had to drop back and help the team in a futile bid to close the gap. This error cost them the team prize and compounded what was, for them, a disastrous Vuelta.

Maertens received his trophy with barely a flicker of emotion. An extremely driven man, his mind was already concentrated on the Giro d'Italia, due to start later in the week. *Dicen* had reported that after each stage Maertens dedicated half an hour to yoga and half an hour to weight-lifting, and published photographs of him in severe cross-legged positions on the masseur's couch. 'The Vuelta has been perfect training for me and I'm going to the Giro in better shape than any of my rivals,' he announced, with a heightened sense of invincibility.

Events wouldn't run quite so smoothly in Italy. Contrary to his plans, the Giro went to Pollentier – which put their relationship out of kilter – after Maertens had to abandon with a fractured wrist. In an act of madness, he reappeared in the Tour of Switzerland with his arm still in a plaster cast. It was the beginning of a decline, as rapid as anything else Maertens did.

The day the Vuelta finished, there were scenes reminiscent of war in Bilbao, the streets barricaded, upturned vehicles burning, right-wing paramilitary groups apparently given free rein. Yet two months later, Spain's first general elections since 1936 were held peacefully, with a massive turn-out. In the run-up, empty wall space had been hard to find, such was the deluge of political propaganda from the 300 parties that had sprouted overnight. Hitherto apolitical Spaniards devoured the guide-books that suddenly appeared on the market, giving crash courses in politics. Fortunately, the situation was simplified by coalitions, such as the winning UCD, a right–centre alliance based on the charisma of Adolfo Suárez. The Socialist Party was the second most voted for, easily outdoing the Communists, who, for a society intent on change, had too many links with the past. The most resounding failure of the election was Alianza Popular, the party most associated with Franco's regime.

One demand for change that had been sweeping Spain, since even before the dictator's death, was for a greater measure of regional independence. It came to be known as *fiebre autonómica* (autonomy fever). Precisely because of the *Caudillo*'s centralist fervour, the most determined opposition to his regime had frequently been articulated in terms of regional nationalism. Although particularly strong throughout Spain, notably in the Basque Country and Catalunya, this demand for regional independence was part of a wider phenomenon in the 1970s. It was the time when Scottish and Welsh nationalists came to the fore in Britain, with similar political movements in Brittany and elsewhere in Europe.

It was a singularly independent-minded young Breton cyclist, on the threshold of stardom, who came to the Vuelta in 1978. Bernard Hinault had caused a stir in 1977 by winning the Liège–Bastogne–Liége and the Dauphiné Libéré and there was talk of a promising future. Perhaps it was their lack of experience of racing abroad, or perhaps because they didn't consider the Renault–Gitane team to be very strong, but the Spaniards didn't regard Hinault as a particular threat.

1978

There was more justification for dismissing the rest of the foreign competition. An Italian team had come with a totally anonymous line-up – the remnants who hadn't been picked for the Giro, which, to avoid clashing with the World Cup in Argentina, overlapped with the Vuelta that year. Another indication of the current status of the Spanish race was the prize money at stake, which had remained frozen for the previous 15 years. While the Tour awarded the equivalent of 21 million pesetas, and the Giro about 14 million, the Vuelta offered a mere 3 million. Taking inflation into account, Mariano Cañardo reckoned he'd earned more in the Vueltas of the Republic!

The route also appeared to favour the home riders. A distinct improvement on the previous year's anodyne affair, it started in the north without the gradual warm-up over a week of flat stages; the early presence of the Fito and the Puerto de Pajares made a welcome change, as did the reduced number of time-trialing kilometres. Teka's director Julio San Emeterio made his view plain: 'The Spaniards can and must win. If not, we deserve to be shot.'

But, after winning the prologue in Gijón, it was Hinault who took the first leader's jersey – yellow once more. One of Kas' climbers, Enrique Cima (whose surname means 'summit') made a bid for it on the second stage when he was first over the top of the Fito; he managed to hold off a pursuing group to win in Cangas de Onís, but his six-second advantage was not quite enough. Kas tried again on the third stage when Pesarrodona's attack, 34 kilometres from the finish in León, cleared the way for a six-man break, which was propelled at a lively pace by a tall, blond Belgian, Ferdi Van den Haute of the Superior team. Hinault chased furiously at the front of the peloton, but the stage went to the Belgian, who became the new race leader. Hinault dropped to fourth overall, 47 seconds down, and shrugged it off: 'I'm free of a responsibility. Others will have to do the work now.' He couldn't quite hide his annoyance, however; he hated to be the one having to chase, instead of taunting the others from out front.

There was no need to fret: 25-year-old Van den Haute saw himself as only a passing race leader. Better informed than the Spaniards, he'd watched Hinault close up in the Belgian classics, and had no doubt the Breton would be the final winner.

Once away from the protection of the mountains, the peloton was exposed to the strong winds of the Meseta. Out of his element, Cima found himself stranded in the second echelon *en route* to Valladolid, dropping from 6th to 19th on general classification. The weather continued to frustrate the climbers: the Sierra de Madrid stage was reduced to its final flat 46 kilometres because of heavy May Day snowfalls. But two days later, the peloton rode itself free of winter when it arrived at the Mediterranean town of Benicassim.

Hinault was biding his time, awaiting the Catalan mountains. He'd stated with bold precision that he would be in yellow again on stage 12 at the summit finish of La Tossa de Monbuí. Another rider with plans for that day was Andrés Gandarias of Novostil. He'd tasted glory in the Giro of 1976, winning the *etapa reina*, and was hungry for more. He made his move after only 35 kilometres, and by the penultimate climb of Can Massana was still ahead. Chasing him was a 13-strong group, including the best climbers from Kas and Teka, who'd managed to open up a gap of two minutes on the main bunch.

At this juncture Hinault's prospects were looking uncertain but when he judged the moment was right, he caught up the break with insulting ease. There he tucked in behind his *domestique,* Jean Bernardeau, who swiftly powered what remained of the group to the foot of the final climb, reeling in Gandarias in the process. Pesarrodona, who'd followed Hinault all the way, had a difficult moment when he punctured, but Cima helped him back on, and the two Kas men were able to witness Hinault's triumphant crossing of the line for his third stage-win. With Van den Haute definitively dropped, he was the new leader.

That morning, Cyrille Guimard, Renault's director, had given his verdict on the local competition. 'The Spaniards don't worry me.' It was a truly wounding comment to make, especially before a mountain stage. But he was right; Hinault had won easily. Afterwards, surrounded by grimacing, gasping riders, he looked remarkably relaxed. Every photograph of Hinault in that Vuelta shows him grinning from ear to ear, having the time of his life. For the second year running, Spanish hopes were concentrated on the second place on the podium, now held by Pesarrodona, who openly declared the race was out of his reach. Positioned third was Bernaudeau, Hinault's team-mate. The most difficult week still lay ahead, yet the podium was as good as settled.

Over the next few days, Hinault took advantage of the intermediate sprints to widen his gap on Pesarrodona. His team played an obstructive role, thwarting anyone else who might be interested in picking up bonuses; it was a task that Lucien Didier, in particular, enjoyed. The Spaniards felt powerless, especially Kas, whose ranks were weakened by illness. The growing tension between them and Renault surfaced on the stage to Miranda del Ebro, when Cima grabbed Didier's handlebars, and pushed him over as they began the descent of the Herrera. Later he explained: 'Didier blocked my way and then he punched me. I was tired of putting up with his dirty tricks.' The Frenchman indignantly denied any wrongdoing. As far as he was concerned, he was merely defending the interests of his team. Both riders were fined, and Guimard's histrionic outburst ignored; no one took his threats of pulling out seriously. In defence of Spanish honour, González Linares asserted that 'we are the most honest riders in the world'. It seemed scant consolation for not winning races.

The hostility flared up again the next day, when there was nearly a fist-fight between Hinault and Kas' Enrique Martínez Heredia. Another Kas rider, Andrés Oliva, trying to break up the tension, rode up alongside the Breton and 'roared at him like a lion', as he related afterwards. 'Then Hinault grabbed me by the back of the neck and, shook me, in fun, but as he's so strong, my handlebar moved and we both hit the ground.' But there was some consolation for the Spanish fans that day, when Vicente Belda won the stage. The diminutive climber – who today directs the Kelme team – had been excused military service for being so short – 1.53 metres – and weighing 52 kilos.

In his autobiography, Hinault writes, 'I was the true Breton in our family: stubborn, belligerent and afraid of nothing.' At school, he waited impatiently for classes to finish, looking forward to the scraps on the way home and he clearly hadn't lost his taste for a punch-up after becoming a professional cyclist. His equivalent of rolling up his sleeves before wading in was to undo his toe-straps.

What he describes with most relish about the '78 Vuelta is clashing with the Spanish peloton, both on and off the bike. In the run-in with Martínez Heredia, he says: 'There were 25 of them against me. War almost broke out that day.' There was nothing he liked more than the idea of himself taking everyone on, John Wayne-style, and of course, winning. But even Hinault showed some empathy: 'The Spaniards were not happy at the prospect of being shown up by a foreigner and their injured pride produced reactions that I could understand.'

While the scraps, stand-offs and bluster are described in detail in Hinault's book, he is surprisingly reticent about the brilliant display he gave on the penultimate stage. It was one that won him many admirers, and convinced everyone they were witnessing the arrival of a new champion who would go on to define an era.

The stage began in Bilbao, before taking the riders into the hills, and the main action occurred after 52 kilometres on the first-category Orduña, whose summit lies in the province of Burgos. When Belda suddenly accelerated, Hinault immediately retaliated and by the top, pounding tremendous gears, he'd distanced the peloton by 35 seconds. Then he launched himself down the other side in pursuit of a duo who were over four minutes ahead. A more conservative rider might have considered the move an unnecessary risk, since the race was already safely won. But not Hinault.

Within 25 kilometres, he'd reached the leading pair – Leone Pizzini and the luckless Gandarias – and after a brief rest to replenish his forces, he took over at the front. Quickly realising they were of no use to him, the Breton dropped his two surplus companions like so much jetsam, and crested the final two climbs alone, finishing 1'–56" ahead of the main field. After the stage, Gandarias described his experience of trying to hold Hinault's wheel: 'He's a type of Eddy Merckx. He encouraged me to take turns at the front. I asked him how he could expect me to do that, if he was going like a motorbike. He roared with laughter and replied, "Yes, yes. I'm going like a motorbike".' As he hobbled off, Gandarias added ruefully, 'He's destroyed my legs.' No wonder Hinault was laughing, intoxicated by his own supremacy, and knowing this was only the beginning. That summer the Tour would also be his.

The race headed towards its customary finish in San Sebastián with trepidation. The previous October, the government led by Adolfo Suárez had finally passed the long-awaited amnesty law, but as Eta stepped up the killings and kidnappings, new political prisoners weren't in short supply. Only a minority of Basques were actively involved in the new pro-amnesty week, but considerable passive support was guaranteed after so many years of repression. Taking into account just the final two years of the dictatorship, more than 6,000 had been arrested in the region for political activities, and an estimated quarter of the Civil Guard had been garrisoned there. The Tour of the Basque Country could pass without hindrance, but the Vuelta would always be an attractive target for the separatists, especially with its contingent of foreign Press.

Thousands of Basques came to watch the last stage, undeterred as always by the steady rain. In Durango, after 50 kilometres, the peloton found the road strewn with stones, nails and wooden planks. Forced to a halt, the riders were taken by bus to Zarauz and only the last 34 kilometres were raced into San Sebastián, where Txomin Perurena – now at the end of a long, fruitful career – won his second stage, expertly shoving Van den Haute out of his way. Surprisingly, in view of the turbulent atmosphere, the organisers went ahead with the concluding time-trial, but the results had to be annulled, since many cyclists were pelted with objects or had earth thrown in their faces, some even being forced to dismount. It made no difference to the top three positions, which had remained unchanged ever since La Tossa de Montbuí.

Depressed by the national performance, *Dicen* asked Hinault for his opinion on what was wrong with Spanish cycling. His reply afforded no new insights, but was damning all the same. 'The Spaniards don't know how to ride. They don't go abroad, except to the Giro and Tour. And from what I've seen and heard, they're only interested in fighting each other to the death in Spanish races.' Events in the ongoing Giro seemed like another admonishment: the Italians had formed a solid front to defeat Thurau, just as they'd done to Anquetil, before settling the race among themselves.

As for the scenes in Durango, the consequences are still felt to this day. In January of 1979 Bergareche announced there would be no Vuelta that year. After 33 years, *El Correo Español-Pueblo Vasco* had had enough. Their official reason of 'financial difficulties' convinced no one; it simply wasn't feasible for a Basque newspaper to continue sponsoring a race that could no longer enter the Basque Country, as the Spanish Cycling Federation had decided. Twenty-five years later, the Vuelta is still waiting for the all-clear to sound.

When he heard the news, Luis Puig, President of the Federation, was in Italy at the Cyclo-cross World Championships. Spanish cycling might be struggling, but without a home tour, it had no future whatsoever. He was galvanised into action and caught the first plane home. An eternal optimist, and armed with the necessary connections and experience, Puig was miraculously able to set up the Vuelta in only three months – a repeat of what Pujol had accomplished back in 1935. He contracted Unipublic, a company specialising in organising and commercialising sporting events, obtained the sponsorship of the clothes company Lois, and roped in the provincial federations to help arrange the route.

Three weeks before the Vuelta was due to start, *Dicen* interviewed Luis Puig and found him busy with the paraphernalia necessary for stage finishes – barriers, podiums, time-trial ramps. He was confident he could obtain all the necessary material from the long-established Catalan races. 'Everything will be sorted out,' he assured the journalist. He showed equal faith in the future of Spanish cycling: it was all a question of patience and continuity.

1979

The guests of honour were to be Joop Zoetemelk and Lucien Van Impe, who, in the words of Geoffrey Nicholson, were 'far better climbers than men from their low countries have any right to be'. Zoetemelk, in fact, in his one previous appearance in the Vuelta, back in 1971, had won the Mountains prize. Now riding for Miko-Mercier, he was 32 years old but his career was far from over. In 1974, a fractured skull had left him in hospital fighting for his life, but when he recovered, he achieved better results than ever. Perhaps unfairly, the Dutchman was often dismissed as an eternal bridesmaid (he'd already accumulated four second-places in the Tour de France) and condemned for perpetually clinging to someone else's wheel, too cautious to stick his own neck out. But shortly before arriving in Spain, he'd won the Paris–Nice, and was judged to be in excellent form. His potential rival, Van Impe, was leading Kas, who'd signed up a contingent of Belgians with a view to expanding their sale of soft drinks into foreign markets.

The other Belgian big name was Pollentier, who'd missed most of the early season because of illness. He was still smarting from the indignity of being thrown off the previous year's Tour, after being caught with a plastic pipe down his shorts, trying to pass off a team-mate's urine as his own. When he broke away from Freddy

Maertens, he took Sean Kelly with him to Splendor. The 22-year-old Irishman was eager to spread his wings after buying himself out of his previous contract, and he'd win two stages, before retiring on stage 17, in his Vuelta debut.

As the race got underway, Zoetemelk was not the only one to exhibit caution. With the Basque Country now off-bounds, new climbs had to be found, and the first loomed up as early as stage three, which finished in the Sierra Nevada. In the proceeding days, the peloton had rolled along slowly, as if already in the shadow of the 2,100-metre summit finish, which was uncharted territory for most of them. In fact, it was the length of the climb – over 30 kilometres – rather than the gradient that posed the challenge. Zoetemelk, in yellow after the prologue, was indisputably the strongest rider, but instead of showing off his strength, he fell prey to his habitual doubts. 'A collapse in the third stage would've been fatal. That's why I didn't attack,' he confessed.

Instead, it was Novostil's top climber, Felipe Yañez, who seized his opportunity and won the stage, after jumping clear ten kilometres from the top. Pollentier lost nearly two minutes: 'I suffered like a dog,' he admitted. Surprisingly, Van Impe lost a similar amount of time, complaining of cramp. With the two Belgians no longer a threat, the tentative Dutchman could rest more easily, since little trouble would be coming from Spanish quarters, either. The top Spaniards had limited aspirations: they were only interested in fighting each other, satisfied with improving their own classification instead of trying to displace Zoetemelk. The race was dubbed 'the Vuelta of the *gregarios*', for while the leaders sat back, the minor players were allowed to attack.

Everyone expected Zoetemelk to win the 22-kilometre time-trial in Valladolid, but he was beaten by long-legged Alfons de Wolf, who looked more like a basketball player. He was riding in Boule d'Or, a Belgian team full of inexperienced neo-professionals in the hands of veteran 67-year-old director, Guillaume Driessens. This wily old fox had rapidly made an agreement with Miko–Mercier: in return for helping to defend the yellow jersey, his boys would have the support of Zoetemelk's team for stage-wins. Before coming to Spain, Boule d'Or's season had been devoid of victories, but in the Vuelta they scored nine, de Wolf taking five, as well as the points jersey. 'Our directors were incapable of confronting the French–

Belgian coalition because tactically they don't come up to the soles of Driessens' shoes,' spat *El Mundo Deportivo*. The problem with Spanish cycling was clearly not only with the riders.

The last opportunity to put Zoetemelk under any pressure came on the penultimate day. This was a split stage, its first sector a tough 155 kilometres from Ávila to Colmenar Viejo, with the first-category Morcuera very near the finish. But the chance was thrown away in an act of petulance.

Split-stages were still a common feature of stage races – with two arrival towns in one day, more money could be squeezed from the route (the Tour de France was even known to organise triple sectors). The three days leading up to Sunday's finale – an urban circuit in Madrid – were particularly cramped, with the riders having to ride one full stage and four sectors, covering almost 700 kilometres, which was nearly a quarter of the entire race. Disgruntled, the Spaniards organised a go-slow on the Saturday morning and, unsurprisingly, they had the full co-operation of the foreigners. Now Zoetemelk could relax and climb up the Morcuera without fear of an ambush.

The stage-winner was decided in advance, as if it were a criterium: Lasa would be allowed to escape, since only his team, Moliner–Vereco, were still without a victory. When challenged about the sanity of having wasted such an occasion, Paco Galdos, who'd replaced Van Impe as Kas' leader and was positioned second overall, saw it in a different, if somewhat pathetic, light: 'What if the one to get a *pájara* had been me?'

After his unspectacular victory, Zoetemelk reflected on the lack of resistance he'd encountered: 'The Spaniards allowed themselves to be carried along by my team without any kind of ambition.' But even an effortless win can be an inspiration, and although he'd be unable to get the better of Hinault in July (scoring his fifth second place), Zoetemelk's great moment in the Tour would finally arrive in 1980.

For the Vuelta, the most important goal had been survival, and the huge crowds thronging the centre of Madrid to cheer on the peloton were a heartening sight for Puig and Unipublic, who'd organised the event at such short notice. They were congratulated for having saved a national cycling institution. Yet, as events proved, it was too early for celebrations. Just three days before the 1980 race was due to start, *El País* ran a headline: 'Vuelta in danger of suspension'.

In an attempt to secure a stronger financial footing for the race, Luis Puig had approached RTVE (*Radio Television Española*) with a proposal to extend its live coverage, only to be informed that the already paltry 15-minute daily summaries were to be reduced to a couple of minutes on the evening news. By contrast, Italy was enjoying two hours of Giro a day.

The simple fact was that the director of RTVE took a dim view of cycling. He regarded it as nothing but advertising on wheels and, unmoved by the half a million spectators who'd welcomed the cyclists into Madrid, he was convinced the Spanish public had lost interest in the sport. Puig was incredulous: 'According to their criteria, our cyclists ride around the roads merely to display the names of commercial brands.' The financial backing for the race began to crumble, and team sponsors threatened to pull out. The prospects looked so dire that even the optimistic Puig had an official notice of cancellation ready on his desk.

At the last moment, the Ministry of Culture stepped in with emergency funding and persuaded RTVE to maintain the 15-minute round-ups, on the understanding that the viewer wouldn't even glimpse an advertising banner. After many sleepless nights, Puig was able to launch the Vuelta as planned in La Manga, a coastal resort of Murcia, which had paid one million pesetas to host the Prologue. But, without the aerial TV image of the town shot from a helicopter, which Puig had rather impetuously promised, their fee was reduced to half a million.

During these desperate negotiations, Bernard Hinault won the Liège–Bastogne–Liège in the most heroic style, fighting through a blizzard. He wouldn't be coming to the Vuelta, though, which presented a low-key field and undemanding route, without a single summit finish. Spain had become a cycling backwater, far from the action. The organisers explained that the gentle *parcours* was necessary to ease the way for the high number of neo-professionals taking part: the number of Spanish teams had grown to a record eight, which at least was one hopeful sign for the future. But any aspirations to equal the Giro or approach the Tour had been put very firmly on hold.

Among the Spanish teams making their debut were Zor (cigarette lighters), Reynolds (aluminium foil) and one that was to become an institution in Spanish cycling – Kelme. In 1979 Luis Puig and Enrique Franco, the Director of Unipublic, had asked the Alicante-based shoe and textile company if they'd like to sponsor the *Gran Premio de Montaña*. For four million pesetas they'd have a minute's exposure on TV each day. On the other hand, with 15 million pesetas they could sponsor a whole cycling team. That seemed a better investment, so they accepted a proposal from Rafael Carrasco, who would be Kelme's director for the first 12 years.

1980   A survey of the Spanish field in 1980 revealed ageing veterans like Miguel María Lasa in Zor and Pedro Torres in Kelme amid a mass of young inexperienced unknowns. The only truly competitive foreign squad was the Belgian Splendor, which featured Claude Criquelion, winner of the Setmana Catalana in 1979, Michel Pollentier, third in the previous Vuelta and soldiering on with a metal pin in his collar bone after crashing in the Paris–Roubaix, and 23-year-old Sean Kelly, already with a reputation as a deadly sprinter.

Kelly easily won the first two stages in Benidorm and Cullera. He was still relishing his new-found freedom from Freddy Maertens, especially as the peloton harboured few rivals. He looked set for a third stage two days later in San Quirze when he came up against Teka's Peter Thaler. The German rider launched his sprint early, creating a gap that seemed insurmountable, only to see it bridged by a lightning-fast Kelly. Yet it was Thaler who lifted his arms in triumph, while Kelly sprawled on the tarmac. In the ensuing commotion, veteran sprinting star Miguel Poblet gave his expert opinion: 'If I had to disqualify anyone, it would be Kelly.' With plenty of space at his disposal, the Irishman had chosen to make a bee-line for Thaler, who'd lashed out in self-defence. And, tellingly, Splendor made no official complaint.

As the peloton approached the Pyrenees, the increasingly rugged terrain inspired the Spanish riders to bring the foreign domination to an end. On stage 5, at the foot of the mountains, the attacks were constant, until the reigning Spanish Champion, Faustino Rupérez, of Zor, made the definitive move. On the descent of the Coll de Jeu, 43 kilometres from the finish, he jumped clear and arrived alone at the finish with a substantial 3'–28" lead on the peloton, led in by Sean Kelly in his blue points jersey.

No one expected Rupérez to retain the yellow jersey for long. Yet, as the race moved westwards towards Huesca, he impressed everyone by holding his own in a 15-strong breakaway, whose members tirelessly attacked each other as the finish drew near. It had been a long day, with five *puertos*, harsh road surfaces and incessant rain. Rupérez responded to each attack, fighting tooth and nail not to be dropped, and ending up in the final foursome before taking the stage in Jaca. He was regarded with new respect: perhaps the Vuelta had a solid leader after all.

The problem was that Rupérez hardly needed to prove his worth. He was allowed to retreat deep into the peloton, and hide there untested, as the race placidly toured the north of Spain, through Asturias and rain-soaked Galicia. On the road to Orense, the cyclists encountered a demonstration against the closure of a metalworking factory, and the workers were ruthlessly chased by the Civil Guard, who fired rubber bullets and shot their guns into the air. Even this unexpected turmoil failed to jolt the peloton out of its general inertia, or disturb Splendor from expertly leading out Kelly to his third stage-victory.

The León time-trial created some suspense, when Kelme's Pedro Torres, classified second overall, cut 37 seconds from Rupérez's 2'–55" lead, the more so because it was on the eve of the *etapa reina* in the Sierra de Madrid, with its three consecutive first-category climbs.

This challenging stage began with Zor in control, but on the Puerto de Morcuera, Rupérez was struggling to keep up with his rivals. When he lost sight of Pedro Torres, panic set in, and had he been alone, the race would have had a different resolution. But another veteran, his team-mate Miguel María Lasa, appeared by his side like a guardian angel, and after some cajoling and pushing, they were able to rejoin the leading group on the descent. Rupérez's moment of crisis was over.

For the second year running, half a million spectators lined the Paseo de Castellana in Madrid to watch the peloton ride round the circuit on the last day, while RTVE transmitted a game of billiards. Kelly scored his fifth stage-win, as well as winning the points jersey and finishing fourth overall. Pleased with the way he'd crossed the mountains, he was convinced that one day he could win the Vuelta. Surrounded by hundreds of enthusiastic fans all simultaneously trying to pat him on the back, Faustino Rupérez finally realised the full significance of his victory. The Soria-born cyclist, bewildered to be the centre of so much attention, was the first to admit he was not a new Ocaña: 'I don't see myself as a star'. As for the organisers, once again they could congratulate themselves that the odds had been overcome and another Vuelta had taken place.

* * * * *

'Everyone on the ground!' With these words, Antonio Tejero, a lieutenant-colonel in the Civil Guard, fired his pistol into the ceiling of Congress and, supported by a contingent of his men armed with machine-guns, took hostage almost the whole of Spain's political establishment. It was 23rd February 1981 and, as Spaniards around the country listened to the attempted *coup d'etat* live on their radios, it seemed their worst nightmare was about to be realised. Many destroyed documents, and prepared to flee the country, while in Valencia, one of the principal conspirators, Lieutenant-General Miláns del Bosch, released his tanks onto the street. Throughout that evening the King spoke directly to each of the country's leading generals and demanded their loyalty. The *coup*, he assured them, did not have his support. Late that night, wearing full uniform as head of the nation's armed forces, he appeared on television and gave the same message to the nation and to the conspirators. If they'd hoped to shelter behind his back, they were mistaken: the *coup* was not only an assault on the constitution, but on the king himself. As Paul Preston puts it, by his resolute action that night, 'he had cleared the monarchy of the stigma of Francoism and earned the right to be head of state.'

Events soon revealed, that the moustachioed Tejero, who cut something of a comic-opera figure, was the puppet of a far more serious faction of the ultra-conservative military. Suárez's government had been moving much too fast for their liking. They were particularly incensed by the legalisation of the Communist Party and the increased autonomy given to the regions: the legalisation of the Basque flag had sent them into apoplexy. While the conspirators sat out their prison sentences and the unrepentant Tejero fumed that 'Spain stinks of Marxism', Santiago Carillo, leader of the Communist Party, remarked of King Juan Carlos: 'What an excellent president of a republic he would have made.'

The resounding failure of the *coup* meant the danger of a military take-over abated, but these remained turbulent times, as extremists of all sides continued in their attempts to destabilise the new

democracy. Two months later, as the country was still reeling, the
Vuelta got on the road.

The race was beset with troubles of its own. Crippled by a limited **1981**
budget, the organisers couldn't attract big names, and paralysed by
the intransigence of RTVE, they were unable to offer decent media
exposure. The last straw was Teka's decision not to participate after
an argument over the low prize money and the far better financial
deal on offer to the foreign teams. The personal enmity between
their director, Santiago Revuelta, and Luis Puig meant neither would
back down. It was a tremendous setback to the race, since Teka had
taken over from Kas as Spain's strongest squad. They were led by
two burgeoning talents, Marino Lejarreta and Alberto Fernández,
who had turned up in Santander for the Prologue, only to leave
with their suitcases unpacked.

So it was a small peloton of only 80 riders that set off to complete
the extensive loop around Spain, which included Extremadura as
that year's neglected region to be brought into the fold. The two
outstanding days in the route book were a *crono-escalada* in the Sierra
Nevada, and a Catalan stage finishing at the ski station of Rassos
de Peguera. The only foreign team of note was Inoxpran (the
predecessor of Carrera) led by the intelligent all-rounder Giovanni
Battaglin. After making an impressive debut in 1973, when he
finished third in the Giro, Battaglin had been repeatedly hampered
by falls and bad luck, but at the age of 30 the Italian would enjoy
the best year of his career. The 1981 Vuelta could be summed up in
one line: Battaglin took the yellow jersey after the *crono-escalada* in
the Sierra Nevada and kept it to the end.

The punishing 30.5-kilometre uphill time-trial came after eight
uneventful days during which the yellow jersey had been on the
back of the young French hopeful, Régis Clère: he was the leader of
Miko-Mercier, who'd sent their reserve team – another reflection of
the current low status of the Vuelta. The great favourite was Battaglin
and, despite a puncture, he won easily. He seemed to glide up
effortlessly, although later admitted having suffered in the thick,
freezing fog: 'It was suffocating – you could've cut it with a knife.'
Indeed, various cyclists had to be given oxygen once over the line.
Pedro Muñoz, this year's 'revelation' (he was to finish the race in
second place) came second at 43 seconds, taking over from Rupérez
as Zor's leader.

Yet it had been a close run thing that the stage had taken place at all, because the local police had neglected to close the roads early enough. In the infernal traffic jam, the cyclists had to squeeze between the cars, carrying their bikes over their heads, just to reach the starting-line. Some had gone up without support vehicles, and faced a teeth-chattering wait at the top without warm clothes to change into. The Press bristled at this chaotic image of Spanish organisation the Vuelta was providing.

They had good reason to complain about the organisation of the second time-trial, a week later. In fact, it produced one of the Vuelta's still-unsolved mysteries. It was another of those days divided into two sectors: a morning road-race, won by Pedro Muñoz and an 11-kilometre time-trial in the afternoon, held in Zaragoza's Primo de Rivera park. When the results were announced, there was general astonishment that the most unlikely protagonist, a humble Zor *gregario* called José Luis López Cerrón had been credited with the best time. Perhaps the most shocked of all was the Zor rider himself, who hadn't counted on giving his team a second victory that day. Somehow he'd managed to beat all the specialists, despite crashing half-way through the ride. Miko-Mercier's director began to huff and puff about irregularities: if his rising star Clère, who'd clocked in 39 seconds behind the Spaniard, was not given the stage, they were going home.

The time-trial had taken place on a complex circuit, with various twists and turns, perhaps not as well sign-posted as it could have been, and one theory was that López Cerrón had taken a wrong turning. But he'd been proceeded by a civil guard car throughout, with a support car behind, and neither driver had noticed anything unusual. Those responsible for the timing hotly denied any error, and the wretched López Cerrón said: 'The truth is I can't explain my time, but I swear I didn't get towed by a car.'

In the end, it was decided that, after falling, he must have picked himself up and set off in the wrong direction, inadvertently shortening the route. Two minutes were deducted from his time, but he wasn't expelled, as the judges conceded he hadn't intended to cheat. But two questions were conveniently ignored: if the cyclist had gone the wrong way, why didn't the support car notice? Moreover, what if – instead of modest López Cerrón – the slip up had involved a specialist with serious designs on the overall?

None of this affected Battaglin, who continued his serene progress towards overall victory in Madrid. Only once did he give the impression of being vulnerable, and that was in the foothills of the Pyrenees on the stage to Rassos de Peguera. The climb to this ski station is one of the toughest in Catalunya, with a particularly brutal start to trap the unwary and ramps regularly reaching 11 per-cent throughout its 16.5 kilometres. There'd been constant attacks during the day, but the main contenders had held on for this final showdown. Kelme's Vicente Belda, keen to make up for his disappointing showing in the Sierra Nevada, where two punctures had cost him valuable time, jumped clear with 15 kilometres to go. Behind, Battaglin found himself deprived of any team-mates and surrounded by Spaniards. But the moment he attacked, all his rivals fell away, and it was as much as Belda could do to hang on to a 36-second lead. Battaglin's masterful reaction had dispelled any doubts as to the eventual outcome of the race. Already thinking ahead to the Giro, he wouldn't waste his energy in any further displays of strength.

The Vuelta's lack of suspense was in stark contrast to the tense atmosphere that enveloped the nation, as political violence continued in the aftermath of the failed *coup*, and intruded on the self-contained world of a cycling race. The day before his unlikely time-trial 'victory', López Cerrón had been given free rein to gallop off on a solo adventure through the Catalan heartlands. He won the stage into Belaguer, after news had broken that a group of left wing extremists, striking simultaneously in Madrid and Barcelona, had killed four people. López Cerrón dedicated his victory to the families of the victims – a gesture that was acknowledged the next morning, when a telegram of congratulations arrived from the head of the national police.

Two days later, three members of the military attached to the King's residence were killed and another seriously wounded by an Eta bomb in Madrid. The following day, it was only after almost the entire country had came to a stand-still at noon in an impressive two minute silence that the peloton set out for Segovia. That afternoon, Miguel María Lasa fought off his opponents to win in front of the famous Roman aqueduct. It was a fine way to conclude his last Vuelta and his cycling career, for as he announced after the stage, his retirement was imminent.

As expected, Battaglin carried his lead into Madrid. A picture of Italian elegance, the yellow jersey matching his smart gold watch, he would then go on to take the Giro, and join that élite club of those who have won two of the major stage races in the same year.

If the 1981 Vuelta had been ridden in the shadow of political events, the following year it would be a sporting event – the football World Cup that Spain was hosting in June – which would relegate it to the bottom of the sports pages. Luis Puig's announcement that it was to be a Vuelta 'for the Spaniards', prompted derision from Santiago Revuelta: 'That's what they say when negotiations fall through. It's absolute nonsense. At the moment, the Vuelta is lagging ten years behind the Giro or Tour.' Intentionally or not, there was no big name to dominate the race and no one dared predict a winner. Claude Criquelion of Splendor was tentatively mentioned – he'd come third in 1980 – as was the Swedish rider Sven-Ake Nilsson, of the French Wolber team.

1982 Despite Revuelta's disparaging comments, his team, Teka, were back and led by the promising Alberto Fernández and Marino Lejarreta who, to the intense pride of his fellow Basques, had won the first-ever Clasica San Sebastián. There were other clear signs that Spanish cycling was emerging from the wilderness. The Navarran team Reynolds (predecessor of Banesto) were steadily improving under the direction of José Miguel Echávarri and were currently euphoric after winning the Tour of the Basque Country with José Luis Laguía, and Julián Gorospe in second place. They'd turned all predictions on their head by beating the Italian star Francesco Moser, who'd expected to win at his leisure.

Another hopeful development was a thawing of RTVE's disapproval of cycling. Under Luis Puig's persistent pressure, the tentative step had been taken of transmitting two stages live: the prologue in Santiago de Compostela and the finale in Madrid. The route would be a tour of the northern half of Spain, the peloton leaving Galicia on an eastwards trek along the Cantabrian coast, skirting southwards to avoid the Basque Country, visiting the Catalan Pyrenees before touching the Mediterranean in Barcelona. It would then turn tail and head rapidly for the Sierra of Madrid in the centre.

The traditional antagonism between the Spaniards and Belgians flared up again this year, which, if nothing else, was a sign that the peloton was waking up. The first three stages went to Eddy

Planckaert of Splendor, but stage four, between the coastal town of Santander and Reinosa on the River Ebro, was clearly not designed for a sprinter, with its two first-category climbs, the Sía and Escudo. It was a day for the Spanish: Teka managed to place three men in the successful break – their two leaders plus Antonio Coll, who won the stage – while Reynold's Ángel Arroyo took advantage of their work to move up to second in the overall. But it was Splendor's Criquelion who secured the yellow jersey. It was especially vexing for the Spaniards to see the Belgian thrust himself over the Escudo in first place, collecting a handsome prize of 100,000 pesetas, which was more than the earnings of his team-mate Eddy Planckaert after three sprint wins.

With Splendor taking the lion's share of the money, it was only a matter of time before the smouldering resentment ignited. It occurred after a placid day rolling through the Ebro flatlands. Kelme's Juan Fernández had his eye on this stage, as the final kilometre into Alfajarín was steeply uphill, the kind of finish he enjoyed. He positioned himself at the front and attacked with 50 metres to go, only to be caught by Eddy Planckaert, who deftly grabbed his saddle and cut him off at a sharp corner. With the pair locked in an elbowing match, the Belgian, who'd already won the first four road stages, was ahead as they crossed the line, but the judges disqualified them both, and gave the stage to Reynold's José Laguía. As proof of RTVE's new interest in cycling, television footage was used for the first time as evidence in a dispute. Their daily résumés were a marked improvement on the lingering, picturesque shots of storks on church towers they'd offered in the past.

After the judges' decision, Splendor threatened to leave the race. Their director Albert de Kimpe commented: 'Eddy's victory has been normal. Totally normal. And if they don't think so, the Spanish riders should go abroad to race.' The veteran director's words were uncomfortably close to the bone. He'd been bringing teams to Spain since 1960, when Pérez Francés attacked him with a bike pump, and had witnessed the ups and downs of Spanish cycling at first hand, including this particularly insular phase, when only a handful of their riders were capable of finishing the Tour de France.

Finally, instead of quitting, Splendor opted for revenge. Apart from sprinting, another weak point of the Spaniards was echelon-formation. Taking advantage of the winds of Zaragoza, and enthusiastically helped by the other Belgian team in the race,

Splendor split the peloton in three. As Ángel Arroyo got caught in the second group, Reynolds had to work very hard to defend his second place. It was an exhausting day.

A 'Criquelion psychosis' had taken hold of the peloton ever since his strong performance on the Escudo, but in the first stage through the Catalan Pyrenees he started to show signs of weakness. On the Alto de Super Molina – at 1,950 metres the highest climb in the race – he lost touch with the leaders. There was a general regrouping on the long descent to the finish (a nightmare for Kelme's Vicente Belda, who punctured three times on the ice-cracked asphalt) and Criquelion held on to his jersey, but his vulnerability had been exposed. And the next day the general classification was given an abrupt shake-up.

It was one of those nervous stages, when the roads twist and turn, constantly changing gradient, making it impossible to find a regular rhythm – *rompepiernas* (leg-breaking) in Spanish jargon – and very difficult to control. Splendor wore themselves out chasing escapes – Pedro Delgado, making his Vuelta debut with Reynolds, was particularly active – so they could do nothing when, on the final short climb, Ángel Arroyo escaped. He found an amenable companion in Nilsson, who collaborated perfectly, allowing the pair to cross the line with an advantage of 1'–23". The stage went to the Swede and the yellow jersey to the Spaniard.

Arroyo seemed a precarious leader at first, losing 51 seconds of his gains almost immediately in the five laps of the Montjuic circuit in Barcelona. The yellow jersey, acquired so early in the race, seemed like a dead weight for Reynolds. Yet in the time-trial of La Mancha, it gave the small wiry Arroyo the proverbial wings. On a 35-kilometre circuit of false flats and strong wind, he decided to risk everything. 'I went full tilt throughout, without measuring my forces,' he said. And the gamble paid off, as he won with four seconds on team-mate Gorospe and 1'–45" on Criquelion, who, suffering with a chest infection, would abandon before reaching Madrid. Arroyo was suddenly a much more convincing proposition.

In comparison with recent editions, the '82 Vuelta had certainly been more spirited, although it ran out of steam towards the end. The final chance for a change in the general classification came in the Sierra de Madrid, with a summit finish on the Navacerrada. Teka repeatedly tried to attack but were thwarted by various alliances: Kelme collaborated with Reynolds to defend their team classification, while Zor also helped to chase Teka down because they wanted the stage for Pedro Muñoz. The day ended with the sound of expletives and recriminations: when Kelme's Vicente Belda made his move on the Navacerrada, Muñoz latched on to his wheel, where he clung tenaciously. In the final kilometre his strong acceleration gave him the stage, leaving Belda to fume.

Proclaimed the winner, a jubilant Arroyo went home to a hero's welcome in Barraco, in the province of Ávila. Four days later, the euphoria turned sour. He received a phone call from a journalist of *El Mundo Deportivo*, informing him that four cyclists had tested positive in the Vuelta and his name was among them. Arroyo laughed, thinking he was having his leg pulled.

On the list with Arroyo were Alberto Fernández, Pedro Muñoz and Vicente Belda: four of Spain's top cyclists, each riding in a different team. The product in question was 'Lidepran', taken as an antidepressant. There were 48 hours of suspense until the results of the second analysis appeared, and then it was confirmed that all four had tested positive for the stimulant methylphediate-facetoperane, one of the 39 substances banned in cycling at the time.

There was some readjusting to do: the first three on the Navacerrada (Muñoz, Belda and Arroyo) were penalised by ten minutes, and the stage-win given to Lejarreta who, finishing fourth, hadn't been tested that day. On general classification this penalty relegated Arroyo to thirteenth place, and gave overall victory to Lejarreta. The fourth rider on the list, Alberto Fernández, had tested positive on the last stage in Madrid.

After the shocking news, Lejarreta was not a particularly happy man: 'To win like this is like not winning. Arroyo has already taken away the glory.' He had words of sympathy for the disgraced cyclist: 'I feel sorry for him because he was the best in the race.' He knew full well that the Vuelta would always be remembered for the Arroyo doping case, not his own achievement. In fact, Lejarreta's victory was not officially confirmed until the following year, when Arroyo's appeal was finally rejected. It seemed like a race that nobody won.

Indirectly, the World Cup was to blame for the whole scandal. Clearly, Lidepran was widely used in the peloton – as Alberto Fernández explained: 'We only use it to help bear the suffering – just as someone might turn to a coffee, a drink or cigarette to calm down.' In other words, he argued, it wasn't a stimulant, but served to numb the pain a little. 'We knew it was banned, but those who took it on other occasions never had any problems.' Nobody had suspected that newer, more efficient testing equipment had been bought especially for the football championship.

It was the first (and only) time that the winner of a major stage race has been dishonoured in such a way. The Press tried to cheer themselves up by congratulating the Medical Control Commission of the Spanish Federation for proving that anti-doping controls were strictly applied in Spain. Unlike in France, they insinuated, remembering the widespread rumours of a suppressed positive test when Thévenet won the 1977 Tour.

Arroyo, however, was inconsolable: 'Even if they take my triumph away, I'll always feel like the moral winner of the race. No one can take that away from me.' He was a cyclist with immense potential but it was never properly realised. Luck wasn't on his side. In 1983, he made his debut in the Tour de France, nervous and out of place, thrown together with the even more overawed Colombians. Impressively, despite having to learn as he went along, he finished second overall, behind Laurent Fignon. But even that achievement was somewhat dwarfed by the emergence of Pedro Delgado, more charismatic and spectacular in style, who took up all the column inches back home. Finally, a debilitating illness cut Arroyo off in his prime, whereupon he retired and turned his back on the cycling world. He still runs his car-wash business in Ávila today.

* * * * *

At the end of 1982 the Socialist Party won a landslide victory in the general elections. Political power changed hands, and did so peacefully – a good indication that democracy had taken root. It seemed the Transition was over at last. For the Vuelta it was a propitious moment to draw a curtain on all its recent tribulations. The election results augured a new period of stability for Spain, one in which the national cycling race could flourish again.

Another Belgian sprint victory – Eddy Peelman
winning at Torrelavega in 1973.

The Basque rider Txomin
Perurena, a stalwart of Kas
during the 1970s, rode 14
Vueltas. In 1975 he held the
leader's jersey throughout
the third week, only to lose
it by 14 seconds in the final
time trial.

Luis Ocaña: Vuelta champion in 1970 and second on three other occasions – 'everything he did was tinged with heroism and tragedy'. Winning the Tour de France in 1973 was easier, he said, than winning the Vuelta, when 'it seemed I was expected to win each and every stage'.

José Manuel Fuente, winner in 1972 and '74. 'Restraining him was impossible, when his natural instinct was always to attack, even when tactically it made no sense.' Like his rival, Ocaña, he rose out of poverty to find glory, and an untimely death.

Mundo Deportivo

Marino Lejarreta, knicknamed 'the reed of Berriz'. In 1982 he won the Vuelta without getting to wear the yellow jersey, when Ángel Arroyo had to return his trophy after testing positive for a banned substance on the penultimate stage. Later in his career his speciality was riding all three of the major tours in the same year.

Hinault on the top step of the podium for the second time in 1983, despite the fierce resistance put up the Spaniards, and a crippling tendinitis that would ruin the rest of his season. 'When I got off the bike in Madrid I could scarcely walk, but at least I'd won.'

Cycle Sport

1983

A Vintage Year

After seven years of mediocrity and foreign domination, culminating in the Arroyo scandal, just as it was most needed, the Vuelta returned with one of its best editions ever. There was a vibrant atmosphere in prologue town Almusafes, with all the trappings of a modern cycling race: a television crew for daily live stage transmissions, a helicopter, a publicity caravan, not to mention the stars. The best cyclist in the world, Bernard Hinault, was there, and the Italian World Champion Giuseppe Saronni. A small miracle had taken place.

The route was much harder than it had been for a long time, outdoing the Giro this year with 38 *puertos*, 12 of them first-category. The organisers had prepared a special surprise with a stage in Asturias finishing high in the Picos de Europa by the Lake of Enol, which the cyclists immediately nicknamed the Lake of Hinault.

For, of course, there were fears that Hinault was going to do a Freddy Maertens and take the yellow jersey in the prologue, and keep it till Madrid. Hinault's palmarés was terrifying: four Tours, two Giros and a Vuelta. He fully expected to bag another Vuelta without undue stress, as in 1978, and then concentrate on joining the ranks of Anquetil and Merckx by winning a fifth Tour. As on his first visit to Spain, he was riding for Renault under the guidance of Cyrille Guimard, but their long and fruitful relationship was showing signs of strain.

Unexpectedly, the prologue was won by Hinault's young team-mate, Dominique Gaigne, a 21-year-old neo-professional, who'd gone straight back to the hotel after his turn, job done for the day, and was fined for not showing up for the podium ceremony. The route had some dangerous curves – Saronni fell, a bad omen – and Hinault explained with crushing self-confidence why he wasn't in a hurry: 'With 3,000 kilometres left to dispute, it was absurd to risk everything in the first six. I know when I'll put on the yellow jersey, and as long as I don't have an accident, no one will take it off me.'

The Press echoed Hinault's conviction; after so many lacklustre years and the debacle of '82, there was an entrenched pessimism about the homegrown riders, who seemed as complacent as ever when, at the end of the first stage, Hinault provoked a cut in the peloton just outside Cuenca. Most of the peloton waited for Saronni to take the initiative, which he failed to do, allowing the Breton to gain a few seconds. One who did respond was Juan Fernández of Reynolds, whose familiarity with the steep cobbled rise leading to Cuenca's main square gave him the winning edge.

Those hoping to see a battle between Hinault and Saronni were angered by the Italian's lack of ambition, although he'd been perfectly honest about his intentions: 'I'm coming to the Vuelta to prepare for the Giro, my main goal of this season.' This won him few friends, but clearly the preparation was ideal – he won the Giro the following month. His idea in Spain had been to win the yellow jersey in the prologue and pick up some stages, but events weren't turning out as planned. In Teruel, at the end of an uncomfortably cold and wet stage, Saronni's team, Del Tongo, prepared the ground perfectly. Rudy Pevenage and German Champion Dietrich Thurau took turns at the front, stretching out the peloton with their diabolical pace. As he began his sprint, Saronni failed to notice the young Belgian of Aernodout, Eric Vanderaerden, powering from behind to overtake him on the line. Not a gracious loser, Saronni blamed a motorbike for obstruction, rather than his own lack of form. With stories already circulating of the Italian getting towed up hills, he was carving out a niche for himself as the villain of the race.

As the peloton made their way north through Catalunya, José Antonio Cabrero of Hueso, one of Spain's most modest teams, attacked eight kilometres from the finish in Sant Quirze de Vallès, and Hinault's top *domestique*, 22-year-old Laurent Fignon didn't hesitate to jump on his wheel. This inspired Antonio Coll of Teka and Marino Lejarreta – who'd taken the unusual decision to go abroad and ride for an Italian team, Alfa Lum – to do likewise. The Hueso rider found himself outclassed and was soon dropped, and with Lejarreta doing most of the work, Fignon took the stage, although the Basque was rewarded by moving from 29th to 10th on general classification. Fignon had to listen to harsh words from his leader that evening for having lured Lejarreta out of the peloton, inadvertently cutting Hinault's lead on Marino to only 20 seconds on the eve of the first tough mountain stage. Hinault could never have suspected he was admonishing the winner of the next two Tours de France, and the usurper of his position in the team.

'The Vuelta begins today', proclaimed *El País* before the fifth stage, which finished in a tiny Catalan village, Castellar de N'Hug, high up in the folds of the Pyrenean foothills. With Renault in command, the peloton arrived intact at the base of the final 30-kilometre climb, where Vicente Belda of Kelme launched the hostilities. A group of the strongest formed up front: Lejarreta, Hinault, Fignon and Alberto Fernández of Zor, his morale high after winning the Setmana Catalana. When Alberto jumped, he kept clear of his pursuers to the end, Hinault and Lejarreta coming in three seconds behind. The Breton was the new race leader, and in a fit of pessimism *El País* concluded: 'He will now keep the yellow jersey to the end.' This, after all, had always been the case with foreign superstars who descended upon the Vuelta.

More hardship for the peloton as they moved westwards to Vall d'Aran. Snow-ploughs saved the day, as heavy snowfalls threatened to disrupt the scheduled route over the Port de la Bonaigua, where Alberto Fernández made a powerful attack and was first over the top. Hinault was close behind but he looked uncomfortable, inspiring Lejarreta, and Reynold's Pedro Delgado and Julián Gorospe – winner of this year's Tour of the Basque Country – to break away with Alberto on the vertiginous descent. Marino won the sprint and, for the first time in his career, pulled on the yellow jersey, which was somewhat ironical for a cyclist who already had a Vuelta in his palmarés.

In spite of all his boasting, Hinault's time in yellow had only lasted for 24 hours. His supremacy was suddenly in doubt; a small crack had appeared in his armour. The Breton had unknowingly timed his return to Spain to coincide with the flowering of a new generation of cyclists, who'd given an exhibition that day. The first ten to arrive in Vielha had all been Spanish. Second on general classification was Gorospe with the same time as Lejarreta, and Hinault was third, 22 seconds behind the two Basques. Of course Hinault was still feared, especially with a time-trial coming up, but national morale was sky-high.

Saronni confirmed his role as official blackguard during the Sabiñanigo stage, instigating a strike, which was rapidly backed up by the Belgians. There was a short, neutralised sector to cover the five-kilometre tunnel of Vielha, but on finding snow flurries on the other side, the foreign riders forced the organisers to shorten the stage still further by refusing to ride, and they were taken the next

73 kilometres by car. *Dicen*'s veteran reporter Antonio Vallugera was disgusted: 'The cyclists of a not-far-off past were of a different cast.' He recalled how Jesús Loroño had been forcefully pulled off his bike on the Puerto de Pajares in a blizzard, and reflected that the antics of Saronni and the other *señoritos* (spoilt rich boys) would not be tolerated in the Tour or Giro. Pedro Delgado remembers the day for catching one of the worst bouts of flu of his cycling career, after sitting around in soaked clothes on the drive to the point where the stage was resumed.

The controversy was quickly forgotten as the cyclists turned their thoughts to the difficult 38-kilometre *crono-escalada* to the mountain spa resort of Panticosa in the Huescan Pyrenees. Everyone expected Hinault to reclaim the yellow jersey, but instead of his usual display of brute strength – even on the hardest of ramps, he would stay in the saddle and punish his kidneys – he was reduced to zig-zagging and standing on the pedals. When Alberto Fernández reached the finish, having nearly overtaken Hinault, he was convinced he'd won. Glued to the chronometer, he and everyone else were dumbfounded when Lejarreta came in ten seconds quicker to win the stage: the Basque had been polishing up his time-trialling in Italy, with excellent results.

When the result finally sunk in that Lejarreta had beaten Hinault by over two minutes, the reaction was ecstatic. There was hurt pride to be avenged: 'For the French Press, who until yesterday were ridiculing our cyclists, this is a lesson,' said *Dicen*. Marino was a hero, but so taciturn and grave that his mother voiced her worries about him in public: 'The only thing I ask for is that he gets married. I don't want him at home getting old. He *likes* girls. But he's so serious…'

Lejarreta didn't have an easy time ahead. Alfa Lum were much weaker than Zor or Reynolds and he was justified to be wary of Hinault. The beast was wounded and therefore extremely dangerous: 'When I'm behind on time I get really aggressive. If I'm not wearing the jersey that should be mine, I take every opportunity to snatch a few seconds, regardless of the effort.'

The newly televised Vuelta was an enormous hit with the public, proving that cycling is one of the most television-friendly of sports. In the words of Antonio Vallugera, 'Marino Lejarreta has turned into Bobby and Hinault into J.R.' The other 'baddy', Saronni, had finished in Panticosa over eight minutes down and blamed it on his bronchitis. *El País* noted that: 'It is curious how Saronni increases his rate of coughing whenever a microphone or pen appears in front of him.' Having taken it easy, the Italian had good legs the next day, and won his first sprint.

Two days after the time-trial, Hinault prepared an ambush. On the windy Meseta, 35 kilometres from Soria, Renault's Maurice Le Guilloux and Hennie Kuiper of Aernodout signalled to each other and the Dutchman made a powerful surge, with Hinault immediately on his wheel. Only three Spanish riders were alert, or strong enough, to latch on: Alberto Fernández of Zor, Martínez Heredia of Hueso and Julián Gorospe of Banesto. Hueso's director, Miguel Moreno, had overheard that the foreigners were up to something, and passed on the information to Echávarri, director of Reynolds, which explained Gorospe's presence. Lejarreta had been caught off-guard: he saw the peloton breaking in two and desperately tried to cross to the front group. 'There was a moment when I was about two metres behind ... but I don't know how to ride against the wind,' sighed Marino, nicknamed 'the reed of Berriz' for his skinny build. He lost all his Panticosa gains, and fell to fourth place. Saronni won the stage and the new leader was Gorospe, with only two seconds on Alberto Fernández, and 2'–02" on Hinault. The Badger was back in the race, announcing with satisfaction: 'Today the most dangerous man of the Vuelta has been eliminated.'

What were supposed to be days of transition before the much awaited mountain stage in Asturias became an ordeal for the Spaniards – at the mercy of the wind and Hinault's ruthless attacks, one of which cost Gorospe enough seconds to lose the yellow jersey to Alberto Fernández in Logroño. Hinault and Kuiper provoked another cut on the Burgos stage, only giving up when no one important was caught out. But 13 kilometres from the end, a tireless Hinault lashed out again, jumping clear with Saronni on his wheel and Alberto Fernández had to work strenuously to close the gap. Defending the yellow jersey was using up all his resources: 'Every day is a battle,' said the Zor leader, tired and frazzled after the stage. 'I'm strong, but I don't know how long I'll last. There's still a lot of race left.'

The *etapa reina* culminated in a sinuous 12-kilometre climb beginning by the basilica of Covadonga, a symbol of Asturian identity, and rising to the glacial lake of Enol. The hardest kilometre, a precipitous stretch that grinds upwards at a 15 per-cent gradient, is named *La Huesera*, or 'Bone Deposit', the site of a bloody battle in the eighth century, when the Moors were driven out of Asturias. Nowadays, it's a point of debate among cyclists whether it's better to attack on *La Huesera* or afterwards.

The day began cold and wet. After the Puerto del Pontón, there was a terrible descent of over 40 kilometres, its dangerous curves and loose gravel breaking up the peloton. Rudy Pevenage of Tonga and Carlos Machín of Hueso had escaped, establishing an eight-minute gap, but when they started the final climb, the Belgian seemed nailed to the ground, hardly able to turn the pedals. Lejarreta was desperate to avenge himself after the Soria debacle, and as soon as the peloton were in sight of the basilica, he attacked. Hinault positioned himself at the front of the field and pulled with all his might, aware of the danger, but Lejarreta's gap grew bigger and bigger.

The Spaniards briefly dropped Hinault, but near the lakes, the gradient eases off, which allowed him to recover and even finish the stage in second place, with Alberto Fernández, Gorospe and Muñoz just behind. Marino had won back 1'–11" with his magnificent climb, inscribing his name as the first victor of what is now a Vuelta classic. He had pushed past Hinault to fourth place, but the differences at the top of the overall remained slight. Nothing had been decided.

The yellow jersey changed hands yet again after the León stage. The peloton had to cross the traditional Puerto de Pajares, which was not what it used to be, the road wider and less steep in its modern version – the era of Seat 600s cooling off at the top had gone. On the summit, a 25-strong breakaway had a 15-minute lead, which increased on the descent. Javier Mínguez, Zor's director, had taken a big risk by placing five of his men in this group, leaving Alberto Fernánadez exposed behind. Kelme also had five representatives and the two teams formed an alliance. Although Carlos Hernández of Reynolds won the stage, Zor's Álvaro Pino was the surprise new race leader, overcome by emotion on the podium, declaring loyalty to dethroned Alberto Fernández.

Another alliance had formed that day, with potentially violent consequences. When the main field were approaching León Hinault attacked, and Saronni protected his rear by blocking the Spaniards, allowing the Frenchman to establish a gap and gain 28 seconds on his rivals at the finish. Afterwards, Alberto Fernández approached

Saronni and said to his face, 'As a champion you're not worth shit!' When Mínguez complained on the radio that the foreigners were ganging up together, playing underhand tricks, all hell broke lose. The following day's time-trial in Valladolid was predictably won by Hinault, although he didn't have the satisfaction of putting on the elusive yellow jersey – too slippery for anyone to grasp for long – since this was returned to Gorospe, who only yielded ten seconds. Alberto Fernández's ride was disappointing: he finished seventh at 1'–24" – his team-mate Álvaro Pino did better at 1'–15". Zor's leader was edgy, suffering from bronchitis and sleeping badly. Lejarreta also lost more time than he should have, out of his element on an entirely flat 22-kilometre circuit. In the overall, Pino was second at 27 seconds, and Hinault third at 1'–11". Alberto was fourth, with the same time, and Marino fifth at 2'–23".

There was still work for Hinault to do, but Mínguez's declarations had awakened tremendous public hostility against him. When he climbed on to the podium after the time-trial, the whistling and booing were deafening. He moved to a continuous soundtrack of insults and threats. When a boy patted him on the back just before the start of the Salamanca stage, a snarling Hinault turned round and kicked him, enraging the crowd even further. The tension was reaching exploding point.

What Hinault urgently needed was to redeem himself by winning in style, instead of resorting to sly tricks. The stage to Ávila, with four *puertos*, two of them first-category, provided him with just such an opportunity. The peloton set off quickly in the rain, with Reynolds in control. On the first climb of Peña Negra, Hinault limited himself to giving small accelerations, and the bunch stayed grouped together. His definitive move came on the Puerto de Serranillos, 18 kilometres long with several hard ramps. He had Fignon set the pace, and when he attacked, only Lejarreta could follow. They soon overtook a small breakaway, from which Belda tagged on.

Reynolds and Zor were unable to react in defence of their men. By the top of Serranillos, Gorospe's group was two minutes down, with one *puerto* still to climb. Lejarreta and Belda began to collaborate with Hinault when they realised that those left behind would never catch up, and the Breton sprinted past them to win in the velodrome in Ávila. Glowing with triumph, he declared: 'I dedicate this victory to Mínguez. He said the foreigners were helping me out, but today

I've shown, not with words but with the bicycle, that I don't need anyone's help.' He had praise for Lejarreta: 'Once again Marino has shown his great class ... I have to admit that he lost the Vuelta in Soria.' The exhausted Basque gave his verdict: 'Hinault was unbeatable today. It was hard enough for me just to keep up.'

The Badger had destroyed the peloton. Inexperienced Gorospe paid dearly for trying to match his pace on the climb of Serranillos: he blew up and lost over 20 minutes, although without the support of his team, he might never have arrived at all. Alberto Fernández came in 7th at 3'–58". The final podium was already settled: Lejarreta had moved up to second place at 1'–12", also taking the points jersey, and Alberto was third at 3'-58". The team prize went to Zor, although Mínquez's direction was questionable: he'd placed five men in the final top ten, but failed to protect Alberto for the key stages.

Hinault had shown various facets of his character. He could be what the Spanish call a *chulo*, a rogue, and also incredibly tenacious in pursuit of victory, never giving up, which is what made him such an exciting competitor. The fierce resistance put up by the Spaniards caught him by surprise, but he rose to the challenge, although at a price. The tendinitis that had plagued him at the beginning of the season had crept back, becoming excruciating after the Ávila stage: 'I had to hold on for two days and didn't want to pull out when I was so close to victory.' In *Memories of the Peloton* he describes with typical bravado how he concealed the pain from his rivals, and while a more cautious cyclist would have retired, that was unthinkable for Hinault: 'When I got off the bike [in Madrid] I could scarcely walk, but at least I'd won.'

And destroyed the rest of his season. This Vuelta marked the end of Hinault's relationship with Guimard. There'd been a very public row between them in a restaurant when the director had raged against the Breton for drinking wine. The argument and the knee would give young Fignon (who'd finished the Vuelta in 7th place) the chance of his life.

1984-1989

Becoming European

At the same time as the Socialist Party's electoral victory placed a young dynamic group of people in charge of the country, there was an injection of new blood into cycling. Pedro Delgado explains: 'There was an important change in Spain at the beginning of the eighties; from having only two professional teams, there were suddenly over eleven. Most of the people in charge of these teams were young, without much experience or knowledge of races outside of Spain.' Rather than undergoing a transition, Spanish cycling was starting again from zero.

This decade also saw the breaking down of traditional cycling frontiers, with the appearance of Colombian, American and Russian riders. It was quite reassuring for the Spaniards to have these rookies in the peloton, but the greatest boost to their confidence was the arrival of a new hero, Pedro Delgado, who became a symbol of Spanish cycling's return to the highest international level, and of Spain's arrival in Europe.

* * * * *

Opening his suitcase, Eric Caritoux cursed when he realised he'd **1984** forgotten his slippers. He was in a hotel room in Jerez de la Frontera, a town of whitewashed houses in the hills of Cádiz. He'd packed in a hurry, not expecting to spend Easter in Andalucía, but when the director of French team Skil found he had to fulfil contractual obligations with the Vuelta, he'd hastily rung round to assemble nine riders, and dispatched them to Spain with instructions to do what they could. Caritoux, who was normally Sean Kelly's right hand man, was going to have to get used to the idea of riding without his team leader – busy at the classics – and making do without his slippers for three weeks.

One of the star attractions in 1984 was Francesco Moser with his revolutionary bicycle. He'd just pulverised Eddy Merckx's 1972 world record, breaking through the 50kph barrier, using disc-wheels and a bull-horn bar. The UCI, although a little nonplussed by these technical advances, accepted his time of 51.51kph. There was great curiosity to see Moser on his super machine in the Prologue, but the cobbled streets of Jerez de la Frontera were slippy with melted candle wax from the Easter processions, and he preferred to use his conventional bike. The cobbles must have reminded him of the Paris–Roubaix, which he'd won for three consecutive years, and he took the first yellow jersey, which he would keep through the long coastal trek up to Catalunya.

Any hopes of enjoying the duel currently dominating Italian cycling, between him and his arch-rival Saronni, soon faded. 'Beppe' rode anonymously, until deciding that he'd had enough during a hailstorm on the 16th stage to Valladolid. The Press chased off their favourite villain, snapping at his heels with terms like 'money-grubber' and 'parasite'. Another man who'd marked the Giro as his main goal for the year was Marino Lejarreta, riding in the Italian Alfa Lum team. When questioned about racing in a foreign team, he was adamant: 'If I've progressed in my profession, it's thanks to my decision to go abroad.' When pressed for more details, he was tactful: 'Spanish cycling is different from the rest.'

Lejarreta was unconsciously echoing the famous and ambiguous slogan, 'Spain is different', used by Manuel Fraga to attract foreign tourists when he was Minister for Tourism in the 1960s. Always a controversial phrase, with its echoes of Franco's 'Spaniards are different', which served as a justification of his authoritarian regime, it nevertheless persists to this day, although mostly in bouts of self-criticism rather than promotion. 'Different or stupid?' demanded *Dicen's* veteran reporter, Antonio Vallugera, after the fourth stage between Elche and Valencia. His angry tirade was mainly directed against the Spanish team directors.

There'd been an important breakaway on the second-category climb of La Carresqueta, with potentially interesting consequences for the overall classification, since it included a range of top figures, such as Alberto Fernández and Faustino Rupérez of Zor, Vicente Belda of Kelme and Julián Gorospe of Reynolds. Yet after establishing a three-minute advantage, the escape fell apart, with Belda and Gorospe inexplicably refusing to cooperate. As the group were about to be swallowed by the peloton, Nico Edmonds, one of the Belgians riding for the Spanish team Teka, decided to try his luck solo. It was reasonable to imagine that the Belgian and Italian teams would organise a chase, since the finish was ideal for sprinters, but mystifyingly, it was the Spanish teams who drove the peloton, with yellow jersey Moser comfortably ensconced behind them. For further irony, the eventual mass sprint was won by the other Teka Belgian, Noel Dejonckheere, who, when asked if he found the development of the stage at all strange, shrugged: 'I've been racing in Spain for five years, and nothing surprises me any more.'

The overriding principle, it seemed, was to prevent the victory of any rider in a rival Spanish team at any cost. It was an obsession that had given the Tour of Valencia to the Frenchman Bruno Cornillet and the Catalan Week to the Australian Phil Anderson, after the Spaniards had dominated both races but forgotten about these well-placed foreigners in their zeal to mark each other. 'It's almost impossible for two Spaniards to reach an agreement in cycling,' complained a deeply frustrated Alberto Fernández after Djonckheere's victory in Valencia. 'What's infuriating is that the foreigners laugh at you. Today there could've been an important selection, and yet only Teka and Zor fought for it.'

After a week on the Belgian-dominated flat, the climbers were looking forward to the summit finish of Rassos de Peguera. At the foot of the 16-kilometre climb, Eduardo Chozas launched Zor's attack, and the peloton shattered. Then, with ten kilometres still to go, his leader Alberto Fernández jumped away, to be rapidly joined by Skil's Eric Caritoux. Anxious to shake off his tenacious companion, Alberto repeatedly accelerated, but when a pursuing trio of Pedro Delgado and two of Teka's Colombian riders began advancing from behind, it was Alberto they overtook – he'd been dropped by Caritoux. The Frenchman's more cautious tactics had paid off, and he won the stage by 16 seconds, although it was Delgado who was the new race leader.

This was Perico's* first yellow jersey, at the age of 24. He was on his way to fame and fortune, although it was going to be a roller-coaster ride. There was an aura of the picaresque surrounding Delgado; he was a hero who needed to live off his wits because pitfalls lurked around each corner. One day he might be basking in glory, and the next day grovelling his way through a devastating *pájara*. Fabulous success could dissolve into catastrophe at the drop of a hat. His wife has commented: 'Pedro's most outstanding quality is his positive attitude to all his small disasters ... his innate ability

---

* Perico is a popular nickname for Pedro

to see life as a game.' Such cheerful resilience, coupled with his exciting attacking style, always endeared him to the Spanish public.

Born into a modest family in Segovia, where his father worked as a truck driver, in 1981 he'd been persuaded to give up his Technical Sanitary Assistant studies, and was signed up by the young and ambitious team director Echávarri for his amateur squad Reynolds. 'Ô là là!' was how the French commentator reacted when watching Delgado's extreme aerodynamic descending style in the 1983 Tour, bum in the air, nose nearly rubbing the front wheel. His most famous cycling exploits took place in France, but it was the Vuelta that established him as a national hero. He was enjoying his first taste of glory in 1984, but in a highly precarious position, with Caritoux second at 11 seconds, closely followed by the two Teka Colombians, Edgar Corredor and Patrocinio Jiménez, with Alberto Fernández in fifth place at just 40 seconds.

Although a Spaniard led the Vuelta, the spectators were still waiting for a home stage-win, and it was already more than half-way through the race. The uneasiness became full-blown anxiety when Teka's German rider Raimund Dietzen won stage 12 up to the Lagos de Covadonga, and Caritoux took the yellow jersey from Pedro Delgado, who'd been dropped on the demanding slopes. In a virtual replay of the Rassos de Peguera stage, Alberto Fernández rode with his heart, not his head, accelerating impatiently while Dietzen and Caritoux stuck to his wheel. When he'd worn himself out, they rode off without him. Alberto was left with the consolation of rising to second overall at 32 seconds, and still with the hope of overtaking the Frenchman in the final time-trial.

When the race arrived in Oviedo, a five-strong breakaway fought out the stage: there were four Spaniards and a Belgian. When Guido Van Calster won, there was general despair: the dearth of Spanish victories now matched the record-breaking year of 1977, when there had, at least, been the excuse of an acute shortage of good Spanish cyclists. Julián Gorospe prevented a new record being set by winning the uphill time-trial on the Naranco, outside Oviedo, watched by massive crowds impervious to the torrential rain, but Eric Caritoux showed he had good climbing legs, as well as courage after running the gauntlet of spitting and missile-throwing spectators. He finished second, five seconds ahead of Alberto Fernández.

'Who is this Caritoux?' people asked. Even in France there was a misconception that he was Swiss. A French camera crew was hastily dispatched to Spain when it became clear his bid for the Vuelta was serious. Those who knew him, however, were not surprised by his excellent performance. A native of Provence, where his family cultivated vineyards, one of his regular training grounds was Mont Ventoux.

The *etapa reina* in 1984 was the stage in the Sierra de Madrid that finished in Segovia, Delgado's home town. Less than a minute behind Alberto Fernández and Eric Caritoux in the overall, Perico escaped on the final descent in typical daredevil style, leaving his more cautious rivals behind. They were without any team support, so when the gap reached 30 seconds, he had good reason to think, 'Today's my day!' Yet, with the help of Moser and Simone Masciarelli, they pulled him back. 'I was filled with a terrible rage,' he remembers in his autobiography, 'and I even asked Moser – him an Italian champion and all – what he had stood to gain in chasing me down.' Moser only smiled sarcastically: 'Calm down, *caro*, calm down.' Delgado observed: 'That day I found out about alliances in cycling and I felt cheated.' Robert Millar would echo those sentiments a year later.

Alberto Fernández had stacked all his hopes on the penultimate day's 33-kilometre time-trial, held in the outskirts of Madrid, but the heavy rain betrayed him. The 37-second gap between himself and Caritoux was reduced to six seconds, but that was not enough, and Alberto had to admit defeat: 'This has been the greatest disappointment of my life.' In December he went to Madrid to pick up an award for the best Spanish cyclist of the year and told the audience: 'Next year, I'll be going for the Vuelta again.' Tragically, both he and his wife were killed in a car crash that night while driving home.

As for Caritoux, he went back to Provence, with the Vuelta trophy in his suitcase, and resumed his career as a much-valued *domestique*.

* * * * *

When Robert Millar came to Spain in April of 1985, as team-leader **1985** of French Peugeot, he was still on a high after winning the King of the Mountains prize in the previous year's Tour de France, the only Britain to ever do so. A prickly character, the Scot didn't court journalists, who found him rude and monosyllabic. Yet he was impeccably professional, earning respect in the peloton and among team-mates. In Spain, this diminutive and sharp-faced cyclist cut a somewhat peculiar figure, with his pierced ear, long hair and vegetarian diet. He complained about the stir his ear-ring caused, but it must have been a rather gratifying confirmation of his unconventionality.

The Vuelta had never been so international as it was in 1985. President Ronald Reagan might have been living out his Star Wars fantasy, but Unipublic had no time for the Cold War, and booked into the same Valladolid hotel were the amateur squad Union Sovietica and the American Xerox-Philadelphia, directed by Robin Morton – a woman, what ever next? But the team arousing the most fascination was the Colombian Varta, with their numerous entourage and 200 kilos of *panelas* – sweets made of sugar cane juice, which the *escarabajos* (or beetles, as the small Colombian climbers were nicknamed) ate to fuel their attacks in the mountains. They'd chosen a good year for their Vuelta debut since there were four summit finishes and of the 37 puertos, ten were first-category. And to keep Colombia up-to-date on her heroes' exploits, two radio stations – Radio Caracol and Radio Nacional de Colombia – competed with ever more feverish commentary.

The home favourite was Pedro Delgado, who'd been lured away from Reynolds by Orbea–Seat with the biggest contract in the history of Spanish cycling, as the Press never tired of repeating. He and team-mate Pello Ruiz Cabestany, recent winner of the Basque Country Tour and ex-Basque Nordic Ski champion, were hogging all the limelight. They represented a new breed of Spanish cyclist: cheerfully ambitious and self-assured, neither took up cycling to escape poverty or for lack of other opportunities. Some old-school directors viewed them with suspicion as over-educated and overpaid.

Kas reappeared in the '85 peloton, now registered in France and led by Sean Kelly, with Caritoux by his side. There was also the 'best team in the world', Panasonic, directed by Peter Post. Not unexpectedly, it was their leader, Bert Oosterbosch, who won the prologue in Valladolid. Rather more surprising was the young unknown who finished second that day: 20-year-old Miguel Induráin of Reynolds.

The first week was tumultuous. Strong winds, rain and an unwieldy peloton filled with novices made a recipe for tension and crashes, the fourth stage in Galicia being particularly hectic. A sheep dog invaded the peloton and left two cyclists seriously injured. Then, the labyrinthine route through La Coruña tied the race into knots, when for a while the broom wagon was at the head and support cars were driving off in the opposite direction. At the finish in Lugo, as Eddy Planckaert celebrated his second sprint victory, two other Belgians sorted out a private dispute in a fist fight.

The Colombians were also to blame for toughening up the race. Aware of a whole nation glued to the radio back home, they were raring to go and decided that the moderately hilly second stage between Zamora and Orense would serve nicely for a preliminary attack. The results were impressive. On a third-category climb they dynamited the race and the scene at the finish was redolent of a Pyrenees stage, with riders trailing in exhausted. Oosterbosch lost 20 minutes, two of the Americans were eliminated, and Induráin swapped his white, best neo-professional jersey for yellow, to become the youngest Vuelta leader ever. His director, Echávarri, hailed him as 'the new Francesco Moser' because of his big build and time-trialing abilities. Sean Kelly, strong in this low mountainous terrain, unlike his Panasonic rival, Eddy Planckaert, won the sprint.

The first real test came on stage 6, when the peloton had to confront the Covadonga climb. Lucho Herrera, Varta's leader, attacked first and created a select group up front, including his team-mate Fabio Parra, Zor's Colombian leader Pacho Rodríguez, Orbea's Pedro Delgado and Pello Ruiz Cabestany, and Robert Millar. The Scot was next to accelerate, and he maintained his pace without looking back, the others on his wheel. Delgado waited for the final kilometre to strike, and when he did, no one could follow. In the very place where the previous year he'd lost the yellow jersey he became the new race leader. In the overall, his team-mate Ruiz Cabestany was seven seconds back and Millar was third at 13 seconds. The casualties of the day were Induráin, who lost 13 minutes, and Sean Kelly nearly four minutes.

There was another summit finish on the following stage in the Alto de Campoo ski station in Cantabria. Sean Kelly, out to retrieve his losses on the steep gradients of Covadonga, knew his only chance was to escape early on and tackle the two final first-category climbs ahead of the peloton. So he attacked on the descent of La Carmona on the Asturian–Cantabrian border, but luck deserted him as he punctured at the foot of the woody Puerto de Palombera. It was here that the Colombian Varta team put their plan into action. They sent one rider on the attack to break up the peloton, and created a small leading group of Millar, Pacho Rodríguez, and Ruiz Cabestany – a trio who would become well acquainted with each other in the next couple of weeks – as well as their own José-Antonio 'Tomate' Agudelo. Ruiz Cabestany was not an outstanding climber – his strength was against the clock – but he kept his head and a steady rhythm. On the final climb, as in Covadonga, Millar made constant accelerations, but his adversaries were able to match every one. Then, a kilometre from the top, Agudelo pounced with a successful bid for the stage. 'El Tomate wins. El Tomate wins,' intoned the Colombian broadcasters, over and over, in an ecstatic trance.

Perico had lost 3'–49" after suffering one of his famous *pájaras*, but the yellow jersey stayed with Orbea, on the back of Ruiz Cabestany. Millar, second at only six seconds, was confident it would soon be his, rating the young Basque as a far easier and less experienced rival than Delgado. 'He's young, and classy,' he said, 'but let's see if he can control the race.'

On the ninth stage Ruiz Cabestany knew everyone's eyes were on him, waiting to see if he'd crack on the slopes leading to the Pyrenean spa of Panticosa. Varta's Fabio Parra had attacked, but the situation was under control. Ruiz Cabestany and Delgado had Millar under close surveillance, as the three rode together in the final kilometres. The Basque could feel satisfied with his performance – he was resisting well. Then, to his consternation, Pedro Delgado jumped without any warning, and disappeared up the road in search of the Colombian. Ruiz Cabestany was suddenly left alone with Millar, who didn't hesitate to follow Delgado's example. Fuelled by indignation, the Basque was not only strong enough to stay with Millar but, in a burst of rage, overtook him on the line.

The two Orbea men had a heated row. Fabio Parra had won the stage, and Delgado had put the yellow jersey in danger. For what? A few paltry seconds. The truth was that Perico had been unable to contain his anxiety to win back lost time. He was furious with himself for having cracked the previous day, and his notorious salary made him an easy object of taunts. Txomin Perurena, Orbea's director, held a team meeting to restore harmony, but in any case, circumstances would soon oblige them to put aside their differences.

Stage 10 was in the lower reaches of the Pyrenees, from Sabiñanigo to Tremp, the kind of hard day of constant small climbs that made Sean Kelly rub his hands with anticipation. Colombian Martín Ramírez was first to stir up hostilities, rapidly joined by Kelly, Millar, Pacho Rodríguez, Álvaro Pino, the Russian Ivan Ivanov and Fabio Parra. Stranded behind, Orbea's Dynamic Duo spent a grim day chasing, and with Fagor's help, were able to limit their losses to half a minute. Kelly, in his element, won the stage, having taken the longest stints on the front, though he had plenty of collaboration from Millar, who was riding into the yellow jersey. Ruiz Cabestany dropped to second overall at 24 seconds and Pacho Rodríguez was third at 37 seconds.

The toughness of this Vuelta had defeated the Americans, who'd all given up and gone home. Not so the Soviets, whose team remained intact. Their director Gamady Godunov explained how they functioned: 'In my country professional sport doesn't exist. The State gives us the clothes, bikes and everything we need, but we don't get paid. They only give us what we lose at work when we go to compete.' The team included a railway engineer, PE teacher, soldier and lathe operator. Godunov was angry that he hadn't been sent a route book. If he'd known it was going to be such a mountainous race, he would have brought climbers rather than roadmen.

As the peloton rode into Andorra, there was no respite. 'It seemed more like a motorbike race than a cycle race,' wrote El País. Unable to hold the fierce pace, Sean Kelly was dropped on the first-category Alto de Cantó, and the Orbea pair launched another attack on the six-kilometre drop to the finish, and won back 14 seconds from Millar. After risking their necks, descending fearlessly at speeds of up to 90kph, it seemed like scant reward, but with the overall so tight, every second was crucial: Ruiz Cabestany was now only ten seconds behind the Scot. The stage-winner was Pacho Rodríguez, and while he was still trying to recover – 'The descent was terrifying,' he gasped, wide-eyed – the Colombian broadcasters hustled him away. They'd set up a connection with his wife back home, so she could congratulate him live on air for maximum emotional impact.

The position at the top of the general classification changed significantly the following day, when the Vuelta's visit to Andorra was completed by a *cronoescalada* to the ski station in Pal. Pacho Rodríguez won, despite losing precious seconds by mistakenly switching to the big chain-ring just as he began the hardest final five kilometres. Millar had the second-best time, only ten seconds slower, but Ruiz Cabestany lost a hefty 1'–58" – a hard blow to his morale.

When people remember the 1985 Vuelta, inevitably there is talk of team alliances, as these played such a big role in the outcome of the race. But pacts and coalitions are all part of a day's work in cycling, and as a reaction to the particularly fratricidal '84 season, there was now a certain reticence among the Spanish team directors to work against each other unless they had a very good reason. For instance, on one of the early stages, when Juan Fernández of Zor escaped, Reynolds, with Induráin in yellow, did not chase. Afterwards, Echávarri wanted to stress that it was 'so no one could accuse us of attacking a Spaniard'.

Hardly a day could pass without some kind of pact. Among the Colombians, there was no doubt about their priorities: when Lucho Herrera abandoned with tendinitis, Varta immediately placed themselves at the disposition of Zor's Pacho Rodríguez, in the interests of national honour. On stage 14, the French teams also showed they could unite forces if it suited them. As the peloton skimmed southwards along the Mediterranean, Peugeot and Skil–Kas took full advantage of the cross-winds, working together to form an echelon. Pacho Rodríguez and Perico Delgado found themselves on the wrong side of the gap, which started to grow alarmingly. Varta were of little use on the flat, so Zor's Javier Mínguez drove nervously back and forth, talking to other directors, looking for help. Kelme agreed to collaborate, and then Teka joined in when their leader Raimund Dietzen punctured. Much hard grafting later, the peloton was compact once more, and Kelme got their reward when José Recio jumped 78 kilometres from the finish in Benidorm and won, with nearly six minutes on the bunch.

Another alliance was born out of Fagor's disappointing performance. Out of contention in the overall classification, all the team could hope for was a stage-win. So before the Albacete to Alcalá de Henares stage, expected to be windy, their director, Luis Ocaña, approached Orbea with a plan. At a feeding station, six members of Fagor attacked, accompanied by Ruiz Cabestany and Delgado, as well as two Soviets. Zor and Peugeot had to chase for all they were worth during 75 kilometres before the battle finally came to an end. The surprise ambush had failed and Kelly won the bunch sprint. Quite clearly, alliances are woven into the fabric of any race; they are the norm rather than the exception.

When it came to the final time-trial, Robert Millar had been in yellow for seven days, and among riders and directors he was the favourite to win the Vuelta. A prominent banner at the roadside read: *'Españoles, valientes, Que no gane El Pendientes'* ('Brave Spaniards, don't let the one with the ear-ring win'). But few believed Ruiz Cabestany could recuperate so much lost time, so it would be between a Scot and a Colombian. Peugeot clearly hadn't taken Millar too seriously, for they had to send over a time-trialing bike á la Moser at the last minute. It was a nervous afternoon for all the top contenders, with punctures and bike changes galore. Ruiz Cabestany won, gaining 37 seconds on Pacho Rodríguez and 40 seconds on Millar, which left the overall with the Colombian ten seconds adrift of Millar and the Basque third at 1'–15". As far as the Scot was concerned, that was it. 'The Vuelta's over. I've won,' he claimed.

Millar had suffered more than he expected to in the time-trial and perhaps it was relief that made him speak so bluntly. He wasn't afraid of the penultimate Segovia stage, with its three *puertos* – Morcuera, Cotos and Los Leones. With the last one 43 kilometres from the finish, a successful attack seemed unlikely. 'I just have to stick to Pacho Rodríguez's wheel and it's done.' But Pacho, cursing the 24 seconds he'd lost by crashing in Compostela, was not going to surrender to a difference of 10 seconds. 'I'll fight to the last moment,' he vowed, 'because you should never give up hope.' Perurena, Orbea's director, hadn't lost faith either, instructing his riders to attack Millar at the slightest opportunity. Delgado, meanwhile, sixth overall and over six minutes down, had long vanished from anyone's predictions.

It was a cold, damp day, sleeting at the top of the puertos, the narrow mountain roads gloomy among the dripping pine forests. A puncture on Cotos, the second climb, was the start of Millar's troubles. Two of his team-mates quickly brought him back to the front group, but then dropped away, exhausted. Peugeot hadn't thought to provide him with some decent climbers for support. The puncture was the trigger for an attack by Kelme's stage-hunter José Recio, who'd won in Segovia the previous year.

When Millar returned to the front group, Ruiz Cabestany realised that he, the Scot, and the Colombian might as well be chained together. Where one went, the others were sure to follow. So he cut Perico loose, thinking his team-mate might at least get a victory in his home town. Delgado jumped and caught up with Recio on Los

Leones. At first, the Kelme rider was suspicious of his unwanted companion, but with the encouragement of his director, Rafael Carrasco, the pair began working hard together. Carrasco had glimpsed the possibility of a miracle and yelled out: 'Go on, Perico! There might be a surprise!' It seemed irrelevant that Delgado belonged to another team. His own director, Perurena, was back with Ruiz Cabestany: that way, Millar's suspicions would not be aroused.

The Scot was happily oblivious to any danger. At the top of Los Leones, the last climb of the '85 Vuelta, he turned to his prospective podium companions and, with a mixture of cockiness and sportsmanship, commiserated with them: 'It wasn't to be. I'm sorry. You tried, but it wasn't to be.'

Then his world shattered: the Peugeot director, Roland Berland, drove up and told him that Recio and Delgado were five minutes up the road, 40 kilometres from the finish. He suddenly realised he was completely isolated, surrounded by enemies. Incredibly, Berland hadn't made any deals beforehand to make up for the limitations of his team, and he was too inept to organise any support now. Afterwards, Millar spoke bitterly against the 15 riders in his group: 'Nobody would ride. They preferred to see me lose and a Spaniard win.' But he was naïve to think he had the right to their support. They needed a good reason for working to the detriment of another cyclist. Millar was trapped: with Pacho Rodríquez breathing down his neck, if he pulled the group too hard on his own, he would lay himself open to attack at the end.

Always a self-contained man, in defeat Millar felt utterly alone: 'It seemed the whole race had wanted me to lose.' When his group entered Segovia at 6'–50", the crowds were going wild. He took it to heart, forgetting that it was a natural response in Delgado's home town. His sense of humiliation was intense. 'The guys in the pack, they acted sympathetic but I felt they were laughing behind my back.' He sought comfort in conspiracy: 'It was so blatant, so scandalous.' Even RENFE (the Spanish equivalent of British Rail) were accused, with dark rumours of Peugeot riders waiting behind closed level crossings and trains that never came: scenes from a cycling thriller. In all his recriminations, Millar never mentioned Roland Berland.

In the jubilant scenes in Segovia, Kelme's director, Carrasco, was carrying Orbea's Delgado around on his shoulders. But just as crucial as Kelme's collaboration – they were well recompensed by winning the stage – was the choice of action of Zor's director, Javier Mínguez. Between Millar's group and the Delgado–Recio duo, there'd been another, intermediate, group including Kelly, Caritoux, and two Zor riders. Surprisingly, Mínguez didn't order them to drop back and help their leader, Pacho Rodríguez. Delgado asked for an explanation, and got a question in response:

'Hey, Perico, do you remember who came second in the '83 Vuelta?'

'No.'

'Nor do I, so you can see what coming second or third means: nothing. Congratulations, lad.'

It was an unprecedented outbreak of national unity. The rare chance to overturn the race in such an audacious way had overcome team rivalries, and in the heady atmosphere the directors forgot their personal quarrels for once. Perico's victory belonged to all of them, and for one brief day, they were a big happy family. His euphoric cry of 'My victory is Spain's' caught the mood.

After the final stage in Salamanca, won by the Soviet, Vladimir Malakhov, the Spanish Press acknowledged that Millar, the best rider in the race, had been badly let down by his team. Their sympathy was tepid though, partly because of his premature crowing of victory, but mainly because Delgado's snatching of victory had been so irresistibly enjoyable.

The international Press were not so enthusiastic, talking scathingly of collusion, but as a footnote, in the Tour de France that year, the blatant assistance given to Hinault by the Colombian Lucho Herrera made the organisers issue a warning to their respective team directors. The complacency among the French journalists prompted Reynold's director Echávarri to protest: 'If you questioned Delgado's victory in the Vuelta because of the collaboration between the Spanish teams, I don't understand why you don't do the same in the case of Hinault and Herrera.' As for Hinault, his reaction to the controversy was to turn up at a Press conference on a motorbike, wearing a traditional Colombian hat.

If nothing else, the '85 Vuelta had shown that the Spaniards were learning to race like their more experienced European peers. In his entertaining autobiography, *Stories of a Cyclist*, Pello Ruiz Cabestany explains how he started racing during 'the era when certain foreign teams came to Spanish races to bully us':

Apart from getting paid a good starting fee by the organisation, they would accept 'offers' from the team of an escaped rider in return for not chasing him down. The system of these strong teams, especially the Dutch, was to only allow solitary breakaways, letting them build up a considerable leeway. These teams, filled with powerful road-men, were so dominant they could close down the escape in the final kilometres unless they found some other 'interest' in the stage.

Ruiz Cabestany conjures up an image of Spanish riders helpless against their bigger, richer and more confident foreign rivals. But change was in the air. When Pedro Delgado was offered a place in Dutch PDM, he jumped at the chance to penetrate the mystique of foreign cycling. He wanted to be initiated into the mysteries of echelons and time-trials, which the foreigners dominated so effortlessly. On his first race in Holland, a strong wind lashed the peloton and Perico observed how the riders cursed and hated the echelons just as much as the Spaniards. It was a revelation: 'There is no formula; simply grit your teeth and get on with it.'

In 1986, Spain (together with Portugal) was at last admitted to the European Community, almost 30 years after Franco's first petition to join the Common Market back in 1957, and although this meant having to struggle with the complexities of VAT, there was a great sense of optimism. At the formal signing of the treaty of accession, the Prime Minister, Felipe González, caught the spirit of the moment when he declared that it was an extremely important step for the overwhelming majority of the population, for whom 'the integration of Spain into Europe has been identified with participation in the ideals of liberty, progress and democracy'.

1986 As if to reinforce the feeling that Spain was irremediably changing, the first week of the 1986 Vuelta no longer had an exclusively Belgian flavour. The Spanish won two stages in bunch sprints, despite the presence of experienced rivals such as Eddy Plankaert and Sean Kelly. It was the spring of the nuclear meltdown in Chernobyl, and all over Europe the direction of the wind was edgily monitored, a common enough pastime among the Spanish cyclists every year in the Vuelta. Yet when the cross-winds blew up on stage 10, as the peloton descended from the Picos de Europa to the plains of Palencia, the Spanish teams were unperturbed. The main losers in the *abanicos* that day were the diminutive Colombians.

Whether or not he had surmounted his bitterness, Robert Millar was back, with improved support from his new team, Panasonic, and everyone expected another duel with his nemesis Delgado. Although Perico was riding, he was saving himself for the Tour, which he would abandon half-way through when his mother died suddenly from a stroke. Instead, Millar had the bad luck to come up against Álvaro Pino in the form of his life.

At the end of the first week, the race had reached Asturias and Millar was looking strong in the yellow jersey after winning the Covadonga stage. Then he was unexpectedly beaten in the uphill time-trial on the Naranco by Pino, who climbed to second overall, eight seconds down on the Scot.

Pino was known as a modest rider with a great capacity for suffering, ready to die on his bicycle, as well as liable to burst into floods of tears at emotional moments. One of the few professional cyclists to emerge from Galicia, when he hung up his wheels, he became a very successful team director, famous for establishing an excellent rapport with his cyclists, first in Kelme and more recently in Phonak. Back in '86, Álvaro was in the hands of director Javier Mínguez in Zor–BH.

In the Valladolid time-trial, after riding as if there were no tomorrow, Pino took 41 seconds out of Millar, who, nevertheless, remained unperturbed. He was biding his time waiting for stage 17, with its summit finish in the Sierra Nevada. He knew it would be the perfect opportunity to win back the yellow jersey, with 30 endless kilometres rising through 1,700 metres. It was a climb for contemplating how fast time can pass – Perico would lose ten minutes.

Millar struck early, still with 22 kilometres to go. But he'd underestimated Pino and, although Javier Mínguez's tactics were sometimes questionable, on this day they worked perfectly. When he lost sight of his rival so far from the finish, Pino momentarily crumpled. It was a propitious moment to call in a favour. A year previously, in the mountains of Segovia, Mínguez had held back from defending Pacho Rodríguez's second place. Some saw it as a sacrifice for the nation, but at this crucial moment in the Sierra Nevada, it might have been viewed as an investment paying timely dividends. Without hesitation, Marino Lejarreta of Orbea, winner of the '82 Vuelta after the Arroyo disgrace, put his wheel at Pino's disposal, pacing him until he recovered. Pino maintained a steady distance behind the Scot, who was dismayed to see his rival draw up alongside, four kilometres from the top.

'I attacked too soon,' Millar admitted afterwards, but he smelt conspiracy all around. 'I never had any time references. I don't understand how Pino had the team-car behind him all the while and they didn't let my director through.' Furthermore, the night before, in Jaen, Panasonic had had to switch hotels at the last minute and the one they were allotted had closed its kitchens; the cyclists had been forced to roam the streets in search of a restaurant. The sense of being in enemy territory was compounded by the terrible dinner they were served.

Plots apart, deep down Millar must have known he'd wasted his chance: no one denied that he was the best climber. If he'd gradually accelerated the pace, patiently squeezing Pino in a vice, a final attack would have seen the Gallego drop like a ripe plum.

The few misguided patriots who thought they were witnessing another united front of Spaniards against the foreigners were disappointed. Two days later on the stage to Puerto Real, near Cádiz, the peloton split, with Millar and Orbea's Lejarreta and Cabestany stranded behind, while Pino was in the front group. The TV commentators spluttered with rage when Orbea collaborated with Panasonic to close the gap. They seemed unable to grasp that the closing of ranks in '85 had occurred in exceptional circumstances, any more than they understood that the Vuelta's international standing would suffer if this were to become a pattern for the future.

Pino, entranced by the Andalucian spectators waving pine branches at the roadsides, was overwhelmed when three coachloads of supporters from Galicia arrived in Jerez to see him hold up the Vuelta trophy. Millar was second, again, and on the bottom step was Sean Kelly, showing how far he'd progressed to be sharing a podium with two climbers, especially as he'd begun the Vuelta suffering from tendinitis. He was going to come back even stronger in 1987, when he'd fight the essential duel of the race with the Colombian Lucho Herrera.

As if to prove they were now proper 'Europeans' and to cheat the French of their smug conviction that 'Africa begins at the Pyrenees', in the Vuelta of 1987 the Spanish riders lost their dominance of the mountains. The speciality that had long been their preserve was appropriated by the Colombians – the new poor relatives of the peloton.

1987

In '87 the race favourites were in a conservative mood, preferring to play a waiting game and let the route eliminate the weakest. Álvaro Pino had to abandon before the race began, with persistent tendinitis in his knee. He was heartbroken because the Vuelta would pay homage to him by beginning a stage in his village, Ponteareas. Delgado was thinking only of the Tour again, so the main attention was focused on Kelly and Fignon. The ambitions of Café de Colombia's leader, Lucho Herrera, were quite modest: he wanted a stage and the Mountain prize, so his excellent form on stage 11, when the Vuelta paid what was becoming an annual visit to the Lagos de Covadonga, took his team completely by surprise. He'd prevailed with such ease, taking the yellow jersey on what happened to be his 26th birthday, that it must have galled his team director, since the stage marked the end of the most mountainous section. Lucho, a deceptively fragile, retiring man who spoke in a barely audible voice, hated to tempt fate: 'I'm not going to win the Vuelta,' he softly assured anyone who was rash enough to think otherwise.

He was right to be cautious, with only a 39-second advantage on Kelly, who'd comfortably crossed the mountains 'in an armchair' – he'd been the main beneficiary of the absence of any serious battle. The steep slopes of the Covadonga climb had defeated him in the past, but this year he finished the stage in a notable third place.

The following stretch in Galicia was uneventful and Lucho kept the yellow jersey in terrain where in theory he should have been quite vulnerable. Only Fignon showed his claws. Now recovered from the flu that had previously kept him at the back of the peloton, he still considered himself to be in the race, and won back over a minute in bonus sprints. The only other excitement was the threat of disruption from workers fearing redundancy as the Socialist government continued their plan to phase out old industries. In Ferrol, the ship yard workers tried to delay the start of the stage, but the tension was diffused when the race organisers handed over their loudspeakers for the strikers to explain their cause. Baton-wielding civil guard were happily absent.

As predicted, Kelly, finishing second behind Jesús Blanco Villar in the Valladolid time-trial, knocked Herrera off the top of the general classification, putting himself 42 seconds ahead in the battle for the overall. But what none of his rivals knew was that Kelly was engaged in another kind of battle – one that would be impossible to win. The excruciating pain from a saddle sore can drive the most hardened, and resilient cyclist to tears. The Irishman had reached the limit of his endurance, and resorted to surgery, but the wound became inflamed, and 14 kilometres into the stage to Ávila, the day after claiming the yellow jersey, he dismounted and got into the team-car. 'What really hurts,' he told the Press, 'is that it was the first time in my sporting career that I was on the point of winning a long stage race.'

The Irishman's departure galvanised the peloton and produced the most exciting stage of the race. The first *puerto* of the day was climbed quite calmly, as new strategies were hurriedly planned. Herrera had inherited the jersey but with only ten seconds on Teka's Raimund Dietzen. It was unusual for a German rider to forge his career in Spain but, although he was the type of cyclist who rarely attacked, his consistency often left him high on general classification (he finished on the Vuelta podium three times). Teka tried to control the race, chasing down an escape group so Dietzen could pick up the bonus at an intermediate sprint. But there was nothing they could do when Fignon's brilliance flared up on the Puerto de Serranillos.

Memories of the '83 Vuelta stirred the Frenchman. This was the spot where his leader, Hinault, had ordered him to set a blistering pace, in preparation for an attack that would dynamite the race. Fignon jumped clear and crossed Serranillos in first place. His descent was awe-inspiring, vehicles hastily pulling over to the side as he swept past, opening up a gap of two minutes. On the final climb, Herrera attacked from the chasing group, and reduced Fignon's lead to 38 seconds. At the end of the day, Fignon had risen to what would be a definitive third place, while Herrera had bolstered his leadership, safely distanced from Dietzen by 1'–04". The Colombian even felt secure enough to tentatively venture that, 'If I'm lucky, I can win the Vuelta.'

What remained of the race turned into a Colombian festival. The lack of movement among the main contenders suggested they had accepted Herrera as the final winner, bowing before his climbing supremacy. The two stages in the Sierras near Madrid were won by Omar Hernández of the other Colombian team, Postobón, who would finish top of the team classification, and Pacho Rodríguez of BH, ending his long drought of victories. Back home in Colombia, the radio commentary and TV coverage had the population mesmerised. With the entire country at a standstill, it made sense to declare the final day of the Vuelta a national holiday. The streets of Bogotá were deserted until Lucho crossed the final line. Then the nation exploded in joy, the first heart attack victim was registered, and the partying began in earnest.

Meanwhile, in Madrid, Lucho was enduring moments of pure terror, unable even to get off his bike, endlessly squeezed and hugged. Kept secret in case it would unduly unnerve him, his parents had been flown over, and they stoically faced the media, with fear in their eyes. By now, the Colombian radio broadcasters were in danger of losing their voices, while Herrera repeated to one and all: 'I'm very happy'.

Herrera flew back to Bogotá to a hero's welcome, greeted by President Barco, who awarded him the highest decoration the government could give. Lucho handed him a yellow jersey in return, which the President immediately donned. Then all the cyclists of Café de Colombia and Postobón drove around the city in a victory parade, perched on fire engines, greeting the flag-waving multitudes, who filled the air with streamers and confetti. The radio endlessly played songs in Lucho's honour, with titles like 'Lucho Campeon' and 'El Matador'. Herrera's triumph, the first time a Colombian* had won a major stage race, was of enormous significance for a country so torn apart by violence and poverty: for his countrymen, Lucho was a symbol of hope.

* * * * *

'Why do I have such bad luck?' sobbed Pino, pounding on the sides of the van with his fists, hemmed in by journalists. For a moment, the pressure had got the better of the '86 Vuelta winner. It was now 1988, and after stage 6 in Valladolid, which had finished with a monumental pile-up during the sprint. Pino crashed with Lejarreta's chain-ring embedded in his delicate right knee, already operated on twice and the cause of his failure to start in '87. Badly shaken, Álvaro's nerves were shredded even more by the rampaging media. Lejarreta and Ruiz Cabestany half-jokingly described their terror as, lying on the ground, they saw a swarm of competing journalists, armed with microphones and cameras, bearing down, in pursuit of quotes and blood.

1988

---

* And only the second by a non-European, after Greg Lemond's win in the Tour de France in 1986

The next day, his leg bandaged and stitched, Pino – without the concentration essential for staying up front – lost seven minutes in the echelon-marked stage to León. It was a set-back for BH, whose 24-year-old climber Laudelino 'Lale' Cubino was in yellow, but in theory only provisionally: his role was to keep it warm for team leader Pino. Cubino had impressed everyone the previous year by winning the Cerler stage, the only Spanish climber able to fend off the Colombians. A year later he suddenly had a great responsibility on his young shoulders. In the León stage he showed the right attitude to handling the *abanicos*,* on a day when Lucho Herrera kissed goodbye to the overall, losing 15 minutes! Cubino explained how it's done: 'It's a pity that Álvaro couldn't enter the *abanico*. If you don't manage it at the beginning, it's very difficult. You've got to be very stroppy to get on. You've got to shove and elbow people out of the way. You're on the point of falling a hundred thousand times. If you have a single moment of doubt, it's the end ... if you have a single moment of weakness, you're done for. Today I was stroppy. If I got shoved, I shoved even more.'

Controversy had marked the prelude to the 1988 Vuelta. The organisers were stunned when Reynolds announced that Delgado, back in the folds of his original team, would race the Giro as his preparation for the Tour de France. It was considered a moral obligation for the Spanish teams to field their best cyclists. The previous July, Perico had kept the nation enthralled as he fought to win the Tour. He came so close, losing the yellow jersey to Stephen Roche in the final time-trial, and finishing second, 40 seconds down in the overall classification. So Reynolds were depriving the public of a chance to see their hero close up, and opting for the Giro, rather than the Vuelta, was nothing short of treachery. The most influential radio sports presenter of the day, José María García, allegedly with financial interests in Unipublic, had always found Delgado far too insubordinate, and his campaign against the Segovian intensified when Perico signed up to do commentary with a rival radio station.

Given the acknowledged impossibility of dislodging the Tour from its pedestal, the Vuelta and Giro found themselves competing for the participation of stars who wanted to warm-up for the French race. The Vuelta was beginning to be prejudiced by its growing reputation for toughness and combativity. Hinault was warning

---

* *abanicos* – echelons

cyclists to stay away, undoubtedly scarred by the memory of the fierce battle the Spanish cyclists had given him in '83, and the ensuing tendinitis that had ruined the rest of his season. In the Giro, it was customary to take the flat stages very calmly for the first 150 kilometres: and often only the last 50 were disputed at high speed, which was ideal if your aim was to build up gradually to top fitness in July.

The Vuelta's *parcours* in '88 was markedly less mountainous than other years, another reason for Perico to choose the Giro, coupled with a desire to avoid the type of media pressure that would send Pino into a frenzy. Little did Delgado know that he was letting himself in for one of the most epic stages in Giro history – the famous crossing of the Gavia in blizzard conditions, when cyclists descending in frozen agony thought they were hallucinating when they discerned others climbing back up towards them through the heavy snow, having turned round in their desperation to get their blood moving and to feel something approaching warmth.

Far from this bitter, wintry image, the Vuelta began in the Canary Islands, situated 1,000 kilometres from Spain, off the African coast, and where summer lasts all year. It was a great publicity stunt, but brought severe logistical headaches, and the cyclists chafed at all the extra travelling. By the time they returned to the mainland, the strongest team in the race, BH, looked very much in control, with young Cubino in yellow. He hoped to keep it until stage 5, which finished in his home town, Béjar, but the team plan was knocked askew after Álvaro Pino's crash and consequent losses in León. With Pino inconsolable and unable to sleep, Mínguez thought a stage-win might be therapeutic and urged him to attack on the first mountainous stage, between León and the Brañillín ski station above the Puerto de Pajares. Pino's attack came early, and he gave an impressive display of strength, riding off alone on the penultimate climb.

This strategy was flawed, however. The main threat to the team was Sean Kelly, and with Pino ahead, they were unable to seize a golden opportunity to pressurize him: if they increased the pace, they might endanger Pino's escape. Untroubled, Kelly was able to climb Pajares at a steady rhythm at the wheel of faithful Caritoux. Cubino and team-mate Anselmo Fuerte had to wait for the final three kilometres before they were free to drop the Irishman. Still, BH had a fully functioning Pino again and the top two placings on general classification, with Fuerte now second at 2'–12", a few seconds ahead of Dietzen and Kelly.

Away from the battle for the overall, 23 kilometres from the finish of the purely transitional stage 12, from Logroño to Jaca, Sean Yates of Fagor and neoprofessional Deno Davie of Carrera organised a British escape. Like surfers, seemingly about to be engulfed by a wave, they maintained the briefest of gaps till the end, where Yates took the stage-win.

The following day came the *etapa reina*, finishing in Cerler, the Pyrenean ski resort. Cubino, still in the yellow jersey and buoyed by his victory there the previous year, was prepared to make the most of his last real chance to distance Kelly before the time-trial. For the second time, BH's strategy came unstuck. It was Pino's job to set the pace, but he did so with such gusto that he put his own team-mate in trouble. At the worst moment, Cubino's chain jammed, and the effort he invested to rejoin the group left him stranded when there was another change of rhythm sparked by the attack of Kelme's Colombian leader, Fabio Parra. Kelly found a useful 'gregario' in Robert Millar, this year riding for Fagor, who paced him to the top, where the Irishman lost a mere 42 seconds. Distraught at having let down his team, Cubino came in at 2'–13". Kelly was now third, just over half a minute behind the race leader, and feeling very confident: 'Having to abandon last year left a thorn in my side. I'm ready to pluck it out.'

Cubino was still tenuously in yellow, with three seconds on his BH team-mate Fuerte, the only one able to follow Parra on Cerler, but the burden of leading the race since the second day would have worn down even a more experienced rider. He lost the top position on the flat stage to Albacete, when Kelly attacked 20 kilometres from the finish, and split the peloton. When they realised that Cubino had missed the cut, Teka and Kas started pulling the front group at a frenetic pace. Fuerte managed to hang on, and so, BH were down to their third and last card.

The Sierra de Madrid was decaffeinated this year, the puertos climbed by their easier sides. On the Ávila–Segovia stage, finishing in the DYC whiskey distilleries, Kelly easily controlled BH's rather timid attacks. Kelme, however, had a tougher offensive planned: José Recio was sent ahead before the Navacerrada, and when the peloton was half-way up, Parra jumped and bridged the gap to his team-mate. Unfortunately, the terrain was not sufficiently hard to inflict real damage, and Recio was not the rider he'd been in '85, when his powerful turns on the front had taken Delgado to victory, so the pair were caught five kilometres from the finish.

It had been a brave try, but the scene was set for Kelly to remove that thorn. After a clear win in the 30-kilometre time-trial – 'the time-trial of my life' – the Vuelta was his. When questioned about the Spanish public's reaction to him, unlike Millar, he had few complaints: 'The day I became leader, some people insulted me, but only a few. They were nearly always encouraging.' Nearly 32, Kelly was conscious that his career was coming to its final phase. Winning the Vuelta was the culmination of an impressive progression: from deadly sprinter to classics specialist, the undisputed king of the Paris–Nice had now conquered a major tour. And how he conquered it: in 20 of the Vuelta's 21 stages he'd finished in the first ten, and, in addition to the overall, he won the Points competition and was third behind Pino in the Mountains prize.

For BH it had been a deeply frustrating race. To their chagrin, Anselmo Fuerte was knocked to third place on the final day when Dietzen picked up a sprint bonus. As a team, they'd been far stronger than Kas, but Kelly had been able to resist them by drawing on his vast experience and an unshakable confidence in his own abilities. His victory was carefully constructed, added to every day, a performance of class and consistency and unmistakable toughness.

In the spring of the following year, Spain was in the grip of Perico-mania, overjoyed to have the '88 Tour de France winner riding the national race. Delgado's victory in France had been a rare occasion to see a climber winning the Tour, something which in recent history seems to happen only about once a decade: Van Impe in 1976 and most recently, Pantani in 1998. In contrast, the Vuelta of the eighties, no longer fixated with copying the Tour, had turned into a race that a climber could aspire to win: Lejarreta, Delgado, Pino, and Lucho Herrera all had their turn during that decade. And the '89 edition was shaping up to be a true climbers' battle between Delgado and Kelme's Colombian leader, Fabio Parra. **1989**

But the battle was slow in coming. Up until the Pyrenees – half-way through the race – the team leaders had been content to watch each other, giving only the occasional display of strength, mainly for psychological effect. Yet no one had been allowed to relax. The cyclists had covered the kilometres in a tense, tightly packed bunch, finishing the stages ahead of schedule. Two of the mass sprints had been won by the Briton, Malcolm Elliott, riding in the Spanish team Teka, who'd beaten Eddy Planckaert with great authority. Those aiming for the overall, however, were saving themselves for a showdown in the final week, when two consecutive summit finishes in Asturias, a time-trial, and a stage in the mountains around Segovia awaited them. It wasn't surprising they bided their time.

In the Pyrenean ski-resort of Cerler, Pedro Delgado won what was surprisingly only his second Vuelta stage victory, when he sprinted past three Colombian rivals. 'They say that in the kingdom of the blind, the one-eyed man is king,' he said afterwards, implying that the Colombians were even worse at sprinting than he was.

After Cerler, the peloton continued its Pyrenean stint westwards to Jaca, on a route that included several unlit tunnels. Cycling is a sport with many inherent risks, but what occurred that day should have been avoided. The organisers had provided generators and strings of light bulbs, but in the Cotefablo tunnel, the arrangements failed. Elliott remembers: 'It was a hell of a long way through and in the middle it was as if you had a bag pulled over your head: we were absolutely blind.' Like bats emitting signals to sense their surroundings, the cyclists began calling, 'Oh! Oh! Oh!' but this only created a disorientating cacophony of echoes. They all made it through except one – Raimund Dietzen, whose crash left him with a fractured skull, his whole season destroyed, and Teka suddenly bereft of a leader. The cyclists were furious, but powerless to do more than organise a sit-down strike at the start of the next stage.

By the time the race arrived in Asturias, Pedro Delgado seemed unassailable. After winning the *crono-escalada* at the Valdezcaray ski-station in La Rioja, nearly a minute faster than Parra, he was a bare two seconds away from the yellow jersey, worn by another Colombian, young Martín Farfán, who was toppled the following day in Cantabria on the dangerous descent of the Puerto de Alisas. Miguel Induráin, who was Delgado's co-leader in Reynolds, still had to hone his climbing skills but was already a brilliant descender, and drove the group down to the coast in torrential rain. Of the Colombians, who were notoriously nervous in these conditions, only Parra held his ground. Teka's German rider Peter Hilse won the stage, and dedicated the victory to his leader and countryman Dietzen, who was still in intensive care, but it was Delgado who was now in yellow and braced for the attacks that were to come in the final demanding week.

Parra's team director, Carrasco, was calling for a united front against Reynolds, although BH were dubious as to whether they could mount a serious challenge. Their leader, Álvaro Pino, had suffered a miserable Vuelta so far: his perennial knee problem, a chest infection and his mother's illness had taken their toll on his performance and morale. However, his luck was about to change. On the Fito, the aperitif regularly served up before the spectacular ascent to the Lagos de Covadonga, Pino's attack broke up the peloton. Reynolds, striving to contain the situation, were halted when Induráin crashed on the descent in full pursuit. They had to let Pino go, no one realising that Induráin had fractured his wrist and would have to abandon the following day. The Fito was destined to be a place of bad memories for him.

Reynolds could afford to cut Pino loose, as he was over three minutes down on general classification, but they faced a much more serious challenge when Fabio Parra attacked 12 kilometres from the finish. Delgado stayed calm, confident that there was plenty of terrain to reel him in. But he misjudged his own strength and that of the Colombian, as Parra drew further and further away, and Delgado, now without team support, began to struggle. After all the predictions of an effortless win, he found himself in deep trouble in one of the most crucial moments. Yet he didn't fall apart – he had too much hard-won experience – but gritted his teeth and continued his grim slog to the top. He was rewarded by retaining his overall lead – by two seconds.

Disappointed, Parra felt he was the rightful owner of the yellow jersey and Kelme planned to seize it without further delay. BH were also pressurising hard, with Pino back in the race, after winning this most prestigious of stages at Covadonga, and now fifth overall at 1'–21", with team-mates placed third and sixth. Delgado suddenly seemed very vulnerable.

The following day, a select group had broken away on the Puerto de Pajares, lost in thick fog. The top climbers – Spaniards Delgado and Pino, and the Colombians Parra and Vargas – were accompanied by Ivan Ivanov, a Russian riding for Italian team Alfa Lum, and himself a fine climber. Ahead, the stage finished at the end of a short, steep turn-off to the ski station of Brañillin. Running through Ivanov's mind were the instructions of his director: 'Attack three kilometres from the top.' Unfamiliar with the climb, and unaware how much was left, he had to rely on his instincts. When the Russian accelerated, the others let the fog swallow him up and continued marking each other. Ivanov thereby became the first professional Russian to take a stage in the Vuelta. Behind him, Delgado was attacked without respite, but he kept his nerve and countered each move, even sprinting to scrape another second at the finish.

The next real test was the time-trial from Valladolid to Medina del Campo of 43.3 relentlessly flat kilometres. Delgado was the only rider to mount two disc wheels, considered inadvisable in a region usually scoured by winds. Yet that day the air was still, and Delgado gave a masterly exhibition of how to win a time-trial: going fast at the beginning, so the intermediate references would demoralise his rivals, measuring his forces in the middle section, before giving his all at the end, where he beat the strong-riding Federico Echave by 29 seconds and, more significantly, Parra by 52 seconds. The crowds went wild: a reporter for *El Mundo Deportivo,* imprisoned in a car with Delgado, described his fear when the fans began rocking it from side to side.

There were some unexpected results in the time-trial: Gorospe, Reynold's leading time-trialist, achieved an uncharacteristically low place, while Parra's best *gregario,* Omar Hernández, who'd worn the yellow jersey for more than a week, finished with the slowest time of all. They were clearly under orders to save their ammunition, as the directors prepared for the final battle in the mountains around Segovia, Perico's home town, on the penultimate stage.

One of the reasons why Pedro Delgado was always such an enthralling cyclist is that he never exuded an air of invulnerable superiority. Unlike his successor, Induráin, he was only too mortal, never an extraterrestrial. That's why the tension before the Segovia stage was so high: it was felt anything might happen. And memories of 1985 were impossible to avoid. Would there be some kind of fateful retribution that would snatch the Vuelta from Perico's hands in the very place he'd won it so brazenly four years before?

With an aggressive strategy, Kelme put Reynolds under pressure from the start. Subjected to constant attacks on the climbs, Delgado responded well, although all his gregarios dropped away. But on the first-category Navacerrada, he was unable to match Fabio Parra. With team-mate Omar Hernández waiting ahead, together with another Colombian from Postobón, Parra's prospects looked very good, as the highly synchronised trio powered their way to the finish at the Dyc Whiskey distilleries.

With the announcement that the Colombian was leader on the road, albeit by only a second, thousands of Segovians hardly dared to breathe. Yet Parra's advantage had peaked and by the finish, Delgado had reduced his losses to only 22 seconds. When the situation had looked quite desperate, what saved him was the ready collaboration he found in his group, particularly from Ivanov. Segovia gave a sigh of relief – although their hero would be making them suffer far more next July, when he arrived late for the Tour prologue. Parra, for his part, accepted the result very sportingly: 'To lose against Delgado,' he declared, 'is an honour.'

But Colombia reacted with indignation, as the 'white envelope scandal' blew up. At the starting-line of the final stage, and in full view of TV cameras, Delgado passed an envelope to Ivanov, who slipped it in his back pocket. Colombian TV, endlessly repeating the film footage, announced that it contained the precise sum of $2,500: 'This has been the payment of Perico to Ivanov for his help in stopping the Colombian Fabio Parra win the Vuelta.' Called upon for an explanation, Delgado revealed that the envelope contained nothing but his home address, so the Russian could visit him on his next trip to Spain. Understandably, the Colombian version of events persists to this day, with its appealing soap-opera overtones.

Rather than relying on opportune alliances, Pedro Delgado had won because of his ability to stay calm under duress and maintain an absolute concentration on the race, despite considerable pressure from the media and fans. As one of Spain's best climbers, he'd also mastered the art of time-trialing. His professional performance had *l'Equipe* comparing him with Anquetil, and in Spain, journalists from outside the field of sport were moved to explore the significance of his victory. Miguel Ángel Bastenier of *El País* saw a symbolic break with the past, remembering the years when the Belgians and French would destroy the home-grown climbers on the flat roads, 'seizing all the hard-won glory of the mountains, leaving the Spanish rider gasping for air in the gutter'. The simple, honest Spaniards had been helpless against the devious foreigners, always ready to stab them in the back.

That's why the 1989 Vuelta marked a new era: 'a Spanish rider has won by applying the exact degree of force at precisely the right time and place.' Instead of offering rash heroics, Delgado had measured his strength, 'turning muscle into intelligence rather than passion.' Bastenier declared it was 'a milestone in the social, political and economic history of Spain' since, while Fabio Parra had taken the role of the 'eternal Spaniard', Perico had ridden like a true cyclist of the European Union.

1990–1994

Swiss on a roll

Almost from the moment they won power in 1982, the Socialist government had been laying plans for a national extravaganza in 1992. On the back of the quincentenary of Columbus' voyage to the Americas, a host of events were planned to draw the world's attention to Spain. It was a testing challenge: would the country be able to simultaneously pull off two events demanding such tremendous organisation as the Olympic Games and the Expo? The hope was to project an image of the country beyond the usual associations with holidays on the beach, siestas, sangria, and during 'Spain's year', the Barcelona Olympics in particular did much to give an impression of a modern, efficient country with an international role to play. Spain became fashionable; all around the world, Spanish language courses were becoming far more popular than French.

It was also a fantastic time for Spanish cycling. At the outset of the '90s few could have dreamed of Miguel Induráin's astonishing five consecutive Tours de France. His biographer, Javier García Sánchez, describes the extraordinary affect the modest farmer's son from Navarra would have on the nation's psyche:

> That was the time when going abroad and saying 'Induráin' was another way of saying 'Spanish' if you wanted to put yourself at a psychological advantage when dealing with someone. And in France the mere mention of his name led to you being treated properly and politely. People admired him, and you felt a kind of pride when you saw that doors opened for you simply because you were of the same nationality as the champion. What a champion, if he had the power to make all that happen and more! Because Miguel became the standard, shield, flag and emblem.

As a true ambassador for Spain, Induráin did his best work abroad, and once his five-year rule of the Tour began, the Vuelta slipped from his schedule, much to Unipublic's vexation. They plotted, cajoled and bullied to have him in their race, all to no avail. He simply preferred the Giro to warm up his great engine for July.

In 1989, the Basque bank Banesto had seamlessly taken over sponsorship from Reynolds, and in 1990 Delgado was still their man for the Tour. His role in the Vuelta was to support Induráin, the principal favourite after having just taken his second Paris–Nice. Without much serious foreign competition, Banesto stood out as the strongest team, but it wasn't going to be a conventional race. As occurred in '84 with Eric Caritoux and further back in '71 with Ferdinand Bracke, an outsider seized a unique opportunity to capture the lead and then stubbornly refused to let go.

1990

A pattern was set when ONCE's director, Manolo Sáiz, refused to defend the yellow jersey awarded to Pello Ruiz Cabestany after the team won the opening stage – a three-up time-trial. It was too early, he said, and, quite frankly, Ruiz Cabestany was not his favoured rider for the overall. His two designated leaders were both climbers, Anselmo Fuerte and the veteran Basque Marino Lejarreta, whose signing for ONCE had been an important step towards the new team obtaining recognition in the Spanish peloton. Lejarreta was showing excellent form in this late stage of his career: in 1989 he'd finished all three of the major tours classified in the top twenty – 5th in the Tour, 10th in the Giro and 19th in the Vuelta.

It was soon apparent that Sáiz's refusal to take responsibility for the race was contagious. The days passed and the Spanish team leaders were reluctant to make any effort to impose themselves, content just to keep an eye on each other. In a stage race, this kind of stalemate between the favourites always provides fruitful opportunities for men of more limited ambition to break clear and win stages – or, occasionally, open up big time-gaps in the overall classification. This is precisely what happened on the second day, when four men went away, unhindered, and finished the short, 108-kilometre, morning stage more than eight minutes clear of the peloton. Best placed of this quartet was the Italian-based Russian, Viktor Klimov, who became the first Soviet professional to lead a major tour.

The pattern was repeated on Stage 5 – from the Mediterranean town of Almería to the 2,510 metre summit of the Sierra Nevada – when, after a 170-kilometre lone break, the Frenchman Patrice Esnault was allowed to finish three minutes clear of the main contenders, who remained bunched together throughout the final 25 kilometres of continuous climbing. And it was repeated again the following day in the mountains of southern Andalucia, at the end of which Julián Gorospe, third string in Banesto's bow, found himself the new race leader. He held a slender, 25-second lead over the Italian Marco Giovanetti, with all the race favourites some minutes adrift.

That night, several of the team directors commented on the strange way the race was unfolding. Kelme's Rafael Carrasco predicted that unless something changed, none of the favoured men were going to win this Vuelta. Banesto's José Miguel Echávarri admitted they were all taking risks: 'Up to now we've put our queens and jacks on the table, and kept our aces and kings in reserve. But it's a very dangerous game. Nobody can feel comfortable with this situation, although our position is better than others.'

Gorospe might have the yellow jersey but it was uncertain how long Banesto's 'jack' would last, or how much the team should invest in defending him. Once one of the great hopes of Spanish cycling, Gorospe's confidence had never recovered from the trauma of losing the yellow jersey to Hinault in the Vuelta of '83, just three days before the end; ever since he'd been living in the shadow of Delgado and Induráin.

Eventually, the dilemma resolved itself on the difficult eleventh stage. By now, the peloton had left the south, and had to cover 203 mountainous kilometres, moving north from León to the ski station of San Isidro on the Asturian border. The stage was enlivened from the start by an attack initiated by Lejarreta, but ONCE's plans came to nothing when the Basque crashed some 60 kilometres from the finish. The yellow jersey arrived at the foot of the final 14-kilometre climb in a select group which had been shedding members along the way. Sensing Gorospe's fragility, Álvaro Pino attacked and shouted to his Seur team-mate, second-placed Marco Giovannetti, to follow his wheel. When Gorospe started to slip back, Banesto left him to his own devices. 'This has just begun,' said a jubilant Álvaro Pino at the finish – where victory was once again reserved for a *gregario*, Carlos Hernández – 'The Vuelta begins today.'

But Giovannetti, the new race leader was, if anything, even more self-effacing than the man he'd displaced. 'I'll try and keep the jersey as long as possible,' he promised, 'but with two time-trials to come, I won't have it in Madrid' – an opinion shared by virtually everyone else. The overall classification was, at last, looking a little more respectable, with ONCE's Fuerte poised two minutes behind the Italian, and Banesto's duo – Induráin and Delgado – a further one minute back. But Giovannetti was a man who'd finished sixth in the Giro two years before – suggesting he could climb – and he'd been a member of the Italian 100 kilometre time-trial team that had taken gold at the 1984 Olympics – so presumably he knew something about riding against the clock.

As the race continued moving northwards, the favourites were still a long way from imposing their authority. The mountain-top finish on the Alto de Naranco in the outskirts of Oviedo produced time differences of just seconds, while Giovannetti held on to his jersey, thanks largely to the tireless efforts and exhortations of Pino. 'I told him to leave me, but he refused,' confessed the unfancied race leader.

By the *cronoescalada* on stage 15, a 24-kilometre climb to the 1,950-metre ski station of Valdezcaray in the Sierra de la Demanda, the Italian had gathered enough self-confidence to hold his ground alone. Run in appalling weather, the stage produced a set of results entirely in keeping with the unlikely way the race was developing. Once again, the aces and kings faded into the background. Induráin – whose five victories in the Tour de France were forged during a cycle of particularly hot summers – hated the cold and finished behind Giovannetti, dropping to eighth overall (he was destined to finish the race in 7th place, more than six minutes down), and ONCE's Anselmo Fuerte remained stuck in second place at 1'–31". Meanwhile, the forgotten men re-emerged: Gorospe, recording the best time among the Banestos, was back to fifth overall, while Ruiz Cabestany, barely mentioned in dispatches since day one, moved up to third place, a solitary second behind his ONCE team leader.

'I've had to show that I'm still here,' the Basque rider said, pointedly. 'Now I'm going to try and achieve my objective, which is to win the Vuelta. I've trained for it better than ever before and I think I have a chance of doing it.' His director didn't rise to the bait. 'The stage has been positive for us' was Sáiz's only comment.

The following day was a disaster in every respect. For more than 20 years the Vuelta had shunned the Basque Country, the organisers arguing that it was preferable to take the race through regions where cycling required a major promotion. What's more, they said, the cycling-crazy Basques had their own tour with an international reputation. If that were truly the case, they should, by the same token, have boycotted Catalunya – which also had an internationally recognised tour – but that was a region that was rarely off the Vuelta route. The reality, of course, was a fear of another Eta bomb attack, like the one that had scarred the 1968 race, or the disruptions the separatists had caused in 1978.

Over the intervening years, however, the route had often skirted the Basque borders and made excursions into the neighbouring province of Navarra, as occurred on stage 16, from Logroño to the Navarran capital of Pamplona. This time Eta decided to pay the race another visit and two small bombs exploded by the roadside. Nobody was hurt, but the race was stopped for an hour and a half. The stage might well have been abandoned altogether, but for Álvaro Pino persuading the anxious foreigners, particularly the Colombians, to continue. Eventually the peloton set out again, pedalling slowly and huddled together, until some 20 kilometres from the finish, when racing in earnest began again. And as it did, the heavens opened in a dramatic thunderstorm with lashing hailstones, making for a treacherous final sprint in which for the second time the East German Uwe Raab won by inches from Malcolm Elliott. The irony was that in those dangerous final metres, Pino slipped and came down heavily, to end his race that night in a hospital bed. As Echávarri said: 'It was a day to forget.'

Losing Pino was a considerable blow for Giovanetti; without his mentor, he felt like a sitting duck. He particularly feared stage 18 with its summit finish in the Pyrenean ski resort of Cerler, where Fuerte and Delgado were aiming to pull back lost time, but it turned into an anti-climax, with all the leading men finishing together. Next to set him in his sights was Ruiz Cabestany in the 39-kilometre time-trial at Zaragoza, but he was slightly off target: 24 seconds still separated him from the yellow jersey.

The final chance to attack the immovable Italian was in the mountains of Segovia. 'The race will go mad,' threatened Delgado, who was third overall at 1'–24". 'Everyone will attack, as the first col is very hard.' The Segovian was as good as his word, attacking without respite, but Giovannetti raced with extraordinary sang froid. A big man, he refused the temptation to try and follow Delgado's violent accelerations. There were times when he lagged by as much as 20 seconds, riding at his own tempo, but that always proved good enough to bring him back to the Spaniard's wheel.

On the Navacerrada, the last climb of the race, Ruiz Cabestany, who'd been in the thick of the action all day, suddenly lost ground, which would relegate him to fourth on general classification, and Delgado's attempts to claw back that tantalising minute and a half lacked conviction. 'I was wrong to have attacked so early,' he subsequently admitted. 'Later, on the Navacerrada, I paid for that and I didn't have the strength to get away from Giovannetti.' Gracious in defeat, he had no complaints about the support the race leader got from the Italian-based Russian, Ivan Ivanov, on that last ascent. After all, didn't he know everything about penultimate-day alliances?

So, the Italian who hadn't figured on anybody's list of potential winners carried his yellow jersey into Madrid the next day. The directors had paid for their over-cautious tactics. One of the riders who felt strongly that the 1990 Vuelta was a lost opportunity was its first leader, Ruiz Cabestany. He'd always swear that 'another cock would've crowed in that Vuelta' if Manolo Sáiz had only shown a little more faith in him. Such reticence hardly fits in with the image ONCE would soon be displaying: a voracious bright yellow formation always at the head of the peloton – the notorious 'yellow peril'.

What distinguished Sáiz from the other directors, and what sometimes caused him to be treated with suspicion, was that he hadn't served his apprenticeship as a professional cyclist, going instead to university to acquire a degree in sport science. He brought a breath of innovation into a sport where folklore and oral tradition held sway. Although the other directors often resented him – for his loud mouth and generous sponsors – they were quick to pick up on his ideas. ONCE was the first Spanish team to provide a comfortable, well-equipped team bus for their cyclists or to use permanent radio contact during the races.

The discipline that fascinated Sáiz most of all, as it gave full vent to his scientific approach, was the time-trial. Always procuring the best equipment, he experimented with positions and bicycle design and the results were quick to come. Since he also took great pains to generate a strong team spirit, the event that gave him the greatest satisfaction of all was the team time-trial, which had the added factor of testing the capacity of the riders to work harmoniously together.

1991   While Sáiz never admitted making an error with Ruiz Cabestany, he must have learned from the experience, as he employed a very different strategy in the 1991 Vuelta. Once again, it was an ONCE *gregario* – Melchor Mauri – who found himself in the leader's jersey at the end of the three-up prologue time-trial. Mauri had been one of the ONCE trio that had won the prologue the year before and, just like Ruiz Cabestany, he was there essentially to support his team leaders – Anselmo Fuerte and Marino Lejarreta. This time, however, Sáiz had no intention of letting that advantage slip away. On the contrary, he was keenly awaiting the second day's 40-kilometre team time-trial in Badajoz. His meticulous preparations and exhortations bellowed from the team-car drove the squad to a crushing victory. With the race barely begun, already everybody's race-favourite, Induráin, was at more than two minutes, the Mexican, Raúl Alcalá, in the strong PDM team was at 1'–03", and the Colombians were nowhere. Never before in the Vuelta had the team time-trial produced such gaps in the overall classification, and Sáiz was jubilant: 'At this event we're the best in the world.'

Mauri's yellow jersey was 'lent' to another of his ONCE team-mates for just one day as the Vuelta made its progress up the Mediterranean coast. But on Stage 8 – the individual time-trial on the island of Mallorca – it was back on his shoulders, and he was back to winning form, taking a further 11 seconds from Alcalá, and beating Induráin by 56 seconds. Nonetheless, he continued to be seen as merely a provisional leader: he was simply keeping the jersey warm for one or other of his team leaders, most probably Lejarreta since Fuerte had lost serious time in the individual time-trial – his Achilles heel. Not that Mauri was dismayed at the thought that his status was temporary. Quite the opposite: it was, he said, 'my dream come true' simply to arrive in his home region of Catalunya in the yellow jersey. 'I'm a *gregario* and I'll be the first to fight for my leaders. I'll try to keep the lead as far as the big mountain stages, but I don't know if I'll be able to hang on in the mountains.'

The Pyrenees, however, were to be dominated not by any of the young Catalan's rivals, nor by his team leaders, but by the climate. On stage 10, the peloton began the long journey from the Costa Brava to Andorra, their ambitions hampered by freezing cold rain, which turned to snow as they climbed. The following day, the *etapa reina*, was scheduled to finish in the Pla de Beret in the north-facing Vall d'Aran, near Spain's most exclusive ski-resort. When other slopes in the Pyrenees are struggling to stay open, here snow is guaranteed.

This year the ski season was a long one, and the race found deep snow blocking the final two cols, which forced the stage to be cancelled. It was no easy decision: it had been widely predicted that this stage, with its two first-category and final special-category climbs, would be decisive. Race-director, Albert Gadea, finally left it to the team directors to decide: curtail the stage at the first climb, or annul it completely? The climbers were anxious to race at least as far as the snow would permit – the Colombians especially, and also Seur, who wanted to pit their Soviet riders against them – but the majority opted for cancellation. It was a decision that thoroughly irritated Rafael Carrasco, Kelme's director: 'Cycling is a very hard sport,' he reminded everyone, and 'I believe that every possibility should have been exhausted before the stage was suspended.'

The climbing specialists who felt they'd been denied their opportunity were in a rampant mood the following day, with its summit-finish at Cerler. Seur's Ivan Ivanov won, ahead of a clutch of Colombians who, like the Spaniards of old, had attacked indiscriminately from the foot of the final climb. But the real action was further back: Induráin and Lejarreta finished together, with Mauri only a minute behind them. Today he'd hung on, which was more than could be said for many: a total of 34 retired or finished outside the time-limit.

Mauri's inspired resistance was drawing admiration, but Sáiz was implacable. 'I can't mortgage the Vuelta for what's only a dream. I have to be realistic… it'll be a couple of years before [Mauri] can deal with the climbs with any certainty.' He was still fully committed to Lejarreta, as this might be the veteran's last chance of an overall victory.

Winter was reluctant to leave the north of Spain. On stage 14, there was a repeat of the previous year's *crono-escalada* in the Sierra de la Demanda, and the snow-ploughs worked feverishly to clear the road to the Valdezcaray ski-station in time. The conditions were dire, as Malcolm Elliott described: 'The tarmac was ripped to shreds. In other places it was undamaged, but your wheels sunk into it and you wondered why you were riding so slowly.'

The cliché about yellow jerseys and wings proved true once more, when Mauri soared up through the fog, overtaking Raúl Alcalá, recapturing 42 seconds from Induráin, and losing only a handful of seconds to Lejarreta, whose ride had lifted him to second overall. Alcalá was the main loser on the stage, dropping from second to sixth. His day was not improved when he crashed into the gaggle of photographers and reporters surrounding Mauri in the mist just beyond the finishing-line.

As the race moved into its final week, ONCE continued to dominate the classification: Mauri's advantage over his 34-year-old team captain stood at 1'–43", with Induráin a further 50 seconds back, now just three seconds ahead of the Colombian, Fabio Parra, whose handsome victory in the mountain time-trial had brought him back into the reckoning. It was impossible to predict the outcome – the Vuelta has always shown a propensity to develop like a Hitchcock thriller, the suspense maintained to the end. But for the first time, Sáiz was acknowledging Mauri's chances. How he survived the stage to the Lagos de Covadonga in the Picos de Europa would be crucial.

In the event, Mauri climbed with the same intelligence he'd displayed on the ascent to Cerler. He ignored Parra's initial (and ultimately suicidal) attack and stayed shoulder to shoulder with the men who mattered – Lejarreta and Induráin. And when they accelerated and dropped him in the final kilometres, he made sure he kept them constantly in sight. His losses on the day were a mere 28 seconds. There were critical voices complaining that the Catalan had been left alone to sink or swim, and it's true that Sáiz played the Lejarreta card to the very end, just in case Mauri cracked. The Basque rider had the delicate task of trying to protect his second place from Induráin, while not prejudicing his own team-mate.

In the final time-trial in Valladolid of over 53 kilometres, Mauri, who'd perfected his skills against the clock under Sáiz's expert tutelage, made his director proud. There was not another rider within a minute of him. The only disappointment for ONCE was that Induráin, 1'–06" slower, had leap-frogged Lejarreta into second overall; it was the closest he'd ever come to winning the Spanish tour. Lejarreta, nearing the end of his career, would have loved to add a second Vuelta to his palmarés, but, as he commented wryly: 'Cycling is getting ever more complicated. All the riders now are fluent over every terrain. Mauri has been sensational.'

* * * * *

With the 1992 celebrations in full swing, it was impressive to think that only 25 years previously, Spain had been struggling to enter the modern world under a repressive regime, an under-developed economy forcing many of her people to emigrate. One of the most common destinations was Switzerland, where Spaniards went to work as waiters, builders, domestic servants, anything that was going. Even today, it's a country that is viewed as the antithesis of Spain: order and discipline versus fiestas and fun. Stereotypes aside, one of the ways they differ is that Switzerland has little cycling tradition – despite having produced aces like Hugo Koblet and Ferdi Kubler. For a long while, the sight of a peloton was greeted with hostility in the conservative rural areas – it was feared the cyclists would frighten the livestock. Even in the 1980s, cycle races were often viewed as a nuisance. Pedro Delgado remembers Switzerland as the most dangerous country to race in, having witnessed car drivers pointedly ignore all the warning signals and invade established events like the Tour of Switzerland and the Championship of Zurich. In the 1990s, Swiss cycling entered a new golden age with the rise of Tony Rominger and Alex Zülle, but it was a sign of the times that to find success *they* had to emigrate to Spain.

1992   In the 1992 Vuelta, Induráin was palpable by his absence. An interview published in *Miroir du Cyclisme* the previous autumn had revealed his ambition to win the Giro. In any case, he'd said, it would be a better preparation than the Vuelta for his bid for a second Tour. Doubtless delighted at his participation, the Giro organisers might also have felt a twinge of indignation to hear their race spoken of as training for another event in another country – a cross the Vuelta had always had to bear.

For Banesto, the situation was made simple: they would ride in Spain with one undisputed leader – Pedro Delgado, who aimed to be the first to secure that elusive triple. His major obstacle would presumably be ONCE, now recognised as one of the strongest teams in world cycling, although they'd suffered a setback when a serious crash in the Basque Country had not only made Lejarreta a non-starter for the Vuelta, but would also bring about his premature retirement from cycling. Nevertheless, a string of early-season stage-race victories had put their ever-voluble director in an ebullient mood: Mauri was the appointed team leader, but Sáiz boldly asserted he could win the race with various of his riders.

The boasting was backed up on stage 4, when in the final 30 kilometres into Albacete, the cyclists were exposed to a fierce side wind and, here, in a perfectly co-ordinated attack, ONCE shattered the peloton into smithereens. It was a demonstration of how far Spanish cycling had come since the times when, year after year, it was the marauding Belgians who demonstrated the art of the echelon. Delgado, relegated to the second group, lost half a minute. So did other significant men, like Tony Rominger and Fabio Parra, while the other Colombian hopefuls fared even worse, finishing nearly two and a half minutes back.

The first week was turning into a protracted ordeal for Rominger. The day after losing time in Albacete, he crashed, and for several hours couldn't remember where he was. He finished the stage in considerable pain, worrying if he'd fractured his collar bone, and his left knee was disconcertingly swollen. As the race approached the Pyrenees, he was doubtful about continuing. Crashing again on stage 6 – without consequences this time – didn't help his morale.

In fact, before beginning the race, Rominger was already riddled with self-doubts. His new team, CLAS – sponsored by an Asturian dairy company – had hired him because they had an excellent troop of strong riders, but no one to lead them. It was a match made in heaven. A rather uptight, serious man, Rominger began to thaw out after coming to Spain. The warm friendly atmosphere in Clas melted his reserve and he was transformed, both as a cyclist and a person. But at the start of this Vuelta, he still had a reputation as a cyclist limited to winning one-week stage races like the Paris–Nice or the Tour de Romandie. It took much careful tending – psychological and physical – from both director Juan Fernández and the masseurs to persuade Rominger that all was not lost.

The well-worn excuse of Bergareche when fending off complaints about the insipid *parcours* of the Vuelta, especially in the 1960s, used to be 'we can't bring the Tourmalet to Spain.' In 1992, the altogether more ambitious organisers, Unipublic, decided to take the Vuelta to the Tourmalet. The *etapa reina* could have been plucked straight from a Tour de France route book, with its five cols, the last two of special-category: the feared Tourmalet itself, and Luz Ardiden. It was the along the route the Tour pioneers had named 'The Circle of Death'.

With the Pyrenees in sight, the race leader was the somewhat unfairly under-rated cyclist from Amaya Seguros, the diminutive Jesús Montoya, who'd ridden an exceptionally good time-trial. Closing in on him were four ONCE men, including two of their new recruits – Johan Bruyneel and Alex Zülle. But three icy stages later, the ONCE challenge was over.

On the first day, to the snow-bound Pla de Beret in Catalunya, Mauri was burning to prove himself, anxious to silence those accusing voices that alleged he owed his '91 Vuelta victory to the cancellation of this particular stage. He was disappointed to lose three minutes, not knowing far worse was to come.

That night, it was predicted that the following day's *etapa reina* would dynamite the race, as the Pyrenean cols are far more savage on the French side. A new leader was assured, bearing in mind that Montoya had arrived at the Pla de Beret exhausted, a wan figure wrapped in blankets, unable to stand up unassisted. His hold on the yellow jersey was a tenuous five seconds.

The toughness of the route was exacerbated by the harsh wintry conditions. For the spectator, it was satisfyingly epic, but from the cyclists' point of view, it was 'pretty diabolical', as Robert Millar put it, and he was one of the strongest on the day, finishing eighth and moving up to 11th overall. He described the hair-raising descents: 'You could only see five metres in front of you – you'd see the snow banks suddenly appearing, but you were only going ten kilometres per hour, anyway. I caught two guys in front of me because their hands were frozen and they couldn't hold the brakes. I was OK because I had big gloves.'

Among those who fared badly were Mauri, who lost a massive 34 minutes, while team-mate Anselmo Fuerte abandoned the struggle altogether, Bruyneel disappeared from the leader board, and Zülle dropped to ninth, before he, too, quit the next day. ONCE's catastrophe was put down to the absence of Marino Lejarreta, who suffered for his team-mates from afar, while recovering from his crash in hospital. The Australian, Stephen Hodge, had no doubts: 'Marino is such as quiet modest guy that you don't notice how important his presence is in the team until he's not there... In the Pyrenean stage he would've been in the front and we would've had greater motivation.'

The hero of the day was Laudelino Cubino of Amaya. He knew the route well enough: he'd won that stage in the 1988 Tour, thoroughly in his element on a July afternoon when the sun was melting the tarmac. 'When I see my shadow on the ground I feel happy,' he always said. Then he'd ridden along a narrow corridor between tightly packed lines of cheering *aficionados;* on this grey day of late-winter snow in 1992, he had to wind his way up the Tourmalet through a silent, deserted gorge carved out by the snowploughs. His solo attack had given him two minutes at the top, and he survived the perilous descent to finish on Luz Ardiden 19 seconds clear of Rominger.

There were several surprised faces to see the Swiss cyclist appear so soon. He'd profited from a classic case of two Spaniards engaged in an obsessive duel, while the foreigner gets away. On the Tourmalet, Montoya had concentrated on marking Delgado, and Amaya's director, Javier Mínguez, repeatedly drove up, leaning out of his car and banging on the door, shouting: 'Montoya! Remember, stay on Perico's wheel!' Delgado finally lost his temper, and began to slow down, eventually coming to a complete standstill. Anxious to obey his bullying director, Montoya did the same, while the others in their group drew away. It was then that Rominger found the conviction to attack.

Letting the Swiss rider escape would prove a costly mistake; few had considered him to be a serious contender, particularly in Amaya's ranks. They were too excited by Montoya, who was in the form of his life. Showing extraordinary powers of recuperation after Pla de Beret, he not only stayed with the select group throughout the day, but finished the stage in third place, putting another 20 seconds into Delgado. It had been a memorable stage, impossible to repeat in today's late summer Vuelta.

The second half of the race became an absorbing three-way battle between Montoya, Rominger and Delgado. After visiting France's illustrious mountain, it was only fitting that the Vuelta should pay homage to its own epic symbol – the equally feared climb to the Lagos de Covadonga. Rominger and Montoya had far stronger team support than Delgado, but his director Echávarri, in one of his poetic moments, compared cycling in the mountains to bull-fighting. 'I compare the team's task to that of the *subalternos* [subordinates who prepare the ground by goading the bull] ... but the one who has to do the killing is the *torero*. And he is always alone.'

Delgado lived up to his director's expectations. The Clas gregario, Fabio Rodríguez, had orders to lift the pace on the final climb, but he was so centred on his task, he didn't hear his struggling team-mates Rominger and Federico Etxabe asking him to slow down. Delgado told himself, 'now or never' and accelerated, his rivals dropping away. It was a fearless display that brought back memories of Perico's best years, although his gains would be measured in seconds rather than minutes.

The next day, on the considerably gentler slopes of the Alto de Naranco, the positions were reversed; this time it was Delgado losing a few seconds to his two rivals. And the net result? With six stages remaining, one minute covered all three riders – Montoya still holding on to his yellow jersey, with Delgado at 49 seconds and Rominger at 55 seconds. After one of its most mountainous editions, the Vuelta would be resolved in the final 38-kilometre time-trial.

And so it proved, but not before a nerve-wracking day of attack and counter-attack on the eve of the time-trial, as each of the three contenders tried in turn to wrest a few seconds advantage, and wore their teams to a frazzle in the process. There was no truce expected, or offered. Coming under the one-kilometre banner on the cobbled streets of Ávila, Rominger launched a final attack. Montoya responded, caught him, but then, as the pace eased, could only watch as Delgado, who'd never left his wheel, jumped away, while the crowds screamed. Now it was Rominger's turn to be on the defensive. Churning a huge gear, he got back to Delgado, only to misjudge the final bend and crash in the gutter. As the accident had happened in the final kilometre, he was given the same time as Perico – all that battle for just three seconds sliced from the yellow jersey.

This was the third time Rominger had come down. Since his fall on stage 5, not a day had gone by when his swollen knee hadn't been subjected to all manner of attention – from laser treatment to herbal remedies. More than once, he'd considered retiring, and now, as his wife saw him crossing the line in Ávila, shaken and bloody-nosed, she wept and urged him to quit. 'I can't put up with any more of this; you've got to stop, don't fight any more; it's too much.'

Her husband was half-inclined to agree, but he knew that the time-trial course, with its long, gently undulating straights, suited him perfectly. He knew also how important the Vuelta was to his Spanish sponsors, and to his team, whose hotel rooms he was in the habit of visiting each night to thank them for their efforts. And besides, he was conscious that he'd been given an opportunity to bury his reputation as just a one-week race man, unable to survive a full three-week tour. That night he allowed the medical staff to work on him again – more ice packs and ultrasonic treatment.

The morning dawned bright and hot, to Montoya's dismay. Born in hot, arid Murcia, he preferred to live in cool, damp Cantabria. He felt on edge, conscious that he was the outsider who no one wanted to win. It was his performance in the individual time-trial on Stage 7 that had first given him the yellow jersey; but after twelve days spent resisting all the attempts to strip it from his back, his nerves were raw. Amaya's director Javier Mínguez, tried to bolster his rider, but he was every bit as nervous: 48 hours from Madrid, this had too many echoes of the nightmare of 1988 when he'd placed all his eggs in Cubino's basket and, in the end, lost everything.

When Rominger got up that morning he could barely bend his leg, but by the afternoon the stiffness had gone. He rode with the fluency that, the year before, had won him the blue-riband of time-trialling, the Grand Prix des Nations. Ahead of his two Spanish rivals at every check-point, he destroyed their hopes in the final ten kilometres into the head-wind. Carlos Arribas, cycling correspondent of *El País*, was lyrical:

The fundamental thing in the individual time-trial is to quickly find a comfortable position on the bike and to get into a rhythm. The position was no problem – Rominger rides like he is inside a mould. Nothing disturbs him. It was as if an external force prevented him from moving from the line made by his shoulders, his arms and his head over the bars. The symmetry. Everything seems easy when one of the best time-triallists in the world is going well.

It was all over. Rominger's Clas team had no difficulty controlling the race the next day, even on Delgado's home territory, and he would lead Montoya and the Segovian into Madrid the day after to register not only his first victory in a three-week tour, at the age of 31, but the first by any Swiss rider since their glory days of forty years earlier, when Kubler and Koblet were winning the Giro and the Tour.

Clas were not the only team to find reinforcements in Switzerland. When Manolo Sáiz had looked abroad for talent, he signed up a gangling, severely short-sighted Swiss rider, Alex Zülle. Initially a nordic skier, he'd been spotted by his local cycling club when he pedalled past them wearing jeans and baseball boots. The lack of professional teams in Switzerland made him look further afield for a contract, and Sáiz offered him one for three months, not suspecting that this lanky, spectacled youth was, in fact, brimming

1993

over with class. Within days of turning professional, he'd come third in the Volta a Catalunya behind the Banesto pair of Induráin and Delgado, and his contract was hastily extended. In the 1993 Vuelta, he took the lead in the prologue and on stage 6, and consolidated it during a superb ride in foul weather on the Navacerrada *cronoescalada*. In the first 17 kilometres of gradual climbing, he beat all the best *rouleurs*, and in the final steep seven kilometres, as the rain turned to sleet, he was better than any of the climbers. Even Manolo Sáiz was taken aback.

Zülle's impressive win had clarified a number of questions: Delgado, still recovering from a bad dose of flu, lost 3'–20" and was out of the running; Erik Breukink, the Dutch time-trial specialist whom Sáiz had initially nominated as ONCE's leader, was even further back; Cubino had emerged as Amaya's best option; and Rominger was comfortable in second place overall.

It had been a powerful performance but the yellow jersey's inexperience let him down as the race unfolded. On stage 11, an impulsive streak led him to chase down each and every one of Amaya's attacks on the slopes of Cerler. By contrast, a rational, calculating Rominger knew exactly when and where to strike. Reeling in Cubino and Oliverio Rincón, he took the stage, while an isolated Zülle was reduced to damage-limitation. The gap between the two Swiss rivals was down to 18 seconds, and Cubino, like Lejarreta in 1991, lamented that a pure climber like himself could never win a major tour when the time-trialists were now capable of climbing so strongly.

Interrupting the Swiss duel, Melchor Mauri won the 37-kilometre time-trial in Zaragoza, albeit by a solitary second on Rominger. Zülle was third, his overall lead now down to four seconds. Mínguez, Amaya's director, was delighted that Cubino had restricted his deficit to just 1'–16". 'The hardest days are yet to come, and Rominger could break,' he said, optimistically.

Mínguez was right on one point: the last section of the race would certainly be a testing challenge, with four mountain-top finishes in the final eight days. On stage 14, Rominger's CLAS team-mates went into action, thinning out the field with an exhausting rhythm even before the foot of the final ten-kilometre ascent of the Alto de la Demanda. There, Rominger took over, and in a series of brutal accelerations, shed everyone from his back wheel: the also-rans, the hopefuls, Amaya's mountain goats, and finally Zülle himself. Last year's victor was back in the yellow jersey with a 33-second advantage.

'It will be very difficult,' said Mínguez, contemplating the remaining days in the Cantabrian mountains, now with a greater measure of realism. Amaya consoled themselves with stage-wins: Montoya at Alto Campoo and the Colombian Rincón at the Lagos de Covadonga, the following day. And all the time, Zülle stayed glued to Rominger. 'Don't let him out of your sight,' was Sáiz's instruction each morning, and the myopic cyclist took him literally. 'The two Swiss could have shaved in the same mirror,' said Carlos Arribas, so close were they. As Zülle resisted all Rominger's attacks, the final day's time-trial was getting closer, and CLAS's director, Fernández, was becoming increasingly nervous. He admitted that he couldn't sleep easily while his man's advantage remained at only 33 seconds.

The final mountainous stage was in Asturias, the land of Rominger's team, where the Asturians had adopted him as one of their own. Nerves were running high. It was raining: an uncomfortable day was assured. There was talk of alliances, and of Zülle profiting from Amaya's aggressive tactics. By the time they reached the demanding slopes of first-category La Cobertoria, the penultimate climb, the leading group was reduced to ten. Rominger had been warned by his director to position himself at the front in preparation for La Cobertoria's treacherous descent. This steep, very narrow road is regularly used by coal trucks that carve up the asphalt and spray gravel on the corners. Perhaps it was the fervent support he was encountering by the road-side that inspired him, but the normally cautious and methodical Rominger had a sudden moment of madness. After exchanging a stolen glance with his CLAS lieutenant, Iñaki Gastón, the two men broke away, launching themselves on the rain-soaked descent. The finish on the summit of the Naranco was still 50 kilometres away.

Behind them, the surprised Amaya trio tried to organise the chase, and in their wake, blinded by the spray, Zülle skidded as he went into a hairpin corner and came down. He was unhurt, but looked around disorientated, because there was no sign of his bicycle. ONCE's car slid to a halt, and their mechanic leapt out and dived head-first into some brambles to retrieve it. Precious seconds were being lost.

Now began a pursuit that was to last more than an hour. With 20 kilometres still to go, Gastón could do no more for his leader and dropped back exhausted, leaving Rominger powering on in time-trial mould. Behind him, mud-splattered from head to toe, Zülle had, with Breukink's help, rejoined the Amaya-Delgado group, and now he dragged them out into single file. He chased heroically, with his string of climbers hanging on as best they could, but it was a lost battle. Rominger had weighed his effort to perfection, with the added boost of riding up the Naranco between cheering lines of supporters. Zülle had to ride up to jeers and insults, and after withholding any support, Cubino rubbed salt into the Swiss rider's wounds by coming round at the finish to snatch second place.

This year the Vuelta began and ended in Galicia, with a final time-trial stage in Santiago de Compostela, the renowned pilgrim destination, to celebrate the Jacobean Holy Year. The final stage was a difficult 44.6 kilometre time-trial of constantly changing gradients and narrow, bad quality roads. Rominger asserted: 'If nothing happens – a fall or a puncture – one minute and seventeen seconds is a sufficient advantage.' But he was more nervous than he'd let on. Up most of the night with stomach ache, he had to suffer during his ride in the wind and rain, pressurised by the references he was getting of Zülle's intermediate times. Later he described it as 'the hardest day of my cycling life'. His younger rival gave another demonstration of power, but at the end there was still a gap of 29 seconds. Rominger could keep his yellow jersey, as well as the green one for the mountains and the blue points jersey – the first time in the Vuelta's history that a rider had won all three.

The Swiss dominance was underlined by the fact that Cubino, who finished third overall, was almost nine minutes down. The little climber, set among time-trialists who also knew how to scale the high mountains, reflected ruefully that he was a man out of his time: 'If I'd been born ten years earlier I would've had more success.' But there were compensations, which he acknowledged: 'If I'd been born ten years earlier I would've earned less money.'

Rominger had thus joined a select group who had won two Vueltas, and they'd both been exciting, combative races with the result in doubt until the closing stages. Despite that, they'd been watched by a dwindling Spanish television audience; more people preferred to watch the retransmission of Italian television's coverage of the Giro. The reason, of course, was Miguel Induráin. In the month after Rominger's second victory in Spain, the Spaniard was winning his second Giro, and he would go on to capture his third Tour – ahead of Rominger – in July.

This was the issue – Induráin's participation in the Vuelta – which brought together the organisers of the Spanish race, Televisión Española (TVE), and Banesto's director, José Miguel Echávarri, to a meeting in November. Unipublic could no longer tolerate the fact that the best stage-race rider in the world, and the best Spain had ever produced, shunned his national tour year after year. As for TVE, they needed him – it was as simple as that. But Echávarri's horizons were wider; as he had repeatedly argued, the prime objective was the Tour de France in July, and for that, the route, the timing and the more advanced spring weather of the Giro made it a better preparation that the Vuelta.

It was an old battle-ground which they'd fought on before. In 1988, Unipublic had rounded on Reynolds for keeping Spain's favourite son, Perico Delgado, out of the Vuelta and sending him to Italy, at precisely the time when they were attempting to usurp the Giro's status as the second most important of the three-week races. With Induráin, the stakes were higher still, and Unipublic's director, Enrique Franco, had attempted to accommodate the Vuelta to his requirements. Whereas the organisers of the French and Italian tours had been steadily reducing the number of time-trialling kilometres in an attempt to curb Induráin's dominance, in the Vuelta they'd been increased. Only once before had that happened – when *El Correo*, the previous organisers, had set the lure to catch Anquetil. Unipublic had even tried to arrange the weather to Indurain's liking, with the 1994 Vuelta routed immediately to the south, leaving the northern mountains to the final week, when there would be less likelihood of the riders encountering the rain and icy winds of late-winter. But Echávarri would not budge: this was essentially a power struggle between organisers and team directors, and he was there to uphold the general principle of the director's right to determine who would ride, where and when.

Unipublic were not prepared to give up, however. In the New Year, they announced a new condition with which the Spanish teams (and only the Spanish teams) would have to comply if they wanted to participate in the Vuelta – the 60 per-cent rule. The total number of the UCI points of the nine riders selected by each team director would, when added together, have to constitute at least 60 per-cent of all that team's UCI points. A bizarre ruling, and a pointed one. It was aimed directly at Banesto, half of whose UCI total was accumulated by one man – Miguel Induráin. The implication was clear – if he didn't ride, neither would Banesto.

A series of lengthy, exhausting meetings took place in January and February between Unipublic and the directors of Spain's seven professional teams. In theory, the directors of the smaller outfits, such as Kelme and Euskadi, upheld their right to field who they wished, but in practice, the rule didn't affect them, as the Vuelta was the centre of their season, and their life-blood. The more powerful directors weren't too disturbed either: Manolo Sáiz had every intention of putting out ONCE's strongest line-up and Juan Fernández never considered leaving Rominger out of Clas. They both insisted they would negotiate their own financial terms with Unipublic. Only Banesto held out.

At the beginning of March, and only through the intervention of the Minister of Sport, a compromise was hammered out: Banesto could ride the 1994 Vuelta without Induráin, in exchange for a signed document that he would ride in 1995. The Minister was pleased: 'All Spaniards want to see Induráin ride and win the Vuelta.' Unipublic seemed satisfied. 'What is good for the Vuelta is good for Spanish cycling,' asserted Enrique Franco, although many Spanish fans were more of the opinion that what was best for Spanish cycling was the sight of a Spaniard in a yellow jersey on the Champs Elysées. Echavárri was less sanguine. As he pointed out, not only was 1995 a long way off, but there was one man in all this who hadn't been consulted – Miguel Induráin, himself.

1994   In the 1994 Vuelta, Rominger, whose team were now called Mapei-Clas, was in his own universe. His absolute superiority made his rivals feel impotent. It was a feeling well-known by Induráin's rivals in the Tour de France, but the Spaniard never showed quite such a voracious appetite. Rominger won six stages: all three time-trials and three summit finishes. There was only one Spanish stage-win, by Banesto's Marino Alonso.

Even discounting the monotony of the race, it was hardly surprising that attention wandered elsewhere, as news broke of yet more scandals involving the Spanish government. A seemingly endless stream of corruption cases were being uncovered and fed to the public by the right-wing Press, who were desperate to wear out the charismatic prime minister Felipe González. The most spectacular was the affair of Roldán, the head of the Civil Guard, who had siphoned off astronomical quantities of funds into his private bank accounts, and who, while under investigation that May, skipped the country. The minister of the Interior became the latest cabinet member to resign, as the twelve-year period of the Socialist party headed towards an ignominious end.

As the Vuelta played itself out, people chose to ignore Rominger altogether and concentrated on the limited suspense concerning who would finish third, since Banesto's young Basque rider, Mikel Zarrabeitia, had also consolidated himself in second place.

On the eve of the final time-trial in Segovia, Zülle – who was building up his form more slowly this year – was pressing hard on Pedro Delgado's heels. During the race, Perico had acted as Zarrabeitia's godfather, advising and protecting his team-mate, who was ten years his junior. It was Delgado's last season as a professional – he'd announced his forthcoming retirement and was disappointed to feel that he wouldn't get to stand on the podium in Madrid for one last time. Yet on the day, helped by an intimate knowledge of the roads and the warmth of the crowds, he pulled off a polished, expert ride. What finally sealed his podium place was Zülle's litany of troubles. After 11 kilometres, his electronic gear changer failed – for once Sáiz's enthusiasm for the latest technology hadn't paid off. On kilometre 25, the chain of the new bike broke, as did his concentration. On kilometre 34, he changed bike yet again, because he didn't feel comfortable. Four kilometres later, he punctured.

It was an edition for checking the statistics: no one had worn the yellow jersey from start to finish since Freddy Maertens in 1977; the last time the race had been won by so wide a margin as 7'–28" was in 1960; and Rominger was the first to reach the hat-trick, in three consecutive years. In July he would go to France with more confidence than ever before to take on Induráin, who'd only managed third in the Giro. There, nearly eight minutes down and ill with stomach problems, he retired in the Pyrenees while Induráin went on to win his fourth consecutive Tour, and by his biggest winning margin.

1995–1997

Last Chance Saloon

When the UCI suggested to the organisers of the Giro that their race be moved to September, the idea was rejected out of hand, but Unipublic, when they were offered the new slot for the Vuelta, were immediately interested. For a while in the 1980s it seemed the Vuelta was gaining ground on the Italian race but now the battle to be the second best tour was turning against them. In the early '90s, the Giro was the scene of memorable battles between some of the best cyclists in the world – Italy's own heroes, Bugno and Chiappucci, were taking on foreign stars like Induráin and Berzin. This was, of course, still a time when trying to win two major tours a year was seen as perfectly feasible, at least for the best riders.

The underlying reason for changing the racing calendar was primarily commercial. The UCI's president, Hein Verbruggen, wanted to lengthen the racing season to give the sponsors their money's worth. Currently, the 63-days of publicity they received from the tours were crammed into an almost continuous, twelve-week period from the start of the Vuelta, at the end of April, through to the end of the Tour in late July. This, he suggested, didn't offer them the best return on their investment.

By accepting Verbruggen's proposal, Unipublic saw a chance to improve the status of their race. One thing was certain: in September, they would never have to complain about riders coming just to prepare for the Tour. On the contrary, the Vuelta would offer a last opportunity to redeem a disappointing ride in France. The other question was financial: attracting sponsors to the Vuelta would be easier if the race had greater repercussions beyond Spain's borders. The more international the line-up, the better.

Next came the delicate task of broaching the issue with the Spanish team directors. Their initial response, when the proposal was first muted in 1992, was strong disapproval. As far as they were concerned, moving the race from its comfortably established April/May slot was akin to turning the world upside-down. All their annual routines would be upset. 'It's not good for Spanish cycling,' stated Amaya's Javier Mínguez flatly. 'The future of the team – getting reinforcements, the continuity of the sponsor, the budget – that's all decided at the end of May, depending on how things have gone in the Vuelta. It would be impossible in September when the contract market is closed.'

The concern of the smaller teams was understandable, as their fate has always been inextricably entwined with that of their national tour; they simply wouldn't exist without it. (In France the pressure on Jean Marie Leblanc is enormous when it comes to allocating the 'wild card' invitations to the Tour, as the minor French teams have such strong international competition.) But when even the most powerful directors joined the opposition, Unipublic opted to keep a public silence, while continuing to negotiate with Verbruggen. Apart from a satisfactory deal on television rights, they demanded a free run in September: there would be no other major competing races, and the World Championships would be put back to October.

When it was announced in November 1992 as a *fait accompli* that from 1995 the Vuelta would be run in September, the negative reaction was predictable. The Spanish cycling establishment expressed its disapproval to Verbruggen, and Mínguez threatened a boycott: 'Unipublic provides the scenery, but the teams are the actors. And in 1995 we could well decide to take part in the Giro and the Tour, which are televised in Spain, and not the Vuelta.' It was pure hot air; however reluctantly, the directors had no option but to accept the decision.

It was Unipublic's turn to feel betrayed when the UCI published the racing calendar for 1995: contrary to what had been agreed, there were to be a host of one-day races in September. To make matters worse, with the World Championships taking place in Colombia, it was feared that many of the world's best riders would travel there some three weeks beforehand – half-way through the Vuelta – to acclimatise to racing at that particularly high altitude.

One of those who absented himself from the Spanish race so as to arrive early in Colombia was Miguel Induráin, now with a record five consecutive Tour wins to his name. Despite Banesto's written pledge, once again he would not be seen in the Vuelta. Unipublic's director, Enrique Franco, summed up his bitter disappointment: 'In Spain we grow oranges and export them to France, while we eat mandarins.'

Despite all the controversy, the race looked promising. Prize money was some 30 times greater than it had been in 1979 when Unipublic first took charge of the Vuelta, and part of that was contributed by the British NatWest bank, which was sponsoring the 'combine competition'. There was also more international media interest than ever before: *Eurosport*, for instance, was transmitting the same extended coverage as it did for the Tour, and in Britain, *Cycling Weekly* was, for the first time, printing as many pages of detailed stage-by-stage reporting as they normally reserved for the other two grand tours.

A total of 180 riders took the starting-line, with such top figures as Marco Pantani, Bjarne Riis, Richard Virenque among them. For the Spanish, there was Abraham Olano in Mapei, but the clear favourite was Alex Zülle, who in July had shown himself to be the best of the rest behind Induráin in the Tour de France. His director, Manolo Sáiz, was not reticent in promoting his number one: 'Alex had two goals at the start of the season – to finish in the top five in the Tour, and to go for the overall win in the Vuelta. So far, so good.'

In fact, that was as good as it was going to get. Zülle was one of the worst affected of some 50-odd riders who were struck down with stomach trouble on Stage 6, attributed to food poisoning in their hotel in Orense the night before. Collective diarrhoea, which brought about an informal truce among the riders for the first half of the stage, was not the only problem to beset the race in the first week. Any thoughts that the change to a September date would ensure better weather proved to be wishful thinking. The remnants of a Caribbean hurricane, playing itself out in northern Spain during the first two or three days, brought torrential rain and horrendous winds, which provoked even more than the usual catalogue of crashes, as cyclists were blown into fields and publicity stands disappeared into the sky.

If Zülle's challenge was effectively over after what one director defined as 'the day of the toilet paper', it certainly didn't spell the end for his team. The mid-nineties saw ONCE reach the height of their domination. The prologue had given an indication of their strength in depth, with four placed in the first eight. Among them was Laurent Jalabert, the rider Sáiz had originally signed as an antidote to the 'Induráin factor'. Fed up with being ignored by the Spanish media, he wanted a cyclist who would shine in the Classics, away from Induráin's territory. In 1994, ONCE's failure to put a man on the podium had been partially compensated by Jalabert winning the points competition and his seven stage-wins, including a controversial victory at the Lagos de Covadonga. Still considered a sprinter, he'd benefited from an early break to 'steal' the prize from the climbers on their hallowed ground; it was an early sign of his renowned versatility. In the new racing calendar of 1995, without the Vuelta to think about in May, he was let lose to win a host of early-season races, including the Paris–Nice and the Milan–San Remo. His excellent form continued in the Tour, where he won the points jersey and finished fourth overall. How much more could Jalabert achieve in one year?

He became the leader of the Vuelta on Stage 3, jumping clear on the six-kilometre first-category climb of the Alto de Naranco, after his ONCE *gregarios*, Neil Stephens and Johan Bruyneel had set a fierce pace through the streets of Oviedo to prohibit any other attacking ventures on the final ascent. On Stage 5, in wet and windy Galician weather, he took his second stage-win – this time in a bunch sprint, after he courageously slipped through into the lead on the last rain-slicked corner. And three days later, on Stage 8, breaking away 60 kilometres from the finish and coming in nearly five minutes clear of all his rivals, he effectively won the race.

This stage followed a classic route – from Salamanca, over the 1,910-metre Puerto de Peñanegra, and slightly lower Puerto de Navalmoral, to the walled city of Ávila. It was on these roads in 1983 that Hinault finally overcame stubborn Spanish resistance to claim his second overall victory, and inevitably Jalabert's exploit recalled memories of that day. 'Jalabert wins à la Hinault' read the headlines, and not without justification, because you would need to return to Hinault's time to find the last occasion in one of the major tours when the wearer of the yellow jersey launched such an audacious attack without warning and with not a single *gregario* at his side.

In his wake, Jalabert had left the peloton in general disarray and disillusion, with only Olano willing and able to take up the chase. That morning, Mapei's leader must have expected an attack from one or other of the ONCE squad because in winning the previous day's 41-kilometre time-trial he'd closed to within six seconds of the yellow jersey. Despite crashing – the consequence of a front tyre puncture – he'd given an ample demonstration of why he was being spoken of as Induráin's successor. But neither in the mountains above Ávila, nor down in the valley with the wind on his back, did he have any answer to Jalabert's flight. However hard he chased, there was never a moment when he could break free from Bruyneel and Mauri and the other ONCE men who were protecting Jalabert's ever-increasing lead. It was to become the abiding motif of the '95 Vuelta – a proud but solitary Olano surrounded by a posse of men in yellow and black. His team-mates in Mapai were just not up to the task. Perhaps things would have been different if their star climber, Fernando Escartín, had been included in the team. But Escartín had signed up with Kelme for the next season, breaking a verbal agreement with Mapei and his director, Juan Fernández, cutting off his nose to spite his face, dropped him on the eve of the race. There would also have been more help for Olano if Bjarne Riis had been in a fit condition to reinforce the pursuit, but he'd crashed in the time-trial when his tyre blew out on a 75kph descent. His damaged back would eventually force him to abandon.

With Jalabert proving that he could win on just about every terrain, and ONCE (now with four in the top six overall) imposing a merciless grip on the race, the subjugated started to chafe under the yoke. *El País* spoke of totalitarianism – 'Orwell would not give a *duro* for this Vuelta'* – and teams weren't slow in reminding Sáiz that he owed them a favour. In the recent Tour, when Jalabert's attack *en route* to Mende had made him the temporary leader on the road, hadn't they refrained from joining in Banesto's counter-attack?

So, in an act of diplomacy, or simple Gallic generosity, Jalabert 'gifted' the twelfth stage to Telekom's Bert Dietz. The German escaped after only 47 kilometres, while the peloton were still on the coast, in Torremolinos. In Granada, where the final climb in the Sierra Nevada began, he still had a 10-minute lead, but he was visibly struggling, and losing time at the rate of 30 seconds per kilometre. Two kilometres from the summit, Jalabert jumped out of the chasing group with characteristic ease, caught the fugitive but gestured to him to take the stage – having first glanced back to be sure that Olano was not going to regain contact. While some praised Jalabert for his gentlemanly deed, others saw it as just another humiliating display of power. Dietz was well and truly cooked by the end; he was 'gifted' the stage but there was no glory in it.

Three days later, in what was effectively a criterium – 11 laps of a 14-kilometre circuit through the city of Barcelona – Jalabert was

---

* *duro* – a five-peseta coin

once again giving full vent to his ambition. Coming under the one-kilometre banner only one man ahead of him – Jesús Montoya – and he was a Banesto. There'd been fierce combat between the two Spanish teams in the Tour de France, with ONCE's attacks on Induráin badly understood in some quarters back home. There was no *entente cordiale* in Barcelona as Jalabert took his fourth stage-win.

The Frenchman's overall lead on Olano was now up to almost six minutes, and it continued to grow as the race wound its way through the Pyrenees. He distanced his rival a little further on the 1,900m Pla de Beret, where he finished second behind Zülle, who'd finally returned to form after his food poisoning and a succession of crashes. And the day after, he meted out more of the same, this time with an impressive stage victory at Luz Ardiden, the scene of ONCE's crushing defeat in 1992. It was a day of bitter cold and lashing rain and, when rumours of snow on the Tourmalet began circulating through the peloton, a number of French riders begged the organisers to shorten the stage. Their petition was rejected: they'd all raced in worse conditions and the snow only existed in their imagination. Perhaps the deserted road-sides disheartened them; there were no Tour holiday crowds to take their minds off their tired legs. Reluctantly, they carried on, although not before Pascal Hervé had threatened to down tools. 'Ride the bike yourself,' he told his Lotus director Miguel Moreno. But Moreno was a veteran. 'If you want to retire, retire, but don't play the fool with strikes,' was his blunt response, and Hervé climbed back on.

There'd been hopes that the French star Richard Virenque would liven up the race on his own territory, but he ran into an intractable ONCE. He was warned not to try one of his hallmark long escapes; they'd only let him go on the final climb. Uninterested in such a gift, he repeatedly tried to break free on the Tourmalet, only to be remorselessly reined in. That final ascent through the clouds to Luz Ardiden epitomised the 1995 Vuelta. With ONCE in complete control, Bruyneel and Mauri forced a pace that gradually wore down the leading group, until Jalabert himself took charge, and only Olano was able to stay anywhere near his back wheel as it disappeared into the dank mist.

The brave Basque rider recouped some of his losses in the final time-trial to guarantee his second-place overall, but the Frenchman, with five stage-wins and a catalogue of intermediate and second-place time-bonuses, was the undisputed winner, his team-mate

Bruyneel taking third. Following Rominger's footsteps, Jalabert also claimed the points, mountains and overall classifications. Needless to say, ONCE won the team competition; dominant from start to finish, they were the only ones to arrive in Madrid with a complete squad, and as if to emphasise the point, they crossed the line in full formation. It'd been an unequal struggle from the beginning, and one in which, as Carlos Arribas told his *El País* readers: 'the gap between the rich and the poor went on increasing'.

For the last five years, the French had had to listen to the Spanish anthem in the the Champs-Elysées, and now in Madrid, the French Minister of Sport was regaled with 'La Marseillaise', as Jalabert stood on top of the podium. An estimated 11,000 blind people wearing yellow ONCE t-shirts had been assembled from all over Spain to celebrate the triumph. A delirious Sáiz declared: 'This is one of the happiest days of my life.' But the hostility of other team directors had marked him deeply, and no amount of success would ever palliate his need to vindicate himself and his particular vision of cycling. He attributed the team's spectacular results to always being one step ahead. 'While the others were busy moaning,' Sáiz had immediately set about adapting ONCE to the new racing calendar.

The UCI immediately declared the September innovation a success, but not everyone was convinced. To be sure, the Jeremiahs who had predicted that a three-week tour so late in the season would produce an alarmingly high retirement rate among tired riders were proved wrong; in fact, it was fairly normal, with 118 of the 180 starters still there in Madrid. Although far more people followed the race on TV, there were noticeably fewer spectators at the stage-finishes. Reasons put forward ranged from insufficient promotion, a public satiated by cycling after the Giro and Tour, competition with the football league, or the absence of Induráin. One of the peculiarities of the new Vuelta was its new function as a market place. It proved to be a perfect arena for finalising deals for the next season and more than 20 riders signed contracts. As for the influence of the World Championships, it was impossible to draw any conclusions. Olano, who'd ridden his heart out in the Vuelta, went to Colombia and took the gold medal in the road race and silver in the time-trial, while Induráin, who'd stayed away, won the time-trial and took the silver in the road race.

In 1996, Unipublic finally got their man. Absent since 1991, when he finished second after Melchor Mauri, Miguel Induráin would be riding the Vuelta. Or rather, Banesto would force him to ride, and the normally amenable and infinitely patient champion openly declared that the decision had been taken against his wishes and better judgement. Coming so soon after his spectacular *pájara* on the climb to Les Arcs in the Tour, the timing could not have been worse. Although he insisted that he had no intention of pulling out before the end, he added: 'I have never started a major race feeling so low.' It says much for Induráin's aura of invincibility that his frank pessimism did little to dampen the expectations that this year's Vuelta would see a genuine battle, rather than just another ONCE festival.

The route indicated a race of two very different halves. Beginning in Valencia, the first nine stages were almost entirely flat; the serious climbing would not begin until stage 12. But, from then on, it would be unremitting, with one mountain-top finish after another. It looked straight-forward enough: for the sprinters there would be numerous opportunities for stage-wins and maybe a day or two in yellow; for the men with higher aspirations, the immediate objective was to get to Ávila, the scene of the stage 10 time-trial, without losing significant amounts of time on their rivals. But that only took account of the topography; it didn't take account of the visionary ambition of Manolo Sáiz. Here was a man who really could build castles in Spain, and on stage 3 ONCE defied that simplistic analysis of the route map by breaking the race apart.

It was the annual visit to Albacete – 167 kilometres into a strong cross-headwind across the flatlands of La Mancha, with a slight rise at kilometre 16 that hardly deserved its third-category status. It's to be assumed that the directors had given orders to be attentive – after all, in the Vuelta Albacete is synonymous with *abanicos*. But no one was expecting an ambush so early. Without warning, three ONCE *gregarios* went to the front on that little climb and, suddenly, the peloton was strung out into single file. Then Jalabert moved to the front: 'I gave a sign to Cuesta to press harder. We got a gap, and more people joined us, and there it all began.' Induráin, intuitively sensing the danger, had rounded up those Banestos he could see and made the bridge.

Before those at the back had fully realised what was happening, there were two groups. Up ahead, 53 had escaped and into the wind they averaged 49kph for the full 167 kilometres (setting a new record for a stage average in the Vuelta). They were driven by the absence

1996

of two of the favourites, Rominger and Fernando Escartín, as well as by Sáiz's exhortations, which were not confined to his own team. Three times he cruised alongside Induráin: 'Come on, Miguel, collaborate.'

'Shut up. You're not my director,' answered Induráin, aware that two of his principal *gregarios*, José María Jiménez and Angel Luis Casero, had missed the break. Then came the instructions from Echávarri. 'Collaborate.'

For a long time, the combined Mapei and Kelme forces in the second group had been tantalisingly close to making contact, but with ONCE and Banesto now in full cry on the front, the cord broke and the gap grew inexorably to an unthinkable seven minutes. No one could have imagined such an outcome. The elimination of two of the top contenders on a completely flat third stage so early in the race in theory seemed impossible, but as Sáiz proudly said: 'The word "impossible" doesn't exist in ONCE's vocabulary.'

Exhausted at the finish – there'd been scant chance to eat or drink – Escartín choked back the tears:

I can't believe what happened. When we were holding the gap at 1'–40" it seemed possible to get back, but then it jumped to three minutes. All year spent working to win the Vuelta and then along comes one of these stages – in principle short and unimportant – and I lose everything.

It was goodbye to the Vuelta for Rominger, too, but he had less invested in the race than the Spaniard; for him it was essentially training for the World Championships that were to be held that year in his native Switzerland. And he had other options: 'What, now?' the journalists asked him in Albacete.

'I will try to win a stage.'

'Time-trial or in the mountains?'

'A mass sprint.'

'Be serious, Tony.'

'I am serious. I've never won a sprint before.'

At least he hadn't lost his sense of humour.

The first time-trial on stage 10 signalled the race was about to change gear. Until now, the leader board was dominated by sprinters, with Italian Fabio Baldato in yellow. The exception was the infiltrator Jalabert, on the basis of his win in Albacete and his relentless pursuit of bonus seconds.

The 46.5-kilometre course into Ávila would have been difficult at the best of times, with countless corners, a long second-category climb and an exposed descent, but it was made all the more so by a strong, capricious wind that boxed the compass. Nobody was going to enjoy this ride. Because of the seven minutes he'd lost earlier, Rominger was the first of the big men to set off. Without references to any other intermediate times, he rode as a man with nothing to lose, and then spent the next hour and a half praying that the wind would not die, nor steady itself. His prayers were answered. Zülle, despite a brave final descent to the walled city, was two seconds slower, and a more cautious Induráin, spurning the use of a specialist time-trial bike on such a technical route and constantly changing gear in search of his characteristic rhythm, was 27 seconds slower. In just 70 minutes Rominger had climbed from 63rd to 22nd overall – not a threat, exactly, but at least back in business.

After Induráin lost time in his own speciality, the first serious doubts set in. He was second overall, but hemmed in on all sides by ONCE men, who occupied the other four places in the top five, with Zülle in yellow. There'd been no Banesto–ONCE confrontation in the Tour that year; the stage of Les Arcs had been catastrophic for both teams, although it was Induráin's downfall that received all the Press attention. The French hope, Jalabert, had abandoned, and Zülle, shaken after two crashes, lost considerable time. During the Tour, in all the most crucial moments, Banesto had failed to support Induráin, and in the Vuelta he cut a similarly solitary figure, with the yellow peril swarming all around. In the words of Manolo Sáiz: 'Banesto is Induráin, while ONCE is the best team in the world.'

The next two testing days were in Asturias, with classic stage-finishes in the Alto de Naranco – named 'Cima Tarangu' in honour of José Manuel Fuente, who'd died that July – and the Lagos de Covadonga. On the road to Oviedo, ONCE assembled their collective strength at the front of the peloton and their pace had reduced the principle group to some 20 riders by the foot of the Naranco. When they reached the steepest section, half-way up, Induráin, who'd appeared completely comfortable all day, began to slip to the back of the group. Disconcerted, Zülle and Jalabert needed a whole kilometre to assimilate the situation. Was Induráin feigning? Could this be a trap? Then the attack came, and it was Les

Arcs all over again – a disconsolate Induráin, pedalling a low gear and barely able to hold the wheel of his *gregario*, Jiménez. As always, his professional dignity wouldn't allow him to give up the fight, but in just two kilometres he lost a minute to the ONCE men, and dropped to third on general classification.

In the inquest, Induráin was his usual phlegmatic self: 'I had difficulties on the last climb. I didn't go as I would have wanted to. I've lost time … and it may be difficult to recuperate the losses.' Eusebio Unzué, co-director at Banesto, was decidedly pessimistic, hinting that his leader might well lose more time the following stage, with its demanding ascent to Covadonga. But was Spain listening?

Induráin's biographer, Javier García Sánchez, notes the religious symbolism that journalists, even in France, tended to adopt when writing about the champion. In *El País*, Carlos Arribas gave full vent to mystical imagery when trying to explain why people had remained so blithely oblivious to all the warning signs:

> In the end, it was all a matter of faith, of wanting to believe that what had happened in the Tour was no more than a temporary loss of form, that if he, the Almighty Induráin, so wished it, the mountains would turn to valleys as he passed through them, and the improbable challenge of riding and winning the Vuelta in September would be feasible for him by a mere act of will, despite the fact that he'd always restricted his best form to three months of the year in order to prolong his career. And although he, he who knows himself and knows his limits, has no faith, faith does not die.

The following day, Induráin retired, not simply from a Vuelta he should never have been required to ride, but also – although he took some months to arrive at this decision – from professional cycling. The end came on the first-category Fito after a vicious attack from Rominger. In the Tour de France, the Swiss rider, who, along with Gianni Bugno, had seen his career stifled by Induráin, had initiated the acceleration on Les Arcs that was to prove the Spaniard's undoing, and now for the second time that year, he again exposed his rival's weakness.

By the summit, Induráin was over four minutes down and had already waved the team-car forward and told his Banesto colleagues to ride on. The TV cameras stayed with him, at the back of the race, and the viewers, transfixed, watched as he consulted his stage itinerary and eventually pulled off the road, shortly before the turn-off to Covadonga. Then he cycled across the forecourt of a two star hotel, calmly dismounted and wheeled his bike into the lobby, where he was greeted by a grave Echávarri and a tearful masseur.

There was nothing more to show, so the television coverage tore itself away to follow the rest of the stage. It was another display of ONCE power, but Manolo Sáiz was frustrated to see his team's performance overshadowed by Induráin yet again, even if for the last time. The next day's headlines would not be 'ONCE spectacular in Covadonga', but 'Induráin abandons Vuelta in *etapa reina*.'

He was not the only great Spanish rider to never win his national tour (or even a stage): like Induráin, Bahamontes always saw the Tour as his race. Similarly, Ocaña, although he won both, commented at the time that winning the Tour had been easier than the Vuelta – where the pressure on him was so much greater. It was, he said, almost as if he was expected to win not just the race, but each and every stage.

The Induráin affair left a bad taste. There'd been hope that some of his grandeur would rub off on the Vuelta, but by forcing him to race, it appeared that the best sportsman Spain has ever produced was being punished for not winning a sixth Tour. And now, without him, the race felt empty. The cyclists immediately noticed a thinning of road-side spectators and missed the cheers, even if they'd been aimed at someone else. People had switched off at home too: the more than four million viewers who'd been watching the Vuelta dropped by half. There were still nine stages left, but the only expectation they held was more ONCE dominance. The superiority of Zülle and Jalabert had been patent in the way they'd swept everyone aside on the way up to the Lagos. They'd finished together, Jalabert taking the stage and Zülle reinforcing his race leadership. It was generally recognised that after accumulating so many second places in his palmarés, he urgently needed to win this Vuelta for his psychological welfare.

There was no threat left for ONCE: Rominger and Escartín had been discounted in Albacete and the Swiss leader of Lotus-Festina, Laurent Dufaux, had lost too much time in the first week while riding himself into form. He was classified third, but at a safe distance of 5'–24". Without an outside enemy to focus on, ONCE seemed in danger of turning on themselves. In particular, Jalabert found it difficult to restrain his attacking nature.

Stage 17, with its summit finish at Cerler, was a bad day for Zülle. First, he'd had to drop back to the team-car for his asthma inhaler, then at the foot of the final ascent he had to ask Jalabert to tell their *gregario*, Oliverio Rincón, to slow down or they'd all be dropped. But the Colombian climber was after a stage-win, and ignored him. Then Escartín attacked and Jalabert, with Dufaux on his wheel, chased them both down. Now Rincón went again, and as the leading group accelerated, the race leader was dropped – by his own team – and suddenly he was isolated. Until, from behind, came Rominger to the rescue. He paced his compatriot back towards the Jalabert/ Dufaux tandem – 'Better for me to help him than Jalabert, wasn't it?' – the two had a long-running grudge from years back when they were riding together in Toshiba. Meanwhile, up ahead, Dufaux stopped working with Jalabert – 'I didn't want Zülle to lose the Vuelta to a Frenchman, who had attacked him.' So, the leading men were reunited, until two hundred metres from the finishing-line when an unrepentant Jalabert jumped again. With this final gesture he took five seconds out of Zülle, plus the eight seconds bonus for second place behind Rincón, the other ONCE renegade.

It was little wonder that people were saying that night that Zülle had been saved by the Swiss Confederation. Sáiz, however, would have none of it. 'Zülle was never in any danger,' he insisted. As for Jalabert, with an insouciance that Hinault would have applauded, he said he was simply demonstrating that 'there is a reserve in the team, if Zülle should falter.'

Two days later, though, it was first-reserve Jalabert who was faltering, losing a massive 25 minutes, and all on the same road to Ávila where just twelve months earlier he'd destroyed the race, and sentenced Olano to a hopeless chase, bereft of allies. The Frenchman wasn't the only one to suffer – Neil Stevens, for instance, lost three-quarters of an hour – as almost the entire ONCE team were weakened by gastro-enteritis, attributed to some suspect meat they'd been served in their hotel. By amazing luck, the one person not to be affected was Zülle.

The day of heavy climbing began with Banesto's Angel Luis Casero setting a riotous 50kph pace, and ended with Dufaux coming in alone after an average of 43kph over 217 switchback kilometres.

Suspicions about ONCE had been aroused when they disappeared from their usual place at the front of the peloton. They tried to bluff it out, responding to the attacks, but soon began to fall apart.

On the first *puerto* Jalabert found himself 'out of gas', and down on the small ring as rider after rider went past. Accompanied by Zarrabeitia, he struggled on, further and further from the real action. Zarrabeitia looked so deathly, that even those who were pleased to see ONCE in trouble felt sorry for him, as he suffered to get to the finish.

While Dufaux's attack was ambitious and brave, his onslaught on the yellow jersey fell short by 55 seconds because Zülle, with his *gregarios* dispersed on the road behind him, was not condemned to the fate Olano had suffered. A mixed group, with varied motives, came to his side. Some were anxious to preserve their position on general classification; others still held out hopes of a stage-win. It was also the time to return favours – Telekom for Dietz's stage-win – or to invest in the future, as in the case of Euskadi. Rominger also lent a hand, although as Zülle said: 'I think that if instead of me it'd been Jalabert, his tactics would've been different.'

The weakness only lasted a day. Despite the retirement of the dedicated and seemingly inexhaustible Stephens, a recovered ONCE were back in control, parading their unity as they surrounded Zülle, the scenes of Cerler forgotten. Dufaux had to be content with second place, while Rominger completed an entirely Swiss podium after winning the final time-trial. The tally for the Spaniards was abysmal; their best placed rider was Escartín, who finished tenth and for the first time in Vuelta history, they hadn't scored a single stage-win – while the spirited Italians broke their 1955 record and won 11 stages. During Induráin's long reign, the Spanish cyclists had been called on to play secondary roles, supporting either him or the foreign stars ONCE had signed to combat him. Without his enormous protective shadow, they seemed unsure of what to do, caught out blinking in the sunlight. 'It's time to give way to the young generation,' said Álvaro Pino, realising an era had ended, 'and to prod some ambition into them.'

Pressurising Induráin to race the Vuelta had been a shabby way to treat a national hero, but come September, others had a genuine need to save their seasons. The new role of the Vuelta as a 'last chance saloon' was very apparent in 1997, with both ONCE and Banesto anxious to make amends for their dismal performances in the Tour de France. Among the foreign riders with something to prove were Rominger and Chris Boardman. The Swiss rider was in his final season and wanted to end his career on a high, and the Briton wanted to show he was something more than just a prologue specialist.

The question was, would ONCE continue their domination for a third year? The onus was on Jalabert, as Zülle had only recently recovered from a fractured collar bone and was very short on competition. He'd crashed on the eve of the Tour de France, where he was supposed to be leading the team, and misguidedly went ahead as planned, only to pull out after four days.

1997 The main novelty of the opening week was that, for the first time, the Vuelta began outside of Spain, with the prologue held in Lisbon. The peloton crossed the Portuguese-Spanish border on stage 3 and would spend the next week baking in Andalucía's soaring temperatures. A day after returning to home ground, in Jerez de la Frontera, there was cause for celebration: 'Anguita breaks the curse' ran *El Mundo Deportivo*'s headline, as the rider of the modest Estepona-Toscaf became the first Spaniard to win a road-stage in the Vuelta since 1994. One of the dominant sprinters that year was Lotus-Festina's Marcel Wüst: after just five days he'd already equalled his '95 tally of three stage-wins.

The first significant battle for the overall was promised on stage 6. It was only 147 kilometres long, but it would take the riders from Málaga on the Costa del Sol, over the 27-kilometre first-category Alto de Cabra Montés and up to Granada, nestling at the foot of the Sierra Nevada. Aside from the altitude to surmount, the oppressive heat on these bare mountain slopes would test the favourites.

When ONCE seized the reins at the foot of the Alto de Cabra Montés, their legendary Basque *gregario* Alberto Leanizbarrutia marking out a suffocating rhythm, there was a feeling of *déjà vu* – didn't this script belong to 1995? The impression intensified when Jalabert, judging the moment to be ripe, rose from the saddle and took off alone. He was shortly joined by Kelme's Escartín, Festina's Dufaux and, riding comfortably on their wheel, team-mate Zülle.

Behind them they'd left a thoroughly disorganised group: two of the top favourites, Banesto's leader Olano and Mapei's Pavel Tonkov were suffering. The Russian had the excuse of a stomach infection, but Olano's weakness disconcerted his team. To compound Banesto's problems, their top climber, José María 'Chaba' Jiménez was struggling to stay in the race.

The powerful quartet in front steadily increased their lead, and by Granada, where Zülle led Jalabert out to victory, they were nearly two minutes clear. The Frenchman was the new race leader, with Dufaux at 16 seconds, Escartín at 21 seconds and Zülle a further five seconds back. Another triumphant day for ONCE while Banesto's director Unzué surveyed the wreckage, at a loss to explain his team's failure. Olano had dropped out of the Tour de France and now his contribution to the Vuelta was also in serious doubt. In fact, he retired the very next day, explaining sadly: 'I haven't got any strength left.' The pressure of having to fill Induráin's shoes was taking its toll: subsequent tests would show he'd been over-training.

The following stage proved too demanding for another team leader. Gan's Chris Boardman, unable to digest a whole major tour, also went home, thus avoiding a tough ride from Guadix, along narrow, badly asphalted roads through the Alpujarras to finish on the Sierra Nevada. At the foot of this mammoth climb, the leading group was already greatly reduced. In their attempts to salvage something from the ruins, both Banesto and Gan sent riders on the attack. It was understandable that ONCE paid scant attention to 'Chaba' Jiménez, as he was a massive 14 minutes down in the overall, but Gan's Yvon Ledanois, who was next to jump, was eighth at 2'–39". As if curious as to why ONCE hadn't reeled the Frenchman in, Escartín attacked, five kilometres from the summit.

The 1997 incarnation of Fernando Escartín was unrecognisable. This small, rather ungainly climber, who grew up in the Huescan Pyrenees, was usually seen hanging on to a leading group, hunched over his bike and apparently suffering terribly. Yet after he'd joined Kelme where, for the first time, he had the responsibilities of a leader, Álvaro Pino coaxed a new racing persona out of him. He'd finished the Tour in fifth place that year, and was one of the main factors why the '97 Vuelta wouldn't turn out to be another ONCE monologue, for, soon after his acceleration, Jalabert cracked. 'My vision clouded,' the Frenchman explained later, 'and I immediately realised what was going to happen.' It was a major *pájara*.

By the finish Jalabert had lost eight minutes and, ashen faced, was reduced almost to walking pace. Joined by Dufaux and Zülle, but working alone, Escartín swept past Jiménez, who'd been unable to stay with the dogged Ledanois. The Gan rider was riding to the best win of his career, while Escartín's attacking performance effectively scuppered all Jalabert's chances of repeating his '95 victory.

The yellow jersey passed to Dufaux, but the top three were classified within 14 seconds, and eyes were turned on Zülle, now ONCE's lone leader. He was suddenly the new race favourite, despite his professed doubts. To some extent, the Córdoba time-trial of stage 9 seemed to confirm his pessimism, as the reigning World Champion against the clock could only finish fourth, unable to establish a significant margin on his two challengers. If the race wasn't going entirely as Manolo Sáiz had planned, at least ONCE hadn't lost any of their mastery in their established speciality. The only "intruder" in the top five was Serguei Gontchar, who finished second while the winner was Melchor Mauri – a conspicuous reminder that no Spaniard had won the Vuelta since 1991.

After Olano's retirement, all of Spain's hopes rested on Escartín, who began the time-trial very strongly, but was unlucky enough to crash on a bend made slippery by a sudden shower. He had to swallow his disappointment, for after his sensational beginning, he went on to lose 2'–15". To maintain his morale he had the prospect of four consecutive summit finishes in the mountains of the north, but the ultimate favourite to win remained Zülle, who was now in yellow and had a team in impressive form behind him. Most of the uncertainty that persisted was down to the Swiss rider's notoriously fragile morale and his famous propensity to crash.

After the disappointing performance of the home-riders in 1996, the second half of the race, in the damper, cooler climes of the north, showed that new Spanish talent was coming to the fore. While Zülle resisted the challenges of Escartín and Dufaux, who were largely dissuaded by the relentless rhythm imposed tirelessly by ONCE, three young Spaniards delighted the spectators with their stage-wins.

On stage 12, after the rest-day, the peloton visited one of Spain's forgotten corners, the Bierzo, a remote mountainous region in the province of León. As the television trucks struggled up a narrow village road to set up the stage-finish on the Puerto del Morredero, they were unable to squeeze past an inopportunely placed barn. There was no alternative: it would have to be dismantled. The owner, sensing a unique opportunity, demanded 10 million pesetas as compensation, but after long talks the negotiators bargained him down to two million, on the strict understanding that everything would be replaced as before. The stage was won by the revelation of the race, Kelme's 23-year old Roberto Heras, who'd go on to finish in fifth place overall.

In Asturias, Banesto could lift up their heads when José García Acosta won on the Naranco and, in the final week, Jiménez, who'd been entertaining the fans with his adventurous attacks, many of them misjudged, finally got his stage-win, as well as clinching the Mountain prize. One of the earlier attackers that day had been Rominger, who managed to build up a 12-minute gap in a last fling of his career.

Without doubt, the most epic day of the race was the Lagos de Covadonga stage, where in cold, drenching rain Escartín again showed his ambition. Still bruised and bandaged from his time-trial crash, he threw caution to the winds, and attacked early – 10 kilometres from the finish – and with every ounce of strength he could muster. He reached a team-mate waiting for him ahead, but by the toughest slopes he was fighting alone, while behind, Jalabert led the chase, with Zülle right on his wheel and Dufaux rapidly losing ground. Only near the end was Escartín caught and overtaken, the stage going to Tonkov, but the Spaniard had secured his second place on the podium, pushing his way in between the two Swiss riders.

The final time-trial of Alcobendas was another opportunity for ONCE to display their collective strength, once more taking four of the top five positions. On this occasion the winner was Zülle, which left his final margin on Escartín a very solid 5'-07". ONCE had completed a remarkable Vuelta triple, without being quite the super-power of other years. They'd been the quickest off the mark to adapt to the September slot, but others were finally getting the hang of it, notably Kelme (who won the best team classification), and the battle had been more evenly matched. Rather than crushing all opposition with brute force, this time ONCE had been more calculating and ready to make alliances.

The debate about the Vuelta's move to September continued. In 1995, Sáiz had boasted that it was possible to remain competitive all season long, but with hindsight, this had only been feasible with an exceptional Jalabert in unrepeatable form. If only there were more where he came from. In 1997, Zülle finished the race by far the strongest rider, but his enforced lay-off from racing through July and most of August had given him a clear edge on his rivals.

For a stage race trying to make its way in a calendar dominated more than ever by the Tour de France, there was no perfect solution. If in May the cyclists had too often been saving their legs for the French race, in September, they came to the Vuelta vulnerable to suffering at least one off-day – as had happened to Jalabert. Yet the peloton could hardly be described as tired: at an average of over 41kph, it had been the fastest three-week tour on record. And at the end of the season there was a guaranteed source of inspiration to overcome fatigue. Gan's Yvon Ledanois had been facing retirement at the age of 28. But after his exploit on the Sierra Nevada, he received offers from no less than ten teams.

Mundo Deportivo

Pedro Delgado, Spain's most popular cyclist after Induraín, delighted the fans by twice winning the Vuelta when all seemed lost. An assiduous participant in his home race, before and after his Tour triumph.

Robert Millar in the yellow jersey he would lose to Pedro Delgado on the penultimate stage in 1985. 'It was so blatant, so scandalous,' said Millar, referring to a rare instance of collaboration among the Spanish teams. In this respect he was certainly unlucky, but a weak, poorly-directed Peugeot team didn't help, either. Millar finished second again in 1986 behind Álvaro Pino.

Lucho Herrera turned the Colombian broadcasters' voices horse with his victory in 1987.

Mundo Deportivo

Phil O'Connor

Sean Kelly rode five Vueltas and won the points jersey four times. Overall victory in 1988 removed the thorn in his side from having to drop out the year before while wearing the leader's jersey.

Tony Rominger celebrating his third consecutive victory in 1994. It was in the Vuelta, supported by an Asturian Clas team fully committed to his cause, that Rominger finally proved that a three-week tour was within his range.

Roberto Heras emerging through the mist to win on the Angliru, 2002.

ONCE winning the opening team time trial at Valencia in 2002. 'The best team in the world,' said Manolo Sáiz.

Alejandro Valverde, Roberto Heras and Isidro Nozal – the principal protagonists of 2003.

1998–2001

The Angliru – the Climbers' Revenge

The Induráin era was now history and the escaladores were reclaiming their position as the heroes of Spanish cycling. The cyclists who followed the Induráin model, dominating the time-trials, and defending their gains in the mountains – highly talented riders like Abraham Olano or Angel Casero – found a Spanish public unmoved by their achievements, even resenting their triumphs. Spectators were tired of large men pounding past in extra-terrestrial outfits – unless they were actually verging on the extra-terrestrial, as in the case of Induráin; they wanted to see fleet climbers escaping lightly away, leaving the heavyweights stranded. Their allegiance shifted to men like Fernando Escartín, José María 'Chaba' Jiménez, Roberto Heras and Oscar Sevilla, whose audacious attacks defied the experts against the clock whenever the road steepened. The two factions would both accuse the Vuelta organisers of favouring the other.

Unipublic also wanted heroics, and they took the Vuelta into a new creative period. It could never rival the Tour de France but, unshackled by tradition, the organisers were free to tinker and innovate, ever on the lookout for tough new climbs, such as the Angliru, which became a classic overnight. The aim was a race that looked good on television and would keep the attention of the spectators. Even the Tour could be plagued by monotony in its first week, before the onset of the mountains: Unipublic's idea was to provide *espectaculo* – the riders had been warned.

Many cyclists are considered unlucky for having coincided with one of the giants – Poulidor with Anquetil, Ocaña and Fuente with Merckx, Bugno with Induráin. The case of the Basque Abraham Olano is particularly unfair, since he had to compete with Induráin even when the five-times Tour winner had retired. Olano could never escape his shadow, never be granted the respect he deserved, because he was forever being compared and found wanting. It didn't help that they had a certain physical similarity and shared the same team colours. Rigged up for a time-trial in matching Darth Vader helmets, the two powerfully-built cyclists were very hard to tell apart.

Superficially, even their characters seemed alike. But while Induráin was quiet in a relaxed way, because nothing could pressurise him into talking if he wasn't so inclined, Olano was painfully shy. He even talked about himself in third person, as if he couldn't bear to use the word 'I' and admit he and Olano were one and the same. His palmarés is impressive, but he obtained results on the basis of tremendous sacrifice and relentless work, starving himself to lose the weight that slowed him down in the mountains.

The aura of suffering and endurance that clung to Olano couldn't contrast more with the carefree approach of his team-mate 'Chaba' Jiménez. Responsibility and perseverance were anathema to Chaba and he was often accused of wasting a prodigious talent. Inexplicably, considering his height and weight – 1.82 metres and 67 kilos – he was, by his own admission, an abysmal time-trialist. Except in the cronoescalada, he never really came to grips with an art that requires discipline and constancy. His preferred scenario was the mountain, thronged with spectators, where instinct and intuition came into play. For Chaba, the prospect of endless, empty flat roads was soul-destroying. 'Maybe on the outside I have the qualities of a time-trialist,' he said, 'but on the inside I'm a pure climber.' His success in the 1998 Vuelta made him a star, and turned what should have one of the highlights of Olano's career into an ordeal.

1998   At the end of stage six, Chaba Jiménez became race leader after an explosive climb of the short but brutal Xorret de Catí. It was the first Vuelta yellow jersey for Banesto since Julián Gorospe wore it in 1990. Still fresh in people's minds was Pantani's spectacular attack on Ullrich on the Galibier in the '98 Tour de France, and there was speculation that a climber might similarly storm the Vuelta. But Chaba's chances of winning the overall were put into perspective when he lost an exhorbitant 4'–05" in the 39-kilometre time-trial in Mallorca on stage 9. He dropped down to fifteenth place, while Olano – the only cyclist to reach an average of over 50kph – gave a performance worthy of Induráin, to ensure that the yellow jersey remained in Banesto's hands. Classified in second place at 41 seconds was Jalabert, at the head of an uncharacteristically low-key ONCE.

As the peloton headed north to the Pyrenees, Kelme prepared their strategy. Powerfully equipped with climbers, their mission was to wear out Olano and put Escartín at the top of the podium. Unfortunately for their interests, the third stage in the Pyrenees had been hastily redesigned to avoid any incursion into France, consequently losing much of its toughness. Since the previous July, when the Tour had nearly been overwhelmed by the 'Festina Affair', and the Spanish teams had walked out mid-race, French–Spanish relations had been strained. There'd been particularly tense confrontations between the Tour organisers and Manolo Sáiz, ONCE's characteristically outspoken director, about their inability to protect the cyclists from heavy-handed police. Throwing Zülle into a police cell, naked and defenceless without his glasses, seemed so shockingly over-the-top that the expelled Festina were welcomed to the Vuelta with open arms, and cheered from the roadsides.

Kelme launched their first massive attack on the etapa reina, which began in the plains of Vic, in the heart of Catalunya, and finished 200 kilometres further north at the ski station of Pal, in Andorra, with three first-category puertos in the last 60 kilometres. On the penultimate climb of the Ordino, a trio of Escartín, Heras and Marcos Serrano escaped, with Chaba Jiménez tagging along for the ride, to sprint past them to victory with insolent ease. Kelme had succeeded in scraping just over a minute on Olano, who crossed the line with Jalabert. It seemed scant reward for their hard work.

Equally effortlessly, Chaba employed the same tactics at the end of the following stage in Cerler, latching onto Escartín and Heras as again they furiously tried to distance Olano. 'I won almost without trying,' he grinned. It was a frustrating position for Kelme, as with every attack they were carrying Jiménez ever closer to the top of the classification. They did all the work, and he stole all the glory. Escartín had risen to third place, at 51 seconds, but Chaba was now fourth at 1'–17". In second place, Jalabert had slightly whittled down his difference to 35 seconds, leaving the top of the general classification very tight.

Although Olano had survived the Pyrenees in yellow, doubts were beginning to form about how solid a leader he might be. The three stages won by Jiménez were a challenge to his position in the team. Even more damning was the image he had presented in the mountains, suffering etched on his face – in this respect, he was very different from Induráin, who'd nearly always worn an impassive mask – guided by his faithful squire, Manolo Beltrán, who would loyally stick with him to the ends of the earth, after his old Mapei team-mate had rescued him from an untimely retirement to olive-picking in Jáen. In contrast, there was Chaba, lifting his arm in triumph yet again, as he crossed the finishing-line, and with more mountains to come.

Kelme had a small but satisfying revenge on what was supposed to be a routinely transitional stage, from Biescas to Zaragoza, as the race turned to the centre of Spain. A 17-strong breakaway was allowed to go clear, made up of powerful well-organised roadmen, all, that is, except for one small climber hidden amongst them. By the time Banesto's director Unzúe realised that Roberto Heras had slipped off unnoticed, and was being born at relentless speed to the finish, it was no easy matter to chase the group down. The result: two and a half hours of hard labour for Banesto, and victory for Festina's sprinter Marcel Wüst, after a stage of the record-breaking average speed of 51.137kph.

Undoubtedly, Banesto had the best team, but cracks began to show when the race returned to the mountains on stage 16, with a summit finish in the Sierra de la Demanda. On the painfully steep final three kilometres, Jiménez didn't wait to follow a Kelme wheel this time, but attacked alone, winning his fourth stage, 33 seconds ahead of Jalabert and Escartín, while Olano came in after 46 seconds, faithfully paced by Beltrán. Banesto's top climber had now overtaken Escartín in the overall, and was only 9 seconds behind Jalabert, who in turn was edging closer to Olano. Chaba was clearly threatening both Kelme and ONCE, but wasn't he also threatening his own leader? Olano's wife and manager, Karmele Zubillaga seemed to think so, and complained on the radio that the team were sidelining her husband: 'Sometimes greed can split the sack,' she warned.

There was furore, as people took sides. Unzúe claimed he'd given Jiménez permission to attack, but his unpredictable climber was difficult to discipline. Paying more attention to his own instincts than team orders, he'd disappeared up the road somewhat sooner than expected. There was also resentment that a woman was butting in, no matter that she was an ex-cyclist. Chaba insisted the team were working for Olano, but admitted he felt he had chances of victory himself.

But the tensions in the team didn't interfere with their hold on the race. The penultimate mountainous day finished in Segovia, and for once Jiménez stayed in the group, and Heras took a stage for Kelme. An excellent descender, Olano was able to rejoin the leaders after running into problems on the Navacerrada, too far from the finish to enter into Escartín's strategy. The same climb featured twice the next day, and since the stage finished at the top, Olano couldn't avoid losing 1'–09", and ceding the yellow jersey to Jiménez, to the delight of the climber's many fans. But it was a calculated move, and only a temporary one, in view of the forthcoming 39-kilometre time-trial in Fuenlabrada. Chaba was keeping the jersey out of Kelme's reach, holding Escartín at bay by 6 seconds, while a very tired-looking Jalabert had lost all chances of making the podium.

As expected, Olano won back the yellow jersey in the final time-trial, which he lost to Zülle by a mere second. Escartín defended his second place, and for once, Chaba Jiménez exerted himself in the discipline he loathed, at least enough to keep Lance Armstrong from ousting him from the podium. The American's come-back from cancer was hailed as a miracle, no one suspecting what was yet to come.

The presence of two climbers on the podium – an accurate reflection of how mountainous a race it had been, lent more prestige to Olano's victory. During his first year and a half with Banesto, plagued by injury and crashes, he had been under tremendous pressure to achieve. Winning the Vuelta should have spelt the end of his troubles, yet people begrudged his victory because he wasn't spectacular enough. Understandably, Olano felt this was unfair: 'It's not often you see the yellow jersey attacking to gain more time on the second man,' he protested. He resented the way the media had tried to cause a rift between him and his wife, and that, instead of celebrating, he was having to excuse himself: 'We can't all be cheerful and talkative … there are people who always have a smile on their lips, and are always telling jokes,' he said, in reference to his team-mate and rival. 'I'm not like that, I'm a man of few words.' It was true that Chaba made the sport look exciting and fun. Young cyclists wanted to be like him; no one wanted to be Olano, grimly defending as if bearing the weight of the world on his back. Few seemed to care that he was the current Spanish rider with by far the best palmarés: among other achievements, this included the World Road-Race title of 1995, third place in the Giro of 1996, an Olympic silver medal in Atlanta, and now the Vuelta, soon to be followed by the 1998 World Time-trial Championship.

For Banesto, the Vuelta had been a resounding success: two men in the top three, the team prize, five stages and the Mountain prize for Chaba Jiménez. In spite of all the controversy, Olano and Jiménez had formed an efficient partnership, acting like the claws of a pincer, in which Kelme struggled. The climber's task had been to wear down Kelme's morale, and without a leader's responsibility, he was free to take stage-wins. But, as Olano pointed out: 'Without me, he wouldn't have reached the podium.' It was the first Spanish win since 1991 and an all-Spanish podium. There were some, like *El País'* long-standing reporter, Luis Gómez, who saw this as a discouraging sign: he dismissed the race as 'a dish for internal consumption'. But the fans had been thrilled by the intensity of the racing, with its ration of scandal included.

* * * * *

1999   The star of the 1999 Vuelta was a mountain track used through the ages for taking livestock to high pasture and discovered by cyclists after being blessed with a layer of asphalt. The infamous Angliru was an answer to all the sceptical critics who avowed the Vuelta could never match the Tour or Giro, because Spain didn't have a Tourmalet or a Mortirolo. As another self-assertive statement, the leader's jersey was officially switched from yellow to gold.

The Angliru was a symbol of defiance. The 1999 Tour de France was all about morality and moderation, the idea being that with less hardship, the cyclists could be persuaded to throw away their stash of EPO. But the Vuelta organisers understood that moderation equals tedium, and had concocted a route that was more mountainous than either the Tour or Giro. The Tour still had the hardest single stage (finishing in Alpe d'Huez) as well as the longest climbs, while the Giro boasted the steepest slopes. But an analysis that took into consideration every climb in the route books, comparing the length, altitude, gradient and distance from the finish, left the Vuelta on top that year.

Obstinately going against the trend, Unipublic had devised no less than three consecutive summit finishes in the Pyrenees, apart from introducing a climb whose severity was already legendary before its official inauguration. Purely as a publicity exercise, the Angliru was a success. Throughout the year, journalists and cyclists had been dispatched to bring back reports, and all returned suitably impressed. Kelme's José Luis 'Chechu' Rubiera swore it was 'the hardest puerto I've climbed in my life.' And Pedro Delgado, after climbing it with his old team mate José Laguía, warned: 'Nothing like it has been seen before. Some will be putting their feet on the ground.' Other visitors included the head of the Basque government, Juan José Ibarretxe, a keen cyclist, and a waiter who went up carrying a tray of drinks in one hand. The interest building up before the stage was intense.

The Vuelta's offer of a last chance to redeem a bad season was taken up by Jan Ullrich. After failing his summer exams, he was obliged to resit them in autumn. The 1997 Tour winner had suffered a disastrous year, apparently with only himself to blame. He'd put on weight, kept an undisciplined training programme and finally had to cancel the Tour because of injury. If anyone needed to save a bad year, it was Ullrich. Taciturn and impassive as ever, the Kaiser hastily played down any ambitions: his form was still bad, he assured everyone, and he was only thinking of the World Championships. Without any other references, his rivals only had the size of his jowls to go on, and they, disconcertingly, had disappeared.

The first selection was expected to occur on stage six, a 51-kilometre time-trial around Salamanca, but the race stirred into life the day before, when the peloton encountered the first serious mountain, the first-category Alto del Portillo. A reshuffle of team line-ups meant that Zülle, who'd finished the Tour in second place behind Armstrong, was now leading Banesto, and Olano had signed with ONCE. Manolo Sáiz wanted to show that in his hands Olano could outshine anything he'd achieved in Banesto. It would be another way of proving ONCE's superiority over their eternal rivals.

Unfortunately for Zülle, the sharp-eyed Sáiz had spotted that his old cyclist was having a bad day, and ONCE's attack was merciless. At the finish in Ciudad Rodrigo, Zülle had lost five minutes, gasping, 'A bad day – I'm very tired.' Rounding off the work of his team, Olano finished the stage in second place behind Ullrich, who recorded his first victory of the season. It was enough to give the Basque rider the maillot oro and the privileged position of starting last in the following day's time-trial.

The parcours of the '99 Vuelta was a snub for Abraham Olano. Rather than paying homage to Spain's top cyclist, it seemed designed to mock him, inviting the country to watch with embarrassment, or exasperation, as he toiled up the most punishing slopes to be found. So there was an air of defiance when he stormed to victory in the Salamanca time-trial. He put almost a minute into Ullrich, and opened up a chasm of time between himself and the climbers: Tonkov, 4'–44"; Heras, 5'–07"; Escartín, 6'–13"; Jiménez, 7'–13". Afterwards, quiet and composed, Olano addressed his enemies, who were stunned into silence: 'They will have to prepare themselves to attack me from afar, and everyone knows such effort can be very costly.'

At last, on a rainy Sunday, came the moment of reckoning. The Angliru was proceeded by two first-category climbs, the Cobertoria and Cordal, all located in Asturias, a region full of vertiginously steep valleys and exuberant vegetation that thrives in the misty wet climate. The central road that comes down from the Puerto de Pajares, leading to Oviedo, is wide with a steady gradient. But take a turning on either side and you invariably find yourself on narrow, suffocatingly steep lanes, observed by handsome, athletic cows clinging impossibly to their near-vertical pasture. This is Angliru territory: there are others lurking there, still to be asphalted. At first glance, the vital statistics of the climb are not overly impressive – 13 kilometres long, reaching an altitude of 1,558 metres – but a more detailed look reveals intimidating ramps of 23%. In comparison, the Tourmalet reaches a maximum of 13% and the Mortirolo 18%.

The stage fulfilled expectations in that it provided an epic day of cycling, which had spectators riveted to the television – in Italy more people watched than during any stage of the Giro. Thousands came to cheer on the cyclists, saturated by the cold rain, livening up the mist with their multicoloured waterproofs. Ironically, the adverse weather meant the descents bore more weight on the final result than the climbs. The notoriously treacherous Cobertoria – where in '93 Zülle lost the race – saw too many crashes to count. Leonardo Piépoli alone fell three times. Escartín, in the best season of his career, having finished third in the Tour, broke three ribs when he landed on a guardrail: 'Tell them not to worry at home. I'll be all right for the wedding' was the message he passed on to the TV commentators. The descent of the Cordal, which led to the Angliru itself, was equally dangerous, and on a corner, Olano disappeared off the road. He was pulled out from the thick mass of leaves and soaking heather, whereupon he immediately remounted and continued the descent, 'like a plane', as the impressed TV commentator described. What was even more impressive was the way Olano, helped at first by team-mate Zarrabeitia, attacked the final climb, storming past everyone in his way.

The Russian Ivanov had been first to reach the Angliru, but closing fast was a group that included Tonkov, Chaba Jiménez, Rubiera, Ullrich and Heras who, with Escartín in hospital, had suddenly become Kelme's leader. Tonkov attacked from the first slopes, but no one reacted. Ullrich must have been thinking the gold jersey was his: all he had to do was maintain a constant rhythm. His calculations were thrown when, incredibly, Olano appeared on his wheel. This was the signal for Heras to react, and Chaba went with him.

They reached the appalling final six kilometres, where Olano, forcing his way up the 18% slopes, left Ullrich behind. Ahead, Jiménez had dropped Heras, but it seemed too late: Tonkov's steady rhythm had taken him nearly to the finish, although at the steepest part, it seemed he would grind to a halt. But just a kilometre from the top, he was caught, and Chaba was first over the line, headlights glowing in the fog behind him.

The stage had given Olano's ex-team-mate and rival a chance to make amends for a disappointing season; he seemed more relieved than ecstatic: "The responsibility was enormous. I knew that the Vuelta had programmed this stage thinking of me and there were many expectant people. I didn't want to let them down.'

The scene at the finish resembled a battlefield, with bloodied legs and torn shorts, and not enough doctors to go round. The overall classification hadn't changed as much as expected, and, ironically, it was Olano who'd profited most of all, putting another minute into Ullrich to secure his position as leader. No one yet knew that he had fractured a rib in the crash. Olano never looked as much of a hero as he did that day, fighting back on the Angliru.

As the peloton moved eastwards to Cantabria on an uncomfortable autumnal day of driving rain and gusting wind, Olano wiped out virtually all the Angliru gains of the climbers by provoking a split on the final downhill stretch. It was his way of telling the organisers he was unimpressed by the newfangled innovations they had strewn in his path. Afterwards he predicted: 'The Vuelta will be decided in the Pyrenees. It's always been so.'

And he was right. On the first of the three Pyreneean stages the peloton showed a reluctance to engage in any battle, preferring to save their strength for the days to come. The climb to the Pla de Beret is long and steady, and the main field were not interested in catching the group that had escaped since kilometre 25. Finally, Santi Blanco of Vitalicio-Seguros decided to move, and unwittingly he exposed Olano. Alone, without any team support, he looked far from strong. His rivals immediately woke up from their lethargy and in four kilometres ONCE's race-leader lost 30 seconds.

The *etapa reina* was short, at 147 kilometres, but with three first-category climbs and an hors catégorie finish at the Arcalís ski station, there would be nowhere to hide. It was Zülle who undertook the task of eliminating Olano. Taking revenge for stage 5, he set a blistering pace on the second climb of the day. As always, Olano didn't take the easy way out. He stoically soldiered on, and managed to catch the leading group on the descent, only for the whole process to be repeated on the following climb. El País reporter Luis Gómez could hardly bear to watch this vision of dignified suffering: 'It doesn't make sense to insist on forcing him into the role of the eternal loser.' He lost over seven minutes at the end, and when the peloton arrived in Barcelona the next day, he visited a hospital for an x-ray, which confirmed that his acute discomfort was due to a fractured rib. Only then did he say goodbye. Shamefully, his doctor was obliged to show the x-rays to the Press, since in some quarters there was disbelief, and suspicion that it was all just an 'excuse'. They were quick to see another failure, where there was only courage.

For Ullrich, Arcalís held only good memories: this was where he'd sealed his victory in the Tour of 1997, leaving behind his role as Riis' gregario, and this was where he now put on the Vuelta's gold jersey. The hero of the day was Igor González de Galdeano of the Spanish Vitalicio team, who escaped on the penultimate climb with 25 kilometres to go. His radio connection wasn't working properly, and he'd mistakenly thought his director was ordering him to attack. It was a profitable mistake because he finished with 40 seconds on Heras and Jiménez, and it left the top three overall extremely close: Ullrich first, with 36 seconds on Igor and 48 seconds on Tonkov.

Forty-five riders had failed to make the cut on the Arcalís stage, but were allowed to continue, a common enough practice in all the major stage races after a gruelling mountain stage. But the perennial problem of over-lenient judges, especially when foreigners were involved, persisted. Festina's sprinter Marcel Wüst, who'd won four stages and worn the gold jersey, was fined 200 Swiss francs for getting towed, but one of the Spanish directors observed that 'Wüst has spent half the Vuelta hanging on to a car'. After the Angliru stage, the grinning German sprinter remarked, 'I hardly noticed the 23-per-cent ramp.' To be fair, neither had a great portion of the peloton, those out of range of the TV cameras, who were propelled upwards by obliging spectators. But, for all Unipublic's self-assertiveness, there still seemed to be a fear of applying the rules too strictly, in case it alienated the foreigners.

The final stage in the Pyrenees was won by Zülle, who'd recovered his form, while Tonkov weakened and lost his third place to Roberto Heras. The peloton faced the final week sapped of their competitive will. There was an Italian-led mutiny in Barcelona, using the excuse of a potentially dangerous urban circuit, which the riders trailed around, assailed by spectators' insults. Providing relief from the general tiredness, Frank Vandenbrouke took two stages with great panache, particularly in Ávila, where the blonde Belgian star, whose earlier escape bid had been curtailed, unleashed his power again on the cobbled rise to the walled city, and crossed the finish alone, fully conscious of his own glamorous image. Vandenbrouke was another rider who needed a boost to his season, in his case marred by accusations of drug-trafficking.

The Belgian had energy to spare, and was hired to work for Ullrich to make up for Telekom's shortcomings. He proved very useful when the German had a bad day in the Sierra de Madrid, the customary final opportunity to attack the race leader. Stage 18 finished on the Alto de Abantos, where Zülle moved to the front and set a torturous pace. Seven kilometres from the top, Ullrich cracked, but the false flats enabled him to minimise his losses; second-placed Igor González de Galdeano only gained 18 seconds. Ullrich arrived at the summit-finish destroyed, but his gold jersey was safe. In the following time-trial, he had no rivals, and shored up his final lead to 4'-15". There wasn't too much regret: it was considered positive for the Vuelta that a foreign rider of the calibre of Ullrich should win, although there was to be a very different view of his performance the following year.

In 2000, Unipublic continued their innovations, slashing the **2000** previous year's route by nearly 700 kilometres, stringing together a series of short, explosive stages, the longest of which was just under 200 kilometres and the majority hovering around 150. It was their response to criticisms of an overly strenuous race at the end of the season, and they hoped the new format would be amenable to cyclists aiming for the World Championships and the Sydney Olympics. Nevertheless, the shortened route was bristling with mountains, with five summit finishes, including both Asturian classics, the Lagos de Covadonga and Angliru. To sweeten the pill, there were two rest days and an attempt to cut down on travelling between stages, several beginning and ending in the same place, giving the riders more time in bed.

Among the foreigners, Ullrich was the star, but he abandoned just before the Asturian challenge, despite being well-classified overall in fourth place. Enrique Franco, Unipublic's boss, couldn't forgive him: 'His withdrawal is his great defeat.' The Vuelta might have saved his desultory '99 season, but he didn't harbour any feelings of gratitude. Given his East German background, the Olympics were particularly important to him and it was unsurprising he'd come to Spain merely to turn pedals in preparation. When the initial fury died down, he was quickly forgotten. The impetus and class of the Spanish riders increasingly undermined the importance of the foreign input.

The race began with an extensive sojourn in Andalucía, where World Champion Oscar Freire won two stages, before moving to the Mediterranean through La Mancha. For all the talk of 'modern' cycling, some things remained reassuringly unchanged: climbers still suffered in the wind. In the echelons of the Albacete stage, not one member of Kelme made it to the first group. Naturally, the instigators were ONCE-Deutschebank. Across the windswept terrain, shorn of trees, the roads are long and straight, but Manolo Sáiz had spotted a curve, where the wind would suddenly pummel the cyclists from the side. On his orders, ONCE drew out the peloton till it snapped and the whole of Kelme were caught out in the second group, coming in at 1'–21". It was a sign of ONCE's declining power that they didn't lose more.

Despite this slip-up, there was no doubt that the strongest team this year was Kelme, under the direction of their ex-cyclist Vicente Belda, who had a taste for unrelentingly aggressive tactics. Their top riders, Oscar Sevilla, Chechu Rubiera and Fernando Escartín, put aside personal glory, and instead of fighting for stage-wins, worked incessantly for their leader, Roberto Heras. At the end of the second week, they gave a master class in the Lagos de

Covadonga stage. By this time, Chaba Jiménez had gone home, ending another poor season, and Vitalicio-Seguros' Igor González de Galdeano, although classified third, was beginning to struggle with a leg injury. Wearing the gold jersey was Ángel Casero, leading a rejuvenated Festina, whose identity was now more Spanish than French. Cool as a cucumber, Casero was a quietly confident rider, whose best result so far had been to finish fifth in the Tour de France in 1999. Excellent against the clock, he didn't appear to struggle in the mountains as much as Olano. He'd taken the leader's jersey on the stage 11 climb to Arcalís, after Kelme had made the essential selection. Behind him, at 1'–15", was Roberto Heras, a rider who never seemed to stop progressing. Small and wiry, in the best tradition of pure-bred climbers, he'd disconcerted Armstrong so much in the Tour that year, that US Postal were at that moment negotiating to sign up both him and team-mate Rubiera.

The climb to the Lagos concluded a short stage of just under 150 kilometres, beginning in Santander. A group had broken away, infiltrated by Kelme's Colombian rider, Felix Cárdenas, while his team-mates maintained a lively tempo that had the main field suffering. Given a jumpstart by Sevilla, whose powerful surge effectively dropped Ángel Casero, Heras escaped with six kilometres to go, Cárdenas falling back to lend a hand. A survivor of the original escape, Andrei Zintchenko, took the stage, but Heras had rounded off the teamwork to secure Kelme's first ever gold, or yellow, jersey.

The race had gone back to zero, with Heras and Casero lying virtually even on general classification. To break this deadlock, Heras had two stages in the final week of racing where he could strike: those finishing on the Angliru and Abantos. But Casero might have the last word in Madrid, for the Vuelta had rediscovered the tradition of finishing with a time-trial, and perhaps his early withdrawal from the Tour de France would leave him fresher for the closing stages. The outcome of the race was still very much up in the air.

As in its inaugural year, the Angliru was proceeded by two first-category climbs, and as on the Lagos stage, Kelme were happy to let an escape go, while remaining in control from behind. On the Alto de la Colladiella, they increased the speed to leave Casero isolated without any team support. Then on the Cordal, they intensified the pace to shrink the leading group even more, Igor González de Galdeano losing touch and then abandoning. On the Angliru, Kelme's old leader Escartín took over from Rubiera at the head of a reduced group of favourites. The mountain was shrouded in fog, but this year the road was mercifully dry. When they reached the toughest ramps, Casero began to drop back, and Heras took off alone, with such zeal it seemed he would overtake all the members of the breakaway, now scattered all over the climb. Finally, only two survived, Jan Hruska and the stage-winner, Gilberto Simoni. Heras crossed the line in a state of euphoria, for as Festina's director, Juan Fernández, ruefully put it: 'The Angliru fits him like a glove.' But even Heras admitted to having suffered: 'You go at 9kph ... it's hell. There's nothing remotely like it.' With Casero losing 3'–41", this year it had been the decisive climb of the race.

As the peloton passed through Castilla, Heras was able to proudly parade his gold jersey through the streets of his home town, Béjar. And on the outskirts of Madrid, in the Alto de Abantos, he experienced the glory of his second stage-win, outdoing Simoni on the line. Casero resisted bravely, but ceded a further 45 seconds, leaving Heras with a four-and-a-half minute margin with which to confront the time-trial in Madrid. It would be more than sufficient. Although Casero finished second, just 6 seconds behind the stage-winner, Once's Santos González, he was able to re-coup less than two minutes on the triumphant Heras.

There was enormous satisfaction that the Vuelta had fallen into the hands of a climber, for the first time since Pedro Delgado won it in 1989. It was also a fitting 20th anniversary present for Kelme, marred only by the disappointing news that Heras would be deserting his old team and riding for US Postal next season, as a gregario de luxe. It seemed that Armstrong had wiped out a rival with his cheque book, and people knew they were being cheated of afternoons of battle and suspense, but the accusations of a lack of ambition were unfair, as Heras was very conscious of his weakness in time-trials. A modern champion is expected to shine in all fields, and like Pedro Delgado before him, who went abroad to PDM to broaden his skills, Heras had every hope that he might learn some new tricks in a foreign team.

His concerns seemed justified when in the Vuelta of 2001, the **2001** climber's ally, the Angliru, was absent, and as the days passed, it became clear that Heras was not the only one in search of a more perfect balance between their abilities in the mountains and against the clock. The race would be marked by a succession of surprise performances, as a result of riders working on their weak points.

The 2001 parcours hadn't left out the other Asturian colossus, the Lagos de Covadonga, and its early presence in the first week meant the contenders had to be in top form from the start. There were many ageing champions in the peloton – Zülle, Olano, Mauri – whose time had passed. Representing the new generation, Banesto's 23-year old Juanmi Mercado attacked seven kilometres from the top, and became the first Spaniard to win the emblematic stage since Delgado in 1992. The only rider able to make a serious pursuit was Kelme's Oscar Sevilla, who became the new race leader. Nicknamed 'El Niño' (the boy) because of his rosy apple cheeks, Sevilla had shone in the Tour de France, finishing in seventh place and winning the white jersey for the best young rider.

The Lagos stage showed that the strongest of the 'all-rounders' were Joseba Beloki, who'd finished third in the Tour de France for the second year running, and Casero, whose contract with Festina was up and his motivation high. It wasn't a good day for Roberto Heras, whose prospects in the overall classification seemed uncertain. His first year in US Postal was not going smoothly, with language problems and a potentially serious knee injury that meant he'd finished the Tour with his leg in plaster. In Kelme, he'd been the undisputed leader, backed by a powerful squad firing on all cylinders. For US Postal, the main goal of the year had already been accomplished, with Armstrong's third Tour in the bag, and Heras had to make do with their B-team.

In fact, US Postal nearly pulled out in the first week because of events outside the race. On 11 September, the peloton were on the road between León and Gijón, completing the fourth stage, when New York's Twin Towers were attacked. As the world held its breath, braced for an apocalyptic reaction from President Bush, US Postal decided to continue, with special police protection for the Americans.

After the Lagos, the top thirteen on general classification were all Spaniards, but there was a group of foreign riders in the race seeking redemption at the end of the season. Unlikely to find it, was Pantani; morally sunk, he'd been dragging himself around various races, trying to recover his old motivation. Another doping casualty, Richard Virenque, had just finished serving out his ban, and the Belgian team Domo-Farm Frites had found space for him. In France, he was still a pariah – at least for the Tour organisers – but in Spain, his determination was admired, and the Vuelta was a chance for rehabilitation.

Then there was David Millar, at the head of Cofidis, anxious to ride a disastrous Tour de France out of his system. He'd crashed in the Prologue, and pulled out a few days later. For him, the Vuelta proved an excellent tonic: he won the opening time-trial in Salamanca and became the first race leader. Then the day after the Lagos, he teamed up with Kelme's Santiago Botero to give the stage an unexpected twist. Mapei were struggling to control the race, trying to set up Oscar Freire for a sprint in his Cantabrian home town, Torrelavega. But the terrain was too rigorous, with three second-category climbs and the third-category San Cipriano situated 13 kilometres from the finish. It was here that Millar, part of a seven-man break, attacked, with Botero quickly on his wheel. By the time the main field realised what was happening it was too late. The pair worked hard together and fought a close sprint, which Millar won. The spectators were delighted by this audacious attack, even though local hero Freire was denied his win. As cycling was no longer the spontaneous sport of the past, any break with the script was well-appreciated.

The surprises continued. The very next day, the blond, blue-eyed Colombian had his revenge on Millar in the stage 7 time-trial. Only the previous year, Botero had gone to the Tour de France and, as befitted a cyclist of his nationality, emerged as King of the Mountains. But after a Jekyll and Hyde struggle, in the Vuelta he found himself winning a flat, 44-kilometre time-trial, and taking over the gold jersey from team-mate Oscar Sevilla. Mountains had become an obstacle for his new, far more muscular physique, but against the clock he was now one of the best. Sevilla was another climber prepared to sacrifice some of his power on the mountains for the same end. His excellent ride – he lost only a second to ONCE's Beloki – revealed he'd been practising.

On stage 8, the peloton faced their second summit finish in La Cruz de la Demanda, and it was expected that Botero would hand the gold jersey back to Sevilla. But Kelme's young leader paid the price for his strong time-trial – and when Chaba Jiménez attacked seven kilometres from the top, he began to struggle. Just as ONCE had almost been written off, Beloki came to the fore and crossed the line 23 seconds behind Chaba. Sevilla gritted his teeth and kept his losses down to 48 seconds, but it was not enough to stop Beloki taking the overall lead, even if the difference was only 14 seconds. In third place was Casero at 51 seconds. When the race halted for its first rest day, after nine stages, there were ten cyclists classified within three and a half minutes, and as Beloki remarked: 'Any of them can win the Vuelta.' The ensuing triple-helping of the Pyrenees promised considerable battle.

To a casual observer, the development of the 168-kilometre stage finishing in the Catalan ski station of La Molina might have seemed quite run-of-the-mill: a long break, culminating in the victory of a relatively unknown rider. But those who knew the story of Santi Blanco were gripped by what unfolded. After years of careful nurturing by Echávarri and Unzúe, Blanco betrayed them and left Banesto for a huge contract with Vitalicio. There he failed to live up to the hype, and at 26, seemed a washout, his career finished. Until his old mentors took him back to the fold.

When a break formed quite soon after the race left Sabadell, a town adjoining Barcelona, Santi Blanco was there, representing Banesto, or iBanesto.com as they were now officially called. Approaching the Pyrenees, on the coll de la Creueta, he attacked his two remaining escape companions, and crested the top alone. With nearly 40 kilometres to go, few had any faith in his chances. But Blanco was well-protected from behind, for when anyone stirred into action they found Chaba Jiménez on their wheel. In the end the prodigal son maintained his lead and rediscovered glory.

They might not have had a clear contender for the overall, but Banesto made an enormous impact on the race, winning in five of the seven summit finishes. The *etapa reina* followed what was now the established Vuelta style, packing five puertos into 158 kilometres, with a finish on the hors catégorie climb to the ski-station of Pal in Andorra. Half-way through the stage, Banesto began marking a relentless pace on the endless Port d'Envalira, and provoked another dramatic upset. The gold jersey Beloki suffered a tremendous old-fashioned pájara and wept as he struggled to the finish, where he lost 20 minutes, mortified at having let down his team. Throwing doubt on the feasibility of being competitive in more than one major stage race, both he and team-mate Igor González de Galdeano shortly abandoned, afflicted with a virus, or more accurately, exhaustion.

The punishing stage was authoritatively won by Chaba Jiménez, after he escaped at the start of the penultimate climb, the Coll d'Ordino, and crossed the line with 1'–44" on the leading group. Drawing considerable comment was the sight of Casero taking turns at the front of the group of favourites, instead of hiding anonymously in the middle, as he usually did. Here was another cyclist in pursuit of an ideal equilibrium. He'd lost weight, and was climbing like never before.

The third and final day in the Pyrenees was a cronoescalada, a 17-kilometre climb to the Andorran ski resort of Arcalís, where Chaba showed that this year he was once more untouchable in the mountains as he took his third stage. It was a sufficiently impressive performance for people to forget his famous irregularity, and to speculate about his podium chances. Yet Jiménez, himself, didn't seem particularly happy with all this success. That summer, tired of his unreliability, Banesto had left him out of the Tour line-up. Unzúe and Echávarri had finally lost their patience and were no longer ready to pardon all his foibles. As Chaba explained: 'They were like parents for me. But now they're just directors.' He seemed disillusioned: 'If once I was passionate about cycling, now I think of it as a job.' It was an early sign that all was not well.

As the peloton pulled out of the Pyrenees towards the Mediterranean, Sevilla was back in gold, but he'd only been able to put four seconds into Casero in the uphill time-trial, which Festina's director took as a very promising omen: 'Casero has taken an important step forward to winning the Vuelta.' He was classified second at 41 seconds. The majority of aficionados were hoping that Sevilla would deal the Valenciano a mortal blow on stage 15, when the Alto de Aitana would make its Vuelta debut. In his column in *Marca*, Perico Delgado felt obliged to defend Casero, pointing out that he 'was racing a very intelligent Vuelta'. He was soaking up the attacks of the climbers like a punch bag, but his admirable consistency didn't ignite much enthusiasm.

Indulging the spectators' insatiable thirst for drama, Unipublic had found a new special-category climb near the coast of Alicante, giving spectacular views of the Mediterranean over its 19 kilometres. Banesto, hoping that Chaba Jiménez would not only win the Alto de Aitana stage, but also make a bid for the podium, for he was fifth at 2'–50", forced the rhythm on what was turning into a gruelling day amid a harsh, dry landscape of terraced mountains. But at the crucial moment, when Chaba realised his legs were not responding, he told the team to stop working, and without the slightest inclination to minimise his losses, ceded 12 minutes in 12 kilometres.

As the group of favourites toiled up, Casero heard a spectator shout at him: 'Attack, attack,' and followed the advice. Sevilla's tired legs initially couldn't respond, but doggedly he fought back. They resembled two heavyweights slugging it out in slow motion, Casero just having the edge. When he accelerated again, Sevilla was left behind – with five long kilometres to go. The crowds were yelling at him, desperately urging him on. He was saved by two things: Santi Blanco appeared, helping Juanmi Mercado to defend his third place, and Sevilla latched on to the Banesto pair like a man overboard grasps a life-belt. Then, Casero began to flag, and his gargantuan effort only rewarded him with 16 seconds, not enough to take the gold jersey. An exhausted Sevilla, having lost some of his youthful bloom, still had a 25-second margin.

Before the climactic last two stages, the peloton had to go though the annual ordeal by wind in Albacete. His two leaders now back home, Manolo Sáiz had given up on the Vuelta, but his pupil Bruyneel was ready to take his place. The US Postal director was a veteran of the famous abanico of 1996 that had eliminated Escartín and Rominger in one fell swoop. This year, the echelons efficiently dispensed with two of Heras' rivals for third place, Casero's gregario in Festina, David Plaza, and Banesto's Mercado. Heras, although far from top form, had been recovering as the days passed, and was at least fighting for the podium. It was ironic that Spain's top climber had his best day on the flat, proof that US Postal hadn't brought a team for the mountains.

The seventh and last summit finish on the Alto de Abantos was won by Gilberto Simoni, after an exciting battle with Chaba. Sevilla and Casero arrived together, drawing out the suspense to the Madrid time-trial, just as the organisers had hoped. The contrast between the two riders was apparent when they were warming up for their decisive duel. While Casero retreated to a secluded corner, Sevilla was still happily chatting to the TV interviewer as the countdown began. Although the majority of spectators were rooting for him, Sevilla stood little chance, and when his triathlon bars broke, his concentration was shattered. Casero remained cool and calm throughout, utterly sure of himself, and although Botero was fastest over the 38-kilometre route, confirming his new identity as an ace time-trialist, it was the Valencian who took the final gold jersey.

By losing the race on the last day, Sevilla was following an established Vuelta tradition in which the outcome remains uncertain until the final day. It's a pattern that distinguishes the Spanish race from the Tour de France, where the winner nearly always has a very clear, unassailable margin. Having lost the gold jersey by 47 seconds he took defeat very gamely, and there was a general conviction that he would come back to win another day. Casero's victory failed to arouse enormous excitement. A commendably regular all-rounder, he hadn't won a single stage and lacked his rival's charisma. Another, more minor, upset was Levi Leipheimer unexpectedly pushing his 'leader' Heras off the podium.

The final paradox in a Vuelta full of oddities was Chaba winning the points jersey, as well as the Mountains prize, becoming only the third rider to do so, after Rominger in '93 and Jalabert in '95. Unfortunately for Erik Zabel, the rules in the Vuelta are not the same as in the Tour, which, offering fewer points in the mountains, aims the prize at sprinters. The German had won three stages in the first week, and had made a great effort to reach Madrid instead of pulling out in conventional sprinter style. He at least had the satisfaction of having survived the fastest Vuelta in history, with an average speed of 42.534kph.

2002–2004

'The crazy rhythm of the Spanish'

The times when a foreign star could come to Spain and find a tailor-made route had long gone. The country's high level of cycling, and the intensity with which the Vuelta was fought, turned it into a challenge few 'outsiders' were willing to take on. The American John Vaughters, reminiscing in *Cycle Sport* about his formative cycling years in Spain, described how he used to suffer to keep up with the peloton, even in minor races. A typical neo-professional experience? Perhaps, but whenever he crossed the border to France, he shot up dramatically in the classifications, finding the comparatively relaxed pace a relief. For decades, when Spanish cyclists had ventured abroad, they had to struggle with the relentlessly fast speeds of the north. A complete reversal had taken place: in 1998, Roger Legeay, manager of Crédit Agricole, explained his team's poor performance in the Vuelta was due to 'the crazy rhythm of the Spanish.'

In 2002, the most successful foreign rider was the sprinter, Mario Cipollini. The Italian's encounters with the Vuelta had never been happy: in 1994, he was hospitalised after a serious crash; in 1997, he sloped off after a couple of stages, claiming illness, and went to judge the Miss Italia beauty contest instead; in 2000, he was expelled for punching Francisco Cerezo the morning after they'd exchanged insults during a typically windy stage around Albacete. It had seemed the act of an ageing prima donna who was frustrated in a peloton where he was no longer powerful or fast enough to command respect. He'd also swung a punch at Oscar Freire, who was quick enough to duck.

Yet in 2002, 35-year-old Cipollini was enjoying a renaissance, winning the Milan–San Remo, a victory he'd always longed for. The only setback was getting snubbed by the Tour, to which he typically over-reacted and announced his immediate retirement. But there was one more event he dreamed of: the World Championships in Zolder, where the circuit suited him to the ground. So when he came to the Vuelta, it was known in advance that after a week he'd be gone, to finish his preparations, but it didn't matter, since he

2002

gave the organisers their money's worth, winning three stages. Expertly set up by his new team Acqua & Sapone, flamboyantly clad in lycra zebra skins, he destroyed all competition: Zabel, Freire and Petacchi.

As the Vuelta got on the road, the media gave it scant attention, absorbed as they were by the wedding of prime minister Aznar's daughter. He'd organised it with full pomp in the Escorial, no less, as if it were a royal affair: a clear sign of hubris. Even the sporting press seemed more concerned with Real Madrid's signing of Ronaldo, yet by the end of stage 10, the race situation was holding plenty of attention. Classified in first place was the popular Oscar Sevilla, while behind him, separated by only one second, was team-mate Aitor González. How would Kelme resolve the situation? Who would win the struggle for team leadership? After winning the time trial in Córdoba with consummate authority, taking a minute on favourite David Millar, Aitor, whose contract with the team finished that season, reflected that 'Labarta, the director who was following me in the car, never gave me any references from Sevilla.' He didn't press the issue and there was apparently no rancour; Aitor* was always supremely relaxed and unworried.

People had first begun to take note of Aitor González on the tough 8th stage to Ubrique, a hot day of incessant climbing in the mountains around Ronda. After cresting the first-category Puerto de Palomas, there were 33 kilometres to the finish, virtually all downhill. Luis Pérez of Coast hurled himself down the technical descent, taking some spine-chilling risks, only to be overtaken on the uphill finish by Aitor. On the eve of the time trial, he was sending a clear message: 'Winning the Vuelta is a possibility. Both Oscar and me have freedom in the team.'

In an earlier interview, Sevilla had admitted how badly he wanted to win the Vuelta, especially after a stomach infection had forced him to abandon the Tour de France, and he'd made his ambition plain as soon as the race began. Unlike anything in the Tour, where the opening week is invariably flat and the suspense of the early stages is largely provided by the sprinters – and often the crashes – the peloton came up against the first mountains very early, with two of the race's four summit-finishes in the first week. The

---

* González is so common a name in Spain that it is usual to use the Christian name only.

absence of Chaba Jiménez was immediately felt. His lifestyle had finally become incompatible with cycling; there were alarming rumours of night-clubs, drugs and crippling depression.

Stage 5 had been a testing run through the Alpujarras, finished off by the 37 kilometre climb of the Sierra Nevada. Sevilla attacked six kilometres from the summit, and although the stage ws won by the Italian, Guido Trentin, he gained 40 seconds on his main rivals and plenty of morale in the process. Stage 6 saw the inauguration of La Pandera, 'the Angliru of the south', a nasty climb in Jaen that reached gradients of 15%. There were overtones of Lance Armstrong when Roberto Heras set his best *gregario*, Christian Vandevelde, to mark the rhythm at the start of the climb, and until they had nearly reached Gilberto Simoni's breakaway group. By the time Heras accelerated away on his own, Joseba Beloki and Francisco Mancebo, the leaders of ONCE and Banesto, were having trouble coping with the steep ramps. Although Simoni resisted, he couldn't hold off Heras, who powered over the finishing-line, without even pausing for a gesture of triumph. The Italian came in second, and Sevilla was third, sufficiently close behind to secure the gold jersey.

Before the Córdoba time trial, which concluded the southern part of the race, Sevilla fully expected to lose the leadership to Aitor González, although he didn't rate him as a serious, long-term threat – 'he tends to be irregular' – with the mountains of the north still to come. Yet Sevilla stunned everyone by finishing the time trial in second place, just 40 seconds behind Aitor, and keeping him at bay in the overall by one second. He'd pushed himself to new limits, because of a fierce desire to thwart his smiling, but deadly, rival/team-mate, who wanted the gold jersey for himself.

On the rest day, the cyclists were transported to another world by a sleek 350kph AVE high-speed train – the much vaunted symbol of Spain's modernisation – and the Vuelta of the north began. After a year's break, the race saw the return of the iconic Angliru. The mountain was often described with religious overtones as a 'shrine' and its ascension, a 'pilgrimage'. This time, Unipublic were determined that all the cyclists would do penance, with plans for stricter crowd control and a clampdown on pushing.

Whatever the complaints about excess, the Angliru was a guaranteed media attraction, and invaluable for this reason alone. Belts were being tightened in cycling; sponsors were becoming wary. Incredibly, despite winning the Vuelta the previous year, Casero had been forced to take a cut in salary. The image of the sport was not improved by the high profile, if bizarre, positive tests of Garzelli and Simoni in the 2002 Giro d'Italia, which kept the issue of doping in the headlines.

On the Angliru, it seems the sun never shines, but Roberto Heras, fighting alone under the deluge of rain, was in his element. The other riders had disappeared from his consciousness. With six kilometres to go, nothing existed beyond the fog, the rain streaming off him, and the walls of shouting people, as he strove to keep his spark alight on the implacable ramps.

A true Castillian, he'd always been taciturn, but after stepping into the unfamiliar environment of US Postal, leaving behind his small town of Béjar to live in Barcelona, Roberto Heras retreated deep inside his shell. Journalists found him uncommunicative, and missed the bright-eyed enthusiasm of the younger Heras who won the 2000 Vuelta. But in those last metres of the Angliru, he was at his most expressive, fighting for every second, seizing the chance the dreaded mountain offered to the few equipped to take it, and he became the new race leader.

Lower down, other struggles were taking place. This year the spectators had to look on and not touch. Afterwards, Juan Antonio Flecha of iBanesto.com described the loneliness of the experience: 'You feel like an alpinist ... fighting against yourself.' In his isolation, Oscar Sevilla had to suppress an irresistible urge to stand up on the pedals, his natural climbing style, because on those slopes in the rain, the back wheel immediately began to slide. Ahead of him, there were ten riders, including Aitor.

When the group of favourites had reached the foot of the Angliru, Kelme took charge, but it was soon obvious that Sevilla, drifting towards the back of the group, was having a bad day. At this point, Aitor took over at the front, raising the pressure. Heras and Beloki immediately stationed themselves behind him, Heras settling comfortably on Aitor's wheel. When Heras accelerated, Aitor struggled a while to keep up, but had to let go. In his ambition, he'd effectively served as Heras' *gregario*, launching the US Postal's leader's attack. More devastatingly, he'd succeeded in exposing Oscar Sevilla, who lost contact with the group. In the end, Aitor lost 2'–16" to Heras, and gained 34 seconds on Sevilla, who resisted with all his might, but couldn't defend the gold jersey: 'Aitor has eliminated me,' was all he said afterwards.

Kelme's director, Vicente Belda, was visibly annoyed by Aitor's attack, considering that if he'd ridden up on someone's wheel, he'd have won time on Sevilla anyway. All he'd achieved was to poison the atmosphere in the team. Belda wanted Sevilla to be leader, but had to bite his tongue, as Aitor was stronger. Heras' climb had been impressive, but not a definitive blow, as in the overall Aitor stood only 35 seconds behind him, while Sevilla was now third at 1'–08".

The stage was described as belonging to a more epic age, but not all the cyclists were prepared to be heroes. It had been a bad day for David Millar, who crashed on the slick asphalt of the Cordal, got knocked over by the Big Mat team-car at the foot of the Angliru, and flung off his number before crossing the line, crying: 'We're not animals and this is inhuman.' His protest left many bemused. It seemed a betrayal of his team, although in recent declarations, Millar has explained that Cofidis never had much of a team-spirit. Quite rightly, the judges ignored his director's pleas to have Millar reinstated. He would never have dared to pull such a stunt in the Tour de France, which has its fair share of dangerous stages. The image of Zülle comes back, on the seaweed-slimy Gois causeway, an absurd booby-trap where he lost six minutes in 1999. He might have wanted to fling his bike into the sea, but kept on fighting to finish second overall.

Among all the controversy, Carlos Arribas in *El País* wrote a strong defence of the climb. 'The Angliru has contributed to the legend of the Vuelta; the stage was extraordinary. And if the cars burn out, let the mechanics go up on motorbikes.' He argued that cycling has managed to survive chiefly because of the epic tales in its history. The television statistics spoke clearly: over three and a half million spectators in Spain, and two and a half million in Italy.

After the second rest day, the peloton confronted the final week, and Aitor was greeted by whistles. Santiago Botero won the stage in León, which was good for Kelme's morale. The race moved southwest to Heras' home province of Salamanca, and on stage 18 the fourth, and last, summit finish was above the village of Candelario, where he'd recently got married. The Alto de Covatilla was a new climb for the Vuelta, the site of a small ski station at just over 2,000metres, with an average gradient of 8 per-cent over its ten kilometres. It was Heras' last chance to bolster his defences before the Madrid time trial. To celebrate Real Madrid 's centenary, the cyclists would be riding into the Santiago Bernabeu stadium, where the final award ceremony would take place. In this vast arena, triumph or defeat would be very spectacular and exposed.

The other local hero was Santi Blanco, who was so impatient to win he attacked his escape partners 50 kilometres from the finish. He set up a two-mintes gap with a comfortable six minutes on the bunch, but as his strength waned, and with the pursuers closing in, he seemed ready to drop off the bike in exhaustion, but for his compatriots at the sides of the road willing him onwards. Everyone heaved a sigh of relief when he won the stage. Heras came in at 39 seconds, disappointed to see Aitor González appear only 37 seconds later. Heras' lead was up to 1'–12" but that would be a precariously small margin to take into the final time trial.

Aitor crossed the line at the limit of his strength, and would surely have lost far more but for Sevilla. When Aitor began to struggle, Sevilla was torn between chasing after Beloki and securing his own podium position, or lending a hand to his team-mate. If ideas of revenge for the Angliru passed through his head, loyalty to Kelme proved stronger, and he paused to let his suffering team-mate take his wheel, guiding him up the final kilometres. In contrast, Heras had limited support, and US Postal's manager, Bruyneel, resorted to roping in two survivors of Cipollini's team. One of them, Miguel Perdiguero, happened to be a good friend of Aitor González. 'A true friend doesn't do that,' stormed Belda after the stage. Others called it 'the Vuelta of Betrayals'.

In the mountains, Aitor had felt the strain, but he wiped out the memory of his suffering the following day, when he attacked on the cobbled ramps leading to the walls of Ávila. He took four seconds, but more importantly, it was a flourish of strength to taunt Heras. On the eve of the final time trial, Aitor was as unconcerned and relaxed as ever: 'The one who has to be nervous is Roberto Heras, for we've arrived at my territory.'

After the event, Heras would confess to the intense humiliation he felt on that last day. Pedalling alone through the streets of Madrid, wearing the gold jersey but knowing the Vuelta was lost, was a bitter moment. In the earlier time-trial of Córdoba it seemed the wind-tunnel training was bearing fruit: he'd looked more aerodynamic, pedalling with an efficient cadence, but in Madrid, he fell apart and lost a massive 3'–22" to Aitor González, who won easily, 1'–23" faster than Casero.

The day also turned into a nightmare for Oscar Sevilla. No sooner had he rolled off the ramp, when he punctured. Then his handlebar broke. When they gave him his third bike, the gears didn't work properly. The result was he didn't even have the consolation of third place on the podium, losing out by 15 seconds to Beloki. It was quite a feat for ONCE's leader, who'd finished second in the Tour de France. Getting on the podium in two major tours in the same season has become a rarity.

Sevilla was on an exceptionally long run of bad-luck, which would continue into the following seasons and cut off his progression. Yet he remains one of Spain's most appreciated cyclists. Popular for his youthful demeanour and communicative ways, he is also respected for his strong team loyalty, courage and resilience – highly valued qualities in a cyclist.

Had a new star been born? Intoxicated with victory, Aitor González allowed Real Madrid's president, Florentino Pérez, ever the canny businessman, to dress him in the white team strip. It was only for a moment, but long enough for the photographs to appear the next morning, much to the displeasure of Kelme and non-Real Madrid supporters. But Aitor was always unfazed by controversy. As a cyclist, he brought to mind riders like Hinault or Fignon, who, while excellent against the clock, didn't suffer unduly in the mountains, and also had a fast finish. But although only 27 years old, the ambition he'd shown would dissipate, and until now the Vuelta seems to have been the peak of his career rather than the beginning.

Although the Vuelta was producing thrilling racing, sometimes it seemed there was no one to see it, outside of the towns and cities. The problem of empty roadsides was particularly acute in 2003, as the peloton sped along kilometres of national highways, through depopulated countryside. Unipublic had a slick show in motion, but this was an aspect of the event they'd neglected.

As a television spectacle, however, it continued to be a great success. Cutting to the penultimate stage of the 2003 Vuelta, an uphill time-trial on the Alto de Abantos, viewers were riveted by the sight of Roberto Heras – usually self-contained, emotions tightly reigned in – riding as if his life were at stake. The intensity of the moment was perfectly transmitted by the camera focused on his normally serious face but now transfigured by the immense effort. Another scene that had the viewers gaping had occurred the previous day, when Manolo Sáiz drove a TV motorbike off the road and unleashed an astonishing tirade of invective straight into the camera and into people's homes. Two extraordinary moments, and both connected with the discovery of a new young star in ONCE's ranks, Isidro Nozal.

2003   It was to be the last major race for Banesto and ONCE as, by a coincidence, both sponsors were pulling out at the end of the season. The two teams had been the pillars of Spanish cycling for over twenty years and although there was great faith that replacement sponsors would be found, allowing the team structures to continue, it seemed an era was coming to an end. It also meant that both squads were highly motivated to finish on a high note.

The route, as usual, was appraised to see who it favoured most: the climbers mourned the absence of the Angliru, and the all-rounders could be heartened by the four time trials. Yet the first of these was for teams, and the last was uphill, which might conceivably give the climbing contingent the upper hand.

The team time trial was the opening stage in Gijón, with a predictable victory for ONCE. 'All of us give everything for the team,' said Igor González de Galdeano afterwards. 'No one keeps anything back.' To celebrate this team spirit, Manolo Sáiz planned to keep the gold jersey rotating among the men he had occupying the top seven positions overall. He chose Igor as the first race leader, to reflect his status as the rider Sáiz most wanted to win the Vuelta. With ONCE it was sometimes difficult to talk of a 'team leader', as this role seemed already fully occupied by their director.

The master plan to distribute the gold jersey proved quite unwieldy. It was supposed to fall to Marcos Serrano to celebrate his birthday, but in Cangas de Onís, ONCE's neo-professional Joaquín Rodríguez ended up wearing it, and to his horror, he kept it for a second day in Santander. It's rare to see a cyclist looking so unhappy to be the race leader. Fearing Sáiz's wrath, he'd desperately tried to lose his position in the final metres of the stage, since local boy Isidro Nozal had been designated to have his turn in gold, but the wet autumnal weather brought chaotic conditions. Still, everything worked out well because the following day, Nozal was part of the successful break, and earned the *maillot oro* fair and square.

The first individual time trial came on stage 6, with 43.8 windy kilometres around Zaragoza. Once again Sáiz's plans for the team were knocked askew, when Nozal swept aside all the competition, pulverising David Millar's time by 1'–20". 'I really surprised myself,' admitted the strapping 25 year-old, refusing to entertain any ambitions for himself: 'I will fight hard to help Igor win the race.' The first week had been glorious for ONCE. No one else had been let anywhere near the gold jersey, and they had three riders in the top four, with Igor in second place at 2'–24", presumably ready to take over when Nozal lost time in the mountains.

The peloton prepared itself for the Pyrenees, whose first stage overlapped with Tour de France territory, climbing the Aubisque and finishing in Cauterets. When Heras attacked on the Aubisque, ONCE tried to control the gap, but one by one their riders fell back. Two kilometres from the top, only Igor and Nozal remained in a group that was struggling to organise a serious pursuit. That's when Nozal took charge of the situation and neutralised Heras on the descent. On the final climb, Nozal paid for his effort and lost over a minute on both Heras and Igor. Having emptied his reserves, at the end the race leader could barely stand.

It was a display that confounded all expectations. Some used it as an excuse to berate Manolo Sáiz, for his apparent obstinacy in making Nozal work for Igor, whose form was beginning to be suspect. Yet the young Cantabrian was enthusiastic about his role as *gregario*, regardless of the colour of his jersey. He dismissed himself with disarming modesty: 'I'm not a good climber, that's a fact.'

On closer inspection, the Pyrenees were an enormous disappointment for the purebred climbers like Roberto Heras. The subsequent two stages finished on the Pla de Beret and the Port d'Envalira, long monotonous climbs with steady gradients, exposed to the winds – nowhere for a specialist to test his rivals – so Nozal was able to avoid losing any more time. In the Pla de Beret, ONCE augmented their winnings even more when Joaquín Rodríguez beat Banesto's Aitor Osa on the line. The race was nearly half-way through and Banesto had still to taste victory. The other main force, Kelme, had got off to a bad start when Oscar Sevilla crashed on the rainy stage to Santander, but on the Port d'Envalira, twenty-three year-old Alejandro Valverde emerged as their new leader, his explosive finish allowing him to outsprint Dario Frigo.

The journalists spent the rest day trying to sniff out any rivalry between Nozal and Igor. They wanted a Cain and Abel situation, which drove Manolo Sáiz to distraction. The public began to learn about Nozal: that his father was a long-distance lorry driver, a job

Nozal quite fancied for himself; that he was an unpretentious soul, who wore tartan slippers in the hotels, and the peak of his cap turned upwards in the old style; that he would happily lend a hand cleaning up the team bus if necessary. And officially, Igor was still ONCE's leader.

The next time trial, held on stage 13 on the windy plains of Albacete, put everyone in their place. Nozal again beat David Millar, on this occasion by a more moderate 13 seconds, while Igor's time was discreet, only 30 seconds faster than Heras, whose impressive, newly found confidence against the clock took him to third place overall. After the stage, Nozal wept, comforted by Manolo Sáiz, in the realisation that there could be no more pretence, no hiding: he'd been disclosed as ONCE's undisputed leader, with all the responsibilities that entailed. His powerful riding and comfortable cushion of time – 3'–03" on Igor and 5'–13" on Heras – led everyone to predict the Vuelta was his.

Roberto Heras had a different kind of responsibility: people were counting on him to liven up the last week of the race in Andalucía. He wasn't greatly inspired at the prospect: only la Pandera held out any promise, but even this was tucked at the end of a dreary day spent on a dual carriageway. Then there was the Sierra Nevada, and a couple of days in the Sierra de Madrid.

Unconvinced, Heras set about his task with a workmanlike approach: at each opportunity he attacked, and whittled down Nozal's lead. While he eroded, Nozal resisted; it became the established routine. There was an unexpected finish on la Pandera: the spectators, prepared to see a tussle between Heras and the Colombian Cárdenas, who had ridden up on the Spaniard's wheel, were amazed to see Valverde zip past them, apparently from nowhere, to take the stage. He'd been assisted by Sevilla, now recovered from his injuries, and wholeheartedly supporting his younger team-mate. 'He has that killer instinct', said Vicente Belda, proudly. Carlos Arribas described Valverde as 'a Vandenbroucke who doesn't need a psychoanalyst.' Nozal contained his losses on Heras to 1'–11", protectively escorted by Marcos Serrano and Igor.

On the Sierra Nevada, Nozal's suffering was plain to see, but again he hung on and only ceded 54 seconds to Heras. At the foot of the climb, US Postal moved into position in Tour de France style, but they were far from that level, despite the presence of Floyd Landis. It reflected Heras' status in the team that George Hincapie had been let off home that morning to prepare for the world championships. The stage went to Cárdenas, who beat Juanmi Mercado of Banesto. Heras was still third overall, but only 6 seconds behind Igor: the second place was within his reach, but Nozal was still comfortably ahead at 3'–09".

In Córdoba, David Millar made up for his defeat in the time trials with a classy stage win, after attacking on the Alto de San Jerónimo, 25 kilometres from the finish, but the big news of the day was that Banesto's director Echávarri had been offered a four-year deal by the government of the Illes Balears. The Spanish government, stung by the prospect of the Basque team Euskaltel-Euskadi being the sole representative from Spain in the Tour de France, were encouraging other autonomous communities to sponsor cycling. The Vuelta might be eluding Banesto, but in securing their future, Echávarri was one step ahead of Sáiz.

The announcement could only have increased the pressure on ONCE's director. Conscious that the livelihood of a large group of people depended on him, he was dedicating every spare moment to the pursuit of a sponsor. The final week of the race was becoming very stressful. He was worried about Nozal, who looked increasingly tired, but Sáiz could at least reassure himself that although the forthcoming Sierra de Madrid stage was demanding, the Alto de Navacerrada lay 25 kilometres from the finish, which would give plenty of margin for defence. It was also generally accepted that the mountains of Madrid rarely changed the race outcome.

But ONCE's problem was that they'd been too greedy. In Sáiz's obsession to recreate their triumphant days of the mid-nineties, they'd cut themselves too big a slice of the cake: they wanted the overall, two thirds of the podium, the team prize, as well as stage wins. The Vuelta was coming to an end, but their rivals were still hungry, and Heras might find a helping hand if their interests coincided. On the Alto de los Leónes, when Kelme and Banesto began forcing the pace, Igor dropped back, but Nozal looked comfortable, and his team-mate was able to rejoin him on the descent. Then at the foot of the Navacerrada, Heras performed his daily duty and attacked. Nozal again responded well, at least initially. But after a while, he was clearly straining, so Heras immediately relaunched his assault, and this time Nozal was helpless to react. What Manolo Sáiz had feared was finally happening: ONCE were tired from shouldering the responsibility of the race since day one, the price for seizing the gold jersey so early, and now their young leader was isolated, and floundering on the first slopes of a 14-kilometre first-category climb. That was when Sáiz lost control and, convinced Heras was taking advantage of the camera motorbike in front, aggressively overtook Heras' group and dangerously ran the motorbike off the road. That evening he was expelled from the race.

At the top of the Navacerrada, Heras had 1'–29"on Nozal and on the long downhill run he found plenty of cooperation in his group: Banesto were well-represented, determined to win the team prize, and Kelme wanted to put Valverde on the podium. ONCE, who had gathered round Nozal and shepherded him to the top, were only able to reduce the gap slightly to 1'–14" on the descent. The race had come alive, and Nozal looked fragile, but he only needed to survive eleven more kilometres – the distance of the following day's *crono-escalada* on the Alto de Abantos. Heras had been chipping away at his lead at roughly a minute per stage, so he would now need to double that rate, as Nozal still had a stockpile of 1'–55", surely enough to get him through.

When psyching himself up for this final test, Heras remembered his own crushing defeat at the hands of Aitor González 12 months before. He knew if he started off strongly, it would gnaw away at Nozal's morale; the psychological element was crucial. Manolo Sáiz had tried to protect the Cantabrian for as long as possible by keeping up the pretence that Igor was still ready to step in as leader, but on Los Leónes this illusion had evaporated. Too much depended on young Nozal, he had too much to lose, and on the big day, he never looked comfortable, losing more time with each kilometre. After giving away 30 seconds in kilometre 8, his resistance seemed to cave in completely, and he ceded a total of 2'–23".

Meanwhile, Heras did the climb of his life. He wept when he realised what he'd achieved, some of the tears pent up since the Bernabeu stadium debacle. For US Postal, it was quite a coup to have won two major tours in one year. For ONCE, it was hard to lose the gold jersey at the very end, and see Igor pushed off the podium by Valverde, as well as the team prize go to Banesto. The peloton rode in relaxed fashion into Madrid, where Petacchi won his fifth sprint.

* * * * *

The political atmosphere in Spain was becoming strained, as Aznar's government imposed a clumsy centralist ideology. This often took the form of trivial but provocative acts, such as hoisting a gargantuan Spanish flag in Madrid, or suppressing regional car number-plates. The government took special delight in fostering anti-Catalan feelings for electoral purposes, which had the effect of successfully converting moderate Catalans into budding separatist extremists. Throughout 2003 there were mass protests: against the mishandling of the Prestige oil-spill in Galicia; and, above all, against the presence of Spanish troops in Iraq. Opinion polls revealed that over 90 percent of the population opposed the war, while Aznar, in the photo shoots with Bush and Blair, seemed a distant, arrogant figure in pursuit of international prominence.

Then, on Thursday, 11th March 2004, four days before the general elections, Spain was devastated by a large-scale terrorist train bombing in Madrid. It happened during the early morning rush-hour, and left 191 people dead and 1,800 injured. There followed four extraordinary days of shock and grief, as normal life was put on hold, and people demonstrated to express their sorrow and, increasingly, anger. The government panicked, and desperately tried to steer the media into attributing the attack to Eta, despite all the evidence pointing to Islamic extremists. Incensed by this gross attempt at manipulation, the Spanish voters drove Partido Popular out of office, after a massive turn-out.

Factions in favour of Spain's involvement in the Iraq war tried to portray the election results as a capitulation to terrorism. Most, however, saw it as a victory for democracy, for it's not often that the people have the power to act so decisively at such a crucial moment in their nation's history. In Spain it had happened before in the summer of 1936 when, across the country, large sections of the population spontaneously took up arms to resist the generals' rebellion against the recently-formed Republic, but that had ended in defeat, and four decades of dictatorship. When democracy was finally restored in the period of the transition, it was embraced with enthusiasm, but by the end of the century the country was growing increasingly disaffected with politics – a common enough feeling throughout Europe. A large part of the population felt unrepresented, or disenchanted by all of the major political parties, and the general election of 2000 was marked by a high rate of voter abstention. But in the aftermath of 11th March 2004 there came a unique moment for the people to assert their will, and they seized the opportunity.

So, when the 2004 Vuelta began, there were no Spanish troops in Iraq and at the head of the country was a mild-mannered Socialist, José Luis Rodríguez Zapatero. A new era for Spain, and ongoing changes in professional cycling, as the last season before the introduction of the ProTour drew to an end. The team directors were distinctly nervous and bad-tempered, easily roused into arguments, which rapidly degenerated into personal smears. Manolo Sáiz was involved in more than his fair share.

After a rather dull edition of the Tour de France, that was devoid of any real suspense, fans were hungry for some exciting and unpredictable cycling. The *parcours* of 2004 was a good example of how unrestrained the Vuelta is by tradition. The Tour without the Alps or Pyrenees is almost unthinkable, but Unipublic had designed a route that avoided the entire north of Spain: no Asturias, no Catalunya, no Pyrenees. Merely looking at the route map was hot, thirsty work, as it depicted a meandering progression through some of the country's most sweltering zones, spiked with mountains that in September would be scorched by an unrelenting sun.

2004   Unipublic had reacted with alacrity to the negative comments provoked by the previous year's race, mainly concerning the overdose of national highways, and invited some of the critics to make suggestions. So Vicente Belda, who hails from Alicante, was asked to improve the stage finishing on the Alto de Aitana and he proposed the Puerto de Torremanzanas. Never included in a race before, although well-known among local cyclists, it would add an extra touch of difficulty. Juan Martínez Oliver, the director of the small Spanish team Paternina, suggested the imposing Puerto de Calar Alto in Almería, 20 kilometres long, the home of an astronomical observatory on its 2,168 metre-crest, which gives locals an occasional glimpse of snow. Paco Cabello, one of Kelme's riders, added a couple of twists to the route of the Sierra Nevada time trial, while Laudelino Cubino, who'd been on the Vuelta podium ten years earlier, recommended a return to the ski station of La Covatilla, outside Béjar, his and Roberto Heras' home town.

The race opened in León, its most northerly point, with a team time-trial. Liberty Seguros, the reincarnation of ONCE, were dumbfounded to lose one and a half minutes. The winners were US Postal, who'd keep hold of the gold jersey until stage 12. The previous winter, Roberto Heras, tired of living in Lance Armstrong's shadow, had broken his contract with the American squad and signed with Manolo Sáiz. Their first Tour de France had been an unmitigated disaster, Heras dropping out half-way through. And now their last opportunity to save a bad year had got off to a shaky start.

The first mountain finish came on stage 9, on the Alto de Aitana. Although Isidro Nozal was the best classified rider in Liberty Seguros, the team's pecking order was clarified when Heras used the powerful Cantabrian to eliminate as many rivals as possible, before he, himself, attacked four kilometres from the military radar installation at the top. The tiny Italian, Leonardo Piepoli, won the stage, but Heras had propelled himself to sixth place overall, 1'–35" behind gold jersey Floyd Landis.

Continuing southwards, stage 10 culminated on the Xorret de Catí, where everyone's thoughts were on José Maria Jiménez, who'd died the previous winter, while undergoing treatment for addiction and depression. It seemed the surname 'Jiménez' was essential to win on this climb, since after Chaba's victory on its inauguration in 1998, the only other rider to inscribe his name there was Eladio Jiménez, once in 2000, and again this year.

It had been an outstanding day of racing. The three riders competing for the points jersey, Freire, Zabel and Stuart O'Grady, were caught up in the break of the day while battling for points, and the sight of the three sprinters fighting it out on Xorret de Catí's 20-per-cent slopes was unrepeatable. O'Grady's second place behind Jiménez had a taste of victory about it, although in the end, it was the ever-reliable German who'd go on to win the points competition.

When the peloton embarked on stage 11, they were setting off for Murcia, Valverde's homeland. He was enthusiastically hovering behind Floyd Landis' shoulder, only nine seconds away from the gold jersey. Alejandro Valverde was the apple of Vicente Belda's eye. After the infamous Manzano confessions, Kelme had been refused an invitation to the Tour de France, and were being excluded from the ProTour, which Belda suspected was largely down to Manolo Sáiz, who was heavily involved in its organisation. So it was of some consolation that Kelme still had Spain's brightest new star in their ranks, although his future career might lie elsewhere.

The importance of Valverde, not only for his team, but for the race and the whole nation, became clear when he crashed early on the Murcia stage. His chain jammed, and caterpaulted him over the handlebars. On TV, the national hero's shredded jersey was displayed to the viewers. Bruised, morally and physically, he wanted to abandon, but the cyclists encouraged him to continue, easing the pace till he was over the worst of the shock. David Zabriskie of US Postal had escaped and was out alone when it happened and his gap grew to 20 minutes, enough for him to resist the peloton's acceleration and win.

The rest day gave Kelme's leader a chance to recover in time for the *etapa reina* in Almería. When Martínez Oliver had recommended Calar Alto, he wasn't sure which approach Unipublic would pick. In the end, they chose both: the first-category north side would be the prelude, and the south-facing *hors catégorie* climb would be the climax. Beforehand, after passing through the desert landscape of the Sergio Léone westerns, the peloton encountered the first-category Alto de Velefique, where a local rider, Paco Lara, broke off alone in pursuit of the improbable. US Postal still held the gold jersey, but they were bowing out, as Liberty Seguros took over the control of the peloton. On the final climb, when Marcos Serrano moved to the front, his pace caused considerable pain. Then Valverde generated a stir by attacking. He was soon caught, but in the flurry, Landis was definitively dropped. Fulfilling his responsibility as chief lieutenant to Heras, Nozal was next to test the reduced group's resistance. It was common knowledge that Nozal was a sweet-natured soul, but as he set a gruelling pace up the parched mountainside, his bared teeth and the wild fixed look in his eye would have frightened many a small child.

Finally, Heras himself took off, unstoppable, to an impressive solo victory, after such impeccable team-work. The gold jersey was his, while second at 35 seconds was Paco Mancebo of Illes Balears-Banesto, and third at 49 seconds was Valverde, bandaged but holding up. Nothing had been decided, with complicated terrain ahead in an exhausting final week.

The first-category Alto de Monachil overlooks Granada, and the cyclist who crests it is rewarded by a 20-kilometre swoop down to the city, which hosted the finish of stage 14. As the leading group approached the top of this last obstacle, Valverde made it clear he had no intention of giving Heras a quiet ride to Madrid, and attacked. But Heras was too wily and was instantly on his wheel. As they descended through the pine trees, Valverde tested Heras' nerve, but the Bejarano showed he was equally prepared to push it to the limit: when the young Murcian took one corner wide, Heras slipped straight across in front of him. It was Valverde's flair for upsetting the status quo that made him so exciting.

Ahead of them was a little known Phonak rider, Santi Pérez, who had escaped on the climb, and gained more advantage on the descent. When he was awarded the stage, he dedicated it to his girlfriend, killed in a car crash two years ago. Shy, quiet Santi Pérez had already appeared on the Calar Altar stage, coming in second, and on the demanding *crono-escalada* of the Sierra Nevada he would confirm himself as the latest revelation, recording the fastest time, and taking over a minute on Valverde and nearly two on Heras.

Under hot blue skies, with spectators sticking to the shade, an uncharacteristically stiff-looking Heras, suffered on the lower slopes. In contrast, Valverde was exuding spirit, and while Manolo Sáiz looked worried, Belda grinned. The two pugnacious directors, whose dark brows furrowed at the mere sight of each other, had crossed swords on the airwaves after Sáiz was spotted chatting to Valverde in a hotel lobby. The idea of his prize rider getting signed up by his sworn enemy made Belda's blood boil over. Eventually, after a hard struggle, Heras managed to find his normal rhythm in the final kilometres, which suggested he wasn't to be discounted yet. All the same, an exuberant Valverde finished the day only five seconds behind on general classification.

The cyclists were airlifted to Extremadura, where the temperatures soared even higher. After a rest day, the peloton mulled over the news of Tyler Hamilton while baking on the road to Cáceres: he'd tested positive after winning the Valencia time-trial, and a similar result in the Olympics suggested blood manipulation. It was a very brief day of transition, for the following stage would finish at the ski station of la Covatilla. The climbers – this year there were no out-and-out time-trialists in the fray – prepared themselves for further combat on another arduously hot day. On home ground, Heras was obliged to attack, and a dehydrated Valverde cracked, losing over three minutes. Afterwards, fans chanted, 'don't give up!' but he seemed to have dropped out of the fight. It had been a long season and, for him, an overcrowded schedule.

When Heras jumped, only Santi Pérez could follow, collaborating for a while to distance Valverde, before attacking in turn, to win the stage with 32 seconds on his rival. What remained would be a duel between these two climbers, separated by 1'–13" on general classification. For the first time in the Vuelta, Heras was being outclassed in his own territory. But while Santi Pérez was taking the role Heras played in 2003, gradually eroding the gold jersey day by day, Heras was not going to play the part of Nozal – he had far too much hard-won experience.

On the penultimate stage, with a summit finish on the Puerto de Navacerrada, Santi Pérez aimed to win a minute off Heras. For once, the weather was mercifully cool. Pérez waited until four kilometres from the top to make his move, and Heras had to work hard to stay on his wheel. When the Asturian lifted the pace even more, Heras wisely backed off, confronting what remained of the climb at his own rhythm. 'I might've cracked if I'd tried not to lose his wheel,' he confessed later. His rival no longer in view, Heras was able to steel his mind and resist, limiting his losses to 29 seconds.

The final day's time trial, fought between climbers, was a test of strength, not specialist skill. The suspense was banished when Heras ceded only 13 seconds – 'I wasn't ever going to let what happened in 2002 happen again' – and he became the first Spaniard to win three Vueltas, equalling Tony Rominger's record. As for Santi Pérez's second place, a new discovery is always welcome, but in this case there is only uncertainty. Perhaps thinking of Aitor González, whose vertiginous rise to stardom did little for his career in the long run, Pérez's representative, Tony Rominger, commented: 'Maybe it's better for Santi that he didn't win the Vuelta.' It was certainly better for the race, considering his positive test later that October in Switzerland, identical to that of team-mate Tyler Hamilton. The Hamilton–Pérez case remains muddied with unanswered questions. The promoters of the new test seem over-hasty in asserting its infallibility, eroding rather than strengthening confidence in the efficiency of doping controls.

The final top ten had been a solid Spanish block, which 'made it strange that they played the national anthem and not the *pasodoble** "La Bejarana",' wrote Juanma Trueba in the sports paper, *As*. It was quite a turnaround from 1996, when Escartín had just managed to scrape in behind nine foreign riders. Back in the 1940s, during Spain's deepest isolation, the Vuelta had a similar Spanish flavour,

---

* The *pasodoble* 'La Bejarana' was a piece of lively 1920s dance music dedicated to a woman from Heras' home town of Béjar.

but today's lack of international input can be attributed to the progressive distillation of the cycling season into a single race.

When comparing his own era to Lance Armstrong's, Eddy Merckx has observed that "the Tour is far more important than it was in my time." The American's lack of interest in other events has been contagious, leading to an obsession with reaching top form exclusively in July. Merckx, with his incomparable palmarés, is disapproving: 'cycling is more than the Tour de France,' he maintains. But unless the ProTour can make any impact, the main motivation in the Vuelta will continue to be Spanish, just as the Giro will remain overwhelmingly contested by Italians.

2005

Viva la Vuelta!

As recently as the nineteenth century, bread in Asturias was more expensive than meat, because of the cost of heaving flour from the wheat fields of the Meseta on mule-back over the Cantabrian Cordillera. Breaching this isolation, the first road fit for vehicles was finally completed, at great cost, in 1834, connecting Oviedo with the province of León over the Puerto de Pajares. Today, Asturians tired of thick mist and *orbayu* – the persistent fine drizzle that blows in off the Bay of Biscay – cross it southwards looking for sun, and landlocked Castillians anxious for bracing sea air pass them heading north.

In cycling, the ascent on the Asturian side has a first-category status, rising nearly a thousand metres over 20 kilometres to a height of 1,379 metres. The road might be wider now, and its surface smoother than when Berrendero and Rebelo fought there elbow to elbow for the Mountains jersey in 1945, but it still has cruel sections of 14 per-cent and 17 per-cent on its upper slopes, and when the Brañillin ski station opened, an additional three kilometres gave the cyclists an extra 100 metres to climb.

Steeped in Vuelta history, Pajares is where Bahamontes and Loroño and, later, Ocaña and Fuente conducted some of their fiercest duels. It was on its slopes that Julio Jiménez secured his one and only Vuelta yellow jersey after a scintillating ascent, while behind him, Ferrys, a team replete with climbers of great, and unruly, talent, wasted their opportunity to thwart Poulidor's ambitions. It was on Pajares that Pedro Delgado fought to save his leadership in 1989, on the day when Ivanov became the race's first Russian stage-winner. And almost invariably, Asturian weather is at its most raw when the peloton reaches Pajares. The first time a stage of the Vuelta was annulled was in 1957 when a blizzard made the summit impassable, and a recalcitrant Loroño had to be hauled, protesting, from his bike. In 1968, in hail and near zero visibility, and on an ice-rink of a descent, Altig opted for discretion, and surrendered his yellow jersey to the fearless Pérez Francés.

In recent Vuelta editions, its more spectacular neighbours, the Lagos de Covadonga and Angliru, as well as the host of novel climbs Unipublic has unveiled around the country, have upstaged the Puerto de Pajares. But in 2005, its legend was restored, when the race was won and lost there in an epic stage.

Since its move to September, ten years ago, the Vuelta has stood at the end of the season like a merciful angel, offering a last chance to those who failed in France in July. Nobody has been in greater need of that opportunity for redemption, or made better use of it, than Roberto Heras. After yet another disappointing performance in the 2005 Tour, where he finished 45th, he ruefully concluded: 'The Vuelta gives me prestige, and the Tour takes it away.'

His determination to recapture that prestige and justify his status as race favourite (Valverde being absent with a knee injury), was made visible on stage 6, the first mountain stage, from Cuenca to the summit finish at Valdelinares. On the final, nine-kilometre climb, Liberty Seguros set so strong a pace, with such abrupt changes of rhythm, that all but a handful of riders with the most serious aspirations were burned off. And when Heras, himself, took over at the front, only the Spanish-domiciled Russian, Denis Menchov, could stay with him. At least until the final kilometre, when another surge carried Heras clear to a solo win, and the gold jersey.

Such an exhibition of strength by Heras, and commitment to his cause from his entire team, containing superb *gregarios* such as Joseba Beloki and Michele Scarponi, suggested that the pattern of the race might already have been decided. But Menchov was to prove the surprise package. He was also smarting from a disappointing Tour ride: his determination to make an impression in France had been foiled by illness. In Spain, he made an immediate impact by winning the short opening time trial in Granada, and beating the rest of the field once again to recapture the gold jersey on stage 9, over a 48-kilometre course at the Costa Brava resort of Lloret de Mar. Heras, displaying his vastly improved time-trialling skills, finished fifth, dropping to second place overall, 47 seconds down.

With all the mountains of the Pyrenees and the north of Spain still to come, Menchov's lead hardly seemed an insurmountable problem for the Spaniard. His challengers in such terrain were more likely to be Francisco Mancebo and Carlos Sastre, lying immediately behind him on general classification. And it was Mancebo, buoyed by his fourth-place overall in the Tour, who snatched the next stage in a mountain-top sprint in the Andorran ski station of Arcalís. More to the point, though, despite the fierce pace Sáiz's Liberty Seguros men had set on the opening climbs, and Heras's repeated accelerations on the final stretch to Arcalís, Menchov had looked comfortable all day. So it proved on the next stage in the high mountains. On the easier climb to Cerler, the race leader was never in difficulties and the quartet who led the general classification finished together, 15 seconds back on Euskaltel-Euskadi's veteran, Roberto Laiseka.

In a race of three weeks, there is plenty of room for unexpected disaster. On stage 12, a rolling 133 kilometres from Logroño to Burgos, Heras emerged shaken from a pile-up, his knee gouged and bloodied. The peloton eased up, and although in pain, he reached the finish without losing any time.

Once his knee had been stitched and his fears soothed – mercifully, the injury wouldn't affect his pedalling power – Heras' main preoccupation switched back to that tantalising gap of 47 seconds, which was beginning to look like an eternity. The unfancied Russian, riding for a weak Danish Rabobank team – they'd come to the Vuelta with none of their better climbers to lend him support – seemed capable of resisting all that Liberty Seguros could hurl at him, secure in the knowledge that he had the final time trial to fall back on. It wouldn't have been the first time that the Vuelta had unfolded in this way: in 1991 ONCE's Melchor Mauri had held on to a slender lead for more than a fortnight, resisting Induráin at every stage, and even extending his margin in the last time trial. Manolo Sáiz might well have recognised the parallel, especially after stage 14.

Although billed as the *etapa reina*, with its finish at the Lagos de Covadonga, it proved no more than a re-telling of the story of the Pyrenees. The day before, Menchov had warned: 'I like a steep climb, too.' Liberty Seguros attacked with strength enough to shred the peloton, but in the final kilometres Heras could never shake the Russian off his back wheel. Only Sastre gained the handful of seconds necessary to lift himself above Mancebo into third place, while Eladio Jiménez, a survivor from a small group that had escaped earlier in the day, held on to give the combative Comunidad Valenciana team the prestigious stage-win. A jubilant Vicente Belda declared the victory was worth three: it was his team's way of sticking two fingers up at the ProTour, from which they'd been excluded.

296

Heras had the good grace not to blame his injured knee. 'It barely hurt,' he said, while admitting that he simply hadn't had the strength to dispose of Menchov. He was at a loss – none of his attacks had ruffled the imperturbable Russian, who looked set to ride all the way to Madrid on Heras' wheel.

The following day, a Sunday, as the cyclists assembled in Cangas de Onis, Heras knew he was facing his last chance. After 191 kilometres over two third-category and two first-category climbs, the stage would culminate on Pajares, the last summit finish of the race. The weather soon deteriorated, with rain and low temperatures punishing the cyclists, whose bodies were still recovering from the August heat of the first week's racing in Andalucía. Right from the outset, there were the usual optimistic escapes, four of Sáiz's men among them. It might have seemed that Liberty Seguros had abandoned all hopes of an Heras victory and were settling for a stage-win, but this was a consciously executed plan: they would be there, up the road, when their leader needed them most.

It was not until the penultimate climb, on the first-category Alto de la Colladiella, that Heras showed his hand. Four vicious attacks decimated the main bunch and, for the first time, Menchov was struggling to hold the little Spaniard's wheel. Soon he would lose sight of it altogether.

On the dangerously steep, narrow and rain-sodden road down to the valley, Heras plummeted in what Mancebo described as a suicidal mission: 'He was either going to end up in the gold jersey, or in hospital.' No one could follow. All the Russian race leader could do was cross his fingers and hope to keep the gap within manageable proportions, while Heras was carving out one of the epic moments in the Vuelta's 70-year history. His hair-raising descent conjured up images of Rominger flying down the Cobertoria in similar circumstances in 1992, to dispose of Zülle's lingering threat. Or Gimondi swooping down off the Orduña in 1968 to snatch the jersey from Pérez Francés, when the great Basque climbs were still part of the Vuelta's regular route.

Heras knew the descent, but not too well: "I entered some of the curves without knowing what lay in wait for me," he revealed afterwards. But fear wasn't an option. His director, Sáiz, had come up with the perfect strategy. His team-mates had obeyed orders and successfully infiltrated early escapes. As team leader, the rest was up to him.

When he reached the bottom of the Colladiella, miraculously intact, Heras discerned the advance guard of Beloki, Scarponi and Ángel Vicioso waiting for him, ready to pace him across the valley floor to the foot of Pajares. Later he would say that this vision of his team-mates was the best moment of the entire race, the memory he'd treasure most.

As for Menchov, he arrived too late to jump aboard the Liberty train – only 20 seconds too late, but by then it was already out of sight, with Beloki, a man who'd twice finished second behind Armstrong in the Tour, pulling on the front for all he was worth. By the time the road began to rise again, 20 kilometres later, the now isolated Russian was trailing by more than two minutes, and his week in the gold jersey was effectively over.

On the lower slopes it was Scarponi who took over the pace-making, and all the time the gap was widening. Finally, six kilometres from the summit, Heras went to the front to deliver the *coup de grace* and was immediately out on his own, pedalling to a record-breaking fourth Vuelta victory. Lower down, Menchov's lonely task was reduced to hanging on to a podium position. He lost 5'–17" in those final 50 kilometres, but managed to maintain second overall, 20 seconds ahead of Sastre.

Heras had rediscovered glory. His overall lead was an irrevocable four and a half minutes, which he even extended by six seconds in an extraordinary final time trial, run off at an average of 56.2 kph. With the wind in their favour, the climbers destroyed the specialists: only fractions of a second prevented Heras from taking another stage victory. The *Bejerano* was hailed as the undisputed champion of the Vuelta, always to be remembered against a backdrop of Asturian mist and rain.

This year, the journey into Madrid was enlivened by Alessandro Petacchi: he won all three intermediate sprints and extended his tally of stage-wins to five, capturing the points prize in the process. Few in Spain would have begrudged him if he'd taken the World Championship title a week later, rather than Tom Boonen, who immediately announced: 'It isn't important to win a load of stages in the Vuelta. The only thing that matters is winning here today.'

The race organisers had incorporated the Madrid World Championship course into the final stage to coax the sprinters over the mountains, but apart from Petacchi few took the bait. Other contenders for the Worlds – Thor Hushovd, Bradley McGee, who held the gold jersey for three days in the first week, and Boonen – dropped out after using the race as high quality training. Whether it's May or September, foreign riders will always quit the Vuelta as they see fit. In the past, the organisers would sometimes dish out a fine, as in the case of Edgard Sorgeloos when he retired to chauffeur his boss, a disappointing Rik Van Looy, back to Belgium. Nowadays, only cases of glaring disrespect, such as Ullrich pulling out while classified in fourth place to prepare for the 2000 Olympics, draw any censure.

So had the ProTour made a difference to the foreign contribution? Scarcely: seven of the top 10 were Spaniards. Even the foreign status of Navarran-based Menchov was questioned in some quarters, his cycling career having evolved in Spain. Rabobank, like other foreign teams, sent their second-string riders to back him, opening up speculation on what the outcome might have been otherwise. It's difficult to hear a good word spoken about the ProTour in Spain. Aside from the struggle between Heras and Menchov, some of the best moments in the 2005 Vuelta were provided by the men from the Comunidad Valenciana squad: their performance ridiculed their exclusion from the ProTour. They placed two men in the top half dozen, won the team competition by an hour, and in the spirit of Kelme (of which they are the reincarnation) were constantly on the attack.

Perhaps there lies the problem. The attitude of Belda's team, and the other Spanish riders, helped to confirm the Vuelta's reputation as a hard, uncompromising race. In the first week, after a typical stage of relentless hostilities from the opening kilometres, Boonen declared he'd never suffered so much in his cycling career, no doubt relieved he had an air-ticket out of Spain for after stage 10. After the glamour of the Tour, the Vuelta can be a tough proposition. There is none of the strict hierarchy of the Italian peloton, where the *capos* impose a discipline and keep the pace in check. On home-ground, the Spaniards are unstoppable.

Although the 2005 Vuelta, as a race, was acknowledged to be an undeniable success in Spain, a certain disillusion lingers. Cycling is under siege, suffering a barrage of doping cases, the latest scandal involving the content of Armstrong's frozen urine, vintage 1999, a story L'Equipe unleashed only a few days before the Vuelta got underway. The last straw for the Spanish race was to be caught up in wrangling between TVE and the new owners of Unipublic, who happen to be a rival television channel. The day the Vuelta, a national institution, produced a legendary stage in a mythic setting should have been an occasion for celebrating. Instead, TVE picked up the live action when it was nearly over, long after Heras' attack on the Colladiella. An opportunity to remind Spanish viewers what cycling is really about had been unforgivably lost.

While the Vuelta was in progress, Asturian Fernando Alonso was proclaimed World Champion of Formula One and, for a day, knocked football off the front pages of the Spanish sporting press. It was another sign that Spain is now one of the world's prominent sporting nations. It was also a reminder that nothing ignites the public so much as winning on an international stage and that Heras' failure in the Tour inevitably undermined his triumph at home. If professional cycling is to recover its gradually fading status in one of the countries where it has most tradition, Heras needs to show his worth abroad.

But there's no need for full-scale pessimism yet; the Vuelta has survived far worse. If the home audience is diminishing, in recent years, many cycling fans beyond Spain, frustrated with the recent predictability of the Tour, have discovered that the season doesn't end in July, and that Spain has an abundance of home-grown talent capable of turning their national race into an engrossing and passionate affair. Behind today's Vuelta lies a glorious 70-year history: from the stalwart Cañardo, resolutely fighting to crack the solid Belgian front, the obsessive duels of Bahamontes and Loroño, the tragic heroism of Fuente and Ocaña, the prowess of Kas, the exciting emergence from the wilderness of Pedro Delgado, to the unrelenting ambition of ONCE. Then there were the giants, Anquetil and Merckx, who came and conquered, as did Hinault, twice, and with far more panache. And although Induráin proved elusive for Unipublic once he'd embarked on his victorious reign in France, they're indebted to him for inspiring and leaving in his wake a new wave of figures: Heras – serious, dependable, his victories an exercise of maturity and strong team work that once seemed beyond Spanish capabilities – and the extrovert Valverde, a guarantee for the future.

Appendix

*La Vuelta Ciclista a España, 1935–2005
Facts amd Figures*

La Vuelta Ciclista a España –
the Winners, 1935–2005

YEAR	Starters	Finishers	DIST. (KMS.)	No. of stages	AVGE. SPEED (KPH)	WINNER
1935	50	29	3,425	12	28.54	Gustaaf Deloor (Bel)
1936	50	26	4,407	21	28.99	Gustaaf Deloor (Bel)
1941	32	16	4,406	22	26.11	Julián Berendero (Sp)
1942	40	18	3,688	19	27.51	Julián Berendero (Sp)
1945	51	26	3,803	19	28.02	Delio Rodríguez (Sp)
1946	48	29	3,797	23	27.68	Dalmacio Langarica (Sp)
1947	47	27	3,893	24	29.39	Edouard Van Dyck (Bel)
1948	54	26	3,990	20	25.72	Bernardo Ruiz (Sp)
1950	42	26	3,932	24	29.12	Emilio Rodríguez (Sp)
1955	106	63	2,740	15	33.80	Jean Dotto (Fr)
1956	90	40	3,531	17	33.43	Angelo Conterno (It)
1957	90	54	2,967	16	35.01	Jesús Loroño (Sp)
1958	100	45	3,250	16	32.25	Jean Stablinski (Fr)
1959	90	41	3,048	17	36.01	Antonio Suárez (Sp)
1960	80	24	3,567	17	34.58	Frans de Mulder (Bel)
1961	100	50	2,824	16	36.38	Angelino Soler (Sp)
1962	90	48	2,806	17	35.68	Rudi Altig (Ger)
1963	90	65	2,442	15	37.69	Jacques Anquetil (Fr)
1964	80	49	2,921	17	36.63	Raymond Poulidor (Fr)
1965	100	51	3,410	18	36.95	Rolf Wolfshohl (Ger)
1966	90	55	2,951	18	37.61	Francisco Gabica (Sp)
1967	110	73	2,945	18	38.72	Jan Janssen (Hol)
1968	90	51	2,990	18	37.96	Felice Gimondi (It)
1969	100	68	2,921	18	39.84	Roger Pingeon (Fr)
1970	109	59	3,568	19	39.58	Luis Ocaña (Sp)

WINNING MARGIN	SECOND	THIRD
13′– 28″	Mariano Cañardo (Sp)	Antoon Digneff (Bel)
11′–39″	Alphonse Deloor (Bel)	Antonio Bertola (It)
1′–07″	Fermín Trueba (Sp)	José Jabardo (Sp)
8′–38″	Diego Chafer (Sp)	Antonio Sancho (Sp)
30′–08″	Julián Berendero (Sp)	Juan Gimeno (Sp)
17′–32″	Julián Berendero (Sp)	Jan Lambrichts (Hol)
2′–14″	Manuel Costa (Sp)	Delio Rodríguez (Sp)
9′–07″	Emilio Rodríguez	Bernardo Capó (Sp)
15′–30″	Manuel Rodríguez (Sp)	José Serra (Sp)
3′–06″	Antonio Jiménez (Sp)	Raphaël Géminiani (Fr)
13 seconds	Jesús Loroño (Sp)	Raymond Impanis (Bel)
8′–11″	Federico Bahamontes (Sp)	Bernardo Ruiz (Sp)
2′–51″	Lino Fornara (It)	Fernando Manzaneque (Sp)
1′–06″	José Segú (Sp)	Rik Van Looy (Bel)
15′–27″	Armand de Smet (Bel)	Miguel Pacheco (Sp)
51 seconds	François Mahé (Fr)	José Pérez Francés (Sp)
7′–14″	José Pérez Francés (Sp)	Seamus Elliott (Ire)
3′–06″	Martin Colmenarejo (Sp)	Miguel Pacheco (Sp)
33 seconds	Luis Otaño (Sp)	José Pérez Francés (Sp)
6′–36″	Raymond Poulidor (Fr)	Rik Van Looy (Bel)
39 seconds	Eusebio Vélez (Sp)	Carlos Echeverría (Sp)
1′–43″	Jean Pierre Ducasse (Fr)	Aurelio González (Sp)
2′–15″	José Pérez Francés (Sp)	Eusebio Vélez (Sp)
1′–56″	Luis Ocaña (Sp)	Marinus Wagtmans (Hol)
1′–18″	Agustín Tamames (Sp)	Herman Van Springel (Bel)

YEAR			DIST. (KMS.)		AVGE. SPEED (KPH)	WINNER
1971	110	68	2,983	17	37.83	Ferdinand Bracke (Bel)
1972	100	57	3,079	17	37.28	José Manuel Fuente (Sp)
1973	80	62	3,062	17	36.10	Eddy Merckx (Bel)
1974	88	55	2,987	19	34.42	José Manuel Fuente (Sp)
1975	90	54	3,104	19	34.95	Agustín Tamames (Sp)
1976	100	49	3,341	19	35.81	José Pesarrodona (Sp)
1977	70	54	2,785	19	35.29	Freddy Maertens (Bel)
1978	99	64	2,995	19	35.01	Bernard Hinault (Fr)
1979	90	73	3,373	19	35.53	Joop Zoetemelk (Hol)
1980	110	63	3,225	19	36.49	Faustino Rupérez (Sp)
1981	80	55	3,499	19	35.68	Giovanni Battaglin (It)
1982	100	76	3,442	19	35.93	Marino Lejarreta (Sp)
1983	100	59	3,399	19	35.98	Bernard Hinault (Fr)
1984	130	97	3,354	19	37.21	Eric Caritoux (Fr)
1985	169	101	3,471	19	36.17	Pedro Delgado (Sp)
1986	170	107	3,675	21	37.40	Álvaro Pino (Sp)
1987	179	88	3,922	22	37.15	Luis Herrera (Col)
1988	180	116	3,440	21	38.51	Sean Kelly (Ire)
1989	189	143	3,656	22	39.31	Pedro Delgado (Sp)
1990	198	133	3,711	22	39.22	Marco Giovannetti (It)
1991	198	116	3,212	21	38.80	Melchor Mauri (Sp)
1992	188	139	3,558	21	36.97	Tony Rominger (Swi)
1993	169	114	3,585	21	37.30	Tony Rominger (Swi)
1994	169	122	3,531	20	38.33	Tony Rominger (Swi)
1995	180	118	3,750	21	39.25	Laurent Jalabert (Fr)
1996	180	115	3,898	22	39.99	Alex Zülle (Swi)
1997	198	125	3,784	22	41.34	Alex Zülle (Swi)
1998	198	108	3,781	22	40.47	Abraham Olano (Sp)
1999	189	115	3,576	21	39.79	Jan Ullrich (Ger)
2000	180	124	2,894	21	40.95	Roberto Heras (Sp)
2001	189	139	2,986	21	42.16	Ángel Casero (Sp)
2002	207	132	3,144	21	41.79	Aitor González (Sp)
2003	198	159	2,955	21	42.52	Roberto Heras (Sp)
2004	189	119	3,034	21	39.04	Roberto Heras (Sp)
2005	198	127	3,353	21	40.74	Roberto Heras (Sp)

WINNING MARGIN	SECOND	THIRD
59 seconds	Wilfried David (Bel)	Luis Ocaña (Sp)
6'–34"	Miguel María Lasa (Sp)	Agustín Tamames (Sp)
3'–46"	Luis Ocaña (Sp)	Bernard Thévenet (Fr)
11 seconds	Joaquim Agostinho (Por)	Miguel María Lasa (Sp)
14 seconds	Domingo Perurena (Sp)	Miguel María Lasa (Sp)
1'–03"	Luis Ocaña (Sp)	José Nazábal (Sp)
2'–09"	Miguel María Lasa (Sp)	Peter Thaler (Ger)
2'–52"	José Pesarrodona (Sp)	Jean-Rene Bernaudeau (Fr)
2'–43"	Francisco Galdos (Sp)	Michel Pollentier (Bel)
2'–15"	Pedro Torres (Sp)	Claude Criquilion (Bel)
2'–09"	Pedro Muñoz (Sp)	Vicente Belda (Sp)
18 seconds	Michel Pollentier (Bel)	Sven-Ake Nilsson (Swe)
1'–12"	Marino Lejarreta (Sp)	Alberto Fernández (Sp)
6 seconds	Alberto Fernández (Sp)	Raymond Dietsen (Ger)
36 seconds	Robert Millar (GBr)	Pacho Rodríguez (Col)
1'–06"	Robert Millar (GBr)	Sean Kelly (Ire)
1'–04"	Raimund Dietzen (Ger)	Laurent Fignon (Fr)
1'–27"	Raimund Dietzen (Ger)	Anselmo Fuerte (Sp)
35 seconds	Fabio Parra (Col)	Oscar Vargas (Col)
1'–28"	Pedro Delgado (Sp)	Anselmo Fuerte (Sp)
2'–52"	Miguel Induráin (Sp)	Marino Lejarreta (Sp)
1'–04"	Jesús Montoya (Sp)	Pedro Delgado (Sp)
29 seconds	Alex Zülle (Swi)	Laudelino Cubino (Sp)
7'–28"	Mikel Zarrabeitia (Sp)	Pedro Delgado (Sp)
4'–22"	Abraham Olano (Sp)	Johan Bruyneel (Bel)
6'–23"	Laurent Dufaux (Swi)	Tony Rominger (Swi)
5'–07"	Fernando Escartín (Sp)	Laurent Dufaux (Swi)
1'–23"	Fernando Escartín (Sp)	José María Jiménez (Sp)
4'–15"	Igor Galdeano (Sp)	Roberto Heras (Sp)
2'–33"	Ángel Casero (Sp)	Pavel Tonkov (Rus)
47 seconds	Oscar Sevilla (Sp)	Levi Leipheimer (US)
2'–14"	Roberto Heras (Sp)	Joseba Beloki (Sp)
28 seconds	Isidro Nozal (Sp)	Alejandro Valverde (Sp)
30 seconds	Santiago Pérez (Sp)	Francisco Mancebo (Sp)
4'–36"	Denis Menchov (Rus)	Carlos Sastre (Sp)

Kings of the Mountains

1935 Edoardo Molinar (It)	1976 Andrés Oliva (Sp)
1936 Salvador Molina (Sp)	1977 Pedro Torres (Sp)
1941 Fermín Trueba (Sp)	1978 Andrés Oliva (Sp)
1942 Julián Berendero (Sp)	1979 Felipe Yañez (Sp)
1945 Julián Berendero (Sp)	1980 Juan Fernández (Sp)
1946 Emilio Rodríguez (Sp)	1981 José Luis Laguía (Sp)
1947 Emilio Rodríguez (Sp)	1982 José Luis Laguía (Sp)
1948 Bernardo Ruiz (Sp)	1983 José Luis Laguía (Sp)
1950 Emilio Rodríguez (Sp)	1984 Felipe Yañez (Sp)
1955 Giuseppe Buratti (It)	1985 José Luis Laguía (Sp)
1956 Nino Defilippis (It)	1986 José Luis Laguía (Sp)
1957 Federico Bahamontes (Sp)	1987 Luis Herrera (Col)
1958 Federico Bahamontes (Sp)	1988 Alvaro Pino (Sp)
1959 Antonio Suárez (Sp)	1989 Oscar de Jesús Vargas (Col)
1960 Antonio Karmany (Sp)	1990 Martín Farfan (Col)
1961 Antonio Karmany (Sp)	1991 Luis Herrera (Col)
1962 Antonio Karmany (Sp)	1992 Carlos Hernández (Sp)
1963 Julio Jiménez (Sp)	1993 Tony Rominger (Swi)
1964 Julio Jiménez (Sp)	1994 Luc Leblanc (Fr)
1965 Julio Jiménez (Sp)	1995 Laurent Jalabert (Fr)
1966 Gregorio San Miguel (Sp)	1996 Tony Rominger (Swi)
1967 Mariano Díaz (Sp)	1997 José María Jiménez (Sp)
1968 Francisco Gabica (Sp)	1998 José María Jiménez (Sp)
1969 Luis Ocaña (Sp)	1999 José María Jiménez (Sp)
1970 Agustín Tamames (Sp)	2000 Carlos Sastre (Sp)
1971 Joop Zoetemelk (Hol)	2001 José María Jiménez (Sp)
1972 José Manuel Fuente (Sp)	2002 Aitor Osa (Sp)
1973 José Luis Abilleira (Sp)	2003 Félix Cárdenas (Col)
1974 José Luis Abilleira (Sp)	2004 Félix Cárdenas (Col)
1975 Andrés Oliva (Sp)	2005 Joaquim Rodríguez (Sp)

Points Competition Winners

1945 Julián Berendero (Sp)
1955 Fiorenzo Magni (It)
1956 Rik Van Steenbergen (Bel)
1957 Vicente Iturat (Sp)
1958 Salvador Botella (Sp)
1959 Rik Van Looy (Bel)
1960 Arthur De Cabooter (Bel)
1961 Antonio Suárez (Sp)
1962 Rudi Altig (Ger)
1963 Bas Maliepaard (Hol)
1964 José Pérez Francés (Sp)
1965 Rik Van Looy (Bel)
1966 Jos Van Der Vleuten (Hol)
1967 Jan Janssen (Hol)
1968 Jan Janssen (Hol)
1969 Raymond Steegmans (Bel)
1970 Guido Reybrouck (Bel)
1971 Cyrille Guimard (Fr)
1972 Domingo Perurena (Sp)
1973   Eddy Merckx (Bel)
1974 Domingo Perurena (Sp)
1975 Miguel María Lasa (Sp)
1976 Dietrich Thurau (Ger)
1977 Freddy Maertens (Bel)
1978 Ferdi Van De Haute (Bel)
1979 Alfons De Wolf (Bel)

1980 Sean Kelly (Ire)
1981 Javier Cedena (Sp)
1982 Steffan Mutter (Sui)
1983 Marino Lejarreta (Sp)
1984 Guido Van Calster (Bel)
1985 Sean Kelly (Ire)
1986 Sean Kelly (Ire)
1987 Alfonso Gutiérrez (Sp)
1988 Sean Kelly (Ire)
1989 Malcolm Elliott (GBr)
1990 Uwe Raab (Ger)
1991 Uwe Raab (Ger)
1992 Djamolidine Abdoujaparov (Uzb)
1993 Tony Rominger (Swi)
1994 Laurent Jalabert (Fr)
1995 Laurent Jalabert (Fr)
1996 Laurent Jalabert (Fr)
1997 Laurent Jalabert (Fr)
1998 Fabeizio Guidi (It)
1999 Frank Vandenbroucke (Bel)
2000 Roberto Heras (Sp)
2001 José María Jiménez (Sp)
2002 Erik Zabel (Ger)
2003 Erik Zabel (Ger)
2004 Erik Zabel (Ger)
2005 Alessandro Petacchi (It)

Team Competition Winners

1935 Belgium	1976 Kas (Sp)
1936 Belgium	1977 Teka (Sp)
1941 Spain	1978 Kas (Sp)
1942 F.C. Barcelona (Sp)	1979 Kas-Belgium
1945 Manresa (Sp)	1980 Splendor (Bel)
1946 Spain	1981 Zor-Novostil (Sp)
1947 Spain	1982 Kelme (Sp)
1948 Spain	1983 Zor (Sp)
1950 Spain	1984 Teka (Sp)
1955 France	1985 Zor (Sp)
1956 Spain	1986 Zor-BH (Sp)
1957 Pirenaico (Sp)	1987 Postobon (Col)
1958 Belgium	1989 Kelme (Sp)
1959 Faema-Belgium	1990 Once (Sp)
1960 Groene Leeuw (Bel)	1991 Once (Sp)
1961 Faema-Spain	1992 Amaya Seguros (Sp)
1962 Helyett-St Raphaël (Fr)	1993 Amaya Seguros (Sp)
1963 St Raphaël (Fr)	1994 Banesto (Sp)
1964 Kas (Sp)	1995 Once (Sp)
1965 Mercier-BP (Fr)	1996 Team Polti (It)
1966 Kas (Sp)	1997 Kelme-Costa Blanca (Sp)
1967 Kas (Sp)	1998 Banesto (Sp)
1968 Kas (Sp)	1999 Banesto (Sp)
1969 Bic (Fr)	2000 Kelme-Costa Blanca (Sp)
1970 Werner (Sp)	2001 iBanesto (Sp)
1971 Werner (Sp)	2002 Kelme-Costa Blanca (Sp)
1972 Kas (Sp)	2003 iBanesto (Sp)
1973 La Casera (Sp)	2004 Kelme-Comunidad Valenciana
1974 Kas (Sp)	2005 Comunidad Valenciana
1975 Kas (Sp)	

Stage Winners

1935 (29.4-15.5)
1. Madrid-Valladolid (185 km): Antoon Dignef (B); 2. Santander (251 km): Antonio Escuriet (Sp); 3. Bilbao (199 km): Gustaaf Deloor (B); 4. San Sebastián (235 km): Antoon Dignef (B); 5. Zaragoza (264 km): Mariano Cañardo (Sp); 6. Barcelona (310 km): François Adam (B); 7. Tortosa (188 km): Antonio Montes (Sp); 8. Valencia (188 km): Max Bulla (A); 9. Murcia (265 km): Salvador Cardona (Sp); 10. Granada (125 km): Max Bulla (A); 11. Sevilla (260 km): Gustaaf Deloor (B); 12. Cáceres (270 km): François Adam (B); 13. Zamora (275 km): Eduardo Molinar (It); 14. Madrid (250 km): Gustaaf Deloor (B).

1936 (5.5-31.5)
1. Madrid-Salamanca (210 km): Jozef Huts (B); 2. Cáceres (214 km): Gustaaf Deloor (B); 3. Sevilla (270 km): Vicente Carretero (Sp); 4. Málaga (212 km): Gustaaf Deloor (B); 5. Granada (132 km): Vicente Carretero (Sp); 6. Almería (185 km): Gustaaf Deloor (B); 7. Alicante (306 km): Mariano Cañardo (Sp); 8. Valencia (184 km): Antonio Bertola (It); 9. Tarragona (279 km): Salvador Cardona (Sp); 10. Barcelona (139 km): Vicente Carretero (Sp); 11. Zaragoza (265 km): Alfons Schepers (B); 12. San Sebastián (265 km): Alfons Schepers (B); 13. Bilbao (160 km): Vicente Carretero (Sp); 14. Santander (199 km): Alfons Deloor (B); 15. Gijón (194 km): Mariano Cañardo (Sp); 16. Ribadeo (155 km): Rafael Ramos (Sp); 17. La Coruna (157 km): Alfons Schepers (B); 18. Vigo (175 km): Vicente Carretero (Sp); 19. Verin (178 km): Fermin Trueba (Sp); 20. Zamora (207 km): Antonio Bertola (It); 21. Madrid (250 km): Emiliano Alvarez (Sp).

1941 (12.6-6.7)
1. Madrid-Salamanca (210 km): Julián Berrendero (Sp); 2. Cáceres (214 km): Antonio Montes (Sp); 3. Sevilla (270 km): Delio Rodríguez (Sp); 4. Málaga (212 km): Antonio Escuriet (Sp); 5. Almería (220 km): Delio Rodríguez (Sp); 6. Murcia (223 km): Delio Rodríguez (Sp); 7. Valencia (248 km): Antonio Andrès Sancho (Sp); 8. Tarragona (279 km): Fermin Trueba (Sp); 9. Barcelona (112 km): Antonio Martin (Sp); 10. Zaragoza (294 km): Delio Rodríguez (Sp); 11. Logrono (172 km): Delio Rodríguez (Sp); 12. San Sebastián (209 km): Delio Rodríguez (Sp); 13. Bilbao (160 km): Federico Ezquerra (Sp); 14. Santander (165 km): Fermin Trueba (Sp); 15. Gijón (192 km): Delio Rodríguez (Sp); 16. a) Oviedo (tt 53 km): Delio Rodríguez (Sp); b) Luarca (101 km): Delio Rodríguez (Sp); 17. La Coruna (219 km): Delio Rodríguez (Sp); 18. Vigo (219 km): Delio Rodríguez (Sp); 19. Verín (178 km): Delio Rodríguez (Sp); 20. Valladolid (178 km): Julián Berrendero (Sp); 21. Madrid (198 km): Vicente Carretero (Sp).

1942 (30.6-19.7)
1. Madrid-Albacete (245 km): Julián Berrendero (Sp); 2. Murcia (160 km): Delio Rodríguez (Sp); 3. Valencia (248 km): José Jabardo (Sp); 4. Tarragona (278 km): Delio Rodríguez (Sp); 5. Barcelona (120 km): Delio Rodríguez (Sp); 6. Huesca (279 km): Delio Rodríguez (Sp); 7. San Sebastián (305 km): Delio Rodríguez (Sp); 8. Bilbao (160 km): René Vietto (F); 9. Castro Urdiales (tt 53 km): Delio Rodríguez (Sp); 10. Santander (151 km): Julián Berrendero (Sp); 11. Reinosa (120 km): Piere Brambilla (It); 12. Gijón (199 km): Delio Rodríguez (Sp); 13. Oviedo (75 km): Louis Thiétard (F); 14. Luarca (129 km): Delio Rodríguez (Sp); 15. La Coruna (219 km): Louis Thiétard (F); 16. a) Santiago (tt 63 km): Antonio Andres Sancho (Sp); b) Vigo (110 km): René Vietto (F); 17. Ponferrada (270 km): Joaquin Olmos (Sp); 18. Salamanca (251 km): Celestino Camilla (It); 19. Madrid (248 km): Celestino Camilla (It).

1945 (10.5-31.5)
1. Madrid-Salamanca (212 km): Julián Berrendero (Sp); 2. Cáceres (214 km): Delio Rodríguez (Sp); 3. Badajoz (132 km): Miguel Gual (Sp); 4. Almendralejo (tt 57 km): Juan Gimeno (Sp); 5. Sevilla (171 km): Vicente Miró (Sp); 6. Granada (251 km): Antonio Montes (Sp); 7. Murcia (285 km): Joaquin Olmos (Sp); 8. Valencia (244 km): Delio Rodríguez (Sp); 9. Tortosa (188 km): Delio

Rodríguez (Sp); 10. Barcelona (276 km): Miguel Gual (Sp); 11. Zaragoza (306 km): Miguel Gual (Sp); 12. San Sebastián (276 km): José Gutiérrez (Sp); 13. Bilbao (207 km): Joao Rebelo (P); 14. Santander (188 km): Delio Rodríguez (Sp); 15. Reinosa (110 km): Joao Rebelo (P); 16. Gijón (200 km): Delio Rodríguez (Sp); 17. León (172 km): Julián Berrendero (Sp); 18. Valladolid (132 km): Delio Rodríguez (Sp); 19. Madrid (185 km): Joaquin Olmos (Sp).

1946 (7.5-30.5)
1. Madrid-Salamanca (212 km): Joaquin Olmos (Sp); 2. Béjar (ttt 73 km): Galindo/ Miguel Gual (Sp); 3. Cáceres (141 km): Antonio Andres Sancho (Sp); 4. Badajoz (132 km): Ignacio Orbaiceta (Sp); 5. Sevilla (218 km): Julián Berrendero (Sp); 6. Granada (251 km): John Lambrichts (NL); 7. Baza (107 km): Dalmacio Langarica (Sp); 8. Murcia (178 km): Joao Lourenço (P); 9. Valencia (264 km): Alejandro Fombellida (Sp); 10. Castellón (ttt 67 km): Netherland/John Lambrichts (NL); 11. Tortosa (123 km): Alejandro Fombellida (Sp); 12. Barcelona (215 km): Dalmacio Langarica (Sp); 13. Lérida (162 km): Delio Rodríguez (Sp); 14. Zaragoza (144 km): Delio Rodríguez (Sp); 15. San Sebastián (276 km): Delio Rodríguez (Sp); 16. Bilbao (207 km): Dalmacio Langarica (Sp); 17. Santander (226 km): Delio Rodríguez (Sp); 18. Reinosa (110 km): Dalmacio Langarica (Sp); 19. Gijón (204 km): Delio Rodríguez (Sp); 20. Oviedo (tt 53 km): Dalmacio Langarica (Sp); 21. León (119 km): Julián Berrendero (Sp); 22. Valladolid (134 km): Alejandro Fombellida (Sp); 20. Madrid (220 km): Julián Berrendero (Sp).

1947 (12.5-5.6)
1. Madrid-Albacete (243 km): Delio Rodríguez (Sp); 2. Murcia (146 km): Emilio Rodríguez (Sp); 3. Alcoy (135 km): Julián Berrendero (Sp); 4. Castellón (175 km): Adolfo Deledda (It); 5. Tarragona (221 km): Delio Rodríguez (Sp); 6. Barcelona (119 km): Cipriano Aquirrezábal (Sp); 7. Lérida (162 km): Cipriano Aquirrézabal; 8. Zaragoza (144 km): Delio Rodríguez (Sp); 9. Pamplona (176 km): Felice Adriano (It); 10. San Sebastián (107 km): Delio Rodríguez (Sp); 11. Bilbao (229 km): Felice Adriano (It); 12. Santander (212 km): Felice Adriano (It); 13. Reinosa (201 km): Joaquín Jiménez (Sp); 14. Gijón (204 km): Delio Rodríguez (Sp); 15. Oviedo (107 km): Delio Rodríguez (Sp); 16. a) Luarca (101 km): Adolfo Deledda (It); b) Ribadeo (tt 70 km): Edward Van Dijck (B); 17. El Ferrol (159 km): Senén Mesa (Sp); 18. La Coruna (70 km): Delio Rodríguez (Sp); 19. Vigo (180 km): Alejandro Fombellida (Sp); 20. Orense (105 km): Felice Adriano (It); 20. Astorga (228 km): Alejandro Fombellida (Sp); 21. León (tt 47 km): Edward Van Dijck (B); 22. Valladolid (133 km): Delio Rodríguez (Sp); 23. Madrid (220 km): Joaquin Olmos.

1948 (13.6-4.7)
1. Madrid (tt 14 km): e.a. Julián Berrendero (Sp) & Bernardo Ruiz (Sp); 2. Valdepenas (198 km): Francis Gielen (B); 3. Granada (232 km): Dalmacio Langarica (Sp); 4. Murcia (285 km): Bernardo Ruiz (Sp); 5. Alicante (202 km): Roberto Vercellone (It); 6. Valencia (163 km): Dalmacio Langarica (Sp); 7. Tortosa (201 km): José Perez (Sp); 8. Barcelona (214 km): Senén Mesa (Sp); 9. Lérida (203 km): Miguel Gual (Sp); 10. Zaragoza (160 km): Jean Lesage (B); 11. San Sebastián (276 km): Dalmacio Langarica (Sp); 12. Bilbao (259 km): Bernardo Ruiz (Sp); 13. Santander (212 km): Senén Mesa (Sp); 14. Gijón (225 km): Senén Mesa (Sp); 15. Ribadeo (200 km): Jean Lesage (B); 16. La Coruna (156 km): Miguel Gual (Sp); 17. Orense (261 km): Miguel Gual (Sp); 18. León (276 km): Jean Lesage (B); 19. Segovia (269 km): Miguel Gual; 20. Madrid (94 km): Bernardo Ruiz.

1950 (17.8-10.9)
1. Madrid-Valladolid (190 km): Omer Braeckeveldt (B); 2. León (133 km): Rik Evens (B); 3. Gijón (148 km): Emilio Rodríguez (Sp); 4. a) Santander (167 km): Emilio Rodríguez (Sp); b) Torrelavega (78 km): Emilio Rodríguez (Sp); 5. Bilbao (177 km): Antonio Gelabert (Sp); 6. Irun (240 km): Emilio Rodríguez (Sp); 7. Pamplona (109 km): Emilio Rodríguez (Sp); 8. a) Tudela (90 km): Bernardo Capó (Sp); b) Zaragoza (176 km): Bernardo Ruiz (Sp); 9. Lérida (144 km): Umberto Drei (It); 10. Barcelona (167 km): José Serra (Sp); 11. Tarragona (150 km): Rik Evens (B); 12. Castellón (194 km): Luis Navarro (Sp); 13. Valencia (65 km): Antonio Sanchez (Sp); 14. Murcia (265 km): Umberto Drei (It); 15. Lorca (117 km): Umberto Drei (It); 16. Granada (222 km): Alighiero Ridolfi (It); 17. Málaga (183 km): Umberto Drei (It); 18. Cadiz (268 km): Antonio Gelabert (Sp); 19. a) Jerez (tt 56 km): Andrés Trobat (Sp); b) Sevilla (100 km): José Serra; 20. Mérida (200 km): Victorio Garcia (Sp); 21. Talavera de la Reina (228 km): Bernardo Capó (Sp); 22. Madrid (117 km): Emilio Rodríguez (Sp).

1955 (23.4-8.5)
1. Bilbao-San Sebastián (240 km): Gilbert Bauvin (F); 2. Bayonne (211 km): Gilbert Bauvin (F); 3. Pamplona (157 km): Antonio Gelabert (Sp); 4. Zaragoza (229 km): Jesus Galdeano (Sp); 5. Lérida (195 km): Gabriel Company (Sp); 6. Barcelona (230 km): Pierino Baffi (It); 7. Barcelona (tt 30 km): Fiorenzo Magni (It); 8. Tortosa (213 km): Vicente Iturat (Sp); 9. Valencia (190 km): Pierino Baffi (It); 10. Cuenca (222 km): Antonio Uliana (It);11. Madrid (168 km): Donato Piazza (It); 12. Madrid (ttt 15 km): Italy "A"; 13. Valladolid (222 km): Fiorenzo Magni (It); 14. Bilbao (308 km): Donato Piazza (It); 15. Bilbao (147 km): Fiorenzo Magni (It).

1956 (26.4-13.5)
1. Bilbao-Santander (203 km): Rik Van Steenbergen (B); Oviedo (248 km): Angelo Conterno (It); 3. Valladolid (178 km): Miguel Poblet (Sp); 4. Madrid (212 km): Iaude Le Ber (F); 5. Albacete (241 km): Miguel Poblet (Sp); 6. Madrid (212 km): Miguel Poblet (Sp); 7. Valencia (182 km): Rik Van Steenbergen (B); 8. Tarragona (249 km): Rik Van Steenbergen (B); 9. Barcelona (163 km): Hugo Koblet (Swi); 10. a) Barcelona (ttt 21 km): France; b) Tárrega (133 km): Gilbert Bauvin (F); 11. Zaragoza (238 km): Rik Van Steenbergen (B); 12. Bayonne (274 km): Giancarlo Astrua (It); 13. a) Irun (tt 43 km): Claude Le Ber (F); b) Pamplona (111 km): Roger Walkowiak (F); 14. San Sebastián (195 km): Rik Van Steenbergen (B); 15. Bilbao (225 km): Nino Defilippis (It); 16. Vitoria (207 km): Beningo Azpuru (Sp); 17. Bilbao (190 km): Rik Van Steenbergen (B).

1957 (26.4-12.5)
1. Bilbao-Vitoria (158 km): Miguel Chacón (Sp); 2. Santander (220 km): Carmelo Morales (Sp); 3. Mierès (259 km): Federico Bahamontes (Sp); 4. León (136 km): (stage annulled through snow); 5. Valladolid (172 km): Roger Hassenforder (F); 6. Madrid (212 km): Miguel Chacón (Sp); 7. Madrid (200 km): Jean Adriaensens (B); 8. Cuenca (159 km): Roger Walkowiak (F); 9. Valencia (249 km): Rino Benedetti (It); 10. Tortosa (192 km): Bruno Tognacini (It); 11. Barcelona (199 km): Gilbert Bauvin (F); 12. Zaragoza (229 km): Mario Baroni (It); 13. Huesca (tt 85 km): Jesus Lorono (Sp); 14. Bayonne (249 km): Antonio Ferraz (Sp); 15. San Sebastián (199 km): Roger Baens (B); 16. Bilbao (193 km): Antonio Suarez (Sp).

1958 (30.4-15.5)
1. Bilbao-San Sebastián (164 km): Miguel Pacheco (Sp); 2. Pamplona (150 km): Antonio Jiménez Quilès (Sp); 3. Zaragoza (245 km): Pierino Baffi (It); 4. Barcelona (229 km): Rik Van Looy (B); 5.a) Montjuich (ttt 4 km): France/; 5.b) Tarragona (119 km): Rik Van Looy (B); 6. Valencia (263 km): Rik Van Looy (B); 7. Cuenca (217 km): Gilbert Desmet I (B); 8. Toledo (206 km): Jean Stablinski (F); 9. Madrid (241 km): Rik Van Looy (B); 10. Soria (225 km): Rik Van Looy (B); 11. Vitoria (167 km); René Marigil (Sp); 12. Bilbao (169 km): Fausto Iza (Sp); 13. a) Castro Urdiales (tt 38.4 km): Guido Carlesi (It); b) Santander (105 km): Jean Craczyk (F); 14. Gijón (221 km): Pierino Baffi (It); 15. Oviedo-Palencia (245 km): Rik Luyten (B); 16. Madrid (241 km): Rik Luyten(B)

1959 (24.4-10.5)
1. a) Madrid (ttt 9 km): St.Raphaël-Geminiani (F); b) Toledo (114 km): Rik Van Looy (B); 2. Manzanares-Córdoba (228 km): Antonio Karmany (Sp); 3. Sevilla (140 km): Vicente Iturat (Sp); 4. Granada (240 km): Federico Bahamontes (Sp); 5. Murcia (225 km): Antonio Suárez (Sp); 6. Alicante (173 km): Gabriel Mas (Sp); 7. Castellón (241 km): Antonio Barrutia (Sp); 8. Tortosa (130 km): Rik Van Looy (B); 9. Barcelona (196 km): Rik Van Looy (B); 10. Granollers-Lérida (183 km): Antonio Suárez (Sp); 11. Pamplona (242 km): Rik Van Looy (B); 12. San Sebastián (210 km): José Sousa Cardoso (P); 13. Anoeta (ttt 9 km): St.Raphaël-Geminiani (F); 14. Eibar-Vitoria (tt 62 km): Roger Rivière (F); 15. Santander (230 km): Julio San Emeterio (Sp); 16. Bilbao (187 km): Roger Rivière (F); 17. Bilbao (222 km): Fernando Manzaneque (F).

1960 (29.4-15.5)
1. Gijón (ttt 7.7 km): Faema; 2. La Coruna (235 km): Felipe Alberdi (Sp); 3. Vigo (187 km): Antonio Barrutia (Sp); 4. Orense (105 km): Frans De Mulder (B); 5. Zamora (287 km); Antonio Gómez del Moral; 6. Madrid (250 km): Nino Assirelli (It); 7. Madrid (209 km): Frans De Mulder (B); 8. Zaragoza (264 km): Arthur De Cabooter (B); 9. Barcelona (269 km): Salvador Botella (Sp); 10. Barbastro (259 km): Alfons Sweeck (B); 11. Pamplona (267 km): Vicente Iturat (Sp); 12. Logrono (179 km):

Jesus Galdeano (Sp); 13. San Sebastián (211 km): Federico Bahamontes (Sp); 14. Vitoria (263 km): Antonio Suárez (Sp); 15. Santander (232 km): Arthur De Cabooter (B); 16. Bilbao (192 km): Frans De Mulder (B); 17. a) Guernica (116 km): Frans De Mulder (B); b) Bilbao (tt 53 km): Antonio Karmany.

1961 (29.4-11.5)

1. a) San Sebastián (ttt 10.5 km): Faema; b) Pamplona (91 km): Marcel Rohrbach (F); 2. Pamplona (149 km): François Mahé (F); 3. Huesca (259 km): Vicente Iturat (Sp); 4. Barcelona (199 km): Marcel Seynaeve (B); 5. Tortosa (185 km): Jesus Galdeano (Sp); 6. Valencia (188 km): Angelino Soler (Sp); 7. Benidorm (141 km): René Van Meenen (B); 8. Albacete (211 km): José Perez-Francés (Sp); 9. Madrid (198 km): Alves Barbosa (P); 10. Madrid (195 km): Luis Otaño (Sp); 11. Valladolid (189 km): Arthur De Cabooter (B); 12. Palencia (tt 48 km): Antonio Suárez (Sp); 13. Santander (220 km): Francisco Moreno (Sp); 14. Vitoria (235 km): François Mahé (F); 15. Bilbao (179 km): Antonio Karmany (Sp); 16. Bilbao (159 km): Gabriel Company (Sp).

1962 (13.6-4.7)

1. Barcelona (Montjuich 90 km): Antonio Barrutia (Sp); 2. Tortosa (185 km): Rudi Altig (Ger); 3. Valencia (188 km): Nino Defilippis (It); 4. Benidorm (141 km): Seamus Elliott (Irl); 5. Benidorm (ttt 21 km): St Raphaël-Helyet (F); 6. Cartagena (152 km): Jean Graczyk (F); 7. Murcia-Almería (223 km): Rudi Altig (Ger); 8. Málaga (220 km): Jean-Claude Annaert (F); 9. Córdoba (193 km): Antonio Gomez del Moral (Sp); 10. Valdepenas-Madrid (210 km): Abe Geldermans (NL); 11. Valladolid (189 km): Jean Stablinski (F); 12. Logrono (232 km): Ernesto Bono (It); 13. Pamplona (190 km): Jean Graczyk (F); 14. Bayonne (148 km): Jean Graczyk (F); 15. San Sebastián (tt 82 km): Rudi Altig (Ger); 16. Vitoria (177 km): Jean Graczyk (F); 17. Bilbao (171 km): José Segú (Sp).

1963 (1.5-15.5)

1. a) Gijón-Mieres (45 km): Antonio Barrutia (Sp); b) Gijón (tt 52 km): Jacques Anquetil (F); 2. Torrelavega (175 km): José Segú (Sp); 3. Vitoria (249 km): Anton Barrutia (Sp); 4. Bilbao (104 km): Jan Lauwers (B); 5. Bilbao (187 km): Bas Maliepaard (NL); 6. Eibar (165 km): Guy Ignolin (F); 7. Tolosa (138 km): Valentin Uriona (Sp); 8. Pamplona (169 km): José Pérez-Francés (Sp); 9. Zaragoza (180 km): Roger Baens (B); 10. Lérida (144 km): Jean Stablinski (F); 11. Barcelona (182 km): Jan Lauwers (B); 12. a) Montjuich 80 km): Frans Aerenhouts (B); b) Sitges-Tarragona (tt 56 km): Miguel Pacheco (Sp); 13. Valencia (252 km): Seamus Elliott (Irl); 14. Cuenca-Madrid (177 km): Roger Baens (B); 15. Madrid (87 km): Guy Ignolin (F).

1964 (30.4-16.5)

1. a) Benidorm (42 km): Edward Sels (B); b) Benidorm (tt 11 km): Eusebio Velez (Sp); 2. Nules (199 km): Rik Van Looy (B); 3. Salou (212 km): Frans Melckenbeeck (B); 4. a) Barcelona (115 km): Armand Desmet (B); b) Barcelona (49 km): Antonio Barrutia (Sp); 5. Puigcerda (174 km): Julio Jiménez (Sp); 6. Lérida (187 km): Frans Melckenbeeck (B); 7. Jaca (201 km): Julio Sanz (Sp); 8. Pamplona (205 km): Michael Stolker (NL); 9. San Sebastián (205 km): Luis Otaño (Sp); 10. Bilbao (197 km): Henri Dewolf (B); 11. Vitoria (107 km): Vic Van Schil (B); 12. Santander (211 km): Barry Hoban (GB); 13. Avilés (230 km): Barry Hoban (GB); 14. León (163 km): Julio Jiménez (Sp); 15. Valladolid (tt 65 km): Raymond Poulidor (F); 16. Madrid (209 km): Antonio Barrutia (Sp); 17. Madrid (Caso de Campa 87 km): Frans Melckenbeeck (B).

1965 (29.4-16.5)

1. Vigo (168 km): Rik Van Looy (B); 2. Pontevedra-Lugo (150 km): Rik Van Looy (B); 3. Gijón (247 km): Rudi Altig (Ger); 4. a) Mieres-Puerto Pajares (tt 41 km): Raymond Poulidor (F); b) Palencia (189 km): Carlos Echevarria (Sp); 5. Madrid (238 km): Fernando Manzaneque (Sp); 6. Cuenca (161 km): Manuel Martin Pinera (Sp); 7. Benidorm (212 km): Rik Van Looy (B); 8. Sagunto (174 km): Jean-Claude Wuillemin (F); 9. Salou (237 km): Rik Van Looy (B);10. a) Barcelona (50 km): Frans Melckenbeeck (B); b) Montjuich (49.8 km): Julio Jiménez (Sp); 11. Barcelona-Andorra (241 km): Esteban Martin (Sp); 12. Lérida (158 km): Rik Van Looy (B); 13. Zaragoza (190 km): José Martin Colmenarejo (Sp); 14. Pamplona (193 km): Rik Van Looy (B); 15. Bayonne (149 km): Rik Van Looy (B); 16. San Sebastián (tt 61 km): Raymond Poulidor (F); 17. Vitoria (214 km): Rik Van Looy (B); 18. Bilbao (222 km): Martin Pinera (Sp).

1966 (28.4-15.5)
1. a) Murcia (111 km): Bruno Sivilotti (RA); b) Murcia (tt 3.5 km): José Maria Errandonea (Sp); 2. a) La Manga (81 km): Enzo Pretolani (It); b) Benidorm (153 km): Ramon Mendiburu (Sp); 3. Valencia (148 km): José Antonio Momene (Sp); 4. Cuenca-Madrid (177 km): Valentin Uriona (Sp); 5. Madrid (181 km): Carlos Echeverria (Sp); 6. Catalayud (225 km): Jo De Roo (NL); 7. Zaragoza (105 km): Cees Haast (NL); 8. Lerida (144 km): Henk Nijdam (NL) 9. Las Colinas (128 km): Antonio Gomez del Moral (Sp); 10. a) Sitges-Barcelona (40 km): Luis Otaño (Sp); b) Montjuich (49.8 km): Henk Nijdam (NL); 11. Barcelona-Huesca (266 km): Mario Zanin (It); 12. Pamplona (221 km): Gerben Karstens (NL); 13. San Sebastián (131 km): Cees Haast (NL); 14. Vitoria (178 km): Gregorio San Miguel (Sp); 15. a) Haro (tt 61 km): Francisco Gabica (Sp); b) Logrono (52 km): Gerben Karstens (NL); 16. Burgos (116 km): Henk Nijdam (NL); 17. Santander (226 km): Gerben Karstens (NL); 18. Bilbao (154 km): Domingo Perurena (Sp).

1967 (27.4-14.5)
1. a) Vigo-Bajo Mino (110 km): Guido Reybrouck (B); b) Vigo (tt 4.1 km): s.t. Jan Janssen (NL) & José Maria Errandonea (Sp); 2. Pontevedra-Orense (186 km): Domingo Perurena (Sp); 3. Astorga (230 km): Ramon Saez (Sp); 4. Salamanca (201 km): Ramon Saez (Sp); 5. Madrid (201 km): Tom Simpson (GB); 6. Albacete-Benidorm (212 km): Evert Dolman (NL); 7. Valencia (148 km): Gerben Karstens (NL); 8. Vinaroz (145 km): Gilbert Bellone (F); 9. Sitges (172 km): Jan Lauwers (B); 10. a) Barcelona (39 km): Jan Harings (NL); b) Montjuich (45.4 km): Mariano Diaz (Sp); 11. Barcelona-Andorra (241 km): Mariano Diaz (Sp); 12. Lerida (158 km): Henk Nijdam (NL); 13. Zaragoza (182 km): Angel Ibanez (Sp); 14. Pamplona (193 km): Jos Vander Vleuten (NL); 15. a) Logrono (92 km): Rolf Wolfshohl (Ger); b) Laguardia-Vitoria (tt 44 km): Raymond Poulidor (F); 16. San Sebastián (139 km): Tom Simpson (GB); 17. Villabona-Zarauz (tt 28 km): Gerben Karstens (NL); 18. Bilbao (175 km): Gerben Karstens (NL).

1968 (25.4-12.5)
1. a) Zaragoza (130 km): Jan Janssen (NL); b) Zaragoza (tt 4 km): Jan Janssen (NL); 2. Lerida (105 km): Michael Wright (GB); 3. a) Barcelona (165 km): Tomasso De Pra (It); b) Montjuich (38 km): Rudi Altig (Ger); 4. Barcelona-Salou (108 km): Michael Wright (GB); 5. Vinaroz (106 km): Rudi Altig (Ger); 6. Valencia (148 km): Pietro Guerra (It); 7. Benidorm (144 km): Wilfried Peffgen (Ger); 8. Almansa (167 km): Manuel Martin Pinera (Sp); 9. Alcazar de San Juan (230 km): José Maria Errandona (Sp); 10. Madrid (173 km): Domingo Perurena (Sp); 11. Palencia (242 km): Ramon Saez (Sp); 12. Villalon de Campos-Gijón (236 km): José Perez-Francés (Sp); 13. Santander (203 km): Vic Van Schil (B); 14. Vitoria (244 km): Eduardo Castello (Sp); 15. Pamplona: stage annuled; 16. San Sebastián (204 km): Luis Pedro Santamarina (Sp); 17. Tolosa (tt 67 km): Felice Gimondi (It); 18. Bilbao (206 km): Manuel Martin Pinera (Sp).

1969 (23.4-11.5)
1. a) Badajoz (tt 6 km): equal Luis Ocaña (Sp) and Antonio Gomez del Moral (Sp); b) Badajoz (246 km): Michael Wright (GB); 2. Caceres (135 km): Felice Salina (It); 3. Talavera de la Reina (190 km): Luigi Sgarbozza (It); 4. Madrid (124 km): Domingo Perurena (Sp); 5. Alcazar de San Juan (162 km): Raymond Steegmans (B); 6. Almansa (231 km): Edward Sels (B); 7. Nules (233 km): Ramon Saez (Sp); 8. Benicasim (199 km): Ramon Saez (Sp); 9. Reus (169 km): José Maria Lopez-Rodríguez (Sp); 10. Barcelona (164 km): Manuel Martin Pinera (Sp); 11. San Feliú de Guixois (118 km): Nemesio Jiménez (Sp); 12. Moya (151 km): Roger Pingeon (F); 13. Barbastro (229 km): Michael Wright (GB); 14. a) Zaragoza (125 km): Raymond Steegmans (B); b) Zaragoza (tt 4 km): Roger Pingeon (F); 15. Pamplona (176 km): Mariano Diaz (Sp); 16. Irun-San Sebastián (tt 25 km): Luis Ocaña (Sp); 17. Vitoria (129 km): Gregorio San Miguel (Sp); 18. a) Llodio (76 km): Ercole Gualazzini (It); b) Bilbao (tt 29 km): Luis Ocaña (Sp).

1970 (23.4-12.5)
0. Cadiz (tt 6 km): Luis Ocaña (Sp); 1. Jerez de la Frontera (170 km): Eddy Peelman (B); 2. Fuengirola (217 km): Julian Cuevas (Sp); 3. Almería (249 km): Guido Reybrouck (B); 4. Lorca (161 km): Jean Ronsmans (B); 5. Calpe (209 km): Luis Pedro Santamarina (P); 6. Burriana (198 km): Eddy Peelman (B); 7. Tarragona (201 km): Guido Reybrouck (B); 8. a) Barcelona (100 km): Ramon Saez (Sp); b) Montjuich (48 km): Guido Reybrouck (B); 9. Barcelona-Igualada (189 km): Agustín Tamames

(Sp); 10. Zaragoza (237 km): Anatole Novak (F); 11. Calatayud (118 km): Marinus Wagtmans (NL); 12. Madrid (204 km): Johnny Schleck (L); 13. Soria (221 km): Marino Wagtmans (NL); 14. Valladolid (238 km): Jan Serpenti (NL); 15. Burgos (134 km): Ramon Saez (Sp); 16. Santander (179 km): Roger Rosiers (Sp); 17. Vitoria (191 km): Willy In 't Ven (B); 18. San Sebastián (157 km): José Mariano Errandonea (Sp); 19. a) Llodio (104 km): Jos Vander Vleuten (NL); b) Bilbao (tt 29 km): Luis Ocaña (Sp).

1971 (29.4-16.5)
0. Almería (tt 4.2 km): René Pijnen (NL); 1. Aguilas (126 km): Ger Harings (NL); 2. Calpe (245 km): Eddy Peelman (B); 3. Puebla de Farnals (164 km): Cyrille Guimard (F); 4. Benicasim (175 km): Hubert Hutsebaut (B); 5. Salou (172 km): René Pijnen (NL); 6. Barcelona (149 km): Eddy Peelman (B); 7. Manresa (179 km): Walter Godefroot (B); 8. Balaguer-Jaca (211 km): Walter Godefroot (B); 9. Pamplona (175 km): Agustín Tamames (Sp); 10. San Sebastián (120 km): Gerard Vianen (NL); 11. a) Bilbao (140 km): Gerben Karstens (NL); b) Bilbao (tt 2.65 km): José A. González-Linares (Sp); 12. Vitoria (185 km): Luis Ocaña (Sp); 13. Torrelavega (208 km): Eddy Peelman (B); 14. Burgos (192 km): Wilfried David (B); 15. Segovia (188 km): Cyrille Guimard (F); 16. Ávila (114 km): Joop Zoetemelk (NL); 17. a) Madrid (138 km): Willy Scheers (B); b) Madrid (tt 5.3 km): René Pijnen (NL).

1972 (27.4-14.5)
0. Fuengirola (tt 6 km): René Pijnen (NL); 1. Cabra (167 km): Miguel Maria Lasa (Sp); 2. Granada (206 km): Gerard Vianen (NL); 3. Almería (181 km): Domingo Perurena (Sp); 4. Dehesa de Campoamor (251 km): Ger Harings (NL); 5. Gandia (183 km): Pieter Nassen (B); 6. a) El Saler (120 km): Roger Kindt (B); b) El Saler (ttt 6.6 km): KAS; 7. Valencia-Vinaroz (171 km): Jos Vander Vleuten (NL); 8. Taragona (189 km): Cees Koeken (NL); 9. a) Barcelona (118 km): Ger Harings; b) Montjuich (tt 10 km): Jesus Manzaneque (Sp); 10. Banolas (192 km): Domingo Perurena (Sp); 11. Manresa-Zaragoza (259 km): Luis Balagué (Sp); 12. Formigal (169 km): José Manuel Fuente (Sp); 13. Sanguesa-Eibar-Arrate (201 km): Agustín Tamames; 14. Eibar-Bilbao (145 km): Miguel Maria Lasa (Sp); 15. Torrelavega (148 km): Gerard Vianen (NL); 16. Vitoria (219 km): Agustín Tamames (Sp); 17. a) San Sebastián (138 km): Jesus Aranzabal (Sp); b) San Sebastián (tt 20 km):José A. González-Linares (Sp).

1973 (26.4-13.5)
0. Calpe (tt 6 km): Eddy Merckx (B); 1. Calpe-Murcia (187 km): Pieter Nassen (B); 2. Albacete (156 km): Gerben Karstens (NL); 3. Alcazar de San Juan (146 km): Peter Nassen (B); 4. Cuenca (169 km): Jos Deschoenmaecker (B); 5. Teruel (191 km): Gerben Karstens (NL); 6. a) Puebla de Farnals (150 km): Roger Swerts (B); b) Puebla de Farnals (ttt 5 km): Molteni; 7. Puebla de Farnals-Castellon (165 km): Gerben Karstens; 8. Calafell (245 km): Eddy Merckx (B); 9. a) Barcelona (80 km): Juan Manuel Santisteban (Sp); b) Montjuich (37.9 km): Jacques Esclassan (F); 10. Barcelona-Ampuriabrava (171 km): Eddy Merckx (B); 11. Manresa (225 km): Bernard Thevenet (F); 12. Zaragoza (259 km): Gerben Karstens (NL); 13. Mallen-Irache (175 km): Domingo Perurena (Sp); 14. Bilbao (182 km): Juan Zurano (Sp); 15. a) Torrelavega (154 km): Eddy Peelman (B); b) Torrelavega (tt 4.4 km): Eddy Merckx (B); 16. Miranda (203 km): Eddy Merckx (B); 17. a) Tolosa (127 km): Eddy Peelman (B); b) Hernani-San Sebastián (tt 10.5 km): Eddy Merckx (B).

1974 (23.4-12.5)
0. Almería (tt 5 km): Rog. Swerts (B); 1. Almería (98 km): Eddy Peelman (B); 2. Granada (187 km): Eric Leman (B); 3. Fuengirola (161 km): Rik Van Linden (B); 4. Marbella-Sevilla (206 km): Rik Van Linden (B); 5. Córdoba (139 km): Domingo Perurena (B); 6. Ciudad Real (211 km): Eddy Peelman (B); 7. Toledo (126 km): Domingo Perurena (Sp); 8. Madrid (167 km): Rog. Swerts (B); 9. Los Angeles de San Rafael (158 km): José Manuel Fuente (Sp); 10. a) Los Angeles (tt 5 km): Raymond Delisle (F); b) Ávila (125 km): Mariano Martinez (F); 11. Valladolid (168 km): José Luis Uribezubia (Sp); 12. León (203 km): Roger Swerts (B); 13. Monte Naranco (Oviedo- 128 km): José Manuel Fuente (Sp); 14. Oviedo-Cangas de Onis (134 km): Joaquim Agostinho (P); 15. Laredo (210 km): Juan Manuel Santisteban (Sp); 16. Bilbao (133 km): Gerben Karstens (NL); 17. Miranda de Ebro (157 km): Agustín Tamames (Sp); 18. Eibar (152 km): Agustín Tamamès (Sp); 19. San Sebastián (79 km): Manuel Antonio Garcia (Sp); b) Anoeta/San Sebastián (tt 35.9 km): Joaquim Agostinho (P).

1975 (22.4-11.5)
0. Fuengirola (tt 4.4 km): Roger Swerts (B); 1. Marbella-Marbella (78 km): Wilfried Wesemael (B); 2. Fuengirola-Granada (143 km): Miguel Maria Lasa (Sp); 3. Almería (179 km): Agustín Tamames (Sp); 4. Aguilas (178 km): Marino Basso (It); 5. Murcia (176 km): Luc Leman (B); 6. Benidorm (217 km): Marino Basso (It); 7. Benidorm (tt 8.3 km): Miguel Maria Lasa (Sp); 8. Puebla de Farnals (217 km): Marino Basso (It); 9. Vinaroz (157 km): Marino Basso (It); 10. Cambrils (173 km): Marino Basso (It); 11. a) Barcelona (151 km): Antonio Menendez (Sp); b) Montjuich (30.3 km): Marino Basso (It); 12. Palma de Mallorca (181 km): Agustín Tamames (Sp); 13. Barcelona-Tremp (189 km): Domingo Perurena (Sp); 14. El Formigal (233 km): Agustín Tamames (Sp); 15. Jaca-Irache (160 km): Agustín Tamames (Sp); 16. Urquiola (150 km): Agustín Tamames (Sp); 17. Durango-Bilbao (123 km): Donald Allan (Aus); 18. Miranda de Ebro (186 km): Hennie Kuiper (NL); 19. a) Beasain (110 km): Julien Stevens (B); b) San Sebastián-San Sebastián (tt 31.7 km): Jesus Manzaneque (Sp).

1976 (27.4-16.5)
0. Estepona (tt 4 km): Dietrich Thurau (Ger); 1. Estepona (135 km): José De Cauwer (B); 2. Priego de Córdoba (224 km): Roger Gilson (L); 3. Jaen (177 km): Theo Smit (NL); 4. Baza (166 km): Hennie Kuiper (NL); 5. Cartagena (201 km): Theo Smit (NL); 6. Cartagena (tt 14 km): Joaquim Agostinho (P); 7. Murcia (186 km): Ferdi Van den Haute (B); 8. Almansa (219 km): Georges Pintens (B); 9. Nules (208 km): Dietrich Thurau (Ger); 10. Cambrils (228 km): José A. González-Linares (Sp); 11. Barcelona (151 km): Antonio Vallori (Sp); 12. Pamplona-Logrono (168 km): Gerben Karstens (NL); 13. Palencia (209 km): Dirk Ongenae (B); 14. Gijón (249 km): Cees Priem (NL); 15. Cangas de Onis (141 km): Vicente Lopez-Carril (Sp); 16. Reinosa (156 km): Dietrich Thurau (Ger); 17. Bilbao (183 km): Arthur Van De Vijver (B); 18. Galdacano-Murguia (Sant. de Oro 204 km): Dietrich Thurau (Ger); 19. a) San Sebastián (139 km): Dirk Ongenae (B); b) San Sebastián (tt 31.7 km): Dietrich Thurau (Ger).

1977 (26.4-15.5)
0. Dehesa de Campoamor (tt 8 km): Freddy Maertens (B); 1. La Manga (115 km): Freddy Maertens (B); 2. Murcia (161 km): Freddy Maertens (B); 3. Benidorm (200 km): Fedor Den Hertog (NL); 4. Benidorm (tt 8.3 km): Michel Pollentier (B); 5. El Saler (159 km): Freddy Maertens (B); 6. a) Valencia-Teruel (170 km): Freddy Maertens (B); 7. Las Fuentes (204 km): Freddy Maertens (B); 8. Tortosa (141 km): Freddy Maertens (B); Salou (144 km): Freddy Maertens (B); 10. Barcelona (144 km): Cees Priem (NL); 11. a) Montjuich (tt 3.8 km): Freddy Maertens (B); b) Montjuich (45 km): Freddy Maertens (B); 12. Barcelona-La Tossa de Montbui (198 km): Giuseppe Perletto (It); 13. Igualada-Seo de Urgel (135 km): Freddy Maertens (B); 14. Monzon (200 km): Carlos Melero (Sp); 15. El Formigal (166 km): Pedro Torres (Sp); 16. Cordovilla (170 km): Freddy Maertens (B); 17. Bilbao (183 km): Luis Alberto Ordiales (Sp); 18. Urquiola (126 km): José Nazabal (Sp); 19. Durango-Miranda de Ebro (104 km): Freddy Maertens

1978 (25.4-14.5)
0. Gijón (tt 8.6 km): Bernard Hinault (F); 1. Gijón (144 km): Adri Schipper (NL); 2. Cangas de Onis (94 km): José Enrique Cima (Sp); 3. León (187 km): Ferdi Van den Haute (B); 4. Valladolid (171 km): Patrick Lefevere (B); 5. Ávila (136 km): Willy TeIrlinck (B); 6. Torrelaguna-Torrejon de Ardoz (46 km): Alfons Van Katwijk (NL); 7. Cuenca (160 km): Domingo Perurena (Sp); 8. Benicasim (249 km): Alfons Van Katwijk (NL); 9. Tortosa (156 km): Ferdi Van den Haute (B); 10. Calafell (201 km): Willy TeIrlinck (B); 11. a) Barcelona (67 km): Javier Elorriaga (Sp); b) (tt 3.8 km): Bernard Hinault (F); 12. La Tossa de Montbui (205 km): Bernard Hinault (F); 13. Igualada-Jaca (243 km): Salvatore Maccali (It); 14. Logrono (219 km): Bernard Hinault (F); 15. Miranda de Ebro (131 km): Philip Vandenbrande (B); 16. Santuario Bien Aparecia (208 km): Vicente Belda (Sp); 17. Ampuero-Bilbao (123 km): Enrique Cima (Sp); 18. Amurrio (154 km): Bernard Hinault (F); 19. a) San Sebastián (84 km): Domingo Perurena (Sp); b) (tt 31.7 km): Annulé/Afgelast.

1979 (24.4-13.5)
0. Jerez de la Frontera (tt 6.5 km): Joop Zoetemelk (NL); 1. Sevilla (156 km): Sean Kelly (Irl); 2. Córdoba (188 km): Alfons De Wolf (B); 3. Sierra Nevada (190 km): Felipe Yanez (Sp); 4. Granada-Puerto Lumbreras (222 km): Roger De Cnijf (B); 5. Murcia (139 km): Juan Argudo (Sp); 6. Alcoy

(171 km): Christian Levavasseur (F); 7. Sedavi (173 km): Alfons De Wolf (B); 8. a) Benicasim (145 km): Sean Kelly (Irl); b) Tt (11.3 km): Joop Zoetemelk (NL); 9. Reus (193 km): Alfons De Wolf (B); 10. Zaragoza (230 km): Noël Dejonckheere (B); 11. Pamplona (183 km): Noël Dejonckheere (B); 12. Logrono (149 km): François Van Vlierberghe (B); 13. Santander (180 km): Angel Lopez del Alamo (Sp); 14. Torrelavaga-Gijón (178 km): Bernardo Alfonsel (Sp); 15. León (156 km): Lucien Van Impe (B); 16. a) Valladolid (134 km): Vicente Belda (Sp); b) Tt (22 km): Alfons De Wolf (B); 17. Ávila (204 km): Francisco Ramon Albelda (Sp); 18. a) Colmenar Viejo (155 km): Miguel Maria Lasa (Sp); b) Azuqueca de Henares (104 km): Cees Bal (NL); 19. Madrid (84 km):Alfons De Wolf (B).

1980 (22.4-11.5)

0. La Manga (tt 10 km): Roberto Visentini (It); 1. Benidorm (155 km): Sean Kelly (Irl); 2. Cullera (170 km): Sean Kelly (Irl); 3. Vinaroz (207 km): Giuseppe Martinelli (It); 4. San Quirce (214 km): Klaus-Peter Thaler (Ger); 5. Seo de Urgel (200 km): Faustino Ruperez (Sp); 6. Viella (131 km): Enrique Martinez Heredia (Sp); 7. Jaca (216 km): Faustino Ruperez (Sp); 8. Monasterio de Leyre-Logrono (160 km): Eulalio Garcia (Sp); 9. Burgos (138 km): Jos Lammertink (NL); 10. Santander (178 km): Paul Jesson (NZ); 11. Gijón (219 km): Jesus Jopez-Carril (Sp); 12. Santiago de Compostela-Pontevedra (133 km): Etienne De Wilde (B); 13. Vigo (195 km): Rolf Haller (Ger); 14. Orense (156 km): Sean Kelly (Irl); 15. Ponferrada (164 km): Javier Elorriaga (Sp); 16. a) León (131 km): Dominique Arnaud (F); b) Tt (22.8 km): Roberto Visentini (It); 17. Valladolid (138 km): Sean Kelly (Irl); 18. Los Angeles de San Rafael (197 km): Manuel Esparza (Sp); 19. Madrid (84 km): Sean Kelly (Irl).

1981 (21.4-10.5)

0. Santander (tt 6.3 km): Régis Clère (F); 1. Aviles (221 km): Guido Bontempi (It); 2. León (159 km): Alfredo Chinetti (It); 3. Salamanca (195 km): Guido Bontempi (It); 4. Caceres (206 km): Celestino Prieto (It); 5. Merida (152 km): Heddie Nieuwdorp (NL); 6. Sevilla (199 km): Jos Lammertink (NL); 7. Ecija-Gaen (181 km): Juan Fernandez (Sp); 8. a) Granada (100 km): José Maria Yurrebaso (Sp); b) Sierra Nevada (tt 30.5 km): Giovanni Battaglin (It); 9. Baza-Murcia (204 km): Manuel Murga (Sp); 10. Almusafes (223 km): Kim Andersen (DK); 11. Peniscola (193 km): Jesus Suarez Cueva (Sp); 12. Esparraguera (217 km): Frédéric Vichot (F); 13. Rassos de Peguera (187 km): Vicente Belda (Sp); 14. Gironella-Balaguer (197 km): José Luis Lopez Cerron (Sp); 15. a) Alfajarin (146 km): Pedro Munoz (Sp); b) Zaragoza (tt 11.3 km): Régis Clère (F); 16. Catalayud-Torrejon de Ardoz (209 km): Alvaro Pino (Sp); 17. Segovia (150 km): Miguel Maria Lasa (Sp); 18. Los Angeles de San Rafael (175 km): Angel Arroyo (Sp); 19. Madrid (84 km): Francisco Javier Cedena (Sp).

1982 (20.4-9.5)

0. Santiago de Compostella (tt 6.7 km): Marc Gomez (F); 1. a) La Coruna (97 km): Eddy Planckaert (B); b): Lugo (97 km): Eddy Planckaert (B); 2. Gijón (240 km): Eddy Planckaert (B); 3. Santander (208 km): Eddy Planckaert (B); 4. Reinosa (196 km): Antonio Coll (Sp); 5. Logrono (230 km): Angel Camarillo (Sp); 6. Zaragoza (190 km): José Luis Laguia (Sp); 7. Sabinanigo (146 km): Enrique Martinez-Heredia (Sp); 8. Lerida (216 km): Jesus Hernandez Ubeda (Sp); 9. Artesa de Segre-Puigcerda (182 km): José Luis Laguia (Sp); 10. San Quirze del Valles (181 km): Sven-Ake Nilsson (S); 11. Barcelona (143 km): José Luis Laguia (Sp); 12. Salou-Nules (200 km): Eddy Planckaert (B); 13. Antella (195 km): José Recio (Sp); 14. Albacete (153 km): Dominique Arnaud (F); 15. a) Tomelloso (119 km): Eddy Vanhaerens (B);b) Campo de Criptana (tt 35 km): Angel Arroyo (Sp); 16. San Fernando de Henares (176 km): Willy Sprangers (B); 17. Navacerrada (178 km): Marino Lejarreta (Sp); 18. Segovia-Segovia (184 km): Juan Fernandez (Sp); 19. Madrid-Madrid (84 km): Eddy Vanhaerens (B).

1983 (19.4-8.5)

0. Almusafes (tt 6.8 km): Dominique Gaigne (F); 1. Cuenca (235 km): Juan Fernandez (Sp); 2. Teruel (152 km): Eric Vanderaerden (B); 3. San Carlos de la Rapita (241 km): Giuseppe Petito (It); 4. San Quirze del Valles (192 km): Laurent Fignon (F); 5. Castellar de Nuch (195 km): Alb. Fernandez (Sp); 6. La Pobla de Lillet-Viella (235 km): Marino Lejarreta (Sp); 7. Les-Sabinanigo (144 km): Jesus Suarez-Cueva (Sp); 8. Sabinanigo-Panticosa (tt 38 km): Marino Lejarreta (Sp); 9.

Alfajarin (189 km): Giuseppe Saronni (It); 10. Zaragoza-Soria (174 km): Giuseppe Saronni (It); 11. Logrono (185 km): Eric Vanderaerden (B); 12. Burgos (147 km): Noël Dejonckheere (B); 13. Aguilar de Campo-Lagos Covadonga (188 km): Marino Lejarreta (Sp); 14. León (195 km): Carlos Hernandez (Sp); 15. a) Valladolid (134 km): Pascal Poisson (F); b) Valladolid (tt 22 km): Bernard Hinault (F); 16. Salamanca (162 km): José Luis Laguia (Sp); 17. Avilla (216 km): Bernard Hinault (F); 18. Dyc (204 km): Jesus Hernandez Ubeda (Sp); 19. Segovia-Madrid (135 km): Michael Wilson (AUS).

1984 (17.4-6.5)
0. Jerez de la Frontera (tt 6.6 km): Francesco Moser (It); 1. Málaga (266 km): Noël Dejonckheere (B); 2. Almería (202 km): Guido Van Calster (B); 3. Elche (204 km): Jos Lieckens (B); 4. Valencia (197 km): Noël Dejonckheere (B); 5. Salou (245 km): Jos Lieckens (B); 6. San Quirze del Valles (113 km): Michel Pollentier (B); 7. Cardona-Zaragoza (184 km): Eric Caritoux (F); 8. Cardona-Zaragoza (269 km): Roger De Vlaeminck (B); 9. Soria (159 km): Orlando Maini (It); 10. Burgos (148 km): Palmiro Masciarelli (It); 11. Santander (182 km): Francesco Moser (It); 12. Lagos de Covadonga (199 km): Raimund Dietzen (Ger); 13. Cangas de Onis-Oviedo (170 km): Guido Van Calster (B); 14. Lugones-El Naranco (tt 12 km): Julian Gorospe (Sp); 15. Oviedo-León (121 km): Antonio Coll (Sp); 16. Valladolid (138 km): Daniël Rossel (B); 17. Segovia (258 km): José Recio (Sp); 18. a) Torrejon (145 km): Jesus Suarez-Cueva (Sp); b) Torrejon (tt 33 km): Julian Gorospe (Sp); 19. Madrid (139 km): Noël Dejonckheere (B).

1985 (23.4-12.5)
0. Valladolid (tt 5.6 km); Bert Oosterbosch (NL); 1. Zamora (177 km): Eddy Planckaert (B); 2. Orense (262 km): Sean Kelly (Irl); 3. Santiago de Compostella (197 km): Giambattista Baronchelli (It); 4. Lugo (162 km): Eddy Planckaert (B); 5. Oviedo (238 km): Federico Echave (Sp); 6. Lagos de Covadonga (145 km): Pedro Delgado (Sp); 7. Cangas de Onis-Alto Campoo (190 km): Antonio Agudelo (Col); 8. Tabacalera Logrono (224 km): Angel Camarillo (Sp); 9. Balneario de Panticosa (253 km): Alfons De Wolf (B); 10. Sabinanigo-Tremp (209 km): Sean Kelly (Irl); 11. Andorra (124 km): Francisco Rodríguez (Col); 12. Pal (tt 16 km): Francisco Rodríguez (Col); 13. San Quirze del Valles (193 km): Angel José Sarrapio (Sp); 14. Valencia-Benidorm (201 km): José Recio (Sp); 15. Albacete (208 km): Sean Kelly (Irl); 16. Alcala de Henares (252 km): Isidro Suarez (Sp); 17. Alcala de Henares (tt 43 km): Pello Ruiz-Cabestany (Sp); 18. Dyc (200 km): José Recio (Sp); 19. Salamanca (175 km): Vladimir Malakov (Rus).

1986 (22.4-13.5)
0. Palma de Mallorca (tt 5.7 km): Thierry Marie (F); 1. Palma-Palma (190 km): Marc Gomez (F); 2. Barcelona-Barcelona (182 km): Jorge Dominguez (Sp); 3. Lerida-Zaragoza (212 km): Eddy Planckaert (B); 4. Logrono (192 km): Alfonso Gutierrez (Sp); 5. Haro-Santander (202 km): Jesus Blanco-Villar (Sp); 6. Lagos de Covadonga (191 km): Robert Millar (GB); 7. Cangas de Onis-Oviedo (180 km): Eddy Planckaert (B); 8. Alto de Naranco (tt 9.7 km): Marino Lejarreta (Sp); 9. Oviedo-San Isidro (180 km): Charly Mottet (F); 10. San Isidro-Palencia (193 km): Sean Kelly (Irl); 11. Valladolid (tt 29.1 km): Charly Mottet (F); 12. Segovia (258 km): Raimund Dietzen (Ger); 13. Vilalba (148 km): Sean Kelly (Irl); 14. Gran Madrid-Leganes (165 km): José Recio (Sp); 15. Aranjuez-Albacete (207 km): Jon Eguiarte (Sp); 16. Jaen (264 km): Alain Bondue (F); 17. Sierra Nevada (172 km): Felipe Yanez (Sp); 18. Granada-Benalmadena (191 km): Viktor Demidenko (Rus); 19. Puerto Real (234 km): Jesus Blanco-Villar (Sp); 20. Jerez de la Frontera (239 km): Marc Gomez (F); 21. Jerez (tt 22 km): Alvaro Pino (Sp).

1987 (23.4-15.5)
0. Benidorm (tt 6.6 km): Jean-Luc Vandenbroucke (B); 1. Albacete (219 km): Sean Kelly (Irl); 2. Valencia (217 km): Paolo Rosola (It); 3. Valencia (tt 34.8 km): Sean Kelly (Irl); 4. Villareal (169 km): Alfonso Gutierrez (Sp); 5. Salou-Barcelona (165 km): Roberto Pagnin (It); 6. Andorra (220 km): Inaki Gaston (Sp); 7. Seo de Urgel-Cerler (186 km): Laudelino Cubino (Sp); 8. Benasque-Zaragoza (219 km): Inaki Gaston (Sp); 9. Pamplona (180 km): Antonio Esparza (Sp); 10. Miranda de Ebro-Alto de Campoo (213 km): Enrique Aja (Sp); 11. Santander-Lagos de Covadonga (170 km): Luis Herrera (Col); 12. Cangas de Onis-Oviedo (142 km): Carlos Hernandez (Sp); 13. Luarca-Ferrol (223 km): Carlos Emiro Gutierrez (Col); 14. La Coruna (152 km): Juan Fernandez (Sp); 15. Vigo

(185 km): Antonio Esparza (Sp); 16. Puenteareas-Ponferrada (237 km): Dominique Arnaud (F); 17. Valladolid (221 km): Roberto Pagnin (It); 18. Valladolid (tt 24 km): Jesus Blanco-Villar (Sp); 19. El Barco de Ávila-Ávila (213 km): Laurent Fignon (F); 20. Dyc (183 km): Omar Hernandez (Col); 21. Collado Villalba (160 km): Francisco Rodríguez (Col); 22. Alcala de Henares-Madrid (176 km): Jaime Vilamajo(Sp).

1988 (25.4-15.5)

1. Santa Cruz de Tenerife (17.4 km): Ettore Pastorelli (It); 2. San Cristobal Laguna-Santa Cruz de Tenerife (210 km): Inaki Gaston (Sp); 3. Las Palmas (ttt 34 km): BH; 4. Alcala del Rio-Badajoz (210 km): Mathieu Hermans (NL); 5. Bejar (234 km): Francisco Navarro (Sp); 6. Valladolid (202 km): Mathieu Hermans (NL); 7. León (160 km): Mathieu Hermans (NL); 8. Branilin (176.7 km): Alvaro Pino (Sp); 9. Oviedo-Alto Naranco (tt 6.8 km): Alvaro Pino (Sp); 10. Oviedo-Santander (197.3 km): Mathieu Hermans (NL); 11. Alto Valdezcaray (217.2 km): Sean Kelly (Irl); 12. Logrono-Jaca (197.5 km): Sean Yates (GB); 13. Jaca-Estacion de Cerler (178.2 km): Fabio Parra (Col); 14. Benasque-Andorra (190.3 km): Inaki Gaston (Sp); 15. Seo de Urgel-San Quirze del Valles (166 km): Johnny Weltz (DK); 16. Valencia-Albacete (192.1 km): Mathieu Hermans (NL); 17. Toledo (244.4 km): Malcolm Elliott (GB); 18. Ávila (212.5 km): Juan Martinez Oliver (Sp); 19. Dyc (150 km): Angel Ocaña (Sp); 20. Las Rozas-Villalba (tt 30 km): Sean Kelly (Irl); 21. Madrid (202 km): Mathieu Hermans (NL).

1989 (24.4-15.5)

1. La Coruna (20.1 km): Marnix Lameire (B); 2. Santiago de Compostella (209.2 km): Omar Hernandez (Col); 3. a) Vigo-Vigo (ttt 34.4 km): Caja Rural; 3. b) Orense (101 km): Malcolm Elliott (GB); 4. Ponferrada (160.5 km): Roberto Pagnin (It); 5. La Baneza-Bejar (247 km): Eddy Planckaert (B); 6. Ávila (197.5 km): Luc Suykerbuyk (NL); 7. Toledo (157 km): Massimo Ghirotto (It); 8. Albacete (235.5 km): Stefano Allocchio (It); 9. Gandia (228.1 km): Raimund Dietzen (Ger); 10. Benicasim (202.6 km): Herminio Diaz Zabala (Sp); 11. Vinaroz-Lerida (179.8 km): Malcolm Elliott (GB); 12. Lerida-Estacion de Cerler (186.5 km): Pedro Delgado (Sp); 13. Benasque-Jaca (160.8 km): Mathieu Hermans (NL); 14. Zaragoza (165.3 km): Mathieu Hermans (NL); 15. Ezcaray-Valdezcaray (tt 24 km): Pedro Delgado (Sp); 16. Haro-Santona (193.6 km): Peter Hilse (Ger); 17. Lagos de Covadonga (228 km): Alvaro Pino (Sp); 18. Cangas de Onis-Branilin (153.2 km): Ivan Ivanov (Rus); 19. León-Valladolid (159.4 km): Mathieu Hermans (NL); 20. Valladolid-Medina del Campo (tt 47.5 km): Pedro Delgado (Sp); 21. Collado Villalba-Dyc (188.6 km): Alberto Camargo (Col); 22. Dyc-Madrid (177 km): Jean-Pierre Heynderickx (B).

1990 (24.4-15.5)

1. Benicasim (tt 11.5 km): Pello Ruiz-Cabestany (Sp); 2. a) Oropesa-Castellon (108 km): Emilio Cuadrado (Sp); 2. b) Benicasim-Burriana (ttt 36.3 km): LOTUS; 3. Denia-Murcia (204.3 km): Silvio Martinello (It); 4. Almería (233.2 km): Erwin Nijboer (NL); 5. Sierra Nevada (198 km): Patrice Esnault (F); 6. Loja-Ubrique (195.2 km): Jesper Worre (DK); 7. Jerez-Sevilla (187.3 km): Benny Van Brabant (B); 8. Merida (199.6 km): Atle Pedersen (N); 9. Caceres-Guijuelo (192.7 km): Nestor Mora (Col); 10. Penaranda de Bracamonte-León (230 km): Uwe Raab (Ger); 11. San Isidro (203 km): Carlos Hernandez (Sp); 12. Alto de Naranco (156 km): Alberto Camargo (Col); 13. Oviedo-Santander (193.3 km): Nico Emonds (B); 14. Najera (207 km): Bernd Gröne (Ger); 15. Ezcaray-Valdezcaray (tt 24 km): Jean-François Bernard (F); 16. Logrono-Pamplona (165 km): Uwe Raab (Ger); 17. Jaca (151 km): Federico Echave (Sp); 18. Estacion de Cerler (178 km): Martin Farfan (Col); 19. Benasque-Zaragoza (223 km): Asiat Saitov (Rus); 20. Zaragoza (tt 39 km): Pello Ruiz-Cabestany (Sp); 21. Collada Villalba-Dyc (188 km): Denis Roux (F); 22. Dyc-Madrid (176 km): Uwe Raab (Ger).

1991 (29.4-19.5)

1. Merida (tt 8.8 km): Melchior Mauri (Sp); 2. a) Merida-Caceres (134.5 km): Michel Zanoli (NL); 2. b): Montijo-Badajoz (ttt 40.4 km): Once; 3. Sevilla (233.2 km): Jesper Skibby (DK); 4. Jaen (241 km): Jesus Cruz Martin (Sp); 5. Linares-Albacete (227.8 km):Uwe Raab (Ger); 6. Valencia (236.5 km): Jean-Paul Van Poppel (NL); 7. Palma-Palma (188 km): Jesper Skibby (DK); 8. Cala d'Or-Cala d'Or (tt 47 km): Melchior Mauri (Sp); 9. San Cugat-Lloret de Mar (140 km): Jean-Paul Van Poppel (NL); 10. Andorra (229 km): Guido Bontempi (It); 11. Andorra-Pla de Beret: Annulé à

cause du mauvais temps/Afgelast wegens slecht weer; 12. Bossost-Cerler (111 km): Ivan Ivanov (Rus); 13. Benasque-Zaragoza (219 km): Jean-Paul Van Poppel (NL); 14. Ezcaray-Valdezcaray (tt 24.1 km): Fabio Parra (Col); 15. Santo Domingo de la Calzada-Santander (219.5 km): Guido Bontempi (It); 16. Lagos de Covadonga (186.6 km): Luis Herrera (Col); 17. Cangas de Onis-Alto Naranco: Laudelino Cubino (Sp); 18. León-Valladolid (137.5 km): Antonio Miguel Diaz (Sp); 19. Valladolid (tt 53.2 km): Melchior Mauri (Sp); 20. Dyc-Dyc (212.7 km): Jesus Montoya (Sp); 21. Collado Villalba-Madrid (169.6 km): Jean-Paul Van Poppel (NL).

1992 (27.4-17.5)
1. Jerez de la Frontera (tt 9.2 km): Jelle Nijdam (NL); 2. a) San Fernando-Jerez de la Frontera (135.5 km): Djamolidine Abdoujaparov (Uzb); 2. b) Arcos de la Frontera-Jerez de la Frontera (ttt 32.6 km): Gatorade; 3. Córdoba (205 km): Jean-Paul Van Poppel (NL); 4. Linares-Albacete (229 km): Djamolidine Abdoujaparov (Uzb); 5. Gandia (213.5 km): Jean-Paul Van Poppel (NL); 6. Gandia-Benicasim (202.8 km): Edwig Van Hooydonck (B); 7. Alquerias-Oropesa (tt 49.5 km): Erik Breukink (NL); 8. Lleida-Pla de Beret (240.5 km): Jon Unzaga (Sp); 9. Vielha-Luz Ardiden (144 km): Laudelino Cubino (Sp); 10. Luz-St.Sauveur-Sabinanigo (196 km): Julio Cesar Cadena (Col); 11. Pamplona (162.9 km): Djamolidine Abdoujaparov (Uzb); 12. Burgos (200.1 km): Johan Bruyneel (B); 13. Santander (178.3 km): Roberto Torres (Sp); 14. Lagos de Covadonga (213.4 km): Pedro Delgado (Sp); 15. Cangas de Onis-Alto Naranco (163 km):Francisco-Javier MauLeón (Sp); 16. Oviedo-León (162 km): Tom Cordes (NL); 17. Salamanca (200.6 km): Eric Vanderaerden (B); 18. Ávila (218.9 km): Enrico Zaina (It); 19. Fuenlabrada (tt 37.9 km): Tony Rominger (Swi); 20. Collado Villalba-Dyc: Tony Rominger (Sw); 21. Dyc-Madrid: Djamolidine Abdoujaparov (Uzb).

1993 (26.4-16.5)
1. La Coruna (tt 10 km): Alex Zülle (Swi); 2. Vigo (251.1 km): Alfonso Gutierrez (Sp); 3. Orense (171.4 km): Laurent Jalabert (F); 4. La Gudina-Salamanca (233.4 km): Jean-Paul Van Poppel (NL); 5. Ávila (219.8 km): Marino Alonso (Sp); 6. Dyc-Alto de Navacerrada (tt 24.1 km): Alex Zülle (Swi); 7. Madrid (184 km): Laurent Jalabert (F); 8. Aranjuez-Albacete (225.1 km): Jean-Paul Van Poppel (NL); 9. Valencia (224 km): Djamolidine Abdoujaparov (Uzb); 10. La Senia (206 km): Juan-Carlos González Salvador (Sp); 11. Lerida-Cerler (221 km): Tony Rominger (Swi); 12. Benasque-Zaragoza (220.7 km): Djamolidine Abdoujaparov (Uzb); 13. Zaragoza-Zaragoza (tt 37.1 km): Melchior Mauri (Sp); 14. Tudela-Valdezcaray (197.2 km): Tony Rominger (Swi); 15. Santo Domingo de la Calzada-Santander (226.2 km): Dag-Otto Lauritzen (N); 16. Alto Campoo (160 km): Jesus Montoya (Sp); 17. Santander-Lagos de Covadonga (179.5 km): Oliveiro Rincon (Col); 18. Cangas de Onis-Gijón (170 km): Serguei Outschakov (Ukr); 19. Alto del Naranco (153 km): Tony Rominger (Swi); 20. Salas-Ferrol (247 km): Djamolidine Abdoujaparov (Uzb); 21. Padron-Santiago de Compostella (tt 44.6 km): Alex Zülle (Swi).

1994 (25.4-15.5)
1. Valladolid (tt 9 km): Tony Rominger (Swi); 2. Salamanca (178.4 km): Laurent Jalabert (F); 3. Caceres (239 km): Laurent Jalabert (F); 4. Almendralejo-Córdoba (235.6 km): Endrio Leóni (It); 5. Granada (166.9 km): Laurent Jalabert (F); 6. Sierra Nevada (151.7 km): Tony Rominger (Swi);7. Baza-Alicante (256.5 km): Simone Biasci (It); 8. Benidorm (tt 39.5 km): Tony Rominger (Swi); 9. Valencia (166 km): Jean-Paul Van Poppel (NL); 10. Igualada-Andorra (205 km): Angel Camargo (Col); 11. Cerler (195.3 km): Tony Rominger (Swi); 12. Benasque-Zaragoza (226.7 km): Laurent Jalabert (F); 13. Pamplona (201.6 km): Laurent Jalabert (F); 14. Valdezcaray (174 km): Tony Rominger (Swi); 15. Santo Domingo Calzada-Santander (209.3 km): Alessio Di Basco (It); 16. Lagos de Covadonga (147.7 km): Laurent Jalabert (F); 17. Cangas de Onis-Alto de Naranco (150.4 km): Bart Voskamp (NL); 18. Ávila-Ávila (189 km): Giuseppe Calcaterra (It); 19. Dyc (171 km): Marino Alonso (It); 20. Segovia-Dyc (tt 53 km): Tony Rominger (Swi); 21. Dyc-Madrid (165.7 km): Laurent Jalabert (F).

1995 (2.9-24.9)
0. Zaragoza (tt 7 km): Abraham Olano (Sp); 1. .Logrono (186.6 km): Nicola Minali (It); 2. San Asensio-Santander (223.5 km): Gianluca Pianegonda (It); 3. Alto de Naranco (206 km): Laurent Jalabert (F); 4. Tapia de Casariego-La Coruna (82.6 km): Marcel Wüst (Ger); 5. Orense (179.8 km): Laurent Jalabert (F); 6. Zamora (264 km): Nicola Minali (It); 7. Salamanca-Salamanca (tt 41 km):

Abraham Olano (Sp); 8. Ávila (219.8 km): Laurent Jalabert (F); 9. Dyc (122.5 km): Jesper Skibby (DK); 10. Córdoba-Sevilla (162.5 km): Jeroen Blijlevens (NL); 11. Marbella (187 km): Nicola Minali (It); 12. Sierra Nevada (238 km): Bert Dietz (Ger); 13. Olula del Rio-Murcia (181 km): Christian Henn (Ger); 14. Elche-Valencia (207 km): Marcel Wüst (Ger); 15. Barcelona-Barcelona (154 km): Laurent Jalabert (F); 16. Tarrega-Pla de Beret (197.3 km): Alex Zülle (Swi); 17. Salardu-Luz Ardiden (179.2 km): Laurent Jalabert (F); 18. Luz St.Sauveur-Sabinanigo (157.8 km): Asiat Saitov (Rus); 19. Calatayud (227.7 km): Adriano Baffi (It); 20. Alcala de Henares (tt 41.6 km): Abraham Olano (Sp); 21. Madrid (171.2 km): Marcel Wüst (Ger).

1996 (7.9-29.9)

1. Valencia-Valencia (162 km): Biagio Conte (It); 2. Cuenca (210 km): Nicola Minali (It); 3. Albacete (167.2 km): Laurent Jalabert (F); 4. Murcia (166.5 km): Tom Steels (B); 5. Almería (208.4 km): Jeroen Blijlevens (NL); 6. Málaga (196.5 km): Fabio Baldato (It); 7. Marbella (171.1 km): Fabio Baldato (It); 8. Jerez de la Frontera (220.7 km): Nicola Minali (It); 9. Córdoba (203.5 km): Nicola Minali (It); 10. El Tiemblo-Ávila (tt 46.5 km): Tony Rominger (Swi); 11. Salamanca (188 km): Marco Antonio Di Renzo (It); 12. Benavente-Alto del Naranco (191.7 km): Daniele Nardello (It); 13. Oviedo-Lagos de Covadonga (159 km): Laurent Jalabert (F); 14. Cangas de Onis-Cabarceno (202.6 km): Biagio Conte (It); 15. Alto Cruz de la Domanda (220 km): Alex Zülle (Swi); 16. Logrono-Sabinanigo (220.9 km): Nicola Minali (It); 17. Cerler (176.7 km): Oliveiro Rincon (Col); 18. Benasque-Zaragoza (219.5 km): Dimitri Konyshev (Rus); 19. Getafe-Ávila (217.1 km): Laurent Dufaux (Swi); 20. Dyc (209.5 km): Gianni Bugno (It); 21. Segovia-Dyc (tt 43 km): Tony Rominger (Swi); 22. Madrid-Madrid (157.6 km): Tom Steels (B).

1997 (6.9-28.9)

1. Lisboa-Estoril (155.7 km): Lars Michaelsen (DK); 2. Evora-Vilamoura (225.3 km): Marcel Wüst (Ger); 3. Loulé-Huelva (173.2 km): Marcel Wüst (Ger); 4. Jerez de la Frontera (192.5 km): Eleuterio Anguita (Sp); 5. Málaga (230.8 km): Marcel Wüst (Ger); 6. Málaga-Granada: Laurent Jalabert (F); 7. Guadix-Sierra Nevada (219.2 km): Yvon Ledanois (F); 8. Granada-Córdoba (175.8 km): Bart Voskamp (NL); 9. Córdoba (tt 35 km): Melchior Mauri (Sp); 10. Córdoba-Almendralejo (224.5 km): Mariano Piccoli (It); 11. Plasencia (194.5 km): Jan Svorada (Cze); 12. León-Alto de Morredero (142 km): Roberto Heras (Sp); 13. Ponferrada-Branilin (196 km): Pavel Tonkov (Rus); 14. Oviedo-Alto del Naranco (169.5 km): José Vicente Garcia Acosta (Sp); 15. Oviedo-Lagos de Covadonga (159.8 km): Pavel Tonkov (Rus); 16. Cangas de Onis-Santander (170 km): Jan Svorada (Cze); 17. Burgos (182.7 km): Jan Svorada (Cze); 18. Valladolid (183.7 km): León Van Bon (NL); 19. Los Angeles de San Rafael (193.3 km): José Maria Jiménez (Sp); 20. Ávila (199.4 km): Laurent Jalabert (F); 21. Alcobendas-Alcobendas (tt 43.7 km): Alex Zülle (Swi); 22. Madrid-Madrid (145.5 km): Max Van Heeswijk (NL).

1998 (5.9-27.9)

1. Córdoba (161.7 km): Markus Zberg (Swi); 2. Cadiz (234.6 km): Jeroen Blijlevens (NL); 3. Estepona (192.6 km): Jaan Kirsipuu (Est); 4. Málaga-Granada (173.5 km): Fabrizio Guidi (It);5. Olula del Rio-Murcia (165.5 km): Jeroen Blijlevens (NL); 6. Xorret de Cati (201.5 km): José Maria Jiménez (Sp); 7. Alicante-Valencia (185 km): Giovanni Lombardi (It); 8. Palma de Mallorca-Palma de Mallorca (181.5 km): Fabrizio Guidi (It); 9. Alcudia-Alcudia (tt 39.5 km): Abraham Olano (Sp); 10. Vic-Andorra (199.3 km): José Maria Jiménez (Sp); 11. Cerler (186 km): José Maria Jiménez (Sp); 12. Benasque-Canfranc (187 km): Gianni Bugno (It); 13. Sabinanigo-Sabinanigo (208.5 km): Andreï Zintchenko (Rus); 14. Biescas-Zaragoza (145.5 km): Marcel Wüst (Ger); 15. Soria (178.8 km): Andreï Zintchenko (Rus); 16. Laguna Negra de Neila (143.7 km): José Maria Jiménez (Sp); 17. Burgos-León (188.5 km): Marcel Wüst (Ger); 18. León-Salamanca (230 km): Fabrizio Guidi (It); 19. Ávila-Segovia (170.4 km): Roberto Heras (Sp); 20. Alto de Navacerrada (206 km): Andreï Zinthchenko (Rus); 21. Fuenlabrada-Fuenlabrada (tt 39 km): Alex Zülle (Swi); 22. Madrid-Madrid (163 km): Markus Zberg (Swi).

1999 (4.9-26.9)

0. Murcia (tt 6.1 km): Igor González de Galdeano (Sp); 1. Benidorm (179 km): Robert Hunter (SA); 3. Alicante-Albacete (206 km): Marcel Wüst (Ger); 3. La Roda-Fuenlabrada (233 km): Marcel Wüst (Ger); 4. Las Rozas-Salamanca (185.6 km): Marcel Wüst (Ger); 5. Béjar-Ciudad Rodrigo

(160 km): Jan Ullrich (Ger); 6. Salamanca-Salamanca (tt 46.4 km): Abraham Olano (Sp); 7. Salamanca-León (217 km): Marcel Wüst (Ger); 8. Alto de l'Angliru (175.6 km): José Maria Jiménez (Sp); 9. Gijón-Los Corrales de Buelna (185.8 km): Laurent Brochard (F); 10. Zaragoza-Zaragoza (183.2 km): Serguei Outschakov (Ukr); 11. Huesca-Pla de Beret (201 km): Daniele Nardello (It); 12. Sort-Arcalis (147.4 km): Igor González de Galdeano (Sp); 13. Andorra-Berga (149 km): Alex Zülle (Swi); 14. Barcelona-Barcelona (94.4 km): Fabio Roscioli (It); 15. La Senia-Valencia (193.4 km): Viatcheslav Ekimov (Rus); 16. Teruel (200.4 km): Frank Vandenbroucke (B); 17. Bronchales-Guadalajara (225 km): Cristian Moreni (It); 18. Alto de Abantos (166 km): Roberto Laiseka (Sp); 19. San Lorenzo de El Escorial-Ávila (184.6 km): Frank Vandenbroucke (B); 20. El Tiemblo-Ávila (tt 46.5 km): Jan Ullrich (Ger); 21. Madrid-Madrid (163 km): Jeroen Blijlevens (NL).

2000 (26.8-17.9)
1. Málaga (tt 13.3 km): Alex Zülle (Swi); 2. Córdoba (167.5 km): Oscar Freire (Sp); 3. Montoro-Valdepenas (199 km): Jans Koerts (NL); 4. Albacete (159 km): Oscar Freire (Sp); 5. Xorret de Cati (152.3 km): Eladio Jiménez (Sp); 6. Benidorm-Valencia (155.5 km): Paolo Bossoni (It); 7. Morella (175.4 km): Roberto Heras (Sp); 8. Vinaroz-Port Aventura (168.5 km): Alessandro Petacchi (It); 9. Tarragona-Tarragona (tt 37.6 km): Abraham Olano (Sp); 10. Sabadell-La Molina (165.8 km): Rafael Cardenas (Col); 11. Alp-Arcalis (136.5 km): Roberto Laiseka (Sp); 12. Zaragoza-Zaragoza (131.5 km): Alessandro Petacchi (It); 13. Santander-Santander (143.3 km): Mariano Piccoli (It); 14. Lagos de Covadonga (146.5 km.: Andreï Zintchenko (Rus); 15. Cangas de Onis-Gijón (164.2 km): Alvaro González de Galdeano (Sp); 16. Gijón-Alto de l'Angliru (168 km): Gilberto Simoni (It); 17. Benavente-Salamanca (155.5 km): Davide Bramati (It); 18. Béjar-Ciudad Rodrigo (159 km): Alexandre Vinokourov (Kaz); 19. Salamanca-Ávila (130 km): Mariano Piccoli (It); 20. Alto de Abantos (128.3 km): Roberto Heras (Sp); 21. Madrid-Madrid (tt 38.6 km): Santos González (Sp).

2001 (8.9-30.9)
1. Salamanca (tt 12.3 km): David Millar (GB); 2. Valladolid (147.2 km): Erik Zabel (Ger); 3. León (140.5 km): Erik Zabel (Ger); 4. Gijón (175 km): Erik Zabel (Ger); 5. Lagos de Covadonga (160.8 km): Juan Miguel Mercado (Sp); 6. Cangas de Onis-Torrelavega (180.6 km): David Millar (GB); 7. Torrelavega (tt 44.2 km): Santiago Botero (Col); 8. Reinosa-Cruz de la Demanda (195 km): José Maria Jiménez (Sp); 9. Logrono-Zaragoza (179.2 km): Igor González de Galdeano (Sp); 10. Sabadell-La Molina (168.4 km): Santiago Blanco (Sp); 11. Alp-Estacion de Pal (154.2 km): José Maria Jiménez (Sp); 12. Ordino-Estacion Arcalis (tt 17.1 km): José Maria Jiménez (Sp); 13. Andorra-Port Aventura (206 km):Beat Zberg (Swi); 14. Tarragona-Vinaroz (170.5 km): Juan Manuel Garate (Sp); 15. Valencia-Alto de Aitana (207.2 km): Klaus Möller (DK); 16. Alcoy-Murcia (153.3 km): Tomas Konecny (Cze); 17. Albacete (159.5 km): Robert Hunter (SA); 18. Cuenca (154.2 km): Filippo Simeoni (It); 19. Guadalajara (168 km): Guido Trenti (USA); 20. Alto de Abantos (176.3 km): Gilberto Simoni (It); Madrid-Madrid (tt 38 km): Santiago Botero (Col).

2002 (7.9-29.9)
1.Valencia (ttt 24.6 km): Once-Eroski (Sp); 2. Alcoi (144.7 km): Danilo Di Luca (It); 3. San Vicente del Raspeig-Murcia (132.4 km): Mario Cipollini (It); 4. Aguilas-Roquetas de Mar (149.5 km): Mario Cipollini (It); 5. El Ejido-Sierra Nevada (198 km): Guido Trentin (It); 6. Granada-Sierra de la Pandera (153.1 km): Roberto Heras (Sp); 7. Jaén-Málaga (196.8 km): Mario Cipollini (It); 8. Ubrique (173.6 km): Aitor González (Sp); 9. Córdoba-Córdoba (130.2 km): Pablo Lastras (Sp); 10. Córdoba (tt 38.6 km): Aitor González (Sp); 11. Alcobendas-Collado Villalba (163 km): Pablo Lastras (Sp); 12. Segovia-Burgos (210.5 km): Alessandro Petacchi (It); 13. Burgos-Santander (189.8 km): Giovanni Lombardi (It); 14. Gijón (190.2 km): Serguei Smetanine (Rus); 15. Alto de El Angliru (176.7 km): Roberto Heras (Sp); 16. Avilés-León (154.7 km): Santiago Botero (Col); 17. Benavente-Salamanca (145.6 km): Angelo Furlan (It); 18. La Covatilla (193.7 km): José Vicente García Acosta (Sp); 19. Ávila-Warner Bross Park (141.2 km): Angelo Furlan (It); 20. Warner Bross Park-Madrid/S. Bernabeu/ (tt 41.2 km): Aitor González (Sp).

2003 (6.9-28.9)
1. Gijón (ttt 30 km): Once; 2. Gijón-Cangas de Onis (140 km): Luis Pérez (Sp); 3. Cangas de Onis-Santander (160 km): Alessandro Petacchi (It); 4. Santander-Burgos (158 km): Unal Etxebarria (Ven); 5. Soria-Zaragoza (165 km): Ángel Edo (Sp); 6. Zaragoze (tt 40 km): isidro Nozal (Sp);

Viva la Vuelta!

7.Huesca-Cauterets (190 km): Michael Rasmussen (Den); 8. Cauterets-Pla de Beret (166 km): Joaquin Rodríguez (Sp); 9. Vielha-Port d'Enlavira (176 km): Alejandro Valverde (Sp); 10. Andorra-Sabadell (179 km): Erik Zabel (Ger); 11. Utiel-Cuenca (160 km): Erik Zabel (Ger); 12. Cuenca-Albacete (167 km): Alessandro Petacchi (It); 13. Albacete (tt 53 km): Isidro Nozal; 14. Albacete-Valdepenas (167 km): Alessandro Petacchi (It); 15. Valdepenas-Sierra de la Pandera (172 km): Alejandro Valverde (Sp); 16. Jaen-Sierra Nevada (162 km): Félix Cárdenas (Col); 17. Granada-Córdoba (188 km): David Millar (GBr); 18. Las Rozas-Las Rozas (143.8 km): Pedro Diaz Lobato (Sp); 19. La Vega de Alcobendas-Collado Villalba (164 km): Filippo Simeoni (It); 20. San Lorenzo-Alto de Abantos (tt 11.2 km): Roberto Heras (Sp); 21. Madrid-Madrid (145.8 km): Alessandro Petacchi (It).

2004 (4.9-26.)
1.León (ttt 28 km): US Postal; 2. León-Burgos (207 km): Alessandro Petacchi (It); 3. Burgos-Soria (157 km): Alejandro Valverde (Sp); 4. Soria-Zaragoza (167 km): Alessandro Petacchi (It); 5. Zaragoza-Morella (186.5 km): Denis Menchov (Rus); 6. Benicarlo-Castellon de la Plana (157 km): Oscar Freire (Sp); 7. Castellon de la Plana-Valencia (165 km): Alessandro Petacchi (It); 8. Factoria Ford (tt 40.1 km): Tyler Hamilton (US); 9. Xativa-Alto de Aitana. Alicante (170 km): Leónardo Piepoli (It); 10. Alcoi-Xorret de Cati (174.5 km): Eladio Jiménez (Sp); 11. San Vicente del Raspeig-Caravaca de la Cruz (165 km): David Zabriskie (US); 12. Almería-Calar Alto (145 km): Roberto Heras (Sp); 13. El Ejido-Málaga (170 km): Alessandro Petacchi (It); 14. Málaga-Granada (167 km): Santiago Perez (Sp); 15. Granada-Sierra Nevada (tt 29.6 km): Santiago Perez (Sp); 16. Olivenza-Cáceres (170 km): José Julia (Sp); 17.Plasencia-La Covatilla (178 km): Félix Cardenas (Col); 18. Bejar-Ávila (196 km): Javier Rodríguez (Sp); 19. Ávila-Collado Villalba (150 km): Constantino Zaballa (Sp); 20. La Vega de Alcobendas-Puerto de Navacerrada (175 km): José Gutierrez (Sp); 21. Madrid (tt 30 km): Santiago Perez (Sp)

2005(27.8-18.9)
1. Granada (tt 7 km): Denis Menchov (Rus); 2.Granada-Córdoba (189.3 km): Bradley McGee (Aus); 3. Córdoba-Puertollano (153.3 km): Alessandro Petacchi (It); 4. Ciudad Real-Arganasilla de Alba (232.3 km): Alessandro Petacchi (It); 5. Alcazar de San Juan-Cuenca (176 km): Thor Hushovd (Nor); 6. Cuenca-Valdelinares (217 km): Roberto Heras; 7. Teruel-Vinaros (212.5 km): Max Van Heeswijk (Nl); 8. Tarragona-Lloret de Mar (189 km): Alessandro Petacchi (It); 9. Lloret de Mar (tt 48 km): Denis Menchov (Rus); 10. Girona-Arcalis. Andorra (206.3 km): Francisco Mancebo (Sp); 11. Andorra-Celer (186.6 km): Roberto Laiseka (Sp); 12. Logroño-Burgos (148 km): Alessandro Petacchi (It); 13. Burgos-La Bien Aparecida (196 km): Samuel Sanchez (Sp); 14. Nestlé La Penilla-Covadonga (172.3 km): Eladio Jiménez (Sp); 15. Cangas de Onis-Valgrande Pajares (191 km): Roberto Heras (Sp); 16. León-Valladolid (162.5 km): Paolo Bettini (It); 17. El Espinar-La Granja de San Ildefonso (165.6 km): Carlos García Quesada (Sp); 18. Ávila-Ávila (197.5 km): Nicki Sørensen (Den); 19. San Martin de Valdeiglisias-Alcobendas (142.9 km): Heinrich Haussler (Ger); 20. Guadalajara-Alcala de Henares (tt 38.9 km): Ruben Plaza (Sp); 21. Madrid-Madrid (136.5 km): Alessandro Petacchi (It).

322

Bibliography

Cycling

Arribas, Carlos; López-Egea, Sergi; Pernau, Gabriel: *Locos por el Tour*, RBA libros, 2003

Bastide, Roger: *A la pointe des pelotons*, Presses Pocket, 1972

Berrendero, Julián: *Mis glorias y memorias*, Pérez del Hoyo, 1949

Chico Pérez, F., Guerra, Adrian: *Vuelta Ciclista a España 1935–85,* Caja Postal, 1985

Delgado, Pedro: *A golpe de pedal,* El País-Aguilar, 1995

Díaz, José Antonio: *Loroño, símbolo del ciclismo vasco,* Bilbao Bizkaia Kutxa, 1998

Díaz, José Antonio: *La gran historia del ciclismo vizcaíno 1884–1999*, Bilbao, 2000

Elliot, Malcolm: *Sprinter*, Pelham Books, 1990

Fuente, José Manuel: *Ciclo de Dolor*, 1977

García Sánchez, Javier: *Induráin: a tempered passion*, Mousehold Press and Sport & Publicity, 2003

Hinault, Bernard: *Memories of the peloton*, Springfield Books, 1989

Nicholson, Geoffrey: *The Great Bike Race*, Hodder and Stoughton, 1977

Nicholson, Geoffrey: *Le Tour*, Hodder and Stoughton, 1991

Ocaña, Luis: *Pour un Maillot Jaune*, Calmann-Levy, 1972

Ruiz Cabestany, Pello: *Historias de un Ciclista*, Pamiela, 1997

Urraca, Juan José: *Kas: crónica de una época 1958–1977*, Dorleta, 1996

Yates, Richard: *Master Jacques*, Mousehold Press, 2001

History

Menéndez Pidal: *Historia de España –*. Vol. 41: *La época de Franco (1939-75)* and Vol. 42: *La transición a la democracia y la España de Juan Carlos I*

Brenan, Gerald: *The Face of Spain*, Turnstile Press, 1950

Brenan, Gerald: *The Spanish Labyrinth*, CUP, 1967

Hooper, John: *The New Spaniards*, Penguin Books, 1995
Preston, Paul: *Franco*, Harper Collins, 1993
Thomas, Hugh: *The Spanish Civil War*, Penguin Books, 1965

Newspapers and magazines

El Mundo Deportivo
Rueda Libre
El Correo Catalan
Dicen
La Vanguardia
El País
Ciclismo a Fondo
Bicisport
Cycle Sport
Cycling Weekly

Webpages

www.altimetrias.com
www.cyclingnews.com
www.lavuelta.com
www.memoir-du-cyclisme.net

Index

The following books are also published by
Mousehold Press and Sport & Publicity

Mr Tom - the true story of Tom Simpson
by Chris Sidwells

Master Jacques – the enigma of Jacques Anquetil
by Richard Yates

Induráin – a tempered passion
by Javier García Sánchez (trans. by Jeremy Munday)

From the Pen of J. B. Wadley
selected by Adrian Bell

Golden Stages of the Tour de France
edited by Richard Allchin & Adrian Bell

This Island Race – inside 135 years of British bike racing
by Les Woodland

The Sweat of the Gods
by Menjo Maso (trans. by Michiel Horn)

A Peiper's Tale
by Allan Peiper with Chris Sidwells

A large range of other cycling books can also be obtained
from Sport & Publicity (telephone 0207 794 0915 or visit
www.sportandpublicity.co.uk)

Sport & Publicity is the exclusive distributor in the UK of:
VELO – the annual 'bible' of cycle racing;
VELO PLUS – which has all the racing results since professional
cycle racing began;
GOTHA – Travel Marketing's new work which contains the
palmarés of all the best known cyclists (and many others) in
the history of cycling and was last published in 1984.